Bombing Germany: The Final Phase

To those with the will to resist

Bombing Germany: The Final Phase

The Destruction of Pforzheim and the Closing Months of Bomber Command's War

Tony Redding

Pen & Sword
AVIATION

First published in Great Britain in 2015
and reprinted in paperback format in 2022 by
PEN AND SWORD AVIATION
An imprint of
Pen & Sword Books Ltd
Yorkshire – Philadelphia

Copyright © Tony Redding 2015, 2022

ISBN 978 1 39901 959 0

The right of Tony Redding to be identified as Author of
this work has been asserted by him in accordance with the Copyright,
Designs and Patents Act 1988.

A CIP catalogue record for this book is available from the British Library.

Typeset in the UK
Printed and bound in the UK by CPI Group (UK) Ltd.

Pen & Sword Books Limited incorporates the imprints of Atlas, Archaeology,
Aviation, Discovery, Family History, Fiction, History, Maritime, Military, Military
Classics, Politics, Select, Transport, True Crime, Air World, Frontline Publishing,
Leo Cooper, Remember When, Seaforth Publishing, The Praetorian Press,
Wharncliffe Local History, Wharncliffe Transport, Wharncliffe True Crime and
White Owl.

For a complete list of Pen & Sword titles please contact
PEN & SWORD BOOKS LIMITED
47 Church Street, Barnsley, South Yorkshire, S70 2AS, England
E-mail: enquiries@pen-and-sword.co.uk
Website: www.pen-and-sword.co.uk

Or
PEN AND SWORD BOOKS
1950 Lawrence Rd, Havertown, PA 19083, USA
E-mail: Uspen-and-sword@casematepublishers.com
Website: www.penandswordbooks.com

Contents

Author's Note

Bomber Command made a crucial contribution to the achievement of the Allied victory in Europe in May 1945. Its young volunteers fought a lonely war, each crew confined to the cramped fuselage of a heavy bomber.

Having written about the two operational tours of rear gunner Warrant Officer Sidney Knott, DFC (*Flying for Freedom*, more recently published as *Life and Death in Bomber Command*), I felt the need to tell the story from the other side, the people in the cities who endured the bombing.

This new project began when gunner Don Robson, during an interview for the earlier book, mentioned the murder of aircrew from his squadron at a place called Pforzheim. My original idea was to explore this war crime and tell the story of the victims and the perpetrators. Soon, however, the new book's scope widened. I discovered that the Pforzheim raid killed over 17,000 people and was, in terms of deaths, the third worst raid on a German city, after Hamburg and Dresden. I was surprised that so little had been written about this cataclysmic raid on Pforzheim.

This book focuses on Pforzheim's destruction and the time of the 'whirlwind' – the last seven months of the bombing war, when Germany's cities were finally overwhelmed. It includes the stories of the British aircrew, particularly the crews of 550 Squadron at North Killingholme, and tells the stories of those on the ground. Their accounts give a vivid impression of total war and the courage and resilience required to survive.

Tony Redding
Ash, Canterbury, 2014

Memories

On Friday, 23 February 1945, Margot Geiger, a 16-year-old pupil at Pforzheim's Hildagymnasium, went to work milling fuses at a watchmaking factory. Dawn came with a red sky, a strange herald of the city's fiery destruction later that day.

Margot had said goodbye to skilled watchmaker Werner Schultz, deported as a *Mischling* (half-Jew) for forced labour near Dresden. She had been used to taking 'messed-up' fuses to Werner, who would try to salvage them while talking about things which were not to be discussed.

Eva Kulp was another friend. She had been ballet mistress at Pforzheim's Stadttheater but had been conscripted for fuse work at the factory the previous September. Eva was not afraid to voice her opposition to the Nazis and showed no fear of denunciation.

At the end of the Friday shift, Margot parted from Eva at the corner of Heinrich-Wieland Allee and Bayernstrasse. Eva said she was going to a city pub. Suddenly, the pre-alarm sounded. Pforzheim was just minutes from destruction. Werner survived, thanks to the Nazis' decision to deport him – his train left the doomed city two hours before the bombs fell. Margot survived the catastrophic raid, but Eva disappeared in the inferno.

Acknowledgements

This book is the product of generosity, enthusiasm and support on the part of many people, both in Britain and in Germany. They include veterans of Bomber Command, who shared memories extending back to their youthful years when their lives were on the line. I owe a special debt of thanks to Wing Commander Jack Harris, OBE, DFC, who tolerated my persistent questioning and shared the results of years of research concerning his beloved 550 Squadron.

This project enjoyed much support in Germany. Dr Christian Groh, formerly director of Pforzheim's Stadtarchiv, paved the way. He agreed to an initial interview, suggested contacts for further interviews, gave access to records and provided a base for research and other work. Leo Steinbeis organized and facilitated my visits to Pforzheim and assisted in the research. He also undertook translations and, when required, acted as interpreter during meetings and interviews. He was unswerving in his support and provided valuable advice and suggestions throughout. In the UK, Tony Butter and Tina Lindemann also made important contributions to the substantial task of translation.

I owe thanks to everyone in Britain and Germany who agreed to be interviewed. Some sources talked about very difficult and painful issues. Several local researchers and historians made outstanding contributions. Brigitte and Gerhard Brändle opened their extensive files on victims and resisters and, in doing so, provided insights into German society in the time of the National Socialists. Most importantly, they gave a human face to the victims of Nazi oppression and those with the courage to resist an appalling tyranny. Stephan Paetzold was equally generous in sharing his research into the murders of British airmen and, in particular, the killing of five members of RAF pilot Johnny Wynne's crew. Helmut Schmitt also gave an important overview of the context surrounding the murders following the bombing of Pforzheim.

A panel of readers corrected errors and provided much useful guidance during preparation of the text. They included Sidney Knott, Don Robson, Jack Harris, Jeremy Hayes, Dr Alan Russell, Brigitte and Gerhard Brändle, Stephan Paetzold and Dr Christian Groh. Naturally, the responsibility for remaining errors rests with the author.

This book represents a considerable workload and its completion is thanks in large measure to the extraordinary efforts of Joy Kemp, who did so much to prepare the text. Mandy Taylor, as always, also gave her time and support.

My thanks to all involved.

Tony Redding

Introduction

Britain stared into a precipice in June 1940. France was lost. The British Expeditionary Force had been rescued but its heavy weapons remained at Dunkirk. Britain stood alone. There were the Navy and Fighter Command, but the battle for Britain – to be contested by fighter squadrons during the Battle of Britain – had yet to be fought. Invasion was expected and when Churchill became prime minister the national mood was caught by his chilling comment on the prospect of a landing: 'You can always take one with you!'

The so-called 'Phoney War' had ended in April 1940 with the German invasion of Denmark and Norway, followed soon after by the main offensive in the West. Until then, Bomber Command's aircraft were permitted only to sow mines, bomb German naval vessels when not in port (to avoid killing civilians) and engage in leaflet dropping. Now Germany showed the way in city bombing. With France defeated, Churchill faced immense pressures in ensuring Britain's immediate survival, yet he still found space to look ahead. He sought a way to prosecute the war successfully in the longer term. On 8 July 1940, he sent Minister of Aircraft Production Lord Beaverbrook a perceptive memorandum: 'When I look round to see how we can win the war, I see that there is only one sure path. We have no continental army which can defeat German military power. The blockade is broken and Hitler has Asia and probably Africa to draw on. Should he be repulsed here or not try invasion, he will probably recoil eastwards and we will have nothing to stop him. But there is one sure way that will bring him back and bring him down and that is an absolutely devastating, exterminating attack by very heavy bombers against the Nazi homeland.'[1]

It is a common misconception that Sir Arthur Harris – 'Bomber Harris' – instigated the strategic bombing campaign against Germany. Harris was certainly vigorous in his pursuit of strategic bombing objectives, but the rapid development of Bomber Command and its capabilities sprang from Churchill's recognition of Britain's lack of other offensive options. In 1941, the year before Harris took over at Bomber Command, the Air Staff had already proposed the creation of a force of 4,000 heavy bombers. This goal proved beyond reach, owing to the high cost of building a new British Army capable of contributing to Europe's liberation in the final phase of the war. Bomber Command reached its maximum strength of 1,994 operational heavy aircraft in May 1945.[1]

A July 1941 memorandum from the Chiefs of Staff to Churchill argued for a British bombing offensive on the heaviest possible scale (the only limits being imposed by operational difficulties in the UK). This paper concluded: 'As our forces increase, we intend to pass to a planned attack on civilian morale with the intensity and continuity which are essential if a final breakdown is to be produced.' It added: 'We have every reason to be confident that if we can expand our forces in accordance with our present programme, and if possible beyond it, that effect will be shattering.'[2]

During the evening of Sunday 29 December 1940, Arthur Harris was at work at the Air Ministry when German bombers began a huge fire raid on the City of London. He stood on the Air Ministry roof, in the company of Sir Charles 'Peter' Portal, then Commander-in-Chief, Bomber Command. They looked out over a sea of flames. Harris commented: 'They are sowing the wind.' Later, after the war, he wrote that this was the sole occasion when he felt vengeful.[3]

Harris arrived at Bomber Command headquarters at High Wycombe, Buckinghamshire, on 22 February 1942. A week earlier, on 14 February, a new directive had been issued. This stated that Bomber Command's primary target was now civilian morale, especially that of Germany's industrial workers. This directive included a list of 'area targets' where collateral damage inevitably implied a large loss of civilian lives. Harris' job was to pursue this directive, and he did so with exceptional energy and determination. Yet this strategy came not from him, but from Churchill, the War Cabinet, the Air Ministry and the Chiefs of Staff.[4]

There was a dilemma here. Before the war, Bomber Command trained for and expected to raid Germany in daylight. Experience in conflicts such as the Italian invasion of Abyssinia and German participation in the Spanish Civil War had led to the conviction that 'the bomber will always get through'. It was hoped that RAF day bombers with powered gun turrets would be capable of self-defence. With savage losses of 25 to 50 per cent on the initial daylight raids, it was soon appreciated that if Bomber Command was to operate at all, it would have to operate at night. This made area bombing inevitable. The problem was summed up by Portal: 'Our original idea at the beginning of the war had been to wreck the German oil industry, but we were not then strong enough. Day bombing was not then practicable and we had not got the radar aids which we needed to enable us to hit small targets at night. We were forced to adopt area bombing as a means of generally weakening the German economy.'[5]

Later, in 1944, Portal felt that Bomber Command at last had the strength to destroy the German oil industry. By that time, however, Harris was firmly wedded to the conviction that area bombing was the most effective way of undermining Germany's war-fighting ability. There was nothing new about regarding enemy morale as a legitimate target. A couple of months before Harris watched London burn, Portal had proposed that the BBC should name twenty German cities to be bombed – each to be attacked by over 100 bombers. Later, as Chief of the Air Staff, Portal continued to advocate attacks on German morale, despite the relatively modest size of the British bomber fleet at that time.[6]

Early assessments of Bomber Command's achievements were wildly over-optimistic, both in terms of damage done and its effect on German morale. The true situation was exposed in 1941. Drawing on a scientific analysis of bombing photographs, the Butt Report painted a dismal picture of the British bomber as an instrument of war. It was found that only one in three crews claiming to bomb a German target put their bombs within 5 miles of the target.[7] The bombers could not operate by day without long-range fighter escort, which would not be available until much later in the war. For the present, many bomber crews had trouble *finding* a large city, let alone bombing a specific target within that city. The report commented: 'only about one third of aircraft claiming to reach the target area actually reach it. This figure of one third … relates to the aircraft recorded as having attacked the primary target, not to the total aircraft dispatched. In the raids considered in this analysis 6,130 aircraft were dispatched but 4,065 attacked, i.e. 66 per cent. Thus of the total dispatched not one third but one fifth reached the target area.'[8]

Clearly, in the wake of this grim report, Harris needed a miracle to restore his new command's flagging fortunes. He found it in the 'Thousand Plan'. Cologne was selected as the target for the first of the 1,000 bomber raids, on 30–1 May 1942. Mass raids were also flown against Essen and Bremen in June, but Cologne was the most destructive of the three attacks. It was a public relations coup of tremendous significance, both for the future of Bomber Command and the eventual fate of Germany's cities. Cologne saved Bomber Command from its many critics. After Cologne, Bomber Command was seen as the way forward.[9]

As for Cologne, over 15,000 dwellings were destroyed or damaged and refugees flooded out into the surrounding countryside. Factories and businesses suffered badly, with 1,505 premises totally destroyed and 630 severely damaged. Cologne's main railway station and trams were put out of action. There were 469 dead and just over 5,000 injured. Cologne's police president commented: 'The weight of this attack is most significant because, for the first time, more than 1,000 aircraft took part. This is not an estimate but a concrete number and on the German side one could not imagine such striking power.'[10]

Several milestones in the growth of Bomber Command and its capabilities were reached in rapid succession. The Avro Lancaster – described by Harris as Bomber Command's 'shining sword' – began operations on 3 March 1942. This aircraft, with a wingspan of 102ft and an all-up weight of 67,000lb, carried 15,000lb of bombs with ease. It had a maximum range of 2,530 miles with a 7,000lb bombload.[11] The Lancaster was by far the most successful British bomber of the Second World War. The crews worshipped the 'Lanc' and it was recognized from the first as a war-winner, given its huge lifting capacity and cavernous bomb-bay.

Britain's Lancaster building programme amounted to a national investment. Britain built 7,377 Lancasters; each cost around £59,000, excluding the electronics. Around 1,150,000 men and women were engaged in building Lancasters at some

Bomber Command's 'shining sword': the Lancaster was by far the most effective British bomber of the Second World War. *Photo: Trustees of the Imperial War Museum.*

point during the war. A total of 156,192 Lancaster sorties were flown on war service; 3,431 Lancasters were written off on operations.[11]

The 'Thousand Plan' raid on Cologne was a convincing demonstration of air power. This created a favourable political environment for the continued expansion of Bomber Command. Harris got his Lancasters and his chance to swamp the German defences with a concentrated 'bomber stream', with twenty-five to thirty bombers a minute crossing the target. New initiatives were essential as the German defences grew much stronger in 1942. The airborne interception Lichtenstein radar entered service and the German night fighter force more than doubled, from 152 to 362.[12] Nevertheless, the bomber stream offered safety in numbers, with the concentrated mass of aircraft flying a set route at a set speed, with individual aircraft given specific height bands and times to reduce collision risks.[13]

Bomber Command's strength continued to grow throughout 1942. By early November, the all-Lancaster 5 Group reached its full strength of ten squadrons (representing two-thirds of total Lancaster strength). By 1 January 1943, Bomber Command had 206 Lancasters (31.7 per cent of heavy bomber strength). Bomber Command's six groups totalled fifty-three squadrons, with nearly 1,000 frontline aircraft (including 650 four-engined bombers). By early 1944 Lancaster numbers had risen to 586 (53.8 per cent of heavy bomber strength).[14] This was of great significance as, in terms of bombs dropped per aircraft failing to return, the Lancaster stood head and shoulders above other 'heavies' (Stirling, 41 tons; Halifax, 51 tons; and Lancaster, 132 tons). By May 1943, the strength of each Lancaster squadron had increased to twenty-six aircraft, with two reserves. This expansion of the bomber fleet was accompanied by a massive programme of bomber airfield construction across eastern England. Another important development was the arrival of the Americans. On 17 August 1942, USAAF B.17s began to operate, marking the beginning of what would become round-the-clock bombing, with American daylight raids under fighter escort.[15]

Bomber Command's effectiveness continued to grow. Electronic devices such as Gee overcame long-standing navigational and target-finding problems at night. Navigators used Gee to fix their position to within 6 miles, even at extreme range (the range was limited by the Earth's curvature to 350–400 miles).

Portal's vision of a bombing 'whirlwind' continued to evolve. On 3 November 1942, the Chief of the Air Staff produced a paper setting out his aims for 1943 and 1944. The objective was to drop 1.25 million tons of bombs on Germany (killing an estimated 900,000 people and seriously injuring a million), destroying the enemy's industrial and transportation infrastructures and making 25 million people homeless.[16] At least one-third of German industry would be laid waste.[17]

A new phase in the bombing war began in March 1943. This was the Battle of the Ruhr. There were forty-three major raids during this campaign and crews flew 18,506 sorties. Half the attacks were on targets in the Ruhr, known euphemistically to bomber crews as 'Happy Valley'. In reality, the Ruhr was Bomber Command's graveyard; the near five-month battle cost 872 aircraft, with another 2,126 damaged.[18] The German night fighters were very effective and German flak was deadly, with guns and searchlights under excellent radar control.

Nevertheless, Harris was not to be deflected. His striking power expanded: the enlarged Pathfinder Force emerged as 8 Group and target location improved. During the final fortnight of December 1942 the revolutionary Oboe blind-bombing system was trialled in service. Oboe required two ground stations, 'Cat' and 'Mouse'. Cat sent a signal to the Mosquito and the pilot had to stay within a beam just 35yd wide. This was achieved by keeping an 'equi signal' – a continuous note, rather than dots to one side and dashes to the other. The aircraft flew an arc of a circle to arrive at the bomb release point. The Mouse station sent 'milestone' signals to the Mosquito as it approached release, ending in five dots and a 2.5 second dash, which was the signal to drop. Oboe-equipped Mosquitoes were ideal for pinpoint target-marking. Oboe made accurate, concentrated bombing possible even when targets were obscured. Pathfinder Force Commander Donald Bennett described it as 'probably the most effective single instrument of warfare in our entire armoury'.[19]

The technological advances accelerated. On the night of 30/1 January 1943, Pathfinder aircraft used H_2S airborne radar for the first time during an attack on Hamburg. Earlier in the month improved Target Indicators (TIs) were dropped to mark Berlin. The intention was to perfect techniques for highly accurate, concentrated bombing. Target finding was by visual means or illumination, using Oboe-equipped Mosquitoes whenever possible. These aircraft were followed by flare-dropping illuminators and primary markers dropping TIs. The TIs were topped up

High precision: the Oboe-equipped Mosquito was the key to accurate, concentrated bombing.
Photo: Trustees of the Imperial War Museum.

by backers-up. The main force arrived over the target in a dense stream, swamping the defences. The master bomber provided direct VHF control of the attack over the target.[19]

Bennett described these methods in *Pathfinder*. The finders dropped flares around the aiming point a few minutes before zero hour. A finder or finders would then drop flares on the exact aiming point. The illuminators dropped more flares, followed by the primary markers (using crews with an established reputation for accuracy). The primary markers dropped TIs on the aiming point and the backers-up added more TIs as required.[19]

In early 1943 the Casablanca Directive gave fresh instructions to Harris: 'Your primary object will be the progressive destruction and dislocation of the German military, industrial and economic system and the undermining of the morale of the German people to the point where their capacity for armed resistance is fatally weakened.'[20]

Britain's investment in heavy bombers paid off. Bomber Command was capable of doing real damage. The entire Ruhr was within Oboe marking range, and this was a system never jammed effectively by the Germans. H_2S ground-scanning radar could pick out rivers, lakes and coastlines. Two Pathfinder squadrons received the first H_2S sets in January 1943. Within a few months all Pathfinder aircraft had H_2S and the entire heavy bomber force was so equipped by early 1944. Oboe and, to some extent, H_2S brought Bomber Command's striking power to an unprecedented level. New devices arrived on the squadrons to warn crews of approaching fighters and further confuse the German defences. Mandrel and Tinsel were introduced in the final quarter of 1942. Mandrel jammed German radars controlling night fighters.

Tinsel was an airborne system broadcasting engine noise on German night fighter frequencies.[21]

The new TIs reached the Pathfinder squadrons in January 1943. These pyrotechnics were in various colours, typically red, green, yellow and combinations. One TI in common use was the Red Spot Fire, which burst at 3,000ft, producing a vivid crimson glow.[21]

This was the crucial period in Bomber Command's evolution. In just eight weeks, during early 1943, Harris' squadrons received Oboe, H_2S, more effective TIs and new radio countermeasures. The new all-Canadian 6 Group became operational on 1 January 1943. The Pathfinder Force became 8 Group one week later. Bomber Command's striking power was transformed: the all-Lancaster 5 Group could drop a greater weight of bombs in a single night than the entire Bomber Command main force a year earlier.[21]

The pace of innovation quickened in the closing months of 1943. During October Mosquitoes trialled the new GH blind-bombing aid. Two new radio countermeasures were introduced that month. Corona broadcast false orders to enemy night fighters, using German-speaking RAF personnel. ABC (Airborne Cigar), carried by heavy aircraft, disrupted German voice transmissions.

In 1944 the radio-countermeasures available continued to proliferate:

- Radar jamming: Window (Würzburg/AI), Mandrel (Freya) and Ground Grocer (AI).
- RT jamming: Airborne Cigar (VHF), Ground Cigar (VHF), Special Tinsel (HF), Corona (broadcasting false fighter control reportage) and Dartboard (MF).
- W/T jamming: W/T Corona.[21]

Some electronic aids warned of approaching fighters, such as Fishpond and the Monica tail-warner. There was also Boozer, a passive radar giving cockpit light warnings whenever Würzburg gun-laying radar or Lichtenstein night fighter radar locked on. The German equipment included Flensburg, which homed onto Monica transmissions, and Naxos, which homed onto H_2S transmissions.

Marking techniques were further refined. Flare-dropping illuminators went in first, followed by primary markers. With the target well lit, the first markers would be laid, followed by fresh markers of another colour dropped by backers-up. Crucially, if things went wrong, markers of a different type and/or colour were now used to cancel earlier markers. Visual ground-marking was codenamed Newhaven. If the target was obscured by cloud or smoke, to a degree ruling out Newhaven, blind ground-marking by H_2S radar was used. This was the Parramatta method. Oboe blind-marking was known as Musical Parramatta. If the target was totally obscured, a third technique – Wanganui – was employed. This was blind-marking using parachute-equipped sky markers.[21]

New tactics reduced the so-called 'creep-back' problem. Markers and bombs tended to fall short, reflecting the crews' understandable desire to drop as soon as possible and the poor ballistics of incendiary bombs. The master bomber's job was to focus attention on accurate markers. 'Offset marking' began to be employed. Markers were dropped beyond the target, allowing bombs to 'creep back' into the target zone. Offset marking also overcame the problem of markers being obscured by smoke or overwhelmed by fire in the immediate target area.[21]

It became apparent that the British target of 4,000 heavy bombers was unrealistic, but even bigger numbers could now be attained if Bomber Command and the Americans joined forces and coordinated their attacks on a round-the-clock basis. At this time there was overwhelming public support for intensified bombing (typically on a 'they started it' basis), but there were a few prominent critics within Church and Parliament. Dr George Bell, Bishop of Chichester, was a firm opponent of area bombing, which he believed involved too great a loss of life and would bring about a needless destruction of cultural heritage.[22] The Labour MP Richard Stokes was also among the critics.[23]

Harris, meanwhile, had a doughty critic at his very elbow. His chaplain, John Collins, protested after the Hamburg raids of July 1943 and continued as an outspoken opponent of area bombing. Yet he remained in post, possibly on the grounds that free speech was one of the freedoms being fought for. Later, Collins became a founder of CND, the Campaign for Nuclear Disarmament. Harris and Collins were two of a kind – strong-willed and unbending in their views. Somehow, they developed an understanding based on mutual respect.[24]

One famous clash involved Minister of Aircraft Production Sir Stafford Cripps, who gave a lecture at Bomber Command headquarters. He changed the subject of his address at the last moment, moving from 'The Christian in industry' to 'Is God my co-pilot?' In other words, was God on the side of Bomber Command and its crews? The minister concluded that conscience always has primacy and that it is possible for a man to find himself in a situation where he must follow his conscience, rather than orders.[25] It is hard to imagine Albert Speer giving a lecture to senior Luftwaffe officers on the primacy of conscience.

Cripps had a good reception, although some senior officers were offended. Harris then ordered everyone attending Cripps' lecture to attend a second lecture putting the counter-argument. His personal assistant, Harry Weldon – an Oxford don – talked on 'The ethics of bombing'. Collins was less than impressed. When Weldon had finished, he stood up and suggested an alternative title: 'The bombing of ethics'.[25]

Harris was convinced that, with sufficient resources, he could smash Germany from the air. This would make an opposed seaborne invasion of Continental Europe unnecessary. Yet, crushing Germany required more than raw power. As Neillands points out, it also demanded a new degree of ruthlessness.[26]

By the third quarter of 1944 Bomber Command was approaching the pinnacle of its power and German defences were in terminal decline. Germany felt the whirlwind's full destructive power during the final months of bombing, from October 1944 to April 1945.[27] There were significant differences of opinion between Harris, Portal, the American commander Spaaz and others on how best to use the bombers. The Air Ministry wanted synthetic oil plants destroyed. Others wanted more rail targets attacked. Harris wanted to continue the area bombing of cities.

The bombing entered a new phase in August 1944. City attacks resumed on 16 August with raids on Stettin and Kiel.[28] By late August the ability to raid Germany in daylight underlined the success of Allied long-range fighters in suppressing the German day fighter force.[29] The point was fast approaching where night operations suited the German night fighters more than the British bombers, as daylight air superiority was won over Germany.

The ferocity of the bombing campaign grew to levels unimagined in 1940. During the final quarter of 1944 Bomber Command alone dropped 163,000 tons of bombs.[30] In this period, Bomber Command dropped more bombs than in the whole of 1943 and with greater accuracy.[31]

In the first four months of 1945, Bomber Command dropped another 181,000 tons of bombs (around one-fifth of the aggregate for the entire war).[32] The combined total for the last quarter of 1944 and the first four months of 1945 – over 344,000 tons of blast and fire bombs – was the whirlwind delivered. In high explosive terms, this tonnage was the equivalent of around seventeen atomic bombs of Hiroshima size.

The few German cities that had so far escaped destruction, notably Dresden, were now to suffer along with the rest. The late targets also included the south German city of Pforzheim, relatively untouched although close to heavily bombed Karlsruhe and Stuttgart. While spared in six years of war, Pforzheim was to share the fate of so many other cities. Disaster overtook it just eleven weeks before the German surrender.

Notes

1. Redding, T. (2008), *Flying for Freedom*, 259–60.
2. Terraine, J. (1988), *The Right of the Line*, 291.
3. Probert, H. (2001), *Bomber Harris*, 110.
4. Ibid., 132.
5. Sweetman, J. (2004), *Bomber Crew*, 249.
6. Neillands, R. (2001), *The Bomber War*, 52–3.
7. Ibid., 58.
8. Terraine, J. (1988), *The Right of the Line*, 293.
9. Redding, T. (2008), *Flying for Freedom*, 30–1.
10. Neillands, R. (2001), *The Bomber War*, 122–3.
11. Redding, T. (2008), *Flying for Freedom*, 34–5.
12. Neillands, R. (2001), *The Bomber War*, 187–8.
13. Redding, T. (2008), *Flying for Freedom*, 32.

14. Ibid., 41–2, 58.
15. Ibid., 181.
16. Terraine, J. (1988), *The Right of the Line*, 505.
17. Overy, R. (1997), *Bomber Command, 1939–1945*, 111.
18. Terraine, J. (1988), *The Right of the Line*, 518–19.
19. Redding, T. (2008), *Flying for Freedom*, 45–8.
20. Longmate, N. (1988), *The Bombers*, 232.
21. Redding, T. (2008), *Flying for Freedom*, 181–5.
22. Neillands, R. (2001), *The Bomber War*, 279.
23. Ibid., 371.
24. Ibid., 279.
25. Nichol, J. and Rennell, T. (2004), *Tail-end Charlies*, 202–3.
26. Neillands, R. (2001), *The Bomber War*, 116–17.
27. Redding, T. (2008), *Flying for Freedom*, 181.
28. Ibid., 210–11.
29. Ibid., 181.
30. Ibid., 210–11.
31. Ibid., 181.
32. Ibid., 212.

Chapter One

The Whirlwind Approaches

Pforzheim is a South German town on the fringes of the Black Forest, situated between Karlsruhe and Stuttgart. Some know it as Goldstadt, as it has long been the centre of Germany's jewellery and watchmaking industries. The factory owners formed the Gold Adel (the Gold Aristocracy).

In the late 1930s Pforzheim had a population of around 79,000. The town had a gentle introduction to war, given its close proximity to France. Peacetime activities continued much as usual, but the pressures increased later in 1939 when food stamps were issued to Pforzheimers. Leather goods came under wartime control in late August, causing a Monday morning run on Pforzheim's shoe shops.[1]

When Poland was invaded on 1 September 1939, a blackout was introduced but everything remained quiet. Pforzheim had a solitary air-raid warning on 9 September, but no aircraft appeared. The war in the West failed to touch most people's lives, although this was not the case for evacuees from border areas, who had to be found emergency accommodation in the town. Gradually, tougher wartime measures were introduced. Clothes rationing took effect on 16 November 1939. Important city archives, paintings and other works of art were moved to safer locations in basements. The town's finance office was told to cut spending, to free up funds for war contributions and air-raid protection measures. There was a freeze on all new construction.[1]

The pressures eased in the summer of 1940, with the fall of France and overwhelming German victory in the West. When war began the enemy was very close. Now the enemy was on the other side of the Channel. Pforzheim had thirty-five air-raid warnings in 1940. On 19 August a single aircraft released bombs over the suburb of Brötzingen. Two buildings were destroyed but nobody was hurt. On a more positive note, unemployment was a thing of the past. Indeed, the problem was exactly the opposite – there were not enough workers in Pforzheim.[1]

The city remained a backwater of war in 1941, but there were signs of things to come that October; women took over the city's trams as men were called up for military service. The first shortages were felt in 1942. All the basics were available but luxury items became scarce. Things became tougher still in 1943. Now all men aged up to 65 were required to work, as were women up to the age of 45. War industries had priority in employing workers. Newspapers became smaller and some titles merged. Gardens and fields now grew vegetables and council workers found a new role gardening and harvesting. They also cut wood for constructing and reinforcing air-raid shelters. Soldiers based locally helped with shelter-related work, but they now had more pressing duties. There were still relatively few air-raid warnings, but a growing appreciation of what could happen took hold. From 29 March 1943, older schoolchildren were required to serve as Air Force and flak helpers. From mid-March 1944, however, many of Pforzheim's teenagers were deployed in other centres, such as Karlsruhe.[1]

Pforzheim's long tradition of fine, precision work was harnessed to Germany's war economy. On 17 December 1943, State Police headquarters in Karlsruhe warned the director of Pforzheim's power utility, in a secret memorandum, that the city was an attractive target for bombers given its significance in fuse production. An expansion of Pforzheim's air defences was recommended. Meanwhile, preparations were in hand to deal with the aftermath of a heavy raid. The city's butchers, bakers, grocery wholesalers and dairy suppliers were organized into a 'food group'. They were ordered to create stockpiles beyond the town. By late 1943 there were emergency food stores in twenty villages and other rural locations. In a crisis food would be provided for three days without the need for food stamps or money. Similar steps were taken with regard to clothing, shoes and household goods.[1]

As the tide of war turned, Goebbels' 'total war' began to affect every Pforzheimer. There were 298 air-raid warnings in 1944. People adopted a more flexible approach to life. The Pforzheim 'swap market' opened, allowing people to trade all manner of goods. More allotments were cultivated, to increase local food production. More people were called up and women up to the age of 50 now had to work. By August 1944 Pforzheimers lived at the fundamental level; yet they refused to bend completely, and the training of fine metals and jewellery workers continued. Somehow, a new vocational college opened, despite the many building restrictions in place.[1]

Pforzheim suffered its first major bombing raid on 1 April 1944. Those who were bombed out were found emergency accommodation. Those in need received help from clothing centres and other contingency stores. Efforts to build more shelters redoubled, but only previously approved work went ahead. There were no funds for new shelter projects. The emphasis was on extending and improving existing shelters within residential blocks. According to town records, public shelter places were available for only a small proportion of the population. Everyone was now subject to emergency duty, including the Hitler Youth. Boys aged 15 were sent to dig trenches in the Vosges. Most of Pforzheim's builders were mobilized to work on the Westwall in September. The Oberbürgermeister protested but his arguments were rejected: national defence was more important than local shelter building.[1]

In February 1945 Pforzheim remained largely intact, although nearby Stuttgart and Karlsruhe had been heavily bombed and Freiburg, to the south, had been devastated on 27–8 November 1944. Freiburg had little industry and had not been bombed before. It became a target as French and American troops advanced in the Vosges, some 35 miles to the west. The town was attacked as it had rail facilities and German troops were believed to have concentrated there. On that November night 1,900 tons of bombs rained down in just twenty-five minutes, killing 2,088 people and injuring 4,072. Another 858 people were listed as missing after this raid by 341 Lancaster bombers and 10 Mosquitoes.[2]

The destruction of Freiburg put Pforzheimers on notice. *The Bomber Command War Diaries* stated that, by this time, the bombers were running out of large cities to attack. They began raiding smaller, less industrialized communities – towns such as Darmstadt, Bonn, Freiburg, Heilbronn and Ulm.[3] Towns and cities close to Germany's western frontier were increasingly important rail and road communications centres, as they now faced the Allied armies about to cross the Rhine.

Many Pforzheimers believed there was nothing in their town worth bombing. They were wrong in making this assumption. Dr Christian Groh, a former Stadtarchiv Pforzheim director: 'Much of Pforzheim's industry consisted of "backyard" enterprises. That's how it was before the war and it's still that way today. There is no heavy industry. The city specializes in precision work for the production of jewellery and watches. Pforzheim's workers have always been highly skilled. This is a town of small businesses.'[4]

Pforzheimers should have had a more acute understanding of the realities of war. Their city suffered heavily in historic wars with France. In more recent times, Pforzheim lost 1,600 men in the First World War; it was about to pay a much higher price in the Second. Pforzheim's factories and skilled workers produced a wide range of fuses and other precision components for weaponry. Its railyards were important for the movement of military stores and troops to the front. Pforzheim was also intact and the enemy was fast approaching.

By July 1944 a total of 491,596 tons had been dropped by Bomber Command. By April 1945 this had increased to 954,707 tons. In effect, 58 per cent of all tonnage dropped since the war began was dropped between D-Day (6 June 1944) and the end of hostilities.[5]

In the first sixteen months of war (i.e. to the end of 1940) Bomber Command dropped 13,045 tons of bombs, increasing to 31,704 tons in 1941, 45,561 tons in 1942, 157,257 tons in 1943, 535,308 tons in 1944 and 181,403 tons in the first four months of 1945. During 1944 and the first four months of 1945, Bomber Command dropped more than twice the tonnage of the period 1939 to 1943. The tonnage dropped in the final seven months of the bombing campaign (from 1 October 1944 to 30 April 1945) exceeded the total for the previous sixty-one months of the war.[6]

One of Bomber Command's principal weapons was the 4,000lb high capacity blast bomb, known as the 'Blockbuster' or 'Cookie'. Bomber Command dropped 68,000 Cookies, to open up buildings and make it easier for incendiaries to take hold.[7] This bomb could be dropped in combinations of two or three, producing 8,000lb or 12,000lb weapons. The big Cookie was always hoisted into the bomb bay first, at a position close to the aircraft's centre of gravity. There were fifteen bomb stations in the Lancaster's bomb bay, arranged in three rows of five, and the Cookie was

War stores: bombs available to the squadrons. The 4,000lb weapon is a high capacity blast bomb, the 'Cookie' or 'Blockbuster'. *Photo: Trustees of the Imperial War Museum.*

secured to No.13, the middle station.[8] The Cookie was a product of the British assessment of the effectiveness of the German bombing of 1940–1. It was noted that German parachute mines had very thin casings and, consequently, a very high ratio of explosives to bomb weight. They devastated surrounding buildings as almost all the blast effect went sideways. The Cookie lacked a parachute but was also a thin casing, high capacity blast weapon.

Bomber Command's most destructive weapon, however, was much smaller: the 4lb No. 15 magnesium incendiary. These bomblets had an hexagonal section for easy packing. The incendiaries were carried in cans known as Small Bomb Containers (SBCs), each holding ninety bomblets. Around one in ten incendiaries carried an explosive charge, to kill or maim those attempting to extinguish them. This version was known as No. 15 (X). In February 1943 Bomber Command held stocks of 5 million 4lb incendiaries, with weekly production running at 60,000.[9]

There was also a 30lb incendiary bomb with a filling of phosphorous and other combustibles. This weapon was said to have 'a great morale effect'.[10] A Lancaster could carry a Cookie and twelve containers, each holding eight 30lb incendiaries.[11] The containers of large incendiaries dropped clear of the bomb bay and the weapons were separated by a trigger fired by bariometric fuse. The smaller 4lb incendiaries were held inside the SBC by spring-loaded buttons and two retaining strips. This type of SBC stayed in the bomb bay. When the strips fell away the incendiaries tumbled out as pressure from the spring-loaded buttons was released. These bomblets had no aerodynamic properties – they tumbled to the ground and had a tendency to undershoot. The resulting fires on the ground attracted high explosive bombs and contributed to 'creep back', a tendency for bombs to fall short.[12]

When sending out orders for operations, Bomber Command's headquarters staff used code words for the various warloads. 'Arson' was the rather predictable code word for an area bombing all-incendiary load. 'Cookie/Plumduff' was the code word for an area bombing blast and fire mix, used against heavily industrialized areas. It consisted of an impact-fused short-finned Cookie, smaller short-delay high explosive bombs and containers of 4lb or 30lb incendiaries. 'Usual' was the code word for a typical area blast/maximum incendiary mix – a Cookie and SBCs of incendiaries.[13]

Raimund Frei was born in 1921. His maternal grandparents and his mother lived in Pforzheim. His father, from Allgäu, was a master umbrella maker who arrived in Pforzheim shortly after the end of the First World War, in 1919. A local umbrella manufacturer was looking for someone to run his company and Raimund's father got the job. Later, he had his own shop in Gymnasiumstrasse. Raimund Frei enjoyed the outdoors: 'When I was 16 I became an apprentice forest ranger for the Baden state forest service. Two years later, in 1939, I transferred to Ettlingen, near Karlsruhe, but returned to Pforzheim occasionally to visit family and friends. I missed Pforzheim. At that age I was keen on girls. We used to hang around the Brötzinger Gasse – the "Rennbahn", or racetrack, in the town centre, with its fashionable cafes.

'I regarded Pforzheim as Baden's most beautiful city. The Black Forest is very close – Pforzheim is often referred to as the gateway to the Black Forest. It was easy to get into the countryside and relax but I also liked the city. It was modern for its time.' Pforzheim was badly damaged in the wars of the seventeenth century and by a major fire in 1789. Many buildings in 1930s Pforzheim had been constructed in relatively recent times.[14]

The city changed dramatically in the late 1920s and early 1930s. Raimund Frei: 'Naturally, I joined the Jungvolk and, later, the Hitler Jugend. The Jungvolk was very appealing. There were two Jewish boys in our class, together with two "half-Jews". They were not allowed to join and had to leave our school shortly afterwards. We didn't think much about them. They disappeared from view and, later, we heard they had emigrated. We weren't much interested in racial issues. I only heard about that in passing, until I joined the Hitler Youth. We were more interested in National Socialism's ability to fix national problems, including the high unemployment rate. The NSDAP (Nationalsozialistische Deutsche Arbeiterpartei) seemed to offer a real solution. Pforzheim struggled hard after the First World War. There was mass unemployment and hunger. Our industry was too focused on jewellery and watches and these markets collapsed. The kids in my class, myself included, felt that life would get better with the National Socialists in power.'[14]

The aircrew nickname for Arthur Harris was 'Butch' – short for 'Butcher'. This was not a reference to his attacks on German cities but, rather, a wry observation on the bombing campaign's high cost in British lives.[15] Bomber Command suffered higher casualties, in proportion to size, than any other branch of the British armed forces. Yet it was an all-volunteer force and, throughout a very long war, there was never a shortage of young volunteers.[16] The many thousands who stepped forward included William 'Dave' Davidson, born in 1922. His family lived in Wanstead, Essex. Dave left school in 1938. All he wanted to do was fly, and he got his chance on reaching the age of 18. He wanted fighters but, in due course, was posted to Bomber Command. 'When I volunteered for aircrew, I joined 145 Squadron, flying Spitfires at Catterick. This was a quiet sector and I saw no action. I then went overseas, firstly to the Middle East and then to West Africa. I was posted to Bomber Command when I returned in 1943. I got on well flying Wellingtons but wanted to get back into fighters. That wasn't to be.'[17]

Davidson progressed from Wellingtons to four-engined Halifaxes and, eventually, the Lancasters of 100 Squadron at Grimsby. He was about to begin his operational tour with six other volunteers. Later in life some veterans remarked that, under the stress of combat, they became closer to their crew than to members of their own families. Bonds forged in war often lasted a lifetime. Davidson's flight engineer was Sergeant Fred Decker, 'an amusing, wire-haired Londoner. We got on well together.' The navigator was Flight Sergeant A.V. 'Tiny' Townsend: 'Unlike many people nicknamed "Tiny", our navigator really was small. Later, he received the DFM. Tiny was a character, a real live wire.'[17]

The two gunners were sergeants. 'Paddy' Watson, from Belfast, was in the mid-upper turret. Dave Davidson: 'Paddy was a replacement for a Canadian gunner. I made the change before we started the tour. The Canadian thought he was God's gift to women; I thought he was pretty hopeless.' In the rear turret was Sergeant 'Sherry' Sherratt. Sherry had a difficult young life. His father walked out and he had been raised by his grandmother. He stayed in the Air Force after the war but was killed when his Lincoln bomber crashed. The bomb aimer was Flight Sergeant R.J. 'Dicky' Lloyd and the wireless operator was Howell 'Taffy' Evans.[17]

Evans was born near Swansea in 1924. His father, a draper, was also postmaster for Hendy

No way back to fighters: Flight Lieutenant William 'Dave' Davidson, DFC. *Photo: Jo Cowen (née Davidson).*

village, near Pontarddulais. His son, a bright grammar school pupil, always did his homework. He had been warned that if he didn't put in the effort he would 'end up in the tinworks'. Ironically, with a break for war service, he spent his entire working life in the steelworks, becoming a production foreman. Evans was 15 when war broke out in 1939: 'I went to work in the steelworks office. I had joined the Air Training Corps, although the last thing on my mind was flying. We had a few Morse lessons and I discovered I had an aptitude for it. I took quite a fancy to Morse and that's how my fate was determined!'[18]

Evans was called up in 1942, on reaching the age of 18: 'They asked me what I wanted to do. I said I'd like to be a wireless operator. They assumed I meant aircrew, but I would have been content staying on the ground! Anyway, there were no vacancies for ground-based wireless operators. I passed the medical, went home on deferred service and returned to the steelworks. It wasn't until late March 1943 that I was required to report to the Aircrew Receiving Centre at St John's Wood, London.'[18]

Following his basic training Evans arrived at No. 2 Radio School at Yatesbury, Wiltshire, in June 1943. The school's twin-engined training aircraft took up four or five pupils at a time. There were also some single-engined Percival Proctors. His first flight at Yatesbury lasted one hour twenty minutes: 'I had a bit of a problem – I was airsick every time I went up. People noticed and I began to get very worried. Fortunately, I was "cured" when I began flying in the Proctor during October.'[18]

Yatesbury was a happy posting for Howell Evans, as he met the love of his life: 'Pat lived in nearby Chippenham. I met her in a park on a lovely Sunday afternoon. The RAF was responsible, indirectly, for a marriage that lasted nearly sixty years. Pat was with a friend. I asked them if they wanted to go to the pictures that night. They couldn't – they were Toc H volunteers and on duty that evening. Well, that night my mate and I had had a couple of drinks and we were walking back when we saw the Toc H sign. We decided to check on the girls' alibi and went inside for a cup of tea. There they were. We asked them what time they finished. When Pat said she had to stay on, to do the washing up, I did a foolish thing with implications for our future life together. I vaulted over the counter and went to the sink, to help her – mistake!' Howell Evans passed out as a wireless operator during Christmas 1943.[18]

From his first day in the RAF Howell had been friends with Londoner Jim Coughrey, another wireless operator/gunner. Somehow, they stayed together through a long series of postings, including the move to an Operational Training Unit (OTU): 'We had been inseparable but things changed at OTU, when we had to crew up. Anyone who hadn't found a crew within a fortnight was placed. Jim and I decided to hang back and see who was left at the end. Only two pilots, Dave Davidson and Pilot Officer Pound, still required wireless operators at the end of the two weeks. We tossed a coin; Jim won and picked Pound. That left me with Dave.'[18]

There may have been good reasons why Davidson was still on the market after a fortnight. Howell Evans: 'He soon put us in the picture. He said he was a fighter pilot and wasn't interested in bombers. He had made no effort to recruit a crew. He told us straight: he was going to do everything possible to fail as a bomber pilot. Despite these discouraging words, I liked Dave from the first. We hit it off, despite his terrible landings in Wellingtons!'[18]

Evans got to know the rest of the crew. 'Flight engineer Fred Decker came from Mitcham, in Surrey. He was a lovely chap and a good flight engineer. Bomb aimer Dick Lloyd was from Hereford and became a close friend. He had worked for the Inland Revenue and had married a girl from Pontypool. I was also friendly with navigator Arthur "Tiny" Townsend. He was "Daddy" to the crew, being a few years older. He was married, with a couple of kids. The rear gunner, "Sherry" Sherratt, was a character and the mid-upper gunner, Paddy Watson, was a charmer. Our Belfast boy was easy to wind up. Dick had studied Paddy's table habits while eating his flying breakfast. He handled his egg like a surgeon. Delicately, he cut away the white and ate it. The lonely yolk was then sandwiched between two slices of bread. One day Dick had a word with the WAAF serving us. She came up to Paddy – who was just about to sandwich the yolk – and said: "I see you don't like the yolk!" She took his plate away. Paddy went berserk and we fell about laughing.'[18]

Howell Evans stopped laughing when he lost Jim, his best friend, while at Sandtoft Heavy Conversion Unit. The entire crew died in a Halifax accident: 'We took off just after Pound and saw the mid-air explosion. Over the intercom I said: "Good God! That's Pound and his crew." No-one could survive that.'[18]

'This loss really shook me up. Jim and I had a strange conversation just before take-off. He came up to me, held out his hand and said: "Taff, thanks for being such a great friend." I was startled and said: "What?" He replied: "We've been friends for a long time and I'm grateful for your friendship. I don't think we will meet again." He had had a premonition and his death affected me terribly. That was the only time Dave had to say to me: "Come on, Taff! Pull your finger out." I stopped writing home. My worried mother contacted the CO and asked him what was wrong. I wrote home regularly, but there had been silence since Jim's death. In the end I was called before the adjutant, who ordered me to resume writing immediately.'[18]

Things brightened for Evans when the crew were posted to Lancaster Finishing School at RAF Hemswell, the final step before commencing operational flying. They had their first flight in a Lancaster on 30 September 1944: 'We were thrilled with the Lanc. It was a fantastic aircraft.'[18]

Hans Gerstung was 7 when war began, and now his teenage years approached. His family came from Pforzheim. Young Hans had known nothing but National Socialism: 'Grandfather was an art teacher and jewellery designer and Father was an architect. I was an only child. We were holidaying on Lake Constance when war came. We had to return but found the railway station packed with people, all with the same thought in mind – to get home as quickly as possible. There was an open window in a carriage and Father fed me in. I knew something very important was happening but managed to keep hold of the toy sailing yacht Father had bought me.

'My father was 51 when war began. He had been an NSDAP member since 1937 – as a freelance architect he had to join the Nazi Party. His de-Nazification records class him as a *Mitläufer* [follower] and a *kleiner Pg* [*Parteigenosse*], a minor Party member. He had served in the First World War. Because of his age he wasn't required in the Second World War until 1944, when he supervised the construction of some of the Rhine fortifications. He was away most of the time but came home whenever he could. When the city suffered several small air raids he became the mayor's adviser on building repairs.'[19]

Father said nothing to son about war and the Nazis. Hans Gerstung's elementary school taught no politics. Things soon changed when he attended high school: 'Our teachers wore SA (Sturmabteilung) or Wehrmacht uniform. We learned to snap to attention and give the Nazi salute. There was a lot of pressure to join the Jungvolk, but I was happy to join – everyone else did. It was a fine thing. There were flags and drums.' Hans Gerstung became a Jungenschaftsführer of 15 Richthofen, a Fähnlein (unit) named after First World War fighter ace Manfred von Richthofen. Young Gerstung had up to ten *Pimpfe* ('brats') under his command.[19]

Deeply held religious beliefs prevented some from supporting Hitler's 'New Germany'. Irma Baroni (née Facoltosi) was 10 when war began. Her Italian father had died before she was born. 'My mother, Tina, was a Jehovah's Witness with a reputation for being outspoken. Mum came from Heidenheim and had been a governess in Cologne. My father's family lived in central Pforzheim, but moved to the western suburb of Arlinger two years before I was born. When Grandfather passed away, Mum and Granny set up home at Blauenstrasse 1. Mum worked as a nanny.[20]

'The Italian connection meant we were brought up as Catholics, but the church took a hefty share of my father's assets and that changed minds. Having decided that the Catholic Church was too fond of money, mum became a Jehovah's Witness. This was not without risk in National Socialist Germany. Mum was a woman of honour and would have nothing to do with the Nazis. She refused to vote in 1933 and that made her an enemy of the state in Nazi eyes. She was so outspoken that it was a miracle that she was not put into a concentration camp.

Flags and drums: teenager Hans Gerstung was promoted to Jungenschaftsführer.
Photo: Hans Gerstung.

Granny feared for her. She tried to reason with her, saying: "Tina, you are putting the whole family in danger!"'[20]

Irma's grandmother had good reason to be frightened. The Gestapo visited on several occasions: 'I remember three uniformed men arriving at our door. They marched in, with their great boots on, and started shouting at Mum: "Why didn't you vote? You're an intelligent woman. We need people like you! Why don't you join us? How do you live? Where do you get your money from?" She rose to the occasion and said: "You have entered my house. At least have the decency to treat me with respect." Granny's natural optimism was shattered. She said to me: "I'm not sure if your mum will still be at home with us this evening."'[20]

'Somehow, she escaped serious punishment for being a Jehovah's Witness and refusing to participate in National Socialism. The Gestapo kept a close watch on us. They searched our home for subversive literature, but found only the Bible. No *Watchtower*. As the youngest of three children, I was very frightened. Granny helped – she had a jolly personality. Yet it was always a strain living under the Nazis. At school I was required to give the Hitler salute. I was fearful and complied, but with a bad conscience. My religious upbringing taught me that the word *Heil* belonged to God, rather than the Hitlers of this world. The pressure was always there. I was supposed to join the BDM – the girls' Hitler Youth. They came for me a few times but Mum held firm. She told them I was ill and could not, under any circumstances, go to meetings.'[20]

Karl Mössner was Irma's age. They grew up together, and he remembers her as 'a very smart girl'. As for Tina: 'She was brave. In fact, we were impressed, as a family, with the strength of will of the Jehovah's Witnesses. After the war, we became Jehovah's Witnesses.'

Londoner Sam Lipfriend was a Bomber Command volunteer. Sam was born in 1925; his family were Polish immigrants. On leaving school he found work in an aircraft factory: 'I also joined the Air Training Corps. I had two great years in the ATC – it was the perfect run-up to service in the RAF.'[21]

In January 1943, a few months before his eighteenth birthday, Sam discovered that the RAF had more volunteers than places. He presented himself at the Aircrew Receiving Centre at St John's Wood: 'I was told to come back after my birthday. I did just that and passed all aptitude tests for pilot training, only to be told that I would have to wait eighteen months before being called. I was in a hurry and asked for alternatives. Navigators were waiting fifteen months, bomb aimers twelve months and flight engineers six months. I decided to be a flight engineer and I was called in mid-August 1943.'[21]

In the final phase of training Lipfriend crewed up at 1667 Heavy Conversion Unit, Sandtoft, in May 1944: 'We flew Halifaxes but we were destined for No. 1 Lancaster School at Hemswell, where we arrived that July. We were then posted for operations to 101 Squadron, a 1 Group Lancaster unit at Ludford Magna.'[21]

The fates were against this crew. The new boys took off on a cross-country training flight – their first with the squadron – on 31 July 1944. They crashed at Lichfield aerodrome seven hours forty minutes later: 'We were halfway round the cross-country when we got a wireless message ordering us back. Fog was rolling in from the sea. We arrived just as aircraft were entering Ludford Magna's circuit, on their return from the night's operation. We were told to head west and land at another airfield but the poor visibility stayed ahead of us. We tried airfield after airfield – Lichfield was the ninth! We crashed at 02.43 on 1 August 1944.'[21]

Three of the seven crew were killed on impact: 'The bomb aimer was sitting with the wireless operator, with their backs to the main spar. The aircraft fuselage broke at that point – they fell through and the wreckage fell back on top of them.' Sam Lipfriend was unconscious: 'I was thrown through the canopy and knocked out. I ended up in the trees near Lichfield's domestic site. I struck the trees with my head, back and legs but broke no bones, although my head swelled up bigger than a football. I was in hospital for over a month.'[21]

When Lipfriend woke up at the crash site he could hear someone calling: 'I think I joined in. Anyway, someone found me.' That someone was Corporal Goldsmith, of RAF Lichfield's fire section. Just over a fortnight later he wrote to the flight engineer he had rescued. In his letter of 17 August 1944, he was responding to a note of thanks from the hospital patient: 'It is nice to know you are pulling round.' He then described the events of that night: 'We could hear you stooging around. Then you seemed to be trying for the runway, but the mist was getting worse every second. On your second pass you only just cleared two hangars. We had everything ready as it was obvious that you were going to hit something sooner or later.' Then the Lancaster finally hit the ground. Goldsmith wrote: 'All we could see was a mass of flames travelling along the ground. We found you and another chap near the main body of the kite, which wasn't burning. We found two of your pals at about 6.30 in the morning but, of course, there was nothing we could do for them. Anyway, it was a miracle that you weren't all killed.'[21]

That miracle allowed Sam Lipfriend to complete thirty-two bombing operations. He participated in attacks on some of the most heavily defended targets in the Reich, including Cologne, Dortmund, Duisburg, Essen, Hannover and Merseburg.[21]

An artistic boy with a gentle frame of mind, Wolfram Aichele enjoyed his childhood in a cultured, rather Bohemian haven from the contaminated world of National Socialism. At a time when the vast majority of boys were enjoying the Hitler Youth, Wolfram was more interested in German Gothic craftsmanship and medieval sculpture.[22]

The Aichele family home sat on a hilltop at Eutingen, on the outskirts of Pforzheim. Wolfram's parents, Erwin and Marie Charlotte, held themselves aloof from Pforzheim's *bourgeoisie*. Erwin, a successful wildlife artist, had taught at a jewellery school.[23] There were three children. Wolfram had a brother, Reiner, and a sister,

Gunhild. However, there were limits to this family's ability to insulate itself from life under the Nazis. The first impact on the household was the closure of Erwin's Freemasonry lodge. The stupidity of Nazi officialdom was evident in a decree that all masons who retained membership after January 1933 were banned from joining the Nazi party. This gave Wolfram's father the perfect alibi for not joining! However, this offered only modest protection, as all former masons were 'enemies of the German people'. Erwin saw the market for his artwork dwindle. His main customer, a hunting magazine, was Jewish-owned and ceased publication.[24]

The Weber and Aichele families were friends in Eutingen. Sisters Doris and Sigrid Weber were 5 and 11 respectively at the outbreak of the Second World War. Naturally, the age gap meant they developed a different perspective on the destruction of Pforzheim and its subsequent occupation by French Colonial troops – at which time Doris was 11 and Sigrid 17.[25]

Doris Weber: 'Our father, Max Weber, volunteered at the age of 18 to fight in the First World War and was taken prisoner. He was away for five years. On his return he started studying in Karlsruhe, in order to become a teacher.' Sigrid Kern (née Weber): 'Father's father, who had a barber's shop in town, was killed in 1944 when the hospital he was staying in was bombed. Our father, the eldest of three brothers, played the piano and violin. He also played the organ in church in Eutingen and conducted a mixed choir in Pforzheim. That is how he came to know our mother, Elise Bordné; they married in 1925.[25]

'We knew the Aicheles very well. Erwin Aichele was a well-known painter of animals and landscapes. Gunhild, the youngest of three children, was a close friend of mine. I liked visiting their home. We had rather strict parents, but Gunhild's home environment was very different. It was a relief to be in a more relaxed atmosphere. When the time came for my labour service, I went to the Aicheles as a home help. Their villa was full of old furniture and antiques. The huge garden was full of animals. It was different, however, being in Gunhild's house as an employee. Her father spent his time painting and her mother took care of the big garden. She liked to have her friends around her and tended to daydream of better times.'[25]

When the war began Sigrid remembers the soldiers marching through Eutingen: 'There was a euphoric atmosphere. The buildings were decorated – everywhere was bedecked with flowers.' Doris was less impressed: 'I had to go out "shaking tins", collecting for the war effort by knocking on doors. I didn't like it. I was embarrassed. It's not easy to collect money!' Sigrid, that much older, didn't mind: 'When the Russian campaign began, I collected for Winter Relief. I asked for warm clothing, rabbit fur and wool. By that time the Aicheles' son, Wolfram, was 18 and he went to the Russian Front.'[25]

Doris, at the age of eight, began knitting socks for Wolfram. She had no enthusiasm for National Socialism. She was sent out of class on one occasion for not using the 'Heil Hitler' greeting. Sigrid, that bit older, decided it was best to keep quiet at school: 'I began to feel isolated. I went to BDM meetings once a week and we had to march through Eutingen, singing songs (*Hetzlieder* – marching songs that attacked opponents of the regime). I hated BDM. I resented losing the freedom to think for myself. We were expected to help farmers at harvest time but I refused. The only person I knew who felt the same way was Gunhild Aichele. She didn't go to BDM. I remember the propaganda films, the cinema newsreels and Hitler and Goebbels speaking. All they seemed to talk about was the territory they had conquered.'[25]

In April 1944 the heavy bombers were switched to Eisenhower's command, for the support of ground forces invading Europe. By September they were free to open a fresh phase of strategic bombing. The Allied armies were reaching out towards Germany's western frontier and the Chief of the Air Staff was determined to further damage German industry and make it harder for the enemy to counter-attack. Oil production was 'Peter' Portal's priority target. New directives were issued to Bomber Command and the US strategic air forces. Their overall objective became the progressive destruction and dislocation of German military, industrial and economic systems, together with direct support of Allied land and naval forces. After the oil industry, the priorities were rail and water transport systems, together with tank and motor transport plants and depots. The Luftwaffe and aircraft industry were no longer priorities, given the weakness of the German Air Force and overwhelming Allied air power.[26]

Allied success in France extended the range of Bomber Command's target location and blind bombing systems. Mobile control stations were set up in liberated territory, much closer to Germany. The bombers spent less time over hostile territory and the escort fighters had more time to patrol the combat area.[26] New crews came forward to replace losses and contribute to Bomber Command's expansion. They included Flying Officer Bruce Potter and his crew. His bomb aimer, Bill Thomas, was a Cornishman. With a distinct lack of imagination, everyone called him 'Bombs'. Thomas was proud of his Cornish heritage: his father was an engineer at the famous Levant Mine and his grandfather had been a mine captain. Bill did well at grammar school and went to work at the county council's health department in Truro. He was a keen member of the Air Training Corps, but his age meant he had to wait until 1942 to join the RAF: 'Even then, I had to spend another twelve months on deferred service.'[27]

During pilot training Bill had trouble with his landings and re-mustered as a navigator/bomb aimer. He crossed the Atlantic and continued training in Canada. He returned to Britain in the bomb aimer role and had a minor brush with authority: 'I managed to hang onto my treasured "flying arsehole" observer's badge, refusing to put up the "B" brevet. This caused a row but that was soon resolved by a note in my logbook. I got official permission to continue to display the "O", whatever job I was doing.'[27]

His skipper, Bruce Potter, had wanted to be a fighter pilot but was posted for heavy bomber training: 'He resented this and made up for it by flying the Lanc like a single-engined fighter. Bruce was from Sussex. He was a good pilot but extremely highly strung. He didn't drink much but liked the ladies. Our flight engineer, Gordon Woolley, came from Wood Green in North London. A flight sergeant, he was quiet and efficient at his job. I gave him a hand during take-offs and landings – I was always ready to switch tanks if a problem developed. Our navigator, Flight Sergeant Jack Boyle, came from Blackpool. Jack was quick to notice any deviation in course and would remind Bruce of the desired track. As a married man, he had a vested interest in accurate flying. Our Aussie wireless operator, Warrant Officer J.S. "Digger" Askew, could drink all night. During the day he slept in whenever he could. When on standby we had to get him out of bed and sober him up for the night's op. I remember Bruce shaking him and saying: "Wake up, you bugger!" We put up with this because he did his job well despite the booze. He missed nothing when "listening out".' That left the gunners. Flight Sergeant Douglas Smith was in the mid-upper turret: '"Smithy" was a quiet lad from the Midlands. Our rear gunner was Flight Sergeant Harold "Harry" Hambrook, a cockney. Harry was tall for a rear gunner, at just over 6ft, but he had no trouble getting his spare frame in and out of that cramped turret.'[27]

The crew arrived at Hemswell Lancaster Finishing School in September 1944. Everyone was impressed with the Lanc. Bill Thomas: 'As far as I was concerned, this was the only aircraft in the world. When trimmed out correctly, a pilot could fly the Lanc with just two fingers on the control column, although we got pushed around a bit whenever the gunners rotated their turrets.'[27]

Potter and crew had a lucky escape during training. They were involved in an emergency that mixed danger with farce: 'Our OTU's Wellingtons were absolutely knackered. We were preparing to land when the undercarriage refused to come down. Bruce was told to dive the Wimpy and check whether the G-force, when pulling out, would be powerful enough to shift the undercarriage. We tried but without success. We appeared to have an hydraulic leak and there was more discussion with Flying Control. They asked us to top up the header tank, located just behind the pilot. They suggested, in all seriousness, that we piss into it! This would have been an impossible feat, requiring accuracy beyond our capabilities. Some bright spark on the ground then suggested that we piss into our Thermos flasks and then top up the tank. I'd had enough. I said we would do this only if we were promised new flasks. Fortunately, the wheels then came down and we made a normal landing.'[27]

Flight Lieutenant 'Buzz' Burrows and crew were also getting ready for operations at this time. Ron 'Gerry' Germain, from Plymouth, was the wireless operator. He was 16 when war began. During a period in London young Ron worked for GEC. This was a 'reserved occupation', but Germain soon discovered he was free to volunteer for aircrew. He wanted to be a pilot but became a wireless operator. He logged his first training flight in December 1943, progressed to heavier aircraft, moved to No. 28 OTU and crossed paths with Burrows, his future pilot. 'Buzz looked very young. He was a tall man, pleasant and modest in habit. He didn't go out drinking with us, unlike our navigator, Sergeant Wilson, who liked his beer. The flight engineer was Sergeant "Smithy" Smith, not especially forthright, and the bomb aimer was Flying

'Buzz' Burrows' crew: 'an easy-going lot with a very good pilot'. Standing, left to right: flight engineer Sergeant 'Smithy' Smith, mid-upper gunner Sergeant 'Towse' Towson, pilot Flight Lieutenant 'Buzz' Burrows, bomb aimer Flying Officer 'Watty' Watling and rear gunner Sergeant 'Curly' Miles. Kneeling (left) is wireless operator Sergeant Ron Germain, with the navigator, Sergeant Wilson. *Photo: Lisa Stone.*

Officer "Watty" Watling. A young sergeant, 'Towse' Towson, was in the mid-upper turret. Sergeant "Curly" Miles – a happy-go-lucky chap – was in the rear turret. We were an easy-going lot with a very good pilot.'[28]

Gunner Frank Woodley's father served in the First World War as a medic before re-mustering into the RAF in 1920. Frank's early years were spent in Palestine. In due course the family returned to the UK. When Frank left school he became a messenger at Fawley oil refinery, near Southampton, and witnessed the heavy bombing of 1940. Now approaching his eighteenth birthday, he was anxious to serve. His brother, Roy, felt the same way and they volunteered together for the RAF on 2 February 1941. Their introduction to service life lacked glamour: 'Our first job was to top and tail sugar beet!'[29]

Frank Woodley was an RAF Regiment ground gunner but responded to a call for aircrew volunteers. He craved action and eventually got his share. He was posted to gunnery school and then to 30 OTU. He had five flights with Flight Lieutenant McLean before this pilot died in an accident. When it came to crewing up for operations, he was one of a crowd of awkward young men ushered into a large room and told to get on with it. 'I went up to a chap and asked: "Are you with anybody?" He had been a driver before becoming a rear gunner. We gunners were then joined by a Canadian bomb aimer (a failed pilot), a navigator, a wireless operator and, of course, a pilot. The flight engineer joined us later, when we went into four-engined aircraft. Our pilot was Warrant Officer Ken Sidwell. At 31, he was relatively mature. Ken had run his own building business in the West Country. He was very easy-going, a nice person. Ken survived thirty-five trips and was then posted as an instructor. Sadly, in July 1945 he went out over the North Sea and never came back. Our bomb aimer – the same advanced age as our pilot – was Canadian Jack Banks, a tough man who kept himself to himself. Twenty-one-year-old Glaswegian John Hewitt, our navigator, was also a bit of a loner. Rear gunner Denis Witchmarsh, from Bournemouth, was sociable and keen on the fair sex. Wireless operator John Chapman came from Hull and, at 19, was the baby.'[29]

As the 1920s became the 1930s, Pforzheim was a troubled town. Raimund Frei remembers his father telling him to close the umbrella shop's shutters: 'He got me to do this whenever he was expecting a street riot. He didn't want his windows broken. Before 1933 there was a lot of politically motivated street violence in Pforzheim.

Sidwell's boys: Warrant Officer Ken Sidwell and crew. Back row, left to right: rear gunner Denis Witchmarsh, Ken Sidwell and mid-upper gunner Frank Woodley. Front row: bomb aimer Jack Banks, navigator John Hewitt, flight engineer Jack Allen and wireless operator John Chapman. *Photo: Frank Woodley.*

Three parties held demonstrations and fought it out: the communists, socialists and NSDAP. Our shop had an unfortunate location, with socialist and communist pubs close by. The Nazi pub was on Östliche Karl-Friedrich-Strasse and there was constant friction. Each party had a "better concept" and was prepared to use violence. They got nowhere and ended up with bloody heads.[30]

'Things were different, of course, after 1933. With Hitler in power, our schoolteachers explained the injustices of the Versailles Treaty and its devastating effects on the German people. The insight that Germany had been treated badly formed our ideological background. It was very simple: if the British and French could be patriotic and feel national pride, why should Germans be different?'[30]

Werner Schultz was 21 years old at the time of the catastrophic air attack on Pforzheim. 'My father was Jewish. He was from Posen and came to Pforzheim in 1904 as a 19-year-old watchmaker. Later, he converted to Christianity and married a Christian woman living in Pforzheim. Our home was at Belfortstrasse until 1930, when we moved to Bayenstrasse 51. My father had been married before. He had three children by his first wife, who died in childbirth. Father married my mother in 1917 and had two more kids. I was the youngest.'[31]

Werner's early life was sheltered. He spent little time in the city, preferring the family's Sunday walks in the countryside. He was nine when Hitler came to power. 'I can remember one of the early SA torch parades. It was fascinating – so fascinating that I followed it down to the Saalbau. When it was over I had trouble finding my way home.'[31]

Taking over: the Nazis' Hitler Jugend absorbed all other youth organizations. The Jungschar church band was told to march with the swastika. *Photo: Werner Schultz.*

His father, a Democrat, said nothing at home when the National Socialists took over. 'It took me some time to become aware of my Jewish background. I was more interested in the Jungschar church club and the sports club. Then the Hitler Jugend gradually absorbed all other youth organizations. It began when the Protestant Jungschar had to march with its banner *and* the swastika flag. The local Jungschar's marching band was led by my elder brother, Kuno, who was seven years my senior.'[31]

Life took an ominous turn. In late 1938 Werner and the rest of the family were excluded from their sports club because of 'impure blood'. Werner Schultz: 'This was one of the most cruel experiences of my life. We had been members since 1930 and all our friends were in the sports club. Now the club was in the hands of the Nazis.'[31]

In the first months of Nazi takeover few Jewish people had any inkling of what was in prospect: 'Back in those days most Jewish people hadn't a clue. A lot of Jewish First World War veterans told themselves that their service would be respected. As a young teenager I began to realize that my family background was a problem. On 23 June 1938, the day after my father's birthday, two Gestapo officials arrived at our door. They took Father to prison.[31]

'In the space of an hour I learned from Mother why he had been taken away. The reason had its roots in the 1920s, when Father established his own watchmaking business. Pforzheim watchmakers depended on their ability to buy components in Switzerland. The Swiss were paid in foreign exchange and these transactions required a special permit. This is what Father's Nazi competitors were after – not the business, as such, but his permit to purchase in Switzerland. They pushed him to sell it for a knock-down price. When he refused, one of them hatched the plot to have him arrested. With Father behind bars, this Nazi then began to threaten my mother.'[31]

Such intimidation and graft went under the National Socialist euphemism of 'Aryanization'. The pushiest of the three Nazis got the permit. He was the youngest of the three and his success prompted a complaint from the other two. They argued that it was the usual practice to let an older party member benefit. 'I found out about this when making enquiries at the Landesarchiv in 2012.'[31]

Some men on the bomber squadrons were now on their second or even third tours. They knew everything there was to know about the risks facing new boys. Don Robson had been an apprentice baker at the family's store in a North Kent village. He became an air gunner and was lucky enough to beat the odds and survive his first tour, at a time of heavy losses. Now he was about to put his life on the line again, for a second operational tour.

While Robson had a gruelling first tour with 467 Squadron, he never fired his guns in anger. This was despite the fact that his skipper, Flying Officer John Cairney, DFM, took them to many heavily defended targets in Germany, including Berlin and Essen. Robson saw many aircraft fall to flak: 'The flak barrage was terrific, especially over the Ruhr. My closest call came during a raid on a Ruhr target. The flak was extremely heavy. We had just started our bomb run when the starboard outer was hit, producing an immediate and very fierce fire. I knew things were serious, as flames were streaming back beyond my rear turret. The extinguisher made no impression. John pressed on. The bomb run continued with unbelievable slowness. We were flying high, at 24,000ft. As soon as the bombs left the aircraft, John put the nose down hard and dived to 5,000ft. We reached over 400mph in the dive and this blew the fire out.[32]

'During the entire episode I didn't think about jumping. It never entered my head. I felt sure John and our engineer would get us out of this fix. Once down to 5,000ft we stayed down and flew back on three engines. John was awarded the DFM for holding steady on the bomb run that night.'[32]

Robson often heard shrapnel striking the fuselage: 'One early morning, having landed back from a Ruhr attack, I went to debriefing and then had my meal. I slept in until mid-morning, then took a stroll to the flight office. On the way I ran into one of the ground crew. He said: "You were lucky to get away with it last night." I had no idea what he was talking about, until I went to inspect our aircraft in the light of day. I stopped counting on reaching fifty holes in the rear fuselage and tail. Not one fragment had hit my turret.'[32]

Cairney's crew were reluctant to push their luck after an incident involving their over-enthusiastic bomb aimer: 'We were taking part in a raid on St Nazaire's U-boat pens. The bomb aimer had just wriggled into the front turret as we flew low over the French countryside, when he immediately saw a long convoy of German trucks on the road below. He opened up instinctively and immediately attracted a blizzard of small arms fire. When I went to depress the rear turret guns they wouldn't move. I found out why on landing back. Only three rounds had struck our Lanc, but one had severed my turret's hydraulic line, immobilizing the guns.'[33]

Don Robson was not superstitious. He cultivated a positive attitude and was confident he would survive as a member of an extremely efficient crew. Nonetheless, he wore the St Christopher given to him by his parents. Cairney's aircraft also had a mascot. A small toy bear dangled from a rib in the cockpit. After twenty-nine sorties Cairney's crew were rested. They went to RAF Silverstone as instructors, distinguished by the fact that they were only the second 467 Squadron crew to survive a full tour. Many failed to complete ten operations. The first 467 crew to survive was that of young Lancaster captain Frank Heavery. Robson was a close friend of Heavery's rear gunner, Sidney Knott (later Warrant Officer Sidney Knott, DFC).[34]

The third crew to survive a full tour with 467 was that of pilot Johnny 'Ginger' Ball. Robson had a close call on 17 March 1944, when he climbed into Ball's Wellington for an air-to-air firing exercise. Owing to poor weather inland, this exercise was flown over the sea. The tired Wellington lost an engine and the other then began to overheat. Ball lost his struggle to stay in the air and the aircraft ditched. The fuselage flooded as Robson struggled to free a trapped foot; he pulled savagely, lost a flying boot and floated free through the astrodome.[34]

Don Robson wrote to his girl almost every day. He married Kate on 26 January 1944 when he was 22 and she was 18. They came close to losing their honeymoon when Robson received a second tour operational posting. He went to the flight commander to plead his case. He got a sympathetic hearing but was told he had to go unless he could find someone to take his place. Another gunner in his billet stepped forward. On returning from honeymoon, Robson was told that his substitute was dead. A second operational posting soon followed. Another gunner took it and he was killed in action. Robson had had enough. When the third posting arrived, he took it. His next stop was a special squadron within 100 (Bomber Support) Group.[35]

The Nazis' boundless cruelty towards Jewish people and the populations of Eastern Europe, together with so-called undesirables and 'useless mouths' within Germany itself, is well documented. Perhaps less familiar to non-Germans is the oppressive behaviour of the regime towards *all* Germans who failed to display sufficient enthusiasm for National Socialism. Life in Nazi Germany was controlled through oppression and intimidation, lubricated by an ever-present fear of denunciation. The banker Adolf Katz, destined to become Pforzheim's first post-war Oberbürgermeister, certainly felt such pressures.[36]

Katz was born in 1893 in Markirch, Alsace (now Sainte Marie-aux-Mines). He was eight when his father died of TB. The family struggled – there was no money for young Katz to go to university. Instead, he joined Banque de Mulhouse in Strasbourg. After service as an officer in the First World War, he held positions with the bank in several towns, including Pforzheim. By the summer of 1943 Adolf Katz was director of the Pforzheim branch of Deutsche Bank. He and his family had an apartment at Schwarzwaldstrasse 20. It was a complex home environment, shaped by earlier marriages and stepchildren. The 1930s had not been easy. Katz came to know a great deal about his family background: 'We owe our detailed family tree to the Nazis because, if you had a Jewish name like Katz in 1933, you had to make a big effort to deliver proof of being Aryan.'[36]

Katz's wife was a doctor with a successful homeopathy practice. He had married Ruth in 1937, after experiencing a succession of domestic tragedies – earlier wives had died young, leaving him with three children. Ruth fell under the Nazis' *Rassegesetze* (racial laws) as she had a Jewish grandfather. As a result of this marriage Katz lost seniority at Deutsche Bank and was forbidden to have direct contact with clients. This was one of many factors that gave him a highly jaundiced view of National Socialism. It was no accident that he was known as 'Dolf', rather than 'Adolf'.[36]

Katz was greatly surprised by the success of Hitler and the Nazis. He felt the bourgeoisie could no longer afford to sit on their hands. He decided to join Stahlhelm ('Steel Helmet'), a right wing organization of First World War veterans, set up as a counterweight to the Nazis. Adolf Katz became a Stahlhelm Ortsgruppenleiter. This was to have embarrassing consequences, in both the short and long term. Stahlhelm was eventually absorbed by the SA (the Nazis' own paramilitary organization). Katz became an SA member by default. He took leave of absence. In 1937 this was no longer relevant – he was excluded from the SA (and also the Officer Corps) because of his marriage to Ruth.[36]

Katz served as Oberbürgermeister of Pforzheim from 1945 to 1947. His diaries for the war years 1943–5 were published by Marianne Pross, his youngest daughter. They reveal how his fears of a devastating air raid on Pforzheim began to take hold during 1943. That June, Adolf Katz was assigned to his block's Luftschutzgemeinschaft (air-raid protection group). In July, following the destruction of Hamburg, Katz took up his diary and wrote perceptively: 'If you try to imagine the situation in six or twelve months, then most of the bigger cities will probably be destroyed and the misery will become almost unbearable. There is no way to prevent this, not even if we might be able to destroy London in the meantime. The war will end with pointless annihilation, with the atrocious destruction of our world ...'[36]

On 15 September 1943, following Italy's surrender, Katz wrote in his diary: 'First Director of Deutsche Bank in Stuttgart, Mr Koehler, has been arrested because he said, on a train, that what happened to Mussolini will also happen to Hitler. If they interpret this to be *Wehrkraftzersetzung* (affecting the armed forces) and *Feindbegünstigung* (giving aid and comfort to the enemy) it might cost him his head.' Meanwhile, changes in banking practice, in late September 1943, centralized the bank's business and made it easier to keep customers under surveillance. The threat of air attack had intensified and the Katz family sent their valuables elsewhere in Germany. Other treasured possessions were moved into the cellar at Schwarzwaldstrasse 20.[36]

Katz's diary was an outlet for the worried banker's most intimate thoughts, for example on 27 October 1943: 'I have lots of leisure. Being a bank director in time of war is completely free of problems, as long as the bank or city is not destroyed by bombs. There is only the war industry and there is only one debtor – the State. Of course, we have to grant credits to every company fulfilling armaments orders. There is not much to consider about that ...' In an entry the next day Katz paid tribute to an acquaintance, Arthur Dietschbowski, who had recently been drafted: 'In Ulm, where he had to report to, he declared to his superiors that he wouldn't want to kill and carry a gun. He was arrested immediately and taken to Torgau, where a Reich military tribunal will condemn him. His wife visited him there. She told Ruth that all the officials there told her that he was going to be shot. The first man I ever met who would rather die than kill.'[36]

There is a significant entry in Katz's diary for 31 October 1943. Writing about life in the fifth year of the war, he singled out the manpower shortage as the key problem: 'The most urgent air-raid protection work is on hold because of lack of workers.' There was also the feeling that Pforzheim was running out of time. In late November 1943 Katz noted that two heavy attacks on Berlin had left Deutsche Bank completely burnt out. On 17 December 1943, he wrote: 'rumour in the city has it that a big attack on Pforzheim is pending'. The next day he added: 'There seems to be something serious behind these rumours.' Arrangements were made for some of the children to stay with their grandparents in Baden-Baden. The family's good carpets and paintings were sent for safe keeping to a friend living in Würm.[36]

Katz had deep-rooted fears for the safety of his family. There was the ever-present threat of a mass air raid. He also had specific concerns about his wife. The race laws were being applied with ever-growing ferocity. So-called 'privileged' German Jews in mixed marriages had been safe from deportation, but policy now hardened. They lost protected status the moment their partner died. On 11 January 1944, Katz wrote: 'Yesterday, the Jews from mixed marriages where the Aryan partner has died have been deported. Ruth used to treat Mrs Aggenloder, who was also deported, and thus we get an account of the horrible scenes that ensued. We were worried about Anni Herrmann, but mixed marriages have not been dissolved.'[36]

In late 1944 this household consisted of Adolf Katz, Ruth, Aunt Friederike and two of five children, Marianne and Annina. Marianne Pross (née Katz) was eight when the bombing of Germany intensified during the second half of 1944: 'As a child I was used to alarms and attacks – they happened almost daily. Besides, young children don't worry too much as they have no concept of death. I remember playing outside, watching the planes above. It was fascinating. We collected aluminium foil strips dropped by bombers to confuse German radar – kids used it as a kind of currency. After all these years, however, I can still feel my claustrophobia in that cellar.'[37]

Wing Commander John 'Jack' Harris, OBE, DFC was born in 1920 into a family living in Gillingham, Kent. Money was tight and, like Katz, he didn't go to university. On reaching the age of 17, he became an Air Ministry clerical officer in the Air Intelligence Directorate. This was a reserved occupation but Harris volunteered for aircrew. He arrived at Elementary Flying Training School at Fairoaks, Surrey, in late February 1941. He logged sixty-four hours on the school's Tiger Moth primary trainers: 'I was no "natural" pilot – I had to work quite hard at it. Fortunately, I am an organized chap and always made a careful study of *Pilot's Notes*. Some pupils went solo after nine hours of instruction; it took me thirteen.'[38]

Harris trod the long road to an operational heavy bomber squadron. The next step was training on twin-engined Airspeed Oxfords. He reached a milestone on 14 July 1941, with completion of his first Oxford night solo. This was not without incident – a German intruder disturbed the peace of the grass field of Ingham, north of Lincoln. Just after take-off, at around 50ft, Harris suddenly saw eight bright flashes as bombs exploded. The flare path promptly disappeared. The last two bombs in the stick were close enough to shake the Oxford. He switched off his navigation lights and began orbiting the nearby Pundit Beacon before realizing his error. If he stayed there, he would almost certainly be joined by unwelcome company. Jack eventually landed safely at a nearby night fighter base.[38]

A common bond: Jack Harris and crew. Left to right: Flight Lieutenant Jack Harris, pilot; Flying Officer Ted Hornsby, navigator; Flight Sergeant Ron Richardson, bomb aimer; Flight Sergeant Stan Freeman, flight engineer; Flight Sergeant Peter Flux, wireless operator; Flight Sergeant Bill Barrett, RCAF, mid-upper gunner; and Sergeant Alec Bentley, rear gunner. *Photo: Bob Stone.*

Harris was commissioned as a pilot officer, completed a navigator's course and sailed for Canada. He returned to Britain in March 1944 and flew Wellingtons at 30 OTU, Hixon, near Stafford. He crewed up at the satellite airfield of Seighford before proceeding to 1667 HCU at Sandtoft, north of Doncaster, to fly Halifax four-engined bombers. His crew included flight engineer Stan Freeman, who was just 18: 'I think he misdeclared his age when he volunteered. A live wire and full of ideas, Stan was extremely confident. He was a bit of a "smart alec" but we got on very well together. He now lives in Harrogate and we still talk on the phone every week. He is the only one of my crew who is still alive.'[38]

Navigator Ted Hornsby, a pilot officer, had a Home Counties background: 'He was a charmer. He looked like David Niven, complete with pencil moustache. He was a good dancer and girls regarded him as a treat. Happily, he was also a good navigator. Ted made sure we survived our tour. He always kept us safely tucked into the middle of the bomber stream, away from the night fighters who preferred to pick off stragglers on the fringes of the stream.'[38]

Sergeant Peter Flux was the wireless operator: 'Peter, a lorry driver before the war, was street-wise and had plenty of experience of life. The bomb aimer, Sergeant Ron Richardson, was very young. We all attended his twenty-first birthday party in London while we were at HCU. The rear gunner, Sergeant Alec Bentley, was a railway porter before joining the Air Force. At 32, he was the oldest. Alec was married, with two kids. As for the mid-upper turret, this gave us problems early on. The crew didn't get on with the first mid-upper gunner and I replaced him before we began operations. Sergeant Bill Barratt, RCAF, a young gunner, arrived and soon settled in. Looking back, it was incredible. We were complete strangers yet, with the exception of that problem gunner, we found a common bond. We depended on each other and we knew that any failure could have serious and possibly fatal consequences.'[38]

They reported to No. 1 Lancaster Finishing School, Hemswell, for a two-week introduction to the Lancaster: 'Although heavier than the Lancaster at the controls, the Halifax was sturdier and could take more punishment. The Lancaster, however, was a thoroughbred. Its climb, cruise and engine-out performance were all superior. Indeed, the Lancaster was a revelation – an absolute joy. There was just one problem: the pilot and flight engineer sat more or less in line with the airscrews and noise levels were high. Consequently, many of us suffered hearing problems in later life.'[38]

Harris and crew reported to North Killingholme and joined 550 Squadron on 31 August 1944. The new boys arrived on a bad day. Only a few hours before the squadron had lost its commanding officer, Wing Commander Sisley. The Australian was shot down on a daylight attack on Agenville, a V2 storage site. He was flying with Pilot Officer P.C. Siddall, RNZAF and crew. All eight were killed in what was probably a direct hit by a flak shell. It was Sisley's fifth trip of his second tour.[38]

This was not encouraging and, furthermore, North Killingholme failed to impress. Jack Harris: 'Basically, our new home was a set of potato fields converted into an airfield. Those who were at North Killingholme during the first four or five months must have had a rough time. The station commander, Group Captain McIntyre, had completed a tour with 100 Squadron, finishing with a DFC. The new squadron commander was Brian "Dingle" Bell, who had a close affinity with all the crews and was well respected. We joined B Flight. As was the case on every squadron, 550 had its share of characters. There was Jock Shaw, the Scot who refused to give up operational flying. He completed his tour, dodged all postings as an instructor and remained at North Killingholme – still flying on ops as a "spare bod". He specialized in introducing new crews to operational flying and completed forty-two sorties before finishing. The eccentrics included Squadron Leader Peter Sarll, very much the public school figure. He always took a hunting horn with him on operations and insisted on blowing it upon reaching the target. As for me, I was just glad to have finally made it to an operational squadron. I felt no apprehension. The pilot of a heavy aircraft is the captain, responsible for his crew. I always found there was too much to think about to worry unduly.'[38]

Harris began his tour on 10 September 1944, as 'second dicky' with Flying Officer Thygessen, RCAF and crew. First tour pilots always began by accompanying an experienced crew on an introductory trip. This was a daylight attack on eight German strongpoints around Le Havre. The Allies needed to capture this vital port as soon as possible. No aircraft were lost.[39] Jack Harris: 'This was a round trip of three and a half hours but we spent just ten minutes over hostile territory. We bombed from 9,000ft. This wasn't much use as a second pilot trip, bearing little resemblance to attacks on German targets. Yet it did serve as an introduction to the process, from pre-flight briefing to debriefing on return.'[40]

This process began with a pre-flight meal, followed by the briefing and a visit to the locker room, to don flying clothing and 'Mae West' (life vest) and to collect parachutes. Crews collected their survival packs and escape packs, then boarded buses or trucks for the drive to dispersal, when the pilots signed 'Form 700', to accept their aircraft. There was usually time for a chat with the ground crew before boarding and starting engines. The bombers lined up for take-off. Each, in turn, received a winking green light from the control caravan, signalling clearance to turn onto the runway. The tail wheel was straightened and the throttles advanced. The aircraft was held on the brakes until a steady green was shown. Then the brakes were released and the throttles opened wide for take-off, with the gunners and wireless operator acknowledging waves from spectators. Once airborne a course was set and the outbound flight began. There would be intercom checks but no transmissions would be made. On return, the process was completed with debrief by an intelligence officer and a chat with other crews over coffee. Most men checked the landing times board, to see if anyone was missing, before going to the Mess for the post-op meal.[40]

Harris and crew made their first operational flight, to Frankfurt, on the night of 12/13 September, a trip of seven hours thirty-five minutes. Jack Harris was impressed: 'The Frankfurt/Mainz area was very heavily defended. As new boys we brought up the rear and it was quite a sight as we approached the target. Looking ahead, there were three or four bombers, each coned by twenty to thirty searchlights. We had mixed feelings: relief that it was someone else being coned and pity for the less fortunate crews who were. It was an absolutely clear night – manna from heaven for Frankfurt's flak gunners. We were carrying what was called the "usual" load for a city area attack: one 4,000lb Cookie high capacity blast-bomb and incendiaries. We dropped and turned away.'[40]

Harris' aircraft was one of 378 Lancasters mounting Bomber Command's final major raid on Frankfurt. Records show that 469 people died on the ground. This raid caused severe damage across the city's western districts and it took three days to extinguish all the fires. The RAF lost seventeen Lancasters, 4.5 per cent of the heavy aircraft on the raid.[41] 'This was completely different to my second pilot trip. It was a totally clear night with no cloud. The Frankfurt/Mainz/Wiesbaden/Darmstadt complex of cities was heavily defended by guns and searchlights and it was a good night for night fighters. As a new crew we were in the last wave and could see everything happening in front of us. Within 30 miles of the target around 150 searchlights were at work.'[42]

Nineteen 550 Squadron Lancasters were sent; three returned early owing to various defects. The remaining sixteen bombed and returned safely. Pilot Officer Ansell was last – his Lancaster landed one and a half hours after the others, having been hit by flak and subjected to three attacks by a night fighter. He got down safely after a long, slow return.

The bombing war was growing in complexity, in a form of deadly competition between British and German scientists. Radio countermeasures (RCM) grew more sophisticated, with a galaxy of jamming devices and feints designed to confuse and frustrate German air defences. When the Harris crew began their tour it had long been the practice to use specialized RCM aircraft to provide a 'Mandrel' radar-jamming shield. The idea was to keep the Germans guessing – for as long as possible – about the main force's intended point of penetration through the shield, on its way to a target in Germany. Frequently, the bombers crossed France at low level, climbed quickly to bombing height and broke through the Mandrel screen late enough to make it difficult for German night fighters to be deployed to maximum effect.

There was a new emphasis on electronic security while operating. H_2S radars were used with discretion, as emissions were monitored by the Germans, allowing them to track the main force, and German night fighters had equipment allowing them to home onto the H_2S. The general rule was to activate H_2S only when crossing into Germany, then switch off when leaving the target. Crews were instructed to use H_2S in very short bursts, only activating the radar when confirming ground features promised a strong signature.

During the afternoon of 16 September 1944, Jack Harris and crew joined the briefing at North Killingholme for attacks in support of Operation Market Garden, the airborne landings and ground thrust to seize the Dutch river crossings, including those at Nijmegen and Arnhem. The 550 Squadron crews were briefed to bomb Steenwijk airfield, one of four Luftwaffe bases in the area. These airfields, together with a flak battery, were all bombed. The attacks took place on the eve of the assault and a main force of 200 Lancasters heavily cratered the runways.[43] The flak battery was attacked by fifty-four Lancasters and five Mosquitoes.

Jack Harris was on again the next day, 17 September, attacking German positions at Biggerkerke, Walcheren, prior to an Allied assault. This large-scale daylight attack involved 762 heavy bombers. Around 3,000 tons of bombs were dropped on German emplacements. Harris' Lancaster contributed a stick of fifteen 1,000lb bombs, dropped from 13,000ft. Opposition was light.[44]

After a few days' rest they then took part in a night raid on Neuss. They took off on 23 September as part of a main force of over 500 heavy aircraft. Five Lancasters and two Halifaxes were lost.[45] Jack Harris: 'This was a sortie of four hours fifty minutes. Crossing the target at 17,000ft, we dropped thirteen 1,000lb bombs and four of 500lbs. There was ten-tenths cloud obscuring the target, so we bombed skymarkers.'[46] This raid killed 289 people.

Within forty-eight hours Harris and other 550 Squadron pilots were taking off to attack German troop concentrations around Calais. This was a heavy daylight attack by 430 Lancasters and 397 Halifaxes, supported by 45 Mosquitoes.[47] Low cloud made for disappointing results, although 287 aircraft bombed early in the raid

Bombing Calais: Wing Commander Jack Harris' photo of the 26 September 1944 raid against German troop concentrations around the port. There is a Halifax below them. *Photo: Jack Harris.*

through gaps. Jack Harris: 'We were still approaching when we heard the master bomber tell crews not to bomb due to thickening cloud. We were among those who returned with our bombs. Some had delayed action fuses – timed to explode six to seventy-two hours after being dropped. The fuses had an anti-handling device and were very temperamental. They could go off at any time. At North Killingholme the standard procedure was to take delayed action "returns" for detonation in a pit, in a large field nearby.'[48]

Their bombs were released over the next day's target, German gun positions at Cap Gris Nez. This was an attack made at unusually low level. Harris' bomb aimer, Ron Richardson, dropped thirteen 1,000lb and four 500lb bombs from just 3,000ft.[48] The four targets at Cap Gris Nez were bombed by 531 aircraft; 191 bombers attacked other targets around Calais.[49]

Harris was over Calais again on 28 September, bombing German positions: 'This was another occasion when cloud ruined the attack and we had to return with the bombs. Landing a fully bombed-up Lanc is not everyone's cup of tea. We had to add 10kts to the landing speed as the aircraft was much heavier than usual and the shock of the landing was that much greater. We burst a tyre on touching down but, fortunately, came to no harm.'[50]

Notes

1. *Administration's Report and Statistics for the Town of Pforzheim 1945–1952: City Life 1939–1945.*
2. Middlebrook, M. and Everitt, C. (1990), *The Bomber Command War Diaries*, 623.
3. Ibid., 568.
4. Interview with Christian Groh, May 2013.
5. *Bomber Command Review for 1945, Part 1, War Operations, 1ˢᵗ January to 8ᵗʰ May, 1945.*
6. Richards, D. (1994), *The Hardest Victory*, 291–2.
7. Redding, T. (2008), *Flying for Freedom*, 51.
8. Ibid., 140.
9. Ibid., 51.
10. Harris, Sir Arthur T. (1995), *Despatch on War Operations*, Appendix C, Section ll, 94.
11. Redding, T. (2008), *Flying for Freedom*, 51.
12. Interview with Jack Harris, April 2013.
13. Redding, T. (2008), *Flying for Freedom*, 51.
14. Interview with Raimund Frei, July 2013.
15. Longmate, N. (1988), *The Bombers*, 147–8.
16. Ibid, 363–4.
17. Interview with Dave Davidson, April 2013.
18. Interview with Howell Evans, June 2013.
19. Interview with Hans Gerstung, April 2013.
20. Interviews with Irma Baroni, August 2013.
21. Interview with Sam Lipfriend, March 2013.
22. Milton, G. (2011), *Wolfram*, prologue.
23. Ibid., 11.
24. Ibid., 40–3.
25. Interview with Doris Weber and Sigrid Kern (née Weber), November 2013.
26. Saward, D. (1985), *Victory Denied*, 341–2.
27. Interview with Bill Thomas, June 2013.
28. Interview with Ron Germain, April 2013.
29. Interview with Frank Woodley, March 2013.
30. Interview with Raimund Frei, July 2013.
31. Interview with Werner Schultz, November 2013.
32. Redding, T. (2008), *Flying for Freedom*, 120–1.
33. Ibid., 128.
34. Ibid., 128, 150–3.
35. Ibid., 279–80.
36. Pross, M. (1995), *Die Einschläge kommen näher, Aus den Tagebüchern 1943–45 von Friedrich Adolf Katz, 1945–1947 Oberbürgermeister der Stadt Pforzheim.*
37. Interview with Marianne Pross, September 2013.
38. Interview with Jack Harris, April 2013.
39. Middlebrook, M. and Everitt, C. (1990), *The Bomber Command War Diaries*, 579.
40. Interview with Jack Harris, April 2013.
41. Middlebrook, M. and Everitt, C. (1990), *The Bomber Command War Diaries*, 582.
42. Interview with Jack Harris, April 2013.
43. Middlebrook, M. and Everitt, C. (1990), *The Bomber Command War Diaries*, 585.
44. Interview with Jack Harris, April 2013.
45. Middlebrook, M. and Everitt, C. (1990), *The Bomber Command War Diaries*, 588.
46. Interview with Jack Harris, April 2013.
47. Middlebrook, M. and Everitt, C. (1990), *The Bomber Command War Diaries*, 589.
48. Interview with Jack Harris, April 2013.
49. Middlebrook, M. and Everitt, C. (1990), *The Bomber Command War Diaries*, 589.
50. Interview with Jack Harris, April 2013.

Chapter Two

The Final Phase Takes Shape

O ctober 1944 opened with heavy air attacks in support of British and American armies struggling to penetrate Germany's western defences. Jack Harris and his crew, back at North Killingholme after a week's leave, were briefed during the afternoon of Thursday, 5 October for a night attack on Saarbrücken. The American Third Army requested this raid, to cut German rail and road communications. The town was attacked by 531 Lancasters and 20 Mosquitoes and they destroyed nearly 6,000 houses and killed 344 people.[1]

This was a challenging seven-hour trip for Harris: 'We bombed from 13,000ft, dropping the 'usual' for an area raid – a 4,000lb Cookie and incendiaries. We suffered

The morning after: O-Oboe pictured on Friday 6 October 1944, with rudder and other damage from a night fighter attack during a raid on Saarbrücken. Pilot Les Cameron, DFC, received a fragment of 20mm cannon shell in the thigh and his navigator, Joe Rigby, applied a tourniquet. Cameron received his DFC for an attack on the V-weapons site at Nieppe. His Lancaster was hit by flak. According to Les Cameron's son, Jim, their aircraft also took a flak hit over the Neuss railyards and Joe Rigby and a second crew member suffered burns when fighting the resulting fire. *Photo: Phil Rigby.*

problems on the way to the target. The "Gee" box went unserviceable and then our navigator, Ted Hornsby, had oxygen problems. He kept telling me we were early when, in fact, we bombed twenty minutes late! We had Saarbrücken all to ourselves, while the flak had only our Lanc to concentrate on. We were sitting ducks and lucky to get away with it. Our troubles continued. When we got back the weather was bad and we were diverted to Attlebridge, an American base in Norfolk. We flew back to North Killingholme the morning after a very long night.'[2]

Many new crews reached the squadrons and began operating during October 1944. They included reluctant bomber pilot Dave Davidson. His war in Lancasters began on Saturday, 7 October 1944. Davidson had done everything he could to get back to flying Spitfires, but there he was – taking part in a daylight attack by 340 Lancasters and 10 Mosquitoes on Emmerich. Three Lancasters were lost during this accurate, highly destructive raid. Emmerich was a railhead for reinforcements opposing Allied forces after the failed Market Garden offensive in Holland. More than 2,400 buildings were destroyed and over 700 people died.[3]

Davidson took Lancaster 'S', a reserve aircraft on 100 Squadron's strength. They had arrived at Waltham, 5 miles south of Grimsby, just a few days earlier. Their big bomber now held a 4,000lb Cookie and 10,000lb of incendiaries. Nerves were at full stretch – all other aircraft had taken off but they had remained on the ground, awaiting clearance. Dave Davidson: 'We watched for the green light, or a red to stand down. We got neither. The ground crew wanted to chock the wheels, saying: "You won't be going now." Yet, seventeen minutes after deadline, we got the green light.'[4]

Howell 'Taff' Evans was Davidson's wireless operator: 'It was a beautiful day. The target was clear. My place, when near the target, was in the astrodome – keeping a close lookout. As we approached I looked up at a Lancaster above and in front of us. Its bomb doors opened and it commenced

Navigator: Flight Lieutenant Joe Rigby, DFC, a member of Flight Lieutenant Les Cameron's crew. Joe did his first op with Lancaster captain Bob Stone on 10 August 1944, against a target in the Paris area. The Cameron crew made twenty-eight operational sorties in Lancaster LM273, lost during the Pforzheim raid – around ten weeks after the end of their tour. *Photo: Phil Rigby.*

its bombing run. The bombs dropped and I followed them down with my eyes. They scored a direct hit on a Lancaster below, which was immediately enveloped in a ball of fire. I never forgot that; it was absolutely appalling.'[5]

There was a strong family atmosphere on 100 Squadron. Howell Evans: 'It was marvellous. The camaraderie was great and Grimsby had everything we wanted, with its pubs and dance halls. I soon found myself a very nice girlfriend.' He and his steady girlfriend, Pat, had an understanding: 'I suppose you could call it a pact. We knew we were too young to make a full commitment.'[5]

Having survived Saarbrücken, 550 Squadron pilot Jack Harris had a close call over Emmerich: 'We had a 4,000lb Cookie and incendiaries in the bomb-bay and bombed from 11,000ft. There was plenty of flak and we took a bad hit to port. The flak shell burst about 20–30yds in front of us and 20–30ft below, on the port bow. I saw the red flash as the shell exploded and jumped out of my skin. There was one big bang as the shell fragments hit. The blind landing approach aerial, by my left knee, was shot away. There were sounds of other fragments hitting and all the instruments for the two port engines wound down to zero. Yet the engines remained working and responded to the controls. The instrument cables for these engines were gathered together in one loom, housed in the wing leading edge, en route to the cockpit. A shell fragment had severed them.

Close call over Emmerich: Jack Harris' Lancaster was damaged by a flak shell shortly after releasing the bombs. *Photo: Jack Harris.*

'The No. 2 port fuel tank was holed and our flight engineer, Stan Freeman, quickly switched all four engines to the damaged tank. This drained it as quickly as possible, so minimizing fuel loss. When we got back we were diverted. We were extremely lucky to get away with it. The ground crew later counted over forty holes in the aircraft. We had a week's leave after Emmerich.'[6]

Ken Sidwell's crew had just arrived on 550 Squadron. Sidwell's mid-upper gunner was Frank Woodley: 'This squadron had its share of Canadians, New Zealanders and Australians, including two Aussies with thirty-six ops completed. It was an excellent squadron and the boys knew it. There wasn't a lot of bull. If someone warned aircrew to put their caps on, they'd shout back: "We'll put them on if you come with us tonight".'[7]

Sidwell's crew was joined by flight engineer Jack Allen, an easy-going 27-year-old Londoner who was always laughing. He was one of several reasons why they all got on so well. Their tour opened on 12 October 1944, when they joined a force of eighty-six Lancasters and ten Mosquitoes attacking German gun positions along the Scheldt. The key target was the heavy battery at Breskens. Frank Woodley: 'We flew low over the Channel and straight along the Scheldt estuary. Our target was Fort Fredrik Hendrik. That first op lasted three hours fifteen minutes.'[7] Two of the four gun positions were destroyed; no aircraft were lost.[8]

New boys on the squadrons soon appreciated the realities of war. These realities had already been discovered by Pforzheimer Raimund Frei. When German boys left school they were required to do national labour service. As a young forest ranger, Frei was exempt. In 1940 he and a colleague, another Pforzheimer, volunteered for the military: 'We went together. Naturally, we had swallowed the propaganda.'[9]

As a forest ranger Frei expected to serve as a Pioneer, with mountain troops or as an infantryman: 'When I volunteered my parents weren't thrilled. I needed their written consent. Mother lost a brother in the First World War and Father was an enlisted man in that conflict. Eventually, I got their permission, but also needed approval from the office. My boss, an artillery battery commander in the last war, left me with a parting comment: "Why so fast? You'd better watch out!" That was a risky thing for him to say out loud.

'I went to an infantry training battalion at Karlsruhe, where young men were in a minority. Around 80 per cent were well into their thirties. My forestry colleague, Emil Frey, went to a naval gunnery unit on the North Sea coast. In the autumn of 1940 I was sent to Flanders with the active element of my unit. The fighting in France and the Low Countries had been over for some months. I was a rifleman in a bicycle battalion and we began training for Operation Sealion, the planned invasion of England. Things changed during Easter 1941, when we transferred to East Prussia. On 19 June we were ready for Operation Barbarossa, the invasion of Russia. We were in the north. Our job was to advance via Suwalki – a part of East Prussia that Germany had had to sign over to Lithuania under the Versailles Treaty – then push on through Lithuania.

'We handed over our bicycles to a neighbouring company and marched in. Before the jump off we were lectured on the importance of respecting the Geneva Convention. Pillaging, plundering and abuse of the civil population were strictly forbidden. The attack opened at 04.25 on 22 June. We penetrated 20km on that first day. The vanguard got even further as the enemy fortifications were not particularly effective. We then entered Belarus and met the first real resistance. As the days passed we moved forward, boarded military transports and reached Smolensk, to take part in our first pitched battle. This ended with the encirclement of the Russian armies. I got through it all, thank God, without being wounded.'[9]

Raimund Frei had been surprised at the rapid progress on that first day. It had seemed easy, with only the spearheads doing the fighting. He was shocked, however, when confronted with brutality: 'Our advance parties set up a dressing station. This was attacked at night by Russians who had been overrun. They killed all the wounded and the medics. Later, there was the incident at Witebsk. Russian troops surrendered and came towards us with their hands up. When they got close enough they threw grenades concealed in their hands. There were not so many prisoners from then on. I don't blame the Russian soldiers. They lived in fear of their political commissars, who forced them to do such things. Nevertheless, there were dangers in taking prisoners and we had to be cautious.'[9]

On 25 November 1943, 550 Squadron was formed from C Flight of 100 Squadron. New squadrons began life with a core of experienced crews. The most experienced captains transferring to the new squadron were Warrant Officer G.W. Brook (twenty ops), Pilot Officer D.C. Dripps, RAAF (nineteen), Flying Officer R.H. Mawle (fifteen), Warrant Officer G.F. Peasgood (ten) and Squadron Leader B. Bell (ten). The new squadron's motto boded ill for Pforzheim and other German cities: '*Per ignem vincimus*' ('Through fire we conquer'). Its badge was described thus: 'In front of flames of fire, a sword erect, point upwards'.

The squadron began operating Lancasters from Waltham, Grimsby. In the first six weeks it attacked Berlin seven times, together with other targets such as Leipzig and Frankfurt, before moving to a new airfield at North Killingholme on 3 January 1944. After a full moon group stand-down, 550's first raid from North Killingholme was on 14 January 1944. It sent eleven Lancasters to Brunswick.[10]

During 1944, 550 Squadron developed a reputation for high efficiency, often topping 1 Group's bombing league table. Morale was extremely high. The first commanding officer was Wing Commander J.J. 'Jimmy' Bennett, DFC, an old hand who flew twin-engined Hampden bombers earlier in the war. His flight commanders were Squadron Leader Bell and Squadron Leader G.D. Graham, RAAF. The addition of 550 brought the number of Lancaster squadrons on 1 Group's strength to ten. Typically, each squadron had at least twenty Lancasters.[10] The squadron went on to establish a third flight on 10 September 1944. That month was unique in the annals of 550, as no losses were suffered. October was more typical. After spending months concentrating on targets in support of land forces, the heavy bombers resumed their area raids on cities. In mid-October Duisburg was subjected to two very heavy raids in the space of twenty-four hours; 550 Squadron sent twenty-four aircraft at 06.30 on 14 October for a daylight, the first of these raids. Two crews (Lancasters captained by Flying Officer A. Abrams and Flying Officer H. Dodds) failed to return. The squadron then sent twenty-five aircraft on the night return to Duisburg. In the last two weeks of October, 550's Lancasters attacked targets including Wilhelmshaven, Stuttgart, Essen (twice) and Cologne (three times).[11]

Bomber Command now raided German cities on an unprecedented scale. On 13 October 1944, Sir Arthur Harris received orders for Operation Hurricane. Its purpose was 'to demonstrate to the enemy in Germany generally the overwhelming superiority of the Allied Air Forces in the theatre … the intention is to apply within the shortest practical period the maximum effort of Royal Air Force Bomber Command and the VIII United States Bomber Command against objectives in the densely populated Ruhr'.[12]

Early next morning 1,013 aircraft (519 Lancasters, 474 Halifaxes and 20 Mosquitoes, with fighter escort) opened Hurricane. The target, Duisburg, was an inland port on the Rhine serving the Ruhr. It was also home to Thyssen steelworks. This force included 550 Squadron's Lancasters. The armada dropped 3,574 tons of high explosive bombs and 820 tons of incendiaries on the city. Meanwhile, the Americans sent 1,000 bombers to the Cologne area. Hurricane continued that night. Bomber Command returned to Duisburg with 1,005 aircraft. This force attacked in two waves, two hours apart. A total of 941 aircraft dropped 4,040 tons of high explosive bombs and 500 tons of incendiaries.[12] According to one source (Saward), Duisburg received 9,075 tons of bombs in twenty-four hours. In comparison, the Luftwaffe dropped less than 10,000 tons on London *throughout the entire 1940–41 Blitz*.[13]

On 14 October Ken Sidwell and crew flew both Duisburg raids. That morning they took Lancaster 'C' to the target, taking off at 06.33. They arrived back at North Killingholme four hours and forty-five minutes later, then changed mounts for the night attack, taking Lancaster 'Q'. They took off at 22.42 and landed back at 04.17, after a very long 'day'.[14]

Layer cloud caused problems during the daylight. Only one 550 Lancaster – 'H', piloted by Flying Officer Bond – claimed to have bombed ground markers. Two others bombed on navigational aids. The rest, according to the *Operations Record Book*, 'endeavoured to obey the master bomber's instructions to bomb any built-up area they could see in the vicinity of the target'. Lancaster 'C2', piloted by Flying Officer John, obtained a good photo of a carpet of bomb bursts on the steelworks.

Of the fourteen men in the two 550 Squadron aircraft lost during the daylight, only one was still alive. Canadian pilot Flying Officer Abrams was flying NG133 ('F2') when it was shot down by flak. The Lancaster exploded, throwing Abrams clear; he made a safe landing and became a POW. The other six were killed. Lancaster PD319

'BQ-G' also failed to return; this aircraft went down north-east of Duisburg. Flying Officer Dodds and his crew all died.[15] Two men had belonged to another crew, that of Warrant Officer Tapsell. Pilot Officer R.J. Moran, RAAF, was Dodds' navigator but could not fly that night. His place was taken by Flying Officer D.J.K. White, Tapsell's navigator. As navigator and bomb aimer worked so closely as a team, White asked for Flying Officer H. Black, Tapsell's bomb aimer, to join him. This request was granted and Les Browning, Dodds' bomb aimer, stood down. On such random factors men lived or died. Moran and Browning lived, to complete their tours with other crews.[16] All 550 Squadron aircraft returned safely from the night raid.

New crews soon came to respect the German defences. An average of 1.3 aircrew survived from the seven-man crews of downed Lancasters, as against 1.8 in Stirlings and 2.45 in Halifaxes. The main reason for the poor Lancaster statistic was the problem of negotiating this aircraft's large main spar – a barrier to prompt evacuation in an emergency. There were two escape options for Lancaster crews: the main door to the rear and the narrow escape hatch in the floor of the nose. The pilot, flight engineer, navigator and bomb aimer had to climb over the main spar, while wearing parachutes, to reach the rear door. Getting out from the front hatch was also a challenge. Firstly, the flight engineer's seat and footrest had to be folded and correctly stowed. Parachute harnesses could become snagged on the seat if it was not properly stowed. The escape hatch also opened inwards and the slipstream often made it difficult to open. The hatch was also very narrow and there was the danger of getting stuck. Yet Stirling and Halifax crews still had a greater chance of dying, owing to the higher loss rates of these types.[17]

The July 1943 Hamburg attacks played havoc with the German defences, thanks to the first use of Window (radar-reflecting coated strips of paper). Hamburg was a wake-up call. The Germans responded by increasing the number of flak guns from 14,949 to 20,625 in the year to January 1944. Searchlights increased from 3,726 to 6,880. Twin-engined night fighter strength increased from 577 to 870 in the year to July 1944. A force of single-engined day fighters was deployed to attack night bombers illuminated by flares, searchlights and fires over the target. The rigid 'box' night fighter defence system was succeeded by more flexible night fighting within the concentrated bomber stream. The hunters were assisted by fighter assembly beacons, flare-dropping along the bombers' line of approach and a broadcast 'running commentary' of the raiders' progress, course and height. More effective airborne radars entered service, to assist night interception within the closely packed stream. A second phase of infiltration was timed for when the bombers turned for home, to ensure kills continued for as long as possible.[18]

The scientific struggle intensified. New German ground stations detected H_2S airborne radar emissions at long range. Bomber Command countered by ordering H_2S sets not to be used until aircraft entered German airspace. It was then used only in short bursts, as Naxos night fighter equipment allowed enemy aircraft to home onto concentrations of H_2S emissions from a range of 60 miles. Night fighters also carried Flensburg, which detected emissions from the bombers' 'Monica' tail-warners. On the ground, new German equipment could also pick up Oboe signals, giving early warning of a raid. By early 1944 German night fighters carried the new SN2 airborne interception radar (replacing the earlier Lichtenstein sets undermined by Window). The advantage was short lived. In July 1944 a Ju88 night fighter with SN2 landed at an RAF base. Shortly afterwards, Window was produced to jam SN2. Despite such setbacks, the German night fighter – at this stage in the war – was a highly advanced killing machine. Many were equipped with twin 20mm Schräge Musik upward-firing cannon. The night fighter approached under the bomber, closed to around 80–100m and opened fire, usually aiming at the wing fuel tanks.[18]

Yet the German night fighter force had passed its peak. After the war, the British Bombing Survey Unit commented: 'even though the nightfighter force continued to grow in numbers, reaching a peak of 1,250 aircraft at the end of 1944, only a small part of it could be employed at any one time, owing to a critical shortage of fuel and a lack of trained crews. The enemy, hampered in the use of its equipment by the RAF's intensified radio-countermeasures and feint forces, grew progressively weaker, and from the autumn of 1944 onwards our night bombers were able to penetrate deeply into Germany with an ever-declining loss rate.'[19]

German air defences had the job of protecting industry, the cities and the people, including young Dieter Essig, living in Pforzheim. He was just 20 months old when war began. In his infant years a state of war was normal – he knew nothing else: 'My first memories are from the early 1940s. Father was an enlisted man stationed in southern France. Our household consisted of Mother, a sister five years my senior and myself. My grandparents had a grocery store downtown. We had a first-floor apartment at Pfälzerstrasse 27, in the northern part of town. The building had five floors. I spent many hours in the air-raid shelter, with the other people in our building. The houses in this neighbourhood had been built at the turn of the century and all had cellars. There were eight families in our building and the cellar accommodated around twenty people. Each family had its compartment – a screen of boards divided it off, to give a little privacy. There were shelves down there, full of jars of preserved fruit and vegetables. The space was lit by an electric bulb of a type you can't buy today. There were plenty of candles, as the power often went off. When the light began to flicker the adults knew bombs were dropping somewhere in the area.

'When we went into the cellar, mother took along our emergency suitcase. This contained the essentials, including something to drink and a first aid kit. She carried me downstairs wrapped in a blanket, with big sister following behind.'[20]

The Essig family went into the cellar frequently during October 1944. Mosquitoes flew six 'nuisance raids' against Pforzheim during the month, including three on consecutive nights. Seven aircraft were sent to attack the city on the night of 2/3 October, six the following night and another six on the night of 4/5 October.[21]

The fourth in the series was on the night of 10/11 October. Six of the fast, twin-engined aircraft bombed the northern and eastern districts of Pforzheim.[22] The Mosquito was capable of carrying a 4,000lb Cookie blast bomb. They returned on the night of 18/19 October, when five aircraft attacked the city (one raider failed to return). The final attack in this series, on 21/22 October, was carried out by four Mosquitoes.[23]

Another youngster, Ellen Eberle, was the only child of parents from Ludwigsburg. She was 7 years old at the time of the Pforzheim attack. Her father, a professional soldier, died in Russia, and her mother came to Pforzheim in 1942. 'My grandparents lived in the city. We were an established Pforzheim family – my grandfather was a stonemason who came to Pforzheim in 1918. He worked at Buckenberg barracks but was killed in an accident in 1937. We lived at Ebersteinstrasse 35. My earliest memory is the day my mother learnt of my father's death. It was 26 December 1941, at about noon. Two soldiers came to the front door. Mother was sitting, listening to the radio programme "From Front to Home". They always played the song "Lili Marlene". When the soldiers spoke to her, mother started to scream. I knew Father was dead – there was no need for explanations. We spent each evening praying for him. I was 3½ at the time.'[24]

In 1943 Ellen's mother became increasingly concerned about air raids. They moved in with a childless couple living at Dobel, in the Black Forest: 'Grandmother took care of the Pforzheim apartment. The couple we lived with at Dobel had a "milk and honey" life. The husband was a beekeeper. Mother liked Dobel – she could live "invisibly", without the need for food stamps. We lunched daily at the Hotel Funk. Prior to this, mother had been drafted to work at the post office in Pforzheim. She was then offered a job as a civil servant but sought to avoid the *Beamteneid* – the oath of loyalty to Hitler and National Socialism. She got round this by going to a sympathetic doctor and persuading him to write a note. This explained that I was ill and that she had to leave work to look after me.

Ellen Eberle: seven years old at the time of the Pforzheim attack. *Photo: Ellen Eberle.*

'I remember sitting in our shelter in Pforzheim on 21 July 1944. We were on a short visit from Dobel. We were listening to the radio as Hitler made his special broadcast after the failed attempt on his life. Everyone in our cellar was against Hitler and said they wished it had worked.

'Inside the cellar there were two bunk beds, to the left. Above the beds was the wireless loudspeaker. On the other side there were chairs for everyone. My place was on the top bunk bed. When we took shelter in early December 1944, mother brought the Advent calendar she had made for me. It was a series of matchboxes on a string; each matchbox contained a small gift. There was also a doll on top of the cupboard. I soon discovered that this doll was not for me. Mother had saved her coupons to buy it; she planned to exchange it for food at some point. It was in the cellar for safe-keeping. I wasn't frightened down there as mother was always with me.

'One day in 1944 everyone was together in the Pforzheim apartment when my uncle's wife arrived unexpectedly. I was then told to leave the room. I heard my grandmother scream – just like my mother had screamed a couple of years before. I knew then what had happened. Hans, my mother's 24-year-old brother, had been killed in Russia. Hans was a convinced Nazi, as was his wife. She prepared a special announcement for the newspapers and told the family that she was very proud – in fact, thrilled – that her husband had died for the Führer on the field of battle. There was a legal dispute between my mother and the widow over some of Hans' possessions and they never spoke again.'[24]

Earlier in the year Deutsche Bank's Adolf Katz had made a diary entry for 2 March 1944: 'Last night, once again, we had the scary and wonderful scene of a large-scale attack on Stuttgart, with countless blue and red flares and the glow of the fires colouring the entire horizon. They haven't dropped bombs on Pforzheim so far, only pamphlets and forged food ration cards. Our factories aren't important enough ...'[25] Katz was too hasty. Four weeks later the Americans bombed Pforzheim by day. A force of ninety-eight bombers arrived over the city at just after 11.00 on 1 April 1944. They came in from the south-east and bombed from a height of 6,000–9,000ft. They released 269 tons of bombs, causing relatively minor damage but killing ninety-five people. Many bombs dropped south of the town, missing the built-up areas. The southern areas of Pforzheim received some bombs and 127 families were rendered homeless. The damage was provisionally estimated at 4 million Reichsmark.[26]

The Friedrichsberg pumping station was hit during this raid. Water pipes were destroyed or damaged at various locations and it took several weeks to fully restore supplies. On the day of the attack Katz wrote: 'This morning the first high explosive and incendiary bombs were dropped on Pforzheim. Some incendiary bombs dropped into a neighbour's garden. The worst thing for me is that I am at the bank, with no idea of what is happening at home. Some houses are destroyed or burnt, the Stadtkirche is badly damaged and countless glass windows are shattered. Also, for the time being, we don't have water.' On 6 April he added: 'Only slowly we recognized that the attack was a lot heavier than it had seemed at first.' Katz was an acute observer: 'The most upsetting image is that of an old man sitting the entire night on the heap of rubble that used to be his house. His daughter and her little boy, from Stuttgart, had moved back with her parents. Now they lie buried under the debris, grandmother, daughter and the little boy, and only the old man is sitting on top, in mute despair ...'[27]

There had been a steady increase in air-raid warnings following the D-Day landings in Normandy in June 1944. On 25 July five heavy bombs fell on Pforzheim and thirty-five buildings were damaged.[28] The Americans were back at noon on 3 October, the day after the first Mosquito raid. Sixteen aircraft dropped 46 tons of bombs on the marshalling yards.[29] Only five people were injured but 131 fires were started and there was damage to 106 residential buildings, a factory, ten warehouses and two garages. Later that day, in the evening, a single aircraft dropped bombs on the station buildings, killing nine and injuring sixty-two.[30]

Those Pforzheimers with imagination were alarmed at the destruction of nearby Stuttgart. This city was attacked by Bomber Command in February 1944. It was raided twice the following month, on each occasion with limited results. Stuttgart was devastated, however, in a series of three raids over a five-day period in late July 1944. The assault began on the night of 24/5 July, when 614 heavy aircraft bombed the city. The following night 550 bombers arrived overhead. The third raid was on 28/9 July and involved 494 Lancasters. Bomber Command paid a stiff price for Stuttgart, losing seventy-two aircraft.[31] In return, the attacks 'finally reduced the city to rubble'.[32] The raids killed over 1,000 people and injured another 1,600.[33]

The scale of destruction, however, did not stop Bomber Command visiting Stuttgart again. A force of 204 Lancasters and 13 Mosquitoes flew to the city on the night of 12/13 September, 1944, in a concentrated attack that caused a firestorm. Nearly 1,200 people were killed.[34] The bombers returned once more on the night of 19/20 October 1944. A force of 565 Lancasters and 18 Mosquitoes attacked but, on this occasion, concentrated bombing was not achieved.[35]

With all the horrors of bombing so vividly displayed on their doorstep, Pforzheimers grew increasingly fearful. The banker Adolf Katz became certain that Pforzheim would suffer a catastrophic raid. On 6 October he recorded some disturbing thoughts: 'I find myself imagining a heavy attack on Pforzheim in which we are spared, of course, and all those I dislike are hit.'[36]

Pforzheim was bombed again a few days later, on 10 October. Areas in the north and east of the town (mainly Christophallee, Erbprinzenstrasse, Dammstrasse and Ostliche Karl-Friedrich-Strasse) were hit by bombs from Mosquitoes and suffered damage. Sixty-four people died. The bombed-out found shelter with relatives or neighbours. At this time the support infrastructure was still functioning – with state provision of replacement furniture and other essentials, together with funds to repair buildings. There were air-raid warnings virtually every evening. When the Mosquitoes returned on the night of 18/19 October, they caused only minor damage. They came back on 21 October and killed eleven people around Pfälzerstrasse and Hohenzollernstrasse.[37]

People became more cautious, especially those living near the railway station – a frequent target. Many left their homes, to stay elsewhere. As for Katz, by the end of October he and his family had taken to sleeping in their clothes. They went into the cellar immediately on hearing aircraft noise.[38]

RAF North Killingholme buzzed with activity on the morning of Thursday, 19 October 1944, as twenty-five Lancasters were bombed up and fuelled. The crews were briefed for an attack on Stuttgart's ruins. Flight Lieutenant A. Wynne Thomas and crew failed to return that night. It was their first sortie with 550 Squadron.

There was nine-tenths cloud over the target and sky markers were used, although six 550 crews took advantage of momentary gaps and bombed ground markers. Flying Officer Young's Lancaster ('A') was damaged by flak. The *Operations Record Book* described this aircraft as 'well-peppered', with damage to its fuselage, tailplane and flaps. A second aircraft, 'K' (Flying Officer Daniels), received rough treatment from Karlsruhe's guns. It suffered damage to the port wing and fuselage, together with a punctured main tyre. Both aircraft returned safely to North Killingholme.

Ken Sidwell attacked Stuttgart that night. Frank Woodley was in the mid-upper turret: 'We climbed into Lancaster 'B' and took off at 21.32. We spent seven hours in the air but ended up in a hedge back at North Killingholme! The weather was terrible. When Ken put the Lanc down it aquaplaned along the runway and refused to stop. Ken let it go. It sailed across the perimeter, entered a field and dug its wheels in, its tail pointing to the sky. I was trapped in my turret. This was all very embarrassing as "B" was none other than the legendary "Phantom of the Ruhr". This Lanc had survived 102 operations at that point. I don't remember how I got out of the fuselage but no harm done. The Phantom was flying again within a few days.'[39]

Sidwell and his crew were not alone in getting a fright that night. Stuttgart was the second trip for Dave Davidson, with 100 Squadron at Waltham. During their first operation, earlier that month, Howell Evans, Davidson's wireless operator, had seen a Lancaster destroyed instantly by 'friendly' bombs. Stuttgart proved even more alarming: 'We took a bad flak hit over the target and the hydraulics failed. Dave

Pranging the Phantom: Ken Sidwell and crew ended up in a hedge at North Killingholme when the Lancaster Phantom of the Ruhr aquaplaned. Here, the veteran bomber is shown with Warrant Officer D.H. Town and crew. *Photo: Bob Stone.*

couldn't close the bomb doors or operate the flaps. We turned for home with bomb doors hanging open.'[40]

It was a difficult return. On the last leg Lancaster 'S' was diverted to Carnaby, one of three emergency airfields. Getting down was far from easy. Dave Davidson: 'Unfortunately, when we reached Carnaby there was one hell of a crosswind. Given the condition of the hydraulics and the turbulence, I told the crew to take up crash positions and they braced themselves against the main spar. Fred used the emergency air – a bottle of compressed air connected to the hydraulic system. The undercarriage went down in half a second flat. On the final approach I fought to keep the aircraft level, the sweat rolling down my face, when I suddenly got a whiff of cigarette smoke. I yelled at the crew: "Who the hell is smoking back there?", only to get a calm answer from Tiny: "We all are."'[41]

They landed at Carnaby after seven and a half hours. Howell Evans: 'We were very late back; everyone was surprised when we announced our presence to base. We received a tremendous welcome on our return – they thought we were goners.'[42]

Returning to Waltham was far from easy. Following an inspection, the Lancaster was not considered flyable and the crew spent a miserable Friday at Carnaby. It rained most of the day. Finally, at 21.00, they climbed into a lorry and left for the long drive to Grimsby, a very slow journey in thick fog. On arriving back, stiff after nearly ten hours on the road, they were horrified to discover that they were on the pending battle order. Mercifully, they were removed from the list.[43]

While the Stuttgart attack may have lacked concentration, central and eastern areas of the city took heavy punishment. A total of 376 people died on the ground; six Lancasters were lost.[44]

Dark humour helped ease tensions. One example on 550 Squadron was provided by Flying Officer Markes' rear gunner, Danny Driscoll. Danny was a Londoner, from Battersea – an area heavily bombed during the Blitz. Over a pint in the pub, Danny mentioned he was bombing Germany. His mates then presented him with a brick from a bombed house and asked him to drop it on Germany. He obliged. This became a regular habit. Driscoll returned from each leave with several bricks in his kitbag; he never bought a drink in that pub.[45]

On Monday 23 October, following several days of bad weather, 550 Squadron readied twenty-five Lancasters for a huge raid on Essen. All aircraft returned safely. It was Ken Sidwell's fifth operation. He took Lancaster 'G' from North Killingholme to the Ruhr, in a sortie of five hours twenty-five minutes.[46] At the Waltham dispersal, Dave Davidson and crew climbed into their 100 Squadron Lancaster for this night attack, their third operation. On the first op a Lancaster blew up below them. On the second they took a flak hit. Later, Dave told his wife, Babs, that he was 'a little scared' of the briefing room until he went inside. He also told her that Essen 'was not a bad trip,

Target for tonight: the business end of North Killingholme's briefing room. *Photo: Bob Stone.*

but the weather was ghastly – cloud and ice all the way'. They landed back after five hours thirty-five minutes.[47]

Lancaster captain Jack Harris, of 550 Squadron, remembers the ice that night: 'The weather was bad on the way to the target, with lots of icing. We lost the airspeed indicator. The ASI static vents were located on the starboard side of the fuselage, near the main door. Moisture collected in the vents and froze, making it impossible to get an airspeed reading. The pilot then had to guess the correct throttle settings, according to the aircraft's weight. The ASI packed up as soon as we climbed above 5,000ft and remained out of action until we dropped below 5,000ft on the return. We bombed from 20,000ft on sky markers, with ten-tenths cloud over the target.'[48]

This area attack was on an enormous scale. It was Essen's heaviest raid to date, involving 1,055 aircraft. They dropped 4,538 tons of bombs. Over 90 per cent was high explosive, including 509 4,000lb Cookies. The incendiary load was low as burnable buildings were thought to be already gutted. A total of 662 people died on the ground; eight bombers were lost.[49]

Bomber Command returned to Essen in force within forty-eight hours. North Killingholme's station commander, Group Captain R.V. McIntyre, took 550 Squadron's Lancaster 'R' to Essen on Wednesday, 25 October. All squadron aircraft returned safely from this daylight attack, despite the fact that German high technology put in an appearance. The *Operations Record Book* commented: 'Opposition over the target area was negligible but a fair number of jet-propelled fighters were seen high over the attackers. No attempt was made to interfere with the bombing ...'

In their turrets, Ken Sidwell's gunners – Woodley and Witchmarsh – saw many fighters, including their first jet aircraft.[50] Among those bombing sky markers over this cloud-obscured target was Dave Davidson, in Lancaster 'W'.[51] This was another major attack, involving 771 aircraft. The bombing was scattered but 820 people died, more than in the heavier raid thirty-six hours earlier. There was further damage to the Krupps steelworks; four bombers were lost.[52]

Bomber Command's headquarters ordered a daylight attack on Cologne for Saturday, 28 October. North Killingholme sent twenty-seven Lancasters. They left for Germany just after 13.00, led by 550 commander Wing Commander 'Dingle' Bell. They took off in poor flying conditions, mist and low cloud – only a brief improvement allowed them to get away at all. In contrast, the weather over the target was good. All aircraft returned safely.

The raid was uneventful for Dave Davidson; his aircraft returned unscathed after five hours ten minutes, but four Halifaxes and three Lancasters were lost. The 733 bombers had arrived over Cologne in two waves, causing catastrophic damage to the north-east and south-west of the city centre. At least 630 people died and 1,200 were injured.[53]

This attack on Cologne was Sam Lipfriend's first operation. He had returned to Ludford Magna after the crash that ended his first flight with 101 Squadron. The flight engineer had been posted to Grimsby and 100 Squadron to begin his tour. He joined Flight Lieutenant Carl 'Eddie' Edlund's crew: 'Morale on this squadron was very good. Eddie and his team had only recently started their tour, having done four trips. At that point their original flight engineer had had enough and went LMF (Lack of Moral Fibre).'[54]

On 28 October Edlund's crew boarded their Lancaster for Cologne. The navigator, Flying Officer Wally Dawson, was in his mid-twenties and from Lethbridge, Alberta. The bomb aimer, Flight Sergeant Phil Barber, was from Hatch End in Middlesex. An Australian, Warrant Officer Gordon, was the wireless operator. His home was a station 120 miles west of McKay, in Queensland. Both gunners were from Scotland. The mid-upper, Flight Sergeant Carruthers, was from Glasgow. The rear gunner, Hector McNeil, was from Galashiels. They took off for Cologne at 13.17 and returned safely despite an iced-up elevator trim tab. Lipfriend had acquired a diary. Turning to the first blank page, he wrote: 'Target vis. 4/10ths. Light, medium, heavy flak. Nice and easy.' This would not be the case on many other trips.[54]

Jack Harris and crew certainly found this operation less than easy. They were over Cologne, dropping the 'usual' city mix of a Cookie and incendiaries: 'We bombed from 19,500ft through a gap in the clouds. During the early phase of the attack the flak was heavy and we were hit, receiving damage to the port mainplane, port outer electrical cabling and bomb doors. The weather was difficult on the return. Visibility at base was down to 1,000yd but we got in, following the "Drem" lighting that funnels aircraft onto the runway.'[55]

Battered Cologne suffered a series of heavy raids in quick succession. Eddie Edlund and crew were over the city again within forty-eight hours, but found the target obscured. Dave Davidson also returned without incident, as did Jack Harris and Ken Sidwell. Sunday was a day of rest for Davidson, but his name was on 100

Bombing Cologne:
Jack Harris' aiming
point photograph.
Photo: Jack Harris.

Squadron's battle order for Monday, 30 October. This second attack on Cologne was a night raid by 905 aircraft. They dropped 3,431 tons of high explosive bombs and 610 tons of incendiaries; over 500 people died. No aircraft were lost.[56]

Cologne, now a sea of rubble, received its third blow the following day, Tuesday, 31 October. At North Killingholme, 550 Squadron sent twenty-four Lancasters. They encountered only moderate opposition. The *Operations Record Book* described this raid as 'highly successful'. At Waltham, the 100 Squadron Lancasters began to take off in the late afternoon. Eddie Edlund's Lancaster was in the air at 17.42. They arrived early, began to orbit, were engaged by predicted flak and received their first battle damage. The starboard outer engine had to be feathered when forty-five minutes from base, owing to a coolant leak from the flak hit. They landed back after five hours fifteen minutes in the air.[57]

It is not difficult to imagine Dave Davidson's feelings when he entered 100 Squadron's briefing room at Waltham that Tuesday. The curtain was drawn back and Cologne was revealed, yet again, as the target. Nevertheless, this crew's third sortie to that city in four days was free of incident. Once again, thick cloud obscured the target, but accurate Oboe marking ensured heavy damage to the southern districts.[58] A total of 493 aircraft attacked and two Lancasters were lost; ninety-eight Germans died on the ground.[59] Lancaster captain Jack Harris recalls: 'The city looked like it had taken a real pasting.'[60]

Baptism of fire: Flight Lieutenant Eddie Edlund, DFC, and crew. Sam Lipfriend is pictured centre. Edlund's Lancaster suffered flak damage over Cologne on Tuesday 31 October 1944. *Photo: Bob Stone.*

Ken Sidwell's crew were grateful to be alive after just over two weeks' participation in Bomber Command's war.[61] In his billet at Waltham, Howell Evans, Dave Davidson's wireless operator, reviewed October. They had survived seven operations – less than a quarter of a full tour. They had attacked Emmerich, Stuttgart, Essen on two occasions and Cologne on three: 'These targets were heavily defended and the flak was very thick. I must confess I was frightened.'[62]

Life in Pforzheim narrowed as the war drew closer. The city library closed. On 1 September 1944, the theatre closed. From mid-October there were no trams on Sundays or bank holidays. Public transport dwindled owing to staff and energy shortages. Late evening and night services ceased as air attacks increased. Normal school life came to an end; the school year 1944–5 operated to a slimmed down timetable. Schoolwork was disrupted by constant air-raid alerts and older students were absent, having been conscripted to work in industry. The planners prepared for catastrophe. A large country house was converted into a military hospital during September. A maternity unit was relocated out of town. A soup kitchen – equipped with twelve cauldrons of 300 litres each – was set up at the Seehaus. During early 1944 bunkers had been allocated for the safe storage of the town's archives and valuables. In October, however, orders were given for these bunkers to be cleared. Some archives were moved to the cellars of the Hilda School and the Enz power station.[63]

Given the scale of the air threat, banker Adolf Katz worried about official apathy. On 29 May 1944, he made an acerbic note in his diary: 'To complete the picture of these magical Whitsun days, we are having alarms day and night. Deutsche Bank in Karlsruhe has been hit. We're rather careless, despite everything, as danger is often predicted for our city but nothing happens. Only when the bombs are dropping will everybody go to the air-raid shelters – too late! But we are getting used to living such a dangerous life.'[64]

In June 1944 Katz referred to the Allied landings in Normandy but remained focused on the bombing threat. On 15 June he wrote of Mannheim's fate after visiting the city: 'Mannheim is ruined. Smoke-blackened facades with gigantic piles of rubble behind them. Now and then a house that has been spared. The streets are quiet. Only a few people. The station, the castle destroyed and burned out, a tangled mess of iron girders, heaps of stones, remains of walls. There is still a slight smell of burning and every gust of wind whirls up clouds of dust.' This diary entry is dismissive of the Vl revenge weapon: 'This can cause heavy disruption but in no way can it be of military significance. The Anglo-Saxons have been dropping far bigger explosive loads on German cities for a long time without getting anywhere. So the whole thing mainly serves to satisfy feelings of hate and revenge at home.'[64]

The new crews joining the bombing war in October 1944 included Bruce Potter's team. They arrived at Kirmington, Lincolnshire, to join 166 Squadron's C Flight. They opened their tour with a daylight sortie – the attack on the gun batteries at Fort Fredrik Hendrik, on the south bank of the Scheldt at Breskens. This was their first and last flight with 166. They were then posted to Scampton, to join 153 Squadron's A Flight. This squadron had just re-formed as a heavy bomber unit. Potter's crew knew Scampton was a pre-war station with a well-deserved reputation for excellent food, accommodation and facilities. Bill Thomas was Potter's bomb aimer: 'We took a Lanc to Scampton as soon as possible, as we wanted the best billets. This station was almost empty in October 1944. Some newly arrived aircrew moved into the old married quarters but we found a better home in the mess building, just round the corner from the bar. This station was fantastic – we even had a French chef! That said, wartime rationing had Scampton in its grip. I vividly remember rejecting a dish of stuffed hearts with the comment: "Stuff the hearts."'[65]

A number of crews from 166 Squadron were posted in to make up the core of 153 Squadron; they moved to Scampton on 15 October. Earlier in the war, 153 had been a night fighter unit. Its badge was a bat and its motto was *'Noctividus'* ('Seeing by night'). It began bombing operations immediately.

Bill Thomas remembers the crews as a mixed bunch, including Canadians, Australians and New Zealanders: 'Squadron morale was good, but I do remember one LMF case. Our aircraft was one of three at the dispersal. That evening we finished our run-up and, as usual, got out to have a last smoke. Suddenly, I saw the pilot of one of the other aircraft hiding in a hedge. I pointed him out but someone said he must be having a pee. I didn't think so. This was the night he decided he couldn't take any more. Three staff cars soon appeared and the poor chap was whisked away. We never saw him again.'[65] Bruce Potter and his crew attacked Cologne on 31 October and returned safely from their second operation.

Notes

1. Middlebrook, M. and Everitt, C. (1990), *The Bomber Command War Diaries*, 595.
2. Interview with Jack Harris, April 2013.
3. Middlebrook, M. and Everitt, C. (1990), *The Bomber Command War Diaries*, 596.
4. Interview with Dave Davidson, April 2013.
5. Interview with Howell Evans, June 2013.
6. Interview with Jack Harris, April 2013.
7. Interview with Frank Woodley, March 2013.
8. Middlebrook, M. and Everitt, C. (1990), *The Bomber Command War Diaries*, 599.
9. Interview with Raimund Frei, July 2013.
10. Newsletter 43, 20 May 2009, 550 Squadron and RAF North Killingholme Association.
11. Documents via Wing Commander Jack Harris, OBE, DFC.
12. Middlebrook, M. and Everitt, C. (1990), *The Bomber Command War Diaries*, 601–2.
13. Saward, D. (1985), *Victory Denied*, 343.
14. Interview with Frank Woodley, March 2013.
15. Newsletter 21, 1 November 2000, 550 Squadron and RAF North Killingholme Association.
16. Newsletter 53, 15 October 2012, 550 Squadron and RAF North Killingholme Association.
17. Redding, T. (2008), *Flying for Freedom*, 78.
18. Newsletter 33, 24 October 2005, 550 Squadron and RAF North Killingholme Association.
19. The Strategic Air War against Germany (the official report of the British Bombing Survey Unit) (1998), 51.
20. Interview with Dieter Essig, April 2013.
21. Middlebrook, M. and Everitt, C. (1990), *The Bomber Command War Diaries*, 593–4.
22. Ibid., 598.
23. Ibid., 604–5.
24. Interview with Ellen Eberle, November 2013.
25. Pross, M. (1995), *Die Einschläge kommen näher, Aus den Tagebüchern 1943–45 von Friedrich Adolf Katz, 1945–1947 Oberbürgermeister der Stadt Pforzheim.*
26. Administration's Report and Statistics for the Town of Pforzheim 1945–1952: City Life 1939–1945.
27. Pross, M. (1995), *Die Einschläge kommen näher, Aus den Tagebüchern 1943–45 von Friedrich Adolf Katz, 1945–1947 Oberbürgermeister der Stadt Pforzheim.*
28. Administration's Report and Statistics for the Town of Pforzheim 1945–52: City Life 1939–1945.
29. National Archives, AIR14/3684.
30. Administration's Report and Statistics for the Town of Pforzheim 1945–52: City Life 1939–1945.
31. Middlebrook, M. and Everitt, C. (1990), *The Bomber Command War Diaries*, 549–52.
32. Neillands, R. (2001), *The Bomber War*, 328.
33. Middlebrook, M. and Everitt, C. (1990), *The Bomber Command War Diaries*, 549–52.
34. Ibid., 582.
35. Ibid., 605.
36. Pross, M. (1995), *Die Einschläge kommen näher, Aus den Tagebüchern 1943–45 von Friedrich Adolf Katz, 1945–1947 Oberbürgermeister der Stadt Pforzheim.*

37. Administration's Report and Statistics for the Town of Pforzheim 1945–52: City Life 1939–1945.
38. Pross, M. (1995), *Die Einschläge kommen näher, Aus den Tagebüchern 1943–45 von Friedrich Adolf Katz, 1945–1947 Oberbürgermeister der Stadt Pforzheim*.
39. Interview with Frank Woodley, March 2013.
40. Interview with Howell Evans, June 2013.
41. Interview with Dave Davidson, April 2013.
42. Interview with Howell Evans, June 2013.
43. Interview with Dave Davidson, April 2013.
44. Middlebrook, M. and Everitt, C. (1990), *The Bomber Command War Diaries*, 605.
45. Newsletter 33, 24 October 2005, 550 Squadron and RAF North Killingholme Association.
46. Interview with Frank Woodley, March 2013.
47. Interview with Dave Davidson, April 2013.
48. Interview with Jack Harris, April 2013.
49. Middlebrook, M. and Everitt, C. (1990), *The Bomber Command War Diaries*, 606.
50. Interview with Frank Woodley, March 2013.
51. Interview with Dave Davidson, April 2013.
52. Middlebrook, M. and Everitt, C. (1990), *The Bomber Command War Diaries*, 607.
53. Ibid., 608.
54. Interview with Sam Lipfriend, March 2013.
55. Interview with Jack Harris, April 2013.
56. Middlebrook, M. and Everitt, C. (1990), *The Bomber Command War Diaries*, 611.
57. Interview with Sam Lipfriend, March 2013.
58. Interview with Dave Davidson, April 2013.
59. Middlebrook, M. and Everitt, C. (1990), *The Bomber Command War Diaries*, 611–12.
60. Interview with Jack Harris, April 2013.
61. Interview with Frank Woodley, March 2013.
62. Interview with Howell Evans, June 2013.
63. Administration's Report and Statistics for the Town of Pforzheim 1945–52: City Life 1939–1945.
64. Pross, M. (1995), *Die Einschläge kommen näher, Aus den Tagebüchern 1943–45 von Friedrich Adolf Katz, 1945–1947 Oberbürgermeister der Stadt Pforzheim*.
65. Interview with Bill Thomas, June 2013.

Chapter Three

Crushing the Enemy

The war continued to stalk Pforzheim banker Adolf Katz. Bomber Command sent six Mosquitoes on a 'nuisance raid' to Pforzheim on the night of 9/10 November 1944. According to Katz's diary, they were certainly a nuisance to Deutsche Bank: 'Yesterday evening a heavy bomb hit the big office building of Knoll u. Pregizer, in Goethestrasse. The blast was so powerful that almost all windows in the bank have been shattered; the window frames, iron shutters and doors torn off. My office is unusable. We have had to move the major part of our company into the cellar.' The next day's entry reflects: 'How the appearance of the town has changed! Piles of glass shards and rubble all over the streets. Most shops downtown have wooden planking instead of windows.'[1]

The 9 November raid hit buildings in an area around Goethestrasse, Salierstrasse, Ebersteinstrasse and Zähringerallee. Two people were killed; twenty-three flats were destroyed and twenty-eight severely damaged. A further 150 flats had to be evacuated pending repairs. The total cost was estimated at 4.4 million Reichsmark.[2]

Only weeks earlier Adolf Katz had marvelled at Pforzheim's continued escape from heavy air attack. On 12 September 1944, he wrote: 'It is totally astonishing that Pforzheim is the only [*sic*] city that has been spared so far. Yet, smaller towns are targeted with bombs, many trains machine-gunned, even health resorts are being attacked. Karlsruhe has been struck heavily.' In late August he had commented on morale: 'more and more people, who only a few months ago couldn't praise National Socialism and the plans of annihilation enough, are now telling me about the hopelessness of the situation'.[3]

North Killingholme prepared twenty-seven Lancasters for a night raid on Düsseldorf. They took off in the late afternoon of Thursday, 2 November 1944. The aircraft were heavy in the climb, with bomb bays full of blast bombs and incendiaries. The weather was fine but cloudy. The 550 Squadron *Operations Record Book* noted that conditions improved, leaving the target clear and in bright moonlight: 'Ground markers were punctual and clearly visible, placed accurately on the marshalling yards and, very quickly, a concentrated cloud of bomb smoke developed. The crews were enthusiastic about the fires, which quickly took hold and emitted a rosy glow seen for almost 100 miles on the return journey.'

Ken Sidwell's name appeared on 550's battle order three times during the first week of November. He and his crew returned safely from Düsseldorf. The flak was light at first, then increased to 'intense'. Night fighters entered the bomber stream and combats resulted. Flight Lieutenant D.J. Foster's Lancaster failed to return to North Killingholme that night. Foster's aircraft was PD255 ('T'); there were no survivors. Düsseldorf was their tenth operation.

Düsseldorf was Dave Davidson's eighth operation. The 100 Squadron Lancaster captain said little to his wife about the sortie, beyond the terse remark: 'Rather a hectic night.' There was significant fighter activity and jets put in an appearance.[4] Flying Officer Adam's gunners exchanged fire with a Fw190, Flying Officer Allen's gunners fired on a Ju88 and Flying Officer Ansell's gunners opened up on an unidentified twin-engined aircraft. Eddie Edlund, another 100 Squadron pilot, certainly had a hectic time. His problems developed on the return, when the starboard inner engine developed an oil leak. They reached home safely, touching down at Waltham after five hours fifteen minutes in the air. Edlund's flight engineer, Sam Lipfriend, kept a close eye on that rogue engine. After debrief, Lipfriend put a brief comment in his diary: 'Medium, heavy flak. Numerous searchlights. Saw a plane shot down.'[5]

This heavy attack on Düsseldorf involved 992 aircraft and 19 were lost. At least 678 people died and over 1,000 were injured. More than 5,000 houses were hit and 7 factories destroyed (another 18 severely damaged). This was Bomber Command's last major raid on Düsseldorf.[6]

Ken Sidwell and crew were 'on again' forty-eight hours after Düsseldorf. They climbed into 550 Squadron Lancaster 'J' for a night raid on Bochum. This extremely destructive attack was Bomber Command's last big raid on Bochum, there being no reason to return. The raid, on Saturday, 4 November 1944, involved 749 aircraft. Losses were high: twenty-eight aircraft – equivalent to an entire heavy bomber squadron. The raid was devastating. Over 4,000 buildings were destroyed or seriously damaged and around 1,000 people died.[7] According to 550's *Operations Record Book*, photo reconnaissance 'showed the great damage done in this attack – the two main factories of first priority importance, with extensive blast furnaces, steelworks and rolling mills, all making armaments, suffered severely …'.

Sidwell's squadron had a well-deserved reputation for 'maximum effort'. Twenty-six Lancasters left North Killingholme to bomb Bochum. There should have been twenty-seven but 'G2', Flying Officer Kennedy's aircraft, aborted owing to faulty hydraulics. Another aircraft, 'E2', flown by Flying Officer Marriott, returned with an unserviceable rear turret. This was a wise decision by Marriott, as night fighters were responsible for most of the losses that night.

Twenty-five 550 Squadron Lancasters flew on in nine-tenths cloud. Conditions then cleared, with Bochum free of cloud. The *Operations Record Book* described the marking as punctual and 'fairly accurate'. Markers were refreshed and the bombing well concentrated: 'After the incendiary attack developed, the whole area rapidly became a mass of fire, visible for 100 miles, and there were a number of impressive explosions.'

The ground opposition was rated as moderate to intense. There were around twenty searchlights and some aircraft were coned. Several bombers fought it out with the fighters. Flying Officer Whynacht, in 550 Lancaster 'B2', had no fewer than four engagements and his gunners (Canadian Sergeants Pattison and Hutchins) claimed two aircraft destroyed and one damaged. The other combat was inconclusive. The Lancaster suffered no damage or casualties. Interestingly, the *Operations Record Book* stated: 'All these appeared to be jet-propelled aircraft.' Other 550 crews encountered the *Luftwaffe* jets. Gunners with Flying Officer McCarthy, in Lancaster 'M', and Pilot Officer Franklyn, in Lancaster 'P', opened fire on jets but made no claims. However, Flying Officer Blackler's gunners, in Lancaster 'V', claimed an aircraft believed to be a jet. The *Operations Record Book* was non-committal: 'The appearance of jet-propelled and other rocket phenomena is only of recent origin and the claims are being further investigated. Meanwhile, these claims are accepted with reserve.' One of 550's aircraft was damaged. Flying Officer Ansell's Lancaster, 'F', landed safely at Manston emergency airfield, near Ramsgate.

Dave Davidson, with 100 Squadron, had been almost the last back from Düsseldorf two days before, but he was first back from Bochum, minus his high explosive load of 14,000lbs. He touched down after four hours thirty minutes in the air.[8] Another 100 Squadron crew logged no time. Eddie Edlund's aircraft failed to get off that night. The crew were keyed up and ready to go, but an engine refused to start. As they climbed out of the truculent Lanc they had no idea that Düsseldorf had been their last op with 100 Squadron. They were posted to 550 at North Killingholme.

A fully laden heavy bomber was little more than a huge bomb, with up to 2,154 gallons of fuel, 150 gallons of oil and 15,000lb of blast bombs, incendiaries and pyrotechnics, together with thousands of rounds of belted ammunition.[9] According to Germany's leading night fighter ace, Major Schnaufer, 98 per cent of aircraft shot down by his group (NJG.4) were 'flamers'. The Lancaster caught fire more readily than the Halifax. The favoured aiming point was between the two engines on either side – to hit the fuel tanks – or the rear turret if the gunner opened fire. Night fighter pilots competed, to see who could shoot down the most bombers with the lowest expenditure of ammunition.[10] Schnaufer was interviewed by RAF officers in June 1945. He said a night fighter pilot could expect to see one to three bombers on a dark night once penetrating the stream, but perhaps twenty or more in bright moonlight. An experienced pilot would attack an average of three bombers on a dark night.[11]

Schnaufer's courage was matched by his prowess. On 21 February 1945, he claimed nine kills – two in the early hours of the morning and seven more in the evening. He attacked many heavy bombers with upward-firing Schräge Musik 20mm cannon. His preferred range was around 80m. Only one bomber in ten saw him at a range of 150–200m and corkscrewed before he could fire.[11] Schnaufer added that a Halifax's exhausts could be seen from below at a range of 400–500m. In contrast, a Lancaster's exhausts could be seen only when flying directly astern and in line. On a dark night a Lancaster's exhausts were visible at up to 800m.[12]

Comrades in arms: leading night fighter ace Major Heinz-Wolfgang Schnaufer (centre), pictured with gunner Wilhelm Gänster (left) and radar operator Fritz Rumpelhardt. Schnaufer is wearing the Knight's Cross with Oakleaves, Swords and Diamonds. His crew wear the Knight's Cross. *Photo: Trustees of the Imperial War Museum.*

Failed to return: Lancaster ED531 (T-Tommy) of 467 Squadron hit high tension wires during a raid on Turin. The wreckage, on a Swiss mountainside, was photographed on the morning of 13 July 1943. *Photo: Vincent Holyoak.*

Ken Sidwell's crew were on for Monday, 6 November 1944, a daylight to Gelsenkirchen. Twenty-three of 550 Squadron's Lancasters went to this target, 7 miles north-east of Essen. Conditions for bombing were reasonable at first but then deteriorated. The bombing was concentrated initially but became scattered. Some major fires were reported. A column of black smoke rose to a height of 10,000ft. As usual, the flak was moderate to intense throughout 'Happy Valley'. A total of 738 aircraft attacked Gelsenkirchen, the principal target being the Nordstern synthetic oil plant. The casualties on the ground included 518 dead.[13]

When Jack Harris' Lancaster arrived over Gelsenkirchen, he found the target obscured by nine-tenths cloud. Suddenly, ground markers were seen through a gap and they dropped a Cookie, six 1,000lb bombs and seven 500lb bombs. Harris recalls: 'This daylight was executed in "Base Column" formation. The main force was led in by two leading vics of three aircraft with special recognition markings on their wingtips and tailplanes.'[14] Twenty-two aircraft landed back at North Killingholme. Lancaster PB562 'M', skippered by Flying Officer L.J.T. McCarthy, failed to return. McCarthy and his crew were killed. This was their twenty-fifth trip. Their Lancaster was the fifth aircraft lost by 550 Squadron in three weeks.

It took Dave Davidson three hours fifty-five minutes to fly to Gelsenkirchen, bomb the town and return to 100 Squadron's base at Waltham. In the language of the day, he described it as 'a good trip and a good prang'. This crew had flown their last op with 100 Squadron. Having survived ten sorties, they moved to North Killingholme and 550 Squadron. Dave Davidson: 'We were sent to 550 as replacements. They'd had quite a few losses. The move was a bit disorientating but we coped and North Killingholme turned out to be a good station.'[15]

Casualties: Flying Officer L.J.T. McCarthy and crew – all killed on a daylight raid to Gelsenkirchen on 6 November 1944. *Photo: Bob Stone.*

Within forty-eight hours they were busy with local flying, familiarizing themselves with North Killingholme's layout and approaches, together with local landmarks. Davidson's wireless operator, Howell Evans, was disturbed by the move: 'We didn't take kindly to this change. I was bitterly disappointed at our transfer to a squadron that had taken significant losses in recent weeks. Yet, within a short time we were as committed to 550 as we were to 100. We found 550 to be a great squadron, with excellent commanders. Morale was just as strong as on 100.'[16]

North Killingholme village, however, failed to win hearts: 'There was a pub and that was about it. The station itself was OK but very dispersed; bikes were essential. Our squadron commander was Wing Commander "Dingle" Bell. I was recommended for a commission. As a wireless operator, I had my initial interview with the signals officer. Bell was the next step. All senior officers did one or two ops per month and Bell had just gone on a raid. He never came back. He had been due to interview me the next day, so my application fell through the cracks. It didn't surface for another year and I spent the last months of the war as a warrant officer.'[16]

Davidson, Evans and the others went on leave soon after arriving at North Killingholme. They did not fly operationally with 550 until the end of the month. Meanwhile, twelve complete 550 crews were posted en masse to form the nucleus of 150 Squadron at Fiskerton. The *Operations Record Book* said of their departure: 'All were operationally experienced and had been with the squadron long enough to feel themselves thoroughly at home at North Killingholme and regretted leaving the "old place".'

Nevertheless, 550 put twenty-three Lancasters in the air the next day, Thursday, 9 November for a daylight attack on Wanne-Eickel synthetic oil plant, west of Gelsenkirchen. Once again, the base column close gaggle formation was flown, with Spitfire and Mustang escort. Thick cloud developed on the way out. By the time they reached the target there was thick cumulus at 20,000ft, with layer cloud below. Only one 550 Lancaster caught a fleeting glimpse of the target. All aircraft returned safely. The sky markers dropped by Oboe-equipped Mosquitoes soon disappeared into cloud and the master bomber was forced to give the order 'Freehand', allowing the Lancasters to bomb any visible built-up area.[17]

After a five-day break Ken Sidwell's name appeared on 550's battle order for the Saturday, 11 November attack on Dortmund. Ken flew a new aircraft, 'BQ-M2', recently delivered to North Killingholme. This was the beginning of a long relationship; they were to fly twenty-five operations in this aircraft.[18]

The 209 Lancasters and 19 Mosquitoes briefed for Dortmund attacked and severely damaged the Hoesch Benzin synthetic oil plant.[19] They included twenty-one Lancasters from 550 Squadron. The *Operations Record Book* noted: 'Once again, 10/10ths cloud was encountered over the target. Reflections from ground markers could be seen on clouds and these were systematically bombed. Flak was light to moderate. One Lanc, "G" (Flying Officer Young), was hit and its rear turret became unserviceable.' Dortmund was the Harris crew's twentieth operation. Jack Harris:

Long relationship: Ken Sidwell and crew flew twenty-five operations in BQ-M2, beginning with the Saturday 11 November 1944 attack on Dortmund. *Photo: Frank Woodley.*

'There were no searchlights and the flak was moderate. We bombed from 20,000ft on the glow of markers showing through the cloud.'[20]

Many oil plants and marshalling yards were attacked by Bomber Command during November 1944, but Arthur Harris was still on call to bomb targets in direct support of Allied ground forces. On Thursday, 16 November, for example, three towns were bombed before an attack by the American First and Ninth Armies in the region between Aachen and the Rhine. The targets were Düren, Jülich and Heinsburg. The aim was to cut communications behind the German lines. A massive force of 1,188 Bomber Command aircraft made these attacks. Düren was raided in daylight by 485 Lancasters and 13 Mosquitoes. All three towns were virtually destroyed, but the American attack made slow progress on the ground. The death toll in Düren was severe, totalling 3,127 – including 2,403 local civilians.[21] Flying Officer Bruce Potter of 153 Squadron was over Düren that night. His Lancaster arrived back at Scampton unharmed, after a flight of four hours thirty minutes.

North Killingholme, 550 Squadron's base, had an informal atmosphere, but service discipline occasionally reared its head. When bad weather curtailed flying, the crews were ordered to clean up their sleeping quarters, which, according to the *Operations Record Book*, 'had been allowed to deteriorate to below the squadron's standard of cleanliness'. It was business as usual, however, on Thursday, 16 November. Twenty-six Lancasters were sent to Düren. The weather was hazy, but 'magnificent marking and precise instructions from the Master Bomber contributed to the successful

Music and politics: Gerd Fleig's Jungbann-Spielmannszug – the Jungvolk marching band. Fleig is just visible; he is standing third from the right. *Photo: Gerd Fleig.*

bombing of rail facilities, where the line east of Aachen forks to Düsseldorf and Cologne'. It was a frustrating trip, however, for 550's Flying Officer George and crew, in 'M2'. They were hit by flak over the target and, as a result, the bombs refused to drop. George landed back safely, with a full bombload and a punctured tyre. A post-raid report on Düren stated: 'almost the entire built-up area of the town has been destroyed, except for a small area due west of the marshalling yards. Fires were still burning and heavy cratering extends well south and east beyond the town.'

Gerd Fleig was an extremely lucky young man. In November 1944 he was in Room 35 of the Hindenburg Lazarett (military hospital), in his home town of Pforzheim. He was fortunate to have escaped death or injury during the heavy fighting in Normandy. He was now hospitalized with a bad case of dysentery. Fleig was born in 1926. His father, a music teacher, had established a music school in Pforzheim. His mother was a singer. 'My grandparents, on my mother's side, had the Pforzheim connection. Grandfather had a factory making silver and gold jewellery. He lived on the south side of town, in the Nagold area.'[22]

Gerd Fleig joined the Jungvolk on reaching the age of 10 and later went into the Hitler Youth: 'Father disapproved, despite the fact that I continued the musical tradition. I was the leader of the Jungbann-Spielmannszug – my Jungvolk marching

Leading the marching band: Gerd Fleig in his Hitler Youth uniform, as Spielmannszugführer. *Photo: Gerd Fleig.*

band. I knew, however, that father despised mixing music with "political education". He was opposed to Hitler but could do nothing about my Hitler Youth membership. That was mandatory. Later, however, he stopped me going to a special Waffen SS camp training Hitler Youth musicians. Mother supported him and there were family arguments. I was torn, anyway. Half of me wanted to go to the camp and the other half wanted to stay home and enjoy the security of the family.'[22]

Three years later, when he was 17, Gerd Fleig graduated from high school (a year earlier than usual, under a wartime scheme) and joined the Waffen SS Division Hitlerjugend: 'I was no volunteer. I was sent there and that was that. I became a wireless operator with an infantry unit. I did my training in Prague, spent time in The Netherlands and then went to Deschel in Belgium. When the Allies landed in Normandy, in June 1944, our division deployed south of Caen. I made no progress in the Waffen SS. With a high school education I could expect promotion, but this was blocked when I failed to have a car ready for one of our officers, who was due at a conference. I was punished with eight days *Bau* [the "slammer"].'[22]

When Fleig arrived in one piece at the Lazarett, established at Osterfeld School, his parents were delighted: 'They were relieved to see me back from the front. I was out of harm's way for a time. The hospital staff soon began to use me as a runner, delivering packages to various Army units. I knew the area well, being a local.'[22]

Active service: Gerd Fleig as a
wireless operator with the Waffen
SS Division Hitlerjugend. *Photo:
Gerd Fleig.*

By October 1944 the effectiveness of the German night fighter force was much
reduced. During that month fifty-four Bomber Command aircraft failed to return
from night operations, as against over 300 in January 1944.[23] Beyond the loss of
experienced crews and fuel shortages, the German air defence organization now had
less time to take decisions on night fighter deployment. They had more opportunity
to make mistakes, given the effectiveness of British radio countermeasures and
Bomber Command's ability to attack three or more targets in a single night.

Yet the Germans showed great ingenuity in responding to fresh challenges as the
bombing war evolved. *Wilde Sau* (Wild Boar) tactics – using single-seat day fighters
in the freelance night fighting role over the target – was a rather obvious response
to the growing night bomber threat. Hamburg, however, changed everything. The
catastrophic firestorm of July 1943 and the use of Window to disable the defences
demanded a radical new approach. *Zahme Sau* (Tame Boar) was an intelligent
counter. It produced immediate results and the British struggled to find an effective
response. *Zahme Sau* night fighters simply joined the fringes of the concentrated
bomber stream, stayed with it as long as possible and engaged as many targets as
possible. The deeper the penetration into Germany, the more time the fighters had

The hunter: a Ju88 C.6B night fighter, pictured in 1942. It is equipped with Lichtenstein BC radar and a Flensburg homer. *Photo: Trustees of the Imperial War Museum.*

The hunted: Lancaster DV305 (BQ-O) crash-landed at Woodbridge on 31 January 1944, with damage to the rear turret and tail assembly. *Photo: Bob Stone.*

to find the bombers and amass kills. Those bombers finding themselves outside the stream lost 'safety in numbers'. They were often shot down while continuing to drop Window in splendid isolation – blatantly advertising their presence as a straggler.[24]

Zahme Sau exploited the British tactic of compressing the main force in space and time, to swamp the defences by passing hundreds of aircraft over the target in a matter of minutes. The obvious advantages remained paramount, but a compressed bomber stream presented *Zahme Sau* night fighter pilots with a very large, concentrated cloud of targets. *Zahme Sau* was used for the first time against a raid on Berlin on the night of 23/4 August 1943. Bomber Command dispatched 727 aircraft and 56 (7.9 per cent) failed to return.[24] The Germans introduced Naxos, a device to pick up H_2S emissions and help *Zahme Sau* pilots enter the bomber stream.[25] From the German standpoint, *Zahme Sau* tactics gave all night fighter crews the chance to make kills, replacing the earlier, more rigid box system of night fighting monopolized by *experten*.

When attacks on the German cities eased back in the early spring of 1944, owing to the need to bomb transportation and other targets in France prior to invasion, Bomber Command was approaching exhaustion. The so-called Battle of Berlin had been a grim, bloody campaign: 1,303 aircraft became casualties (625 while actually attacking Berlin).[26] Nevertheless, by the spring of 1944 Bomber Command had an average daily availability of around 1,000 bombers, despite such heavy losses. The bombers remained under the control of General Eisenhower, Supreme Allied Commander in Europe, from 1 April to mid-September, when the area campaign and oil/transportation targeting resumed in earnest. During the months spent supporting the Normandy landings and eventual break-out, Bomber Command gathered strength, benefiting from a 'rest', in relative terms, from German targets. When the bombing of Germany resumed, life became more difficult for *Zahme Sau* pilots. Harris' force was now big enough to deliver hammer blows against several targets in one night, together with 'spoof' (decoy) raids. Gradually, Bomber Command's striking power became too much for the overstretched German night defences. Furthermore, daylight operations became viable as the Germans lost air superiority to the escort fighters.

Yet there remained no effective tactical counter to *Zahme Sau*, as main force concentration was essential to the achievement of devastating bombing results. In May 1944, 550 Squadron took matters into its own hands. As so many fighter attacks came from below, they converted an aircraft to carry an 'undergun'. Lancaster W5005 (BQ-N) had a hole cut in its floor, behind the bomb bay, and a .5 heavy machine gun was mounted on a rail. A deflection plate was fitted, to shield the gunner from the slipstream. This aircraft flew a number of operations with an eighth crew member – the 'mid-under gunner'. Wing Commander Jack Harris remembers this aircraft: 'There were sighs of relief when N-Nan ditched in the Humber on 26 August 1944, after suffering flak damage on a raid to Kiel. The aircraft was attempting a flapless landing but the pilot misjudged the approach and ditched in 3 or 4ft of water off Killingholme Haven. The crew waded ashore, and that was the end of W5005. This aircraft flew very badly.'[27]

The mid-under gunner's field of vision was extremely limited. Nevertheless, 550 was not the only squadron experimenting with this arrangement. Gunner Len Whitehead, with 61 Squadron, found the undergun ineffectual. He made four trips as under gunner with Pilot Officer Aukland in late April/early May 1944. During one sortie they were attacked by a night fighter positioned beneath their Lancaster. Only the bomb aimer – who happened to be checking the bomb bay for a 'hang-up' – spotted it, at the last moment. Whitehead, forced by the undergun arrangement to look towards the rear, saw nothing. The bomb aimer just had time to shout one word – 'Weave!' – before being killed by exploding cannon shells. The damaged bomber limped back to an airfield near Southampton.[28]

Bomber Command returned to Wanne-Eickel on Saturday, 18 November. North Killingholme's 550 Squadron mustered twenty-nine Lancasters for a fresh raid on this synthetic oil plant, situated west of Gelsenkirchen. They began taking off at 15.30 and the cloud cleared during the flight out. Over the target thin cloud obscured ground detail, but markers could be seen. The *Operations Record Book* noted: 'Bombing was reported to have been well concentrated around the markers and, very early in the attack, a large fire developed which, from the column of black smoke which arose, it would seem likely that the oil plant was successfully hit. Numerous orange-coloured explosions were seen during the course of the attack; two, occurring at 19.20 and 19.23, must have been particularly large as some of the crews clearly saw the glow when 40 miles away, on the homeward journey.'

This raid involved 285 Lancasters and 24 Mosquitoes. One Lancaster was lost. There was modest flak and some night fighter engagements (none involving 550's Lancasters). All squadron aircraft bombed, with the exception of 'C', Flying Officer Smith's Lancaster. He returned to North Killingholme on three engines. The skills of another 550 Lancaster captain, Ken Sidwell, were also tested that night. When he and his crew returned in 'M2' they found North Killingholme fogged in. They were diverted to Witchford, where they made a FIDO-assisted landing in the murk. Sidwell struggled during the final approach, as turbulence from the FIDO fires threw his aircraft around.[29]

During the afternoon of Tuesday 21 November twenty-six Lancasters of 550 Squadron taxied from their dispersals at North Killingholme. The crews had been briefed to attack Aschaffenburg's marshalling yards. The *Operations Record Book* commented on the poor weather and problems in marking the target. Yet a small break in the cloud allowed crews to spot well-placed ground markers. This was the first sortie with 550 for Eddie Edlund and crew, having been posted in from 100 Squadron. They took off from North Killingholme at 15.15 and landed back six hours twenty-five minutes later. They had bombed from 14,000ft. Back in his billet, flight engineer Sam Lipfriend made a brief diary entry: 'Target obscured. Little flak.'[30]

The night raid on Aschaffenburg was Dave Davidson's debut with 550, having also been posted in from 100 Squadron. Davidson's run of uneventful sorties continued. He landed back at North Killingholme without incident, after six hours ten minutes.[31] The attack was made by 274 Lancasters and nine Mosquitoes; two Lancasters were lost. The casualties on the ground included 344 dead.[32]

There was a further air attack on Pforzheim on 21 November, a five-minute nuisance raid in the early evening. Bombs fell on the south-western edge of town, nearby Büchenbronn and onto open fields.[33] It was obvious to all but the diehards that the war was lost. Pforzheim would soon be occupied by the French or Americans. In late November French forces in Alsace began to break through. In his diary, Adolf Katz noted that the Allies were advancing on Colmar and there were reports that American forces had entered Strasbourg. Katz dwelt on the threat of a huge air raid. On 28 November his diary refers to the bombing of Offenburg – a town south-west of Pforzheim, near the Rhine – which caused 'great destruction' in residential areas.[34]

Hans Ade was nearly 10 years old in early 1945. His father was a butcher in Pforzheim, who worked at a shop in the centre of town near the river Enz. 'He had his own shop until the Depression, when he went bankrupt. As a master butcher, however, he soon found work with another business.' When the Second World War began, Ade senior was drafted into the Wehrmacht. He served in his trade, as a butcher, with the field kitchens during the French campaign. 'Later, he was ordered back to Pforzheim. The Kreisleitung (Nazi administration) wanted two master butchers to secure local meat supply. Unusually, my father and the other man selected were not Party members. Father stayed in Pforzheim throughout the war. This is surprising, as he had a 'loose mouth' – he was always cracking jokes about Hitler and Goebbels. This never got him into trouble with his boss, but the Blockwart [a Nazi official responsible for the political supervision of a neighbourhood] was displeased. Father was threatened but nothing serious happened. However, whenever there were bombing raids the non-Party members, including my father, were always called in first to help with firefighting and clean-up.'[35]

The Ade household included Hans and his two sisters. The older girl had a secretarial job at the local hospital. Hans' mother worked as a galvanizer during the Second World War. The family lived at Sophienstrasse 10, near the city hospital and the Kunstgewerbeschule (art school).[35]

In 1944, 9-year-old Hans Ade was still too young to join the Jungvolk but there were compensations at school. He was thought big enough to be taught to fire the Panzerfaust – a one-shot, shoulder-fired anti-tank weapon. 'We had trenches behind the school buildings. At the Volksschule I also fired a light machine gun. When firing the Panzerfaust, I was taught to always check behind, as it produced a very long exhaust flame. It was great! I felt very proud.' Hans Ade had other responsibilities. The boy was given binoculars and a whistle and told to station himself in the street or backyard. He kept watch for approaching planes: 'At that late stage in the war we were all used to daily alarms. Aircraft were always overhead; most people didn't even bother going into the cellars.

'My mother and older sister didn't get on. My sister was keen on the Nazis. One day she came home and walked into the kitchen, where mother was preparing potato salad. She said she'd heard that when German soldiers died for the Führer, they died with a smile on their face. Mother told her to stop that bullshit. My sister replied:

"Say that again and you'll end up in a concentration camp." That was it. Mother was so mad she picked up the bowl of potato salad and threw it out of the open window, into the backyard below. Of course, at that time children were always threatening their parents. There was no criticism of the regime at my school. I may have been only nine, but I would have been happy to have used that Panzerfaust, given the chance. The entire war was fascinating to me. All boys were immersed in the "hero cult"; we spent a lot of time drawing tanks and U-boats.'[35]

Nonetheless, Hans knew the meaning of fear: 'The only time I was really afraid was sitting in our shelter. It was the usual type of cellar, reinforced with support beams. Everyone took their place on the benches. I used to sit there, staring up at the beams and wondering what would happen if the ceiling came down, or the whole house collapsed.'[35]

North Killingholme sent a record number of thirty-one Lancasters to bomb Freiburg on Monday, 27 November 1944. This was also a record for 1 Group (which put up 312 Lancasters that night). The squadron had used six days of bad weather stand-downs to bring all available aircraft on line. They took off from around 15.45. The *Operations Record Book* stated: 'Nearly all our crews bombed on ground markers seen through haze. The bombing appeared to be concentrated and a satisfactory fire glow soon developed.' The opposition was modest, with only spasmodic flak. Crews were impressed with their view of the Swiss town of Basle, flooded with light and a sharp contrast to the more familiar blacked-out cities of nations at war.

Freiburg had escaped Bomber Command's attentions until that Monday. Eddie Edlund's Lancaster left North Killingholme for the town just after 16.00. Their flight was plagued with technical difficulties. Later, Sam Lipfriend, the flight engineer, opened his diary and wrote: 'Starboard outer's revs fluctuated from the start. Pressed on. Gee went U/S [unserviceable]. Intercom U/S during circuit. Two overshoots.' Lipfriend wasn't superstitious, but he did carry a lucky charm: 'My brother got me a rabbit's foot and I carried that with me. On one occasion I didn't have it and got a bit bothered. Some men were full of nerves, but I wasn't. I had a good pilot in Eddie and I just thought I would survive.'[36]

Freiburg was the Davidson crew's twelfth operation. It was uneventful and they landed back after six hours thirty minutes.[37] This town was targeted as a rail junction in front of American and French troops advancing in the Vosges, to the west. There were reports of large German troop formations present (although very few soldiers died in this attack). Wireless operator Howell Evans: 'After the war I saw a newspaper story about this raid. It was the only big attack on Freiburg and, apparently, the town now has a monument to an "early warning duck"! It is said that, on the night of the raid, this duck made such a racket that it alerted the locals, saving many lives.'[38]

Jack Harris dropped his bombs from 13,500ft: 'Freiburg was well marked and the raid was an obvious success. The flak was not as bad as over Ruhr targets.'[39] This raid on Freiburg (codenamed Tigerfish) was very destructive and the death toll unusually heavy: 2,088 people killed and 858 missing. Around 30 per cent of homes were destroyed or severely damaged. The 'early warning duck' mentioned by Howell Evans was a drake in the municipal park. A statue commemorating this bird was presented as a gift to the citizens of Freiburg by Mayor Wolfgang Hoffmann on 27 November 1953, the ninth anniversary of the raid.

A total of 341 Lancasters and 10 Mosquitoes attacked Freiburg, and one Lancaster was lost. The flak was light and the main force dropped 1,900 tons of bombs in twenty-five minutes. *The Bomber Command War Diaries* comments: 'The high casualty rate suggests that the population were taken by surprise and had not been properly prepared for air attack. The ratio of more than eight people dead for each heavy bomber attacking is unusually high.'[40]

The lessons of Freiburg's destruction were not lost on Adolf Katz, the Pforzheim banker. Writing in his diary, Katz correctly observed: 'the great danger is that the same thing happens to us that happened to Freiburg'.

Sam Lipfriend's seventh operation (his third with 550 Squadron) was a daylight raid on Dortmund two days later. This was unsuccessful because of the poor weather. The bombing, by a main force of 294 Lancasters, was scattered and six bombers were lost.[41] Jack Harris' Lancaster was over Dortmund: 'The marking was poor. There was five-tenths cloud over the target and ground visibility was poor. Nevertheless, we managed to drop our load on the built-up area.'[42]

Lucky escape: Flying Officer David Summons' Lancaster (PD313-P) at Manston, after surviving a mid-air collision. Summons pressed on to Dortmund and bombed, despite losing two engines. *Photo: Bob Stone.*

Sam Lipfriend sat alongside his pilot, Eddie Edlund, as their Lancaster took off at 11.24 on Wednesday, 29 November. They ran into flak near Cologne. Lipfriend saw two aircraft collide. Their Lancaster pitched and rocked in the flak explosions. The 'gremlins' – those devilish creatures responsible for all mechanical problems affecting RAF aircraft – made a concerted attack on Edlund's Lancaster. He made a flapless landing at North Killingholme.[43]

Thirty 550 Squadron Lancasters took part in the raid on Dortmund. Some crews saw nothing and bombed alternatives, receiving flak damage for their pains. The North Killingholme newsletter *Summary* reported the following day (30 November): 'Marking, never exuberant, appears to have been widely scattered and the Master Bomber's guidance can scarcely be described as either inspiring or inspired.' One 550 pilot, Flying Officer D.W. Summons, RAAF, had a lucky escape. He was flying PD313 ('P') on this raid. He collided with another aircraft before reaching the target but managed to make it back, crash-landing at Manston in Kent. All survived.[44] Summons pressed on to the target and bombed, despite the loss of both starboard engines. This was described by *Summary* as 'a truly remarkable performance, as was disclosed on subsequent inspection of the mangled bomb-bay'.

Notes

1. Pross, M. (1995), *Die Einschläge kommen näher, Aus den Tagebüchern 1943–45 von Friedrich Adolf Katz, 1945–1947 Oberbürgermeister der Stadt Pforzheim.*
2. Administration's Report and Statistics for the Town of Pforzheim 1945–52: City Life 1939–45.
3. Pross, M. (1995), *Die Einschläge kommen näher, Aus den Tagebüchern 1943–45 von Friedrich Adolf Katz, 1945–1947 Oberbürgermeister der Stadt Pforzheim.*
4. Interview with Dave Davidson, April 2013.
5. Interview with Sam Lipfriend, March 2013.
6. Middlebrook, M. and Everitt, C. (1990), *The Bomber Command War Diaries*, 612.
7. Ibid., 613.
8. Interview with Dave Davidson, April 2013.
9. Redding, T. (2008), *Flying for Freedom*, 118.
10. Ibid., 131.
11. Ibid., 72.
12. Ibid., 74.
13. Middlebrook, M. and Everitt, C. (1990), *The Bomber Command War Diaries*, 614–15.
14. Interview with Jack Harris, April 2013.
15. Interview with Dave Davidson, April 2013.
16. Interview with Howell Evans, June 2013.
17. Middlebrook, M. and Everitt, C. (1990), *The Bomber Command War Diaries*, 616.
18. Interview with Frank Woodley, March 2013.
19. Middlebrook, M. and Everitt, C. (1990), *The Bomber Command War Diaries*, 617.
20. Interview with Jack Harris, April 2013.
21. Middlebrook, M. and Everitt, C. (1990), *The Bomber Command War Diaries*, 618.
22. Interview with Gerd Fleig, July 2013.
23. Redding, T. (2008), *Flying for Freedom*, 216.
24. Ibid., 176.
25. Ibid., 189.

26. Middlebrook, M. (1990), *The Berlin Raids*, 306.
27. Interview with Jack Harris, April 2013.
28. Redding, T. (2008), *Flying for Freedom*, 80–1.
29. Interview with Frank Woodley, March 2013.
30. Interview with Sam Lipfriend, March 2013.
31. Interview with Dave Davidson, April 2013.
32. Middlebrook, M. and Everitt, C. (1990), *The Bomber Command War Diaries*, 620.
33. Administration's Report and Statistics for the Town of Pforzheim 1945–52: City Life 1939–45.
34. Pross, M. (1995), *Die Einschläge kommen näher, Aus den Tagebüchern 1943–45 von Friedrich Adolf Katz, 1945–1947 Oberbürgermeister der Stadt Pforzheim.*
35. Interview with Hans Ade, November 2013.
36. Interview with Sam Lipfriend, March 2013.
37. Interview with Dave Davidson, April 2013.
38. Interview with Howell Evans, June 2013.
39. Interview with Jack Harris, April 2013.
40. Middlebrook, M. and Everitt, C. (1990), *The Bomber Command War Diaries*, 623.
41. Ibid., 624.
42. Interview with Jack Harris, April 2013.
43. Interview with Sam Lipfriend, March 2013.
44. Newsletter No. 21, 1 November 2000, 550 Squadron and RAF North Killingholme Association.

Chapter Four

Oil Plants and Railyards

Punishing attacks on German oil and rail targets continued throughout December 1944, whenever the weather allowed. The heavy bombers were also used in support of Allied ground forces. December got off to a poor start for 550 Squadron. The crews of fourteen Lancasters were briefed for a daylight attack on the Urft Dam, in the Eifel, but the weather was appalling. The visibility over the target was so bad that they had to return with their bombs. The weather at North Killingholme was no better. They landed, bombs and all, in the murk, with cloud base down to 600ft. There were several unsuccessful attempts to breach this dam, to prevent the Germans flooding territory in front of advancing American troops.[1]

Eddie Edlund took part in this disappointing operation. Their next briefing was for the 4/5 December night attack on Karlsruhe. At 16.30 the first of twenty-four Lancasters left the airfield, carrying heavy loads of blast bombs. The main target was Karlsruhe's marshalling yards. The rail link between Karlsruhe and Stuttgart was assuming greater importance. The bomb aimers had a difficult time: Karlsruhe

Getting ready: a briefing under way at North Killingholme. *Photo: Bob Stone.*

was covered with nine-tenths cloud, yet some crews identified red and green Target Indicators (TIs) through small gaps. The majority, however, relied on the glow of green TIs below cloud. Despite these problems 550's *Operations Record Book* noted: 'good fires were started in the town, the glow of which could be seen for over 100 miles'. All squadron aircraft returned safely.

Karlsruhe was bombed by 369 Lancasters and 154 Halifaxes, assisted by 12 Mosquitoes. One Lancaster and one Mosquito were lost. The marking was accurate despite the cloud cover and southern and western city districts suffered severe damage. The Durlacher machine tool plant was destroyed and over 400 people died.[2]

Eddie Edlund's flight engineer, Sam Lipfriend, had his first glimpse of the Luftwaffe that night. Their Lancaster ploughed through the bad weather and finally emerged from cloud at 16,000ft. They bombed sky markers and landed back home after six hours. Lipfriend took up his diary and wrote: 'Saw fights. Fighter passed by, 300 yards starboard up.'[3]

Karlsruhe was the eighth operation for 153 Squadron Lancaster captain Bruce Potter. He would fly another five sorties from Scampton in December.[4] The two largest cities close to Pforzheim – Karlsruhe and Stuttgart – were hit hard by Bomber Command. On the same night as the Karlsruhe raid, 5 Group sent 282 Lancasters and 10 Mosquitoes to Heilbronn, on the main north–south railway line and to the north-east of Pforzheim. They dropped 1,254 tons of blast bombs and incendiaries

Bad Penny ll: Flight Lieutenant R.P. Stone in the cockpit of Lancaster BL811, BQ-J. *Photo: Bob Stone.*

in a few minutes. *The Bomber Command War Diaries* comments: 'Much investigation resulted in the reliable estimate that just over 7,000 people died. Most of these victims would have died in fires so intense that there was probably a genuine firestorm.'[5]

Minor air attacks continued to disturb life in Pforzheim. Bombs from what was probably a single raider fell at noon on Saturday, 2 December. There was another nuisance raid the following Monday, 4 December, with blast bombs falling beyond the urban area, at locations near the autobahn in the north, the south near Seehaus and south-west near Büchenbronn. Ordnance specialists dealt with three unexploded bombs. A total of forty-four residential buildings were damaged; many others lost glass. Hostile air activity increased in December, with sixty-one warnings totalling forty-six hours.[6] The writing was on the wall. Yet Adolf Katz, constantly fretting about the possibility of a catastrophic raid, now had something new to worry about. His deferment from military service expired in late November. Earlier, Katz had felt sure he would be called up for work on the Alsace defences. In the second week of September 800 men aged up to 65 had been ordered to work on the Alsace fortifications. At that time he had made a note in his diary: 'I expect to be part of this, since the Party takes advantage of the situation and uses it to get rid of all half-hearted, suspicious and uncomfortable individuals.' Katz was right. On 20 September he received his Kriegs-Sondereinsatz orders, to work on strengthening the Siegfried Line. He was back within twenty-four hours, however, having been diagnosed with nephritis (inflammation of the kidneys). On 4 October he was examined for fitness for military service. He noted, somewhat drily: 'Seven years ago I received my discharge from the Officer Corps because I wanted to marry a non-Aryan woman. Now, all of a sudden, they remember me!' He received a deferment until 30 November.[7]

In early December Katz was called up. His first experience of the Volkssturm left him underwhelmed: 'Battle is the element of youth. How different it was this morning with the Volkssturm. The last stand! There were seriously ill people, amputees, many old, worn out people and extremely young boys. The battalion commander is a *Schreier* [someone who yells a lot] who permanently has to outdo himself and puff himself up to show his importance. The 2,000 men are a reluctant crowd without a trace of enthusiasm. I am ashamed to be part of this motley crew.'[7]

It wasn't too long, however, before Katz's diary returned to his worst nightmare. On Thursday, 7 December he wrote: 'I keep hearing more and more gruesome details about the attacks on Freiburg and Heilbronn. Everybody asks themselves, full of horror, when it will be our turn. Everybody knows there is no way to escape this destiny.'[7]

Clearly, Katz knew it was just a matter of time before the heavy bombers appeared over Pforzheim in their hundreds. In these final weeks of 1944 he arranged for Marianne, Annina and Friederike to stay with relatives near Lake Constance. Margrit, another daughter, had been on Christmas leave from Reichsarbeitsdienst (labour service), but soon returned to her ten-hour shifts at a spinning mill. His oldest son,

Wolfgang, a merchant seaman, had been arrested by British forces in Australia at the outbreak of war in 1939. He was held at a detention centre in Canada.[8]

The journey to Lake Constance was arranged for the second week of January. Bomb-damaged railway stations and lines meant that the journey of 130km took thirty-one hours. Eventually, they reached Überlingen and the Lang family. Marianne was impressed with Lake Constance. They now lived with Adolf and Änne Lang (Ruth's former sister-in-law). Eight-year-old Marianne liked Rudi, the younger of the two Lang sons, and contemplated marriage for a while. Rudi, sadly, was absent most of the time, on labour service. Gradually, however, Lake Constance lost its appeal in the winter fog. Marianne felt the lack of a playmate; the age gap with Annina was too wide.[8]

The crippling attacks on Germany's oil industry continued. On Wednesday, 6 December 475 Lancasters and 12 Mosquitoes made a deep penetration attack on the Leuna synthetic oil plant near the East German town of Merseburg, west of Leipzig. This huge complex, about 1 mile square, produced both oil and chemicals. Conditions were cloudy and the target obscured. Nevertheless, there was significant damage and several large explosions were seen.[9] Five Lancasters were lost, including that of 550 Squadron's Flight Lieutenant J.P. Morris. This crew were in NG251 ('J'). They were hit by flak and the Lancaster crashed with no survivors.[10]

Jack Harris was over the target: 'There was scattered but very heavy flak. We bombed from 20,000ft on skymarkers.'[11] Howell Evans, 550 pilot Dave Davidson's wireless operator, remembers Leuna for reasons other than the defences: 'It was a bloody long way. The round trip took eight hours five minutes and it was one of those rare occasions when I had to use the Elsan (chemical toilet). This was a performance. I had to disconnect from the main oxygen supply, connect up to a small oxygen bottle and carry this with me down the fuselage. I clambered over the main spar, reached the Elsan and fiddled about with my flying clothes. It was a real obstacle course.'[12]

His pilot was more concerned with the opposition. Davidson recalled the extraordinary flak barrage put up to protect this vital fuel plant: 'We had a saying: "The flak was so heavy you could get out and walk on it!" Merseburg was one of those occasions. It was the only time I told the crew to clip on their parachutes and, if they thought we had been hit and were possibly out of control, to bale out and not wait for an order from me!'[13]

Other 550 pilots had unnerving experiences that night. Eddie Edlund guided his Lancaster over the target with flight engineer Sam Lipfriend at his side. They flew through the medium and heavy flak barrage and were suddenly treated to a spectacular view of an Me163 rocket fighter in a vertical climb. On the way back the mischievous 'gremlins' returned to plague Edlund and crew. Lipfriend wrote in his diary: 'Starboard inner cut one hour from base. Port generator U/S. Three-engined landing.'[14]

Several crews had the terrifying experience of flying into clouds of incendiaries. Merseburg was mid-upper gunner Frank Woodley's sixteenth operational flight with Ken Sidwell. It was very nearly his last. The night began badly and got steadily worse. At the dispersal, one of their Lancaster's engines refused to start. They transferred to 'N', the standby aircraft. Later, while over the target, they were hit by flak which smashed the bomber's nose cone. They then flew through a deluge of incendiaries falling from the bomb bay of an aircraft above.[15]

Frank Woodley: 'One penetrated the portside wing-root. It was firmly lodged and burning fiercely. Our flight engineer, Jack Allen, set to work with an axe. He opened up a hole and played an extinguisher on the incendiary, but it had no effect. He got fed up, reached in, grabbed it and put it out on the fuselage floor. He kept it as a paperweight until he died in 2011. It now resides in the 550 Squadron Museum. Our pilot, Ken, got frostbite from freezing air and snow coming in through the shattered nose.

'We were hit all over the place by falling incendiaries. One went through the tailplane on the port side. The skipper took us down to 7,000ft and asked for a direct course for home. We got a shock when we landed back, after eight hours twenty minutes in the air. We knew our aircraft had been badly damaged but we were not prepared for the reality. The ground crew retrieved fifty-two incendiaries from our Lanc! Following an inspection the aircraft was declared a write-off.'[15]

There were more reminders of the fact that their future was in doubt. Frank Woodley: 'A new crew came into our hut. I had a Canadian on one side of me and a Londoner on the other. They never came back from their third or fourth op. In came the replacements. I assumed the earlier lot were dead. Just after the war, however, I saw a photo of that Canadian in the *Daily Sketch*. He had jumped and had been taken prisoner.'[15]

Edlund's crew, including Sam Lipfriend, enjoyed a few days' break owing to bad weather but were on again for the Tuesday, 12 December attack on heavily defended Essen. They left at 16.11 and spent six hours in the air.[16] North Killingholme sent

Souvenir: Ken Sidwell's flight engineer, Jack Allen, put out this incendiary when it penetrated their Lancaster's wing root. Subsequently, he used it as a paperweight. It is now in the 550 Squadron Museum. A cloud of incendiaries hit Sidwell's aircraft, when over the Leuna Works on 6 December 1944. *Photo: Frank Woodley.*

twenty-five Lancasters to Essen, which was obscured by cloud. The aircraft bombed, and 550's *Operations Record Book* noted crew reports of a developing red glow, together with a series of three explosions. Flak was slight to moderate but later increased in intensity. This was Bomber Command's last major night attack on Essen. Over 460 people died. Industrial premises and residential property suffered in this raid by 349 Lancasters, 163 Halifaxes and 28 Mosquitoes. Six Lancasters were lost.

Sam Lipfriend's tour continued to unfold at a brisk pace. The twelfth operation for Eddie Edlund's wireless operator was a night raid on Ludwigshafen, on Friday, 15 December. There were two I.G. Farben chemical plants in the area – one in Ludwigshafen and another in the nearby small town of Oppau. The latter ceased production after this raid, which was delivered by 327 Lancasters and 14 Mosquitoes.[17]

North Killingholme sent thirty Lancasters to Ludwigshafen. Edlund's aircraft got away at 14.35 and landed back at 21.10. Conditions were cloudier than expected and strong winds brought many aircraft to the target early, before the Pathfinders had done their work. Some first wave crews bombed on navigational aids or ETA. Others orbited until markers were dropped. The early bombing was scattered but then a concentration of markers developed. Large fires took hold. For the first time Sam Lipfriend used the phrase 'glittering diamonds' in his diary, to describe the panorama of thousands of small fires and bursting incendiaries far below.[18]

Jack Harris flew across Ludwigshafen and released his high explosive load. They dropped from 17,500ft on TIs.[19] Two crews were singled out in 550's *Operations Record Book* entry for Ludwigshafen. Flight Lieutenant Pyke completed this operation on three engines. Squadron Leader Redmond could not retract an undercarriage leg, and he completed the round trip with a 'swinging leg'. This sortie completed Redmond's second tour.

Dave Davidson was over Ludwigshafen that night. He landed back after six hours fifty minutes and slept in on Saturday. Davidson's name was also on 550's battle order for Sunday, 17 December. Preparations were under way to fuel and bomb-up 550 Squadron's hard-working Lancasters for a night strike on Ulm, near the Swiss border. Davidson's trip began unhappily and continued in that vein. They crossed the coast at Brighton in low cloud and rain, and so the weather remained – filthy throughout. Davidson flew half the sortie entirely on instruments. He and his crew deserved the week's rest that followed.[20]

Twenty-nine Lancasters left North Killingholme to join the attack on Ulm's rail facilities. Ground markers were seen but the master bomber decided that better results would come from bombing well-placed sky markers. The 550 *Operations Record Book* commented: 'A very good concentration of fire developed, with a number of spectacular explosions … Defences were meagre.' Squadron Leader Caldow, flying Lancaster 'B', was unlucky: 'One of the few flak bursts over the target hit a fuel tank, which promptly emptied. There was also damage to the Lanc's tailplane and elevators. Nevertheless, the aircraft made a safe return.'

This was Bomber Command's sole raid on Ulm and its two large truck plants (Magirius-Deutz and Kässbohrer), together with various barracks and depots. The main force consisted of 317 Lancasters, dropping 1,449 tons of bombs and incendiaries in twenty-five minutes. A square kilometre of Ulm was 'engulfed by fire', over 700 people died and more than 20,000 were bombed out. Two Lancasters were lost.[21]

Following a safe return from Ulm and debriefing, Sam Lipfriend, Eddie Edlund's flight engineer, found time to make a diary note about his thirteenth operation: 'Snow on the ground. Could see cars driving on roads near target. Very good prang. Glittering diamonds. Very little opposition.'[22] This is confirmed by Jack Harris: 'We dropped a Cookie and incendiaries from 10,000ft, aiming on skymarkers. There was thin cloud over the target and the defences were negligible.'[23]

Despite winter's snowy grip on Bomber Command's airfields, determined spirits moved heaven and earth to report their stations operational. Sam Lipfriend remembered the afternoon in late December when everyone was ordered to set to with shovels. They made progress on North Killingholme's snowed runway but a persistent layer of compacted ice still worried 550's pilots, who had been briefed to fly that night. Sam Lipfriend: 'As take-off time approached Flight Lieutenant Jock Shaw said: "Leave it to me." He tore down the runway, fully laden with bombs and fuel. He then gave his verdict: "I'm up. So send the buggers up!" Many years later I had the privilege of telling this story to Shaw's daughter and granddaughter. We didn't go that night – we were off on leave.'[24]

More restrictions were introduced in Pforzheim during the last two months of 1944. In November a shortage of coal and gas led to the decision to reduce opening times for the public baths. Tram services were further curtailed. The town council now carried out only essential administrative tasks. Earlier, it had received an order to turn over 10 per cent of its staff for military service. From 17 August 1944, all staff born in or after 1897 had to be made available for Wehrmacht service. Only a skeleton staff was left to respond in the case of a major air attack. During 1944 almost 50 per cent of Pforzheim Council's total budget was used to cover war-related costs.[25]

Fog and ice were frequent hazards for stressed bomber crews taking off and landing back, exhausted, after long and dangerous sorties. There were four days of bad weather stand-downs but on Friday, 22 December 550 Squadron sent twenty Lancasters to attack Koblenz. It was on this occasion that Jock Shaw took the lead and ignored the poor condition of North Killingholme's iced runway. The *Operations Record Book* noted: 'F/L Shaw, in "E", was the first to take to the air and the remainder of the boys decided that if a Scotsman could get off, so could they.' When the Lancasters took off visibility was extremely poor, 300yd at best.

Nineteen 550 Squadron Lancasters bombed Koblenz. Flying Officer Franklyn, in 'H', lost an engine and returned. There was thin cloud over the target and the main fall of bombs missed the rail yards.[26] All squadron aircraft were diverted to Woodbridge on the return, as North Killingholme was fogged in.

During the afternoon of Sunday, 24 December 550's crews were briefed for a night raid on railyards at Cologne/Nippes. A force of ninety-seven Lancasters and five Mosquitoes was dispatched and five Lancasters were lost. Another two crashed in England. The crews were surprised to find totally clear conditions over the target. The Oboe marking and bombing were highly accurate, and the damage was aggravated when an ammunition train blew up.[27]

Dave Davidson was flying 550's Lancaster 'A' that Christmas Eve. He knew he would be diverted on his return because of the fog. His wireless was unserviceable and he was forced to land at Ludford Magna, an airfield equipped with a system for landing in dense fog.[28] Howell Evans: 'This was not a good night. During the attack one of our engines was hit and put out of action. This operated the mid-upper turret, which became useless. The damage also meant limited power for the wireless. We came back on three engines. On reaching England we found ourselves in dense fog. It was awful – we couldn't see a thing. As we neared base I couldn't tune the wireless. Dave called up on the RT, asking North Killingholme for permission to land. They replied with a question: "Why haven't you diverted to Norfolk?" One of our fuel tanks had been holed and we were now low on fuel. When we explained we were short, we were ordered to Ludford Magna, which was equipped with a FIDO [Fog, Intensive Dispersal of] landing system. The fog was terrible. Dave could barely see the runway, even with FIDO doing its best. It was the scariest landing I ever experienced. Our Lanc hit the edge of the runway, sheared off and came to a halt in a field. There was nothing left in the tanks; our fuel gauges were at zero. The aircraft had to stay at Ludford Magna. Happy Christmas Eve! I think about that night every 24 December. Ludford Magna was home to 101 Squadron, who were not operating that night. Everyone was having a good time apart from us. We had no money for beer and no-one made the effort to make us feel welcome. Eventually, Dave managed to scrounge some money for a few pints.'[29]

Despite the poor conditions, 550 Squadron prepared twenty-three Lancasters for Cologne-Nippes. The crews were told this raid was needed to disrupt German reinforcements for the Ardennes offensive (the Battle of the Bulge). One aircraft failed to take off. Another made a three-engined return. The remaining twenty-one contributed to the main force bombing the railyards. All squadron aircraft were diverted on the return but Davidson's wireless problem meant they missed a Christmas treat. The others were told to land at the USAAF Liberator base of Wendling, Norfolk, where they enjoyed lavish American hospitality for three days. The delights included a turkey dinner in the Combat Officers' Mess and ample goodies such as chocolate and cigarettes.[30]

Jack Harris recalls that Wendling's initial welcome was not over enthusiastic: 'We had to tell them what to ask us at debriefing! We were then given a blanket each and told to settle down on the floor of the station gym. The next morning, Christmas Day, things looked up. We were served a wonderful Christmas lunch. Looking back, they did well – they had an extra 100 mouths to feed. When we finally flew back, on 28 December, we were laden with candy, peanut butter and Lucky Strike cigarettes.'[31]

In contrast, Christmas Day was a miserable affair for Dave Davidson's crew. They returned to North Killingholme by truck in the early morning. Lack of friendly company at Ludford Magna had dampened their spirits.[32]

The Christmas spirit was also hard to find in Pforzheim. On Sunday, 17 December blast bombs fell and thirty-five people were killed.[33] On Christmas Eve thirty-six American heavy bombers arrived over the town and dropped 98 tons of bombs on the marshalling yards. In the relatively modest attacks of 1944, Pforzheim had received 473 tons of bombs.[34]

On that Christmas Eve Deutsche Bank director Adolf Katz got a sharp reminder of what was at stake at a personal level. He and his daughter, Margrit, decided to go for a walk. It was a clear, sunny day. Suddenly there was an air-raid alert and American bombers appeared in the sky. Bombs began to fall. Katz described the raid: 'We took cover in the grass because the formations were right above us. There were explosions in front of us and behind. We ran back into town, filled with fear that something might have happened to Ruth and the children. As we ran down Schwarzwaldstrasse we saw the first burning incendiaries right in front of our house, but, with great relief, we realized the house was still standing …'[35]

In this attack, during the early afternoon, bombs fell on Südstadt, Sedan and areas of Nordstadt, Saalbau and the Goldsmiths' School (used as emergency accommodation for evacuees). Ninety people were killed. Rubble blocked roads, hampering access for firefighting teams. Fighter-bombers kept up the pressure on Christmas Day. They made low-level attacks on Messplatz, the station, Sonnenberg and Dillweissenstein.[36]

Teenager Irma Facoltosi heard and felt the bombs in the cellar of her family's apartment in Arlinger: 'The planes came over in waves. We went into the cellar and felt the detonations in the city, some distance away. There were ten of us in the shelter – me, Mum, Granny, Uncle Peter and six others from No. 3, next door.'[37]

The Facoltosi family had worked hard to preserve normality, but normal life gradually disintegrated around them. They had been largely successful before the war, despite Gestapo interest in all Jehovah's Witnesses. Irma Baroni (née Facoltosi): 'We led a sheltered existence and enjoyed a good home life. My sister, eight years older, did well. She studied in Pforzheim and eventually became a jeweller. My brother, Enrico, was interested in fine art. In due course he became a painter and engraver. When war came we tried to hold onto normality. In winter we enjoyed the snow, the slides and the skiing. In summer we spent time in the beautiful countryside. I enjoyed school. The war progressed and I became a teenager. I liked geography, history and sport – especially roller-skating and riding my bike. Mum remained outspoken. She supported the Jews and had several Jewish friends. This did not escape the attention of our neighbours, who could be petty. One day we found small Nazi flags planted in our window boxes. Mum opened the shutters, weeded out the flags from among the petunias, snapped them in two and threw them into the garden.'[37]

When Enrico Facoltosi completed his labour service, he went into the Army. Irma: 'He was on his way to Stalingrad when he became very ill. He went down with dysentery and came home on sick leave. I was also seriously ill at that time, with diphtheria. I spent only three days in hospital. Mum took me home and I was treated by a homeopathic specialist. Enrico recovered and returned to the Russian Front. He was killed near Kiev, in the Ukraine.'[37]

Set against this great sadness was a more positive development in Irma's life. Now approaching 16, she became fond of Arno Baroni, a young delivery boy who occasionally visited their apartment to deliver soaps and toiletries. 'I saw him only once every two months, but that was enough for us to become sweet on each other.' Arno Baroni's grandfather was Italian. Arno and Irma were drawn together as both families were Jehovah's Witnesses. They had first met at a meeting.[37]

Werner, Arno Baroni's older brother, was born in 1927. Grandmother Anna had travelled to Egypt in 1896 to take up the post of German teacher at the English School in Cairo. Werner Baroni: 'It was there that she met my grandfather, Vincenzo Baroni, the Italian vice-consul in the city. My father was born in Cairo in 1898. Later, a diplomatic posting brought the family to New York. Subsequently, Anna became seriously ill and it was for that reason that they returned to Europe. I never knew exactly why we came to live in Pforzheim but my aunt – my father's sister – was born in the city in 1905. My father served in a German infantry division in the First World War and was badly wounded at Verdun. After the war he met my mother, Ida, the daughter of a Pforzheim jewellery manufacturer. My mother was the factory manager. My father joined the family business and, as he spoke fluent Italian, he helped to establish a chainstore in Italy.'[38]

When the Second World War came, things changed forever. Within forty-eight hours Werner's father was drafted into the Army as an infantryman. Werner's mother died only two months later, at the early age of 40. The care of Werner and Arno was now in the hands of their grandmother and Aunt Eliese, known to all as Lisel. 'Aunt Lisel became a mother to us. We lived at grandmother's apartment at Dillsteinerstrasse 2. They were Jehovah's Witnesses and opposed to Hitler and his regime. For these reasons they received attention from the Pforzheim Gestapo and were arrested several times. My grandmother and aunt were "political undesirables". Dillsteinerstrasse 2 was where Pforzheim's Jehovah's Witnesses met during the Third Reich years. Anna and Lisel had Jewish friends, including the Gabriel family, who owned a small shop selling dairy products. In the First World War Mr Gabriel had served in the 109th Infantry Regiment, my father's unit.'[38] Mr Gabriel had two sisters. According to the Stadtarchiv Pforzheim database on Jewish citizens and other sources (via Gerhard Brändle), Emma was deported to Gurs camp in 1940. She died in France in April 1945. Julius and Cilly emigrated to the USA before the outbreak of war.

Lisel Baroni was arrested in 1937, during a second wave of arrests and incarceration of Jehovah's Witnesses. Lisel was imprisoned from 25 November 1937 to 11 May 1938 (Gerhard Brändle). Werner Baroni: 'At this time, the term "Jehovah's Witness" was not used. They were known as Bibelforscher [honest bible students]. Anna was also arrested and taken into Schutzhaft for a time. When Lisel was absent, Arno and I were cared for by Grandmother. Anna had remained defiant. Each week she sent me to buy Jewish bread and eggs at the Gabriels' store. Goebbels told us that Germans do not shop at Jewish stores. In our apartment, Granny would proclaim: "Anna Baroni says buy in Jewish stores!" That's why I made that weekly shopping trip. I was never bothered by SA men.

'At the age of 10 I also had the job of visiting Aunt Lisel in Pforzheim prison, bringing fresh clothes and toiletries. Every week I had the same argument with one of the guards. I turned up and asked to give the toiletries to my Aunt Lisel Baroni. The guard said: "Listen, boy. We don't have any aunts here. Or uncles. Or mothers. We only have prisoners!" I refused to say the word prisoner. This went on for months, until the man finally let it go.'[38]

Lisel was a member of Pforzheim's Piano School – the masterclass of Professor Röhmeyer; she was a concert pianist. Upon her release from prison she lost her licence to give public performances. In response, 'home concerts' were organized. The Gabriels were always invited, until it became too dangerous for all concerned. 'Meanwhile, my aunt, together with my brother and I, had to present ourselves every Wednesday at Gestapo headquarters on Bahnhofstrasse. This went on for several years.' Lisel's custody over the boys was revoked owing to her Jehovah's Witness affiliations. 'An SS man became our legal guardian. He turned up two or three times a year, to check that we were growing up as good National Socialists.'[38]

Things could have been worse. Some of Pforzheim's small community of Jehovah's Witnesses died at the hands of the Nazis, including Fritz Burger, the popular manager of the Pfannkuch store. Werner Baroni: 'I knew Fritz Burger very well. This kind, gentle man refused to join the German Army.' Burger was sent to Welzheim and Dachau camps and then to Mauthausen on 29 September 1939, where he died on 6 March 1940. 'I was present when his widow came to see my grandmother. Destitute and desperate, she asked Anna for the 10 Reichsmark demanded by the Gestapo to hand over her husband's ashes. When they were paid, the Gestapo also returned some of his bloodstained clothing. When Mrs Burger left, Grandmother said: "Well, now the Nazis have killed Fritz!" I told Granny: "How can you say that? In German concentration camps, no-one is killed!" You have to remember I was just a young boy at the time. Anna, who was very tough and just as smart, looked at me and said: "One day you will wake up and see that your Hitler is a criminal."'[38]

Werner Baroni also knew Klara Müssle: 'She had young children. Klara was sent to a concentration camp for being a Jehovah's Witness. She died in Auschwitz. There were other victims too, including Ludwig Stickel, who spent eight years in Dachau but survived the war. There was also Franz Barth, who was imprisoned in Dachau and so badly beaten about the head that he eventually lost his hearing.' In the camps, from 1937, Bibelforscher were required to wear a purple triangle on their camp uniforms, denoting their category.[38]

Werner Baroni: 'My father did what he could to ease the constant pressure on our family. During one leave he went to see the Gestapo boss at Bahnhofstrasse and asked him to leave us alone. Standing there, as a serving soldier, he told the Gestapo man that his family were not criminals and that there was no good reason for the repeated visits and searches. Fortunately, the fact that Dillsteinerstrasse 2 was the main meeting place for Pforzheim's Bibelforscher remained secret.'[38]

Dave Davidson and his crew were still fed up. On their Christmas Eve return from Cologne they had to land at Ludford Magna, where the welcome was less than warm. Meanwhile, other 550 crews were enjoying their wonderful Christmas break at an American base. The unlucky crew returned by road for a depressing Christmas Day at fog-bound North Killingholme. On Boxing Day, Davidson was told he would be operating his Lancaster from Ludford Magna the next day, Wednesday, 27 December. He got this news at tea-time, forcing him to tour Grimsby's smoky pubs and dance halls, rounding up his crew. He finally got to bed at midnight and had to rise at 03.00 for the drive to Ludford Magna. Upon arrival he was told that the morning raid had been postponed until lunchtime.[39]

The target for Wednesday was Rheydt's railyards. Davidson's day unfolded with an element of farce. He had a row with a Ludford Magna armaments officer,

Trying to relax: the ante room of the Officers' Mess at North Killingholme. *Photo: Bob Stone.*

having arrived at dispersal to find his Lanc covered in frost. As the crew threw their parachutes into the aircraft, they noticed that the guns had been removed. 'Later, when we were taken out to get ready for take-off, the guns were back – but there were no parachutes! Only then did we realize that there were TWO Lancs with the letter 'A' on the airfield.'[39]

During the preceding day, 550 Squadron contributed nine Lancasters for an attack on the rail hub of St Vith, just inside Belgium and on the northern side of the Germans' Ardennes offensive. They took off on Tuesday in foggy conditions, with visibility at 600yd. According to the *Operations Record Book*, St Vith 'was being used as a de-training centre for Panzer troops from rearward areas'. Conditions were good and crews found it easy to identify the aiming point: 'An excellent concentration of bombing was achieved. Two large explosions were noted, one in the town and one on the railway to the north-east. Once again, all returning aircraft were diverted.' The bombers were told to land at Waltham. The squadron's scattered Lancasters finally returned to North Killingholme on the Thursday.

The main force bombing Rheydt on Wednesday consisted of 200 Lancasters. Leaving England's fog behind, they found the Continent clear, with good visibility over the target. The *Operations Record Book* commented: 'The first TIs cascaded on the northern end of the marshalling yard, followed by others which were dead on the aiming point.' The bombing was concentrated and accurate; smoke rose thousands of feet into the air. One very large explosion may have involved ammunition wagons. Once again, 550's aircraft were diverted, this time to Finningley.

Things remained untidy for the Davidson crew. They landed at Finningley five hours thirty-five minutes after leaving Ludford Magna. Having stayed the night at Finningley, they flew home to North Killingholme on Thursday morning. This messy, frustrating week was far from over. Davidson was summoned to the CO's office and told by the adjutant that a Ludford Magna armaments officer had made a complaint: the latter was still upset by his hostile telephone conversation with the 550 pilot. The CO wasn't interested in details: he cut the interview short with a brisk command: 'Don't do it again!'[39]

Oil and rail targets dominated Bomber Command's December. At Scampton, for example, 153 Squadron pilot Bruce Potter flew six operations that month. The first three were to Karlsruhe on the 4th (marshalling yards), Essen on the 12th (industrial area) and Ulm on the 17th (industrial and rail facilities). The final three were to Bonn on the 28th (railyards), Scholven-Buer on the 29th (oil production and storage facilities, together with other industry) and Osterfeld (railyards) on 31 December.[40]

During the mid-afternoon of Friday, 29 December 550 Squadron sent twenty-two Lancasters to bomb the Scholven-Buer oil complex, 7 miles north of Gelsenkirchen. There was ten-tenths thin cloud over the target but the TIs were visible. According to the *Operations Record Book*, 'bombing quickly became concentrated round the markers and, almost immediately, a very large explosion was seen and resulted in thick columns of black smoke rising through the clouds. Several good fires developed and explosions were continuous until the last aircraft left. The defences of Cologne, Bochum, Gelsenkirchen and the Essen district were very active but not over the target itself.' All aircraft returned safely.

The last day of a tough year was a Sunday. Fourteen crews at North Killingholme took off in the mid-afternoon of 31 December, to join the attack on Osterfeld's marshalling yards. There was ten-tenths thin cloud over the target, but the markers could be seen. Dave Davidson's aircraft was one of 149 Lancasters over Osterfeld that day. The marshalling yards were assessed as 35 per cent damaged; two Lancasters were lost.[41]

In Pforzheim, Adolf Katz had nothing to look forward to. On 23 December the reserves and Training Battalion 5 took up positions around Pforzheim, to face Allied forces.[42] Ironically, despite his jaundiced view of the Volkssturm, Katz made rapid progress in his unit. On 29 December he was prompted to make a wry entry in his diary: 'Yesterday I was promoted to platoon leader and deputy company commander and thus have the same job as thirty years ago. But woe betide us if we should really go to war with these men.'[43] As for Katz's fellow citizens, this would be the last Christmas for over 17,000 Pforzheimers.

Notes

1. Middlebrook, M. and Everitt, C. (1990), *The Bomber Command War Diaries*, 626–7.
2. Ibid., 627.
3. Interview with Sam Lipfriend, March 2013.
4. Interview with Bill Thomas, June 2013.
5. Middlebrook, M. and Everitt, C. (1990), *The Bomber Command War Diaries*, 627.
6. Administration's Report and Statistics for the Town of Pforzheim 1945–52: City Life 1939–45.
7. Pross, M. (1995), *Die Einschläge kommen näher, Aus den Tagebüchern 1943–45 von Friedrich Adolf Katz, 1945–1947 Oberbürgermeister der Stadt Pforzheim.*
8. Interview with Marianne Pross, September 2013
9. Middlebrook, M. and Everitt, C. (1990), *The Bomber Command War Diaries*, 628.
10. Newsletter 21, 1 November 2000, 550 Squadron and RAF North Killingholme Association.
11. Interview with Jack Harris, April 2013.
12. Interview with Howell Evans, June 2013.
13. Interview with Dave Davidson, April 2013.
14. Interview with Sam Lipfriend, March 2013.
15. Interview with Frank Woodley, March 2013.
16. Interview with Sam Lipfriend, March 2013.
17. Middlebrook, M. and Everitt, C. (1990), *The Bomber Command War Diaries*, 631–2.
18. Interview with Sam Lipfriend, March 2013.
19. Interview with Jack Harris, April 2013.
20. Interview with Dave Davidson, April 2013.
21. Middlebrook, M. and Everitt, C. (1990), *The Bomber Command War Diaries*, 633.
22. Interview with Sam Lipfriend, March 2013.
23. Interview with Jack Harris, April 2013.
24. Interview with Sam Lipfriend, March 2013.

25. Administration's Report and Statistics for the Town of Pforzheim 1945–52: City Life 1939–45.
26. Middlebrook, M. and Everitt, C. (1990), *The Bomber Command War Diaries*, 635.
27. Ibid., 637.
28. Interview with Dave Davidson April, 2013.
29. Interview with Howell Evans, June 2013.
30. Notes provided by Jack Harris and Dave Davidson.
31. Interview with Jack Harris, April 2013.
32. Interview with Dave Davidson, April 2013.
33. Administration's Report and Statistics for the Town of Pforzheim 1945–52: City Life 1939–45.
34. National Archives, AIR 14/3684.
35. Pross, M. (1995), *Die Einschläge kommen näher, Aus den Tagebüchern 1943–45 von Friedrich Adolf Katz, 1945–1947 Oberbürgermeister der Stadt Pforzheim.*
36. Administration's Report and Statistics for the Town of Pforzheim 1945–52: City Life 1939–45.
37. Interviews with Irma Baroni, August 2013.
38. Interviews with Werner Baroni, 2013.
39. Interview with Dave Davidson, April 2013.
40. Interview with Bill Thomas, June 2013.
41. Middlebrook, M. and Everitt, C. (1990), *The Bomber Command War Diaries*, 641.
42. Administration's Report and Statistics for the Town of Pforzheim 1945–52: City Life 1939–45.
43. Pross, M. (1995), *Die Einschläge kommen näher, Aus den Tagebüchern 1943–45 von Friedrich Adolf Katz, 1945–1947 Oberbürgermeister der Stadt Pforzheim.*

Chapter Five

The Whirlwind Arrives

B y December 1944, 80 per cent of all German cities with a pre-war population exceeding 100,000 had been 'devastated or very seriously damaged', according to Bomber Command's Arthur Harris. Nevertheless, the full force of the bombing 'whirlwind' had yet to scourge Germany. The 20 per cent of German towns still relatively undamaged were increasingly conspicuous. The largely intact cities in the east, notably Dresden and Chemnitz, were now more vulnerable as the German air defence organization had lost its early warning networks to the west. Bomber Command's precision bombing systems reached out to these distant targets as the ground stations had been brought up to Germany's western border. The Gee chain and Oboe systems now covered almost the whole of Germany. Harris commented: 'this ensured the success of attacks on many distant objectives when the weather would otherwise have prevented us from finding the target'.[1]

Victory by May 1945 was a real prospect, given a successful Russian offensive supported by massive Bomber Command attacks on the eastern cities and communication centres. Attacks on oil and communication targets intensified, to paralyse the movement of reinforcements and supplies. This meant bombing towns directly in the path of the Russian, British and American advances.[2]

In January 1945 snow and fog disrupted Bomber Command's operations. At North Killingholme, 550 Squadron flew just six raids, all night attacks: Nuremberg, Hannover, Munich and Duisburg, together with oil plants at Merseburg and Zeitz. In mid-January the intrepid Flight Lieutenant Jock Shaw was finally ordered to stop operational flying, having completed forty-two trips.

Dave Davidson was on 550's Battle Order for Nuremberg on the night of 2/3 January 1945. They took off that Tuesday afternoon and returned safely after an exhausting flight of seven hours forty-five minutes. This was a major area attack by 514 Lancasters and seven Mosquitoes. Four Lancasters were lost and two crashed in France. Conditions were clear over the city and the marking was accurate. Nuremberg's centre was laid waste and rail facilities and the MAN and Siemens plants suffered severely. The raid took 1,838 lives, and razed 2,000 medieval buildings and over 4,600 houses and flats.[3]

The weather was cloudy most of the way out but conditions were excellent over Nuremberg, with only a slight ground haze. The built-up area contrasted sharply with the snow-covered countryside, according to 550 Squadron's *Operations Record Book*. The first of the mixed red and green TIs fell across the marshalling yards in the city centre: 'Excellent, concentrated bombing developed, numerous explosions took place and the glow of raging fires could be seen 150 miles away by crews on their return journey. A reconnaissance aircraft flying over the target after the attack reported "three large areas of solid fire" to the north-north-west and one to the south-east, with many smaller ones over the whole area.' Ground opposition declined rapidly as the raid developed.

Jack Harris and his crew were on their thirtieth trip: 'It was a clear night and we bombed from 17,000ft on the TIs. There was night fighter activity in the area – we could see the fighter flares above the bomber stream.'[4]

One 550 aircraft – Lancaster 'E', captained by Flying Officer Smith – developed an oil leak in the port inner engine while outward bound, over France. Following orders, Smith searched for an alternative target just across the German border. A Merlin engine with an oil leak is the reason why Pforzheim received a Lancaster's bombs that night. Pforzheim was also bombed the next day, Wednesday, 3 January, when twenty-five American aircraft dropped 77 tons of bombs on the marshalling yards. This was the first of four daylight raids on the town by the USAAF over a four-week period. The bombs fell at lunchtime, dropping on Südstadt. Most damage was done in the Kupferhammer area, but bombs also fell on the 'war evacuee estate' in the opposite direction, on Wilferdinger Höhe. There was also damage to local utilities. Eight people were killed.[5]

Fear of death from the air held Pforzheim in its grip. Adolf Katz made a sober reference to his daughter, Marianne, in a diary entry for Sunday, 7 January 1945: 'In the evening bomber formations fly by on their way to Munich. In her nightgown and full of fear, Marianne came into the air-raid shelter. When Ruth vigorously put her back to bed she sat there and sobbed and it was almost impossible to calm her. The fear will stay with hundreds of thousands of children for their entire lives.'[6]

On Friday, 5 January 1945, thousands of Bomber Command aircrew prepared for a night raid on Hannover. This was Dave Davidson's twentieth operation. The 550 Squadron pilot described the five-hour sortie as a 'shaky do'. He wrote: 'We lost a crew – one of the best we had, including four married men. Hope they managed to get out by 'chute. They were all great guys.'[7] This loss was Lancaster NG331 ('M'). The aircraft was shot down by flak. Flying Officer J.C. Adams, RCAF, and five others died. The rear gunner, the sole survivor, became a prisoner.[8]

This was the first major attack on Hannover since October 1943. It caused much destruction but was very costly. Around 250 people died on the ground that night, but almost as many died in the air. The losses totalled twenty-three Halifaxes and eight Lancasters – 4.7 per cent of the main force of 650 heavy bombers, a severe casualty rate for so late in the war.[9]

Eddie Edlund and crew felt unsettled as they left for Hannover. Flight engineer Sam Lipfriend: 'We were shaky. It was our first op for three weeks and it was easy to get out of the mood. It was much better with no break. Anyway, by the time we crossed the Dutch coast we had regained our nerve.' Later, back in the billet, he made a diary entry before getting to sleep: 'Medium flak over target. 4/10th cloud. Good prang.'[10]

Twenty-four Lancasters of 550 Squadron began taking off from North Killingholme at 19.00. They were in the second wave attacking Hannover. The *Operations Record Book* stated: 'Our crews were led visually to the target by means of its "blaze of glory", that could be seen for 100 miles. This blaze had been started by an earlier attack, two and a half hours before, by Halifaxes. The town was blazing beautifully and the second instalment of high explosives and incendiaries were added to the holocaust. Flames and smoke increased and could be seen by our crews when over the Zuider Zee on their return.' It added, rather facetiously: 'The attack was an outstanding success and Hannover now has a hangover.'

Bruce Potter and his crew had taken part in a night attack on Royan.[11] They took off from Scampton with other 153 Squadron Lancasters during the evening of Thursday, 4 January. Royan was a heavily fortified town held by the Germans. The enemy retained control of the Gironde estuary, so denying the Allies the use of Bordeaux's docks. The main force of 347 Lancasters attacked in two waves, dropping 1,576 tons of high explosive bombs – including 285 4,000lb Cookies. Between 500 and 800 French civilians died, but probably fewer than 50 Germans were killed. Potter was on again for the 7 January night area attack on Munich. The main force of 645 Lancasters took off from eastern England's many bomber airfields. In Pforzheim, the Katz family listened to their engines a couple of hours later. The aircraft passed over, on the final leg of their outward flight. This was a successful attack and the last on Munich. Eleven Lancasters were lost and another four crashed in France.[12]

Twenty-seven aircraft were bombed-up at North Killingholme for the Munich attack. Three were found to be unserviceable and the remaining twenty-four began taking off at 18.00. The bombers arrived early over Munich owing to stronger than forecast winds. They were forced to dog-leg or orbit as they waited for the markers to go down. Once again, 550's Lancasters were part of the second wave; aircraft of 5 Group had attacked the city several hours before. The second wave crews spotted the glow from burning Munich from some distance.

The 5 Group aircraft had benefited from more favourable conditions. When the second wave Lancasters arrived they found the target completely obscured by thick cloud, with tops up to 12,000ft. According to 550's *Operations Record Book*, there were very few markers. Many second wave crews had bombed the best they could by the time the long-awaited concentration of sky markers was achieved. There was slight to moderate heavy flak over the target and several night fighter combats took place. Once again, 550 Squadron lost an aircraft, that of Flying Officer C.J. Clarke, RCAF. He was flying NG363 ('P'). There was one survivor: the bomb aimer became a prisoner of war.[13]

Meanwhile, in Pforzheim and many other German towns, free-ranging Allied fighter-bombers now added a new dimension to the air threat. During the afternoon of Wednesday, 10 January they dropped bombs on Pforzheim's centre, with hits in areas including Nonnenmühlgasse and Obere Augasse. Ten people were killed.[14]

Following Munich, five days of bad weather restricted Bomber Command's activities. Instead of flying, many bomber crews found themselves snow-clearing in the freezing conditions. At windswept North Killingholme, orders were given on Saturday, 13 January to prepare twenty-four Lancasters for a raid. By 14.00, however, the planned attack was cancelled. Operations finally resumed the next day, when 550 Squadron crews were briefed to attack the Leuna synthetic oil plant near Merseburg. Twenty-seven Lancasters took off, but one returned early when a crew member became ill. The others pressed on in deteriorating weather; they found ten-tenths cloud over the target and bombed sky markers. The *Operations Record Book* described Merseburg's defences as 'active', but all squadron aircraft returned safely.

This attack on much-bombed Leuna meant a long sortie of eight hours thirty-five minutes for 153 Squadron's Bruce Potter. It was even longer for 550 Squadron's Eddie Edlund. His Lancaster arrived back at North Killingholme after eight hours fifty minutes. Flight engineer Sam Lipfriend made a diary note: 'Intense flak over target. Reportedly worse than Berlin. Saw PFF over target, dropping markers. I hope they take some guns away if we have to go there again.' Edlund had to orbit the target, prompting Lipfriend's comment: 'I don't know how they missed us.'[15] Ten bombers were not so fortunate. This raid, involving 573 Lancasters, was delivered in two waves three hours apart. Heavy damage was inflicted on Leuna.[16]

Within forty-eight hours Lipfriend was back in a Lancaster, sitting alongside Edlund, as they carried out checks before taking off for a raid on another synthetic oil plant. They started their take-off run at 17.33.[17] This time the target was the Braunkohle-Benzin complex at Zeitz, 20 miles south of Leipzig. The 16/17 January raid on Zeitz severely damaged the plant's northern area. Once again, a deep penetration to a well-defended target came at a price. Ten Lancasters were lost (around 3 per cent of the force of 328 Lancasters). There were three other Bomber Command raids that night. The targets were: the synthetic oil plant at Brüx, in western Czechoslovakia, the benzol plant at Wanne-Eickel and an area attack on Magdeburg.[18]

Edlund's Lancaster touched down at North Killingholme at 01.38 on Wednesday, 17 January. Despite his fatigue, Sam Lipfriend found the energy to take up his diary. He noted the 'fairly intense' flak barrage and mass of searchlights around Zeitz. He saw many explosions, including a very large blast at around thirty-five minutes into the return.[19]

North Killingholme had sent twenty-eight Lancasters to Zeitz. One crew had a particularly unpleasant experience. Flight Lieutenant Pyke, in Lancaster 'E', got off to a bad start. Soon after take-off, in the climb over base, his port outer engine caught fire. The *Operations Record Book* described what happened: 'Unable to extinguish it or feather the airscrew, F/L Pyke proceeded out to sea to jettison his bombs and to do it quickly as the fire threatened to get out of hand.' Fortunately, all went well

Aborted sortie: Flight Lieutenant F.T. Pyke, DFC, with crew members and others. They lost an engine shortly after take-off for an attack on Zeitz on the night of 16/17 January 1945. The port outer engine caught fire. They jettisoned their bombs over the sea. *Photo: Bob Stone.*

and they landed safely. The other 550 Squadron aircraft found clear weather and good visibility over the target. The *Operations Record Book* added: 'The bombing was highly concentrated in the centre of the target. Nine major explosions and one really super explosion, which belched forth flame and black oily smoke, were seen.' All aircraft returned safely.

Pforzheim was the target on Saturday, 20 January 1945, when nine American aircraft dropped 27 tons of bombs. The following day, forty-five aircraft dropped 135 tons. In both instances the rail yards were the main target.[20]

On that Saturday Adolf Katz was in a grim mood when he turned to his diary: 'The Russian offensive has broken loose with enormous force and shattered our whole front within a few days. The feeling of hopelessness is spreading.'[21] German forces reeled back, beginning their retreat from East and West Prussia. Around 2 million civilians were already trekking west, in fear of Russian retribution.

Pforzheim received its next taste of total war on Sunday, 21 January. It was witnessed by Katz: 'This was about the most uncanny scene I have ever seen. More than a thousand bombers and fast fighter planes flew over the city for an hour. Owing to the cold you could see the condensation trails very clearly in the bright winter sun. I had just written this when the formations came back. We watched them until we saw the flares and then ran down into the cellar, where we waited for the explosions.

At least three flights released their bombs over the city but, to our relief, not over our part of the city.'[21]

Katz checked Deutsche Bank and found the building intact. He went to the Volkssturm muster point but there was no-one around. He moved on to the eastern part of town, where most of the damage was concentrated. Later, he turned again to his diary: 'Burning houses, piles of rubble blocking the streets, countless empty windows and glass splinters, distraught people carrying away mattresses and other personal effects on little carts, every now and then a wounded person or a stretcher with a covered body, in a courtyard some unrecognizable remains that used to be a human being. And lots of people walking through the streets just to have a look.

'I ran into several men from my Volkssturm unit who wanted to help but didn't know how to get started, like me. I asked a policeman who shrugged and said that individuals could not help at all; help would have to be organized. Diagonally across from the School for Master Craftsmen I saw the debris of a house and was told by a man from Technical Emergency Aid that two people were still buried in the cellar. I stayed and helped. However, when I went home tired, at dusk, we had hardly dug a hole as deep as a man and it will take all night and probably all day to unearth the cellar. Fifteen to twenty men were standing around and three or four were able to work. For each man working there were five rubbernecks, including women and girls. Meanwhile, the fires increased and spread to neighbouring houses because the firefighters were at full stretch. The eastern and, again, the northern parts of town were badly hit but two bomb carpets dropped beyond the city perimeter, otherwise the disaster would have been much bigger.'[21]

The damage began at Gesellstrasse and continued into Holzgartenstrasse, the Kunstgewerbeschule (art school), Östliche Karl-Friedrich-Strasse, Lindenstrasse up to Christophallee and Luitgardstrasse. Fifty-eight people lost their lives. There was considerable damage to many buildings.[22]

Teenager Sigrid Kern (née Weber) lived with her family adjacent to Eutingen Town Hall. 'That's where the siren was – the noise was terrible. When the siren started we left our warm beds and went into the damp cellar. Later in the war it seemed that *Bomben-Karle* ['Bomb-Charlie'] came over every night. I got used to his arrival and the dropping of just the one bomb.' When labour service with the Aicheles came to an end, Sigrid had found work as a tailoress. 'Every night our sleep was disturbed and I had to get up for work at 6.00am. I was always tired.'[23]

After a few days off, Eddie Edlund and crew were back on 550 Squadron's battle order, for the Monday, 22 January raid on industrial plants around Duisburg. Edlund's flight engineer, Sam Lipfriend, made an upbeat note in his diary: 'Nice easy trip. Moonlight. Target very visible – Rhine outstanding. A few searchlights but very little flak.'[24] Many bombs fell on the Thyssen steelworks.

The 550 pilots operating that night included Dave Davidson. He and his crew had been unlucky. They had been on leave but were recalled on 15 January, when the squadron suddenly found itself short of crews. On their return the weather changed and conditions became too poor for flying. They had to wait for the Duisburg attack on 22 January. On returning, Dave wrote to his wife, Babs, and mentioned the appalling weather – 'snow and ice everywhere'.[25]

The Duisburg raid struck the benzol plant in the Bruckhausen area, but also damaged the nearby steelworks; local reports estimated that 500 bombs hit Thyssen steelworks. The raid killed 152 people, including 115 foreign workers and prisoners of war.[26]

Before this raid the weather had been poor for nearly a week. At North Killingholme a fierce gale blew down many trees and crews kept warm by sawing logs. The 550 Squadron *Operations Record Book* commented: 'Apart from the fact that snow shovelling is good, healthy exercise, the issue of rum at the conclusion of the task is appreciated by most and it almost amounts to an incentive.'

On the morning of Monday, 22 January 550's crews were in their Lancasters, ready to go, when the operation was 'scrubbed'. The *Operations Record Book* made an unlikely claim: 'Needless to say, the boys were very disappointed for they all, without exception, thoroughly enjoy a daylight operation.' It is more likely that disappointment stemmed from the 'let-down' – the release of the intense nervous strain that built up before any operation, daylight or otherwise. The reaction after a 'scrub' was a strange mixture of relief and appalling anti-climax. These feelings didn't last long. The training programme hastily organized for the day was scrubbed, in turn, when fresh orders were received. Duisburg was on again, but as a night raid. Thirty-one Lancasters were prepared. Conditions over the target were clear, the marking was accurate and the bombing concentrated. The crews saw fires develop, with explosions across the target area. A thick pall of smoke rose. There was little opposition and all squadron aircraft returned safely.

Lancaster Captain Bruce Potter and his crew had one more operation in January. So far, they had flown only one sortie in the month, to Leuna on the 14th, because of the big freeze. They enjoyed the break, but it was back to the war in the late afternoon of Sunday, 28 January. Their Lancaster got the green at Scampton and joined an attack on targets around Stuttgart.[27] The 153 Squadron Lancasters were among 602 aircraft dispatched in two waves. The first hit the Kornwestheim railyards north of Stuttgart. The second bombed the Hirth aero-engine plant at Zuffenhausen. Cloud obscured both targets and the bombing was scattered.[28]

This raid on nearby Stuttgart was Pforzheim's final warning of what was to come. It was the last of many raids on Stuttgart. These attacks destroyed 32,549 apartment buildings and houses (67.8 per cent of the total). After the war, 4.9 million cubic metres of rubble had to be cleared. The raids killed 4,562 people, including 770 foreign workers and prisoners of war. According to *The Bomber Command War Diaries*: 'Stuttgart's experience was not as severe as other German cities. Its location, spread out in a series of deep valleys, had consistently frustrated the Pathfinders and the shelters dug into the sides of the surrounding hills had saved many lives.'[29]

The reality of city bombing: air raid casualties laid out for identification following a December 1943 raid on Berlin. *Photo: Trustees of the Imperial War Museum.*

A few days earlier, on Thursday, 25 January, Adolf Katz's diary entry for the day was filled with gloom: 'Symptoms of decline. All express trains are cancelled. You are not allowed to ride passenger trains for more than 75 kilometres without approval. Letters are no longer carried, only postcards. There is only gas for 2–3 hours a day. Many parts of the city don't have any gas, water, telephone or light. The consumption of electricity is strictly limited. On Fridays, factories are forbidden to use electricity.' Katz then added a very significant sentence, which may explain, in part, why Pforzheim was judged worthy of a heavy raid: 'There are munitions worth 25–30 million sitting here which can't be transported away owing to the difficulties with traffic.'[30]

On the day Katz made this diary entry, Churchill met Secretary of State for Air Sir Archibald Sinclair and discussed RAF deployment in the final phase of the European war. The Yalta 'Big Three' summit was scheduled to begin on 4 February. Churchill planned to use Bomber Command to support the Russians, and he wanted a clear picture of how to go about this before meeting Stalin and Roosevelt. He needed to know how the bombers could be used to best effect as German forces fell back from the Russians.[31]

In December 1944 Bomber Command had directed 30 per cent of its total effort at city attacks, 20 per cent at communications targets and 8 per cent at oil facilities. In

January the emphasis changed: 20 per cent of total effort was directed at oil targets, despite Harris' lack of enthusiasm for the oil campaign.[32]

On 26 January, Sinclair met Portal – who still felt that oil targets should be the general priority but agreed that attacks to support the Russian armies should be the next priority. Portal proposed one huge attack on Berlin 'and attacks on Dresden, Leipzig, Chemnitz or any other cities where a severe blitz will not only cause confusion in the evacuation from the East but will also hamper the movement of troops from the West'.[33]

Sinclair then responded to Churchill's specific questions. He confirmed oil as the top priority, but he added that area attacks on large cities in eastern Germany could be delivered when the weather ruled out attacks on oil targets. The targeting priorities were revised accordingly on Sunday, 28 January to provide for large-scale attacks on Berlin, Dresden, Chemnitz and Leipzig.[33]

Some months before, the planners had prepared Operation Thunderclap. This was to be a catastrophic attack on one city, as an overwhelming demonstration of what would follow if the Germans failed to surrender. This idea was not followed through but it was revived in late January, as a joint Anglo-American action to support the advance of Soviet forces.[34] According to Overy, Thunderclap was 'deliberately intended to create demoralisation and disorder in the cities of central and eastern Germany, in order to hamper the movement of troops and supplies, already confused by the flood of refugees from the Soviet advance'. Overy also makes the point that the new city campaign was not developed by Harris, but by the Air Ministry and, furthermore, was proposed by the Joint Intelligence Subcommittee of the Combined Chiefs of Staff. Churchill progressed the idea. The Americans made the first Thunderclap attack and Bomber Command was ordered to raid Dresden.[35]

There was no awareness in the classroom of the Baroni family's confrontations with the authorities. Nevertheless, brothers Werner and Arno had to put up with childish bullying. Werner: 'I was called "spaghetti" and "macaroni". My big problem was Fritz, the strongest boy in the class. The bullying got out of hand and, at one point, I refused to go to school. My father took me aside, explained that "a Baroni never gives up", handed me some boxing gloves and taught me to box. I beat up Fritz. I made a good job of him. In fact, Fritz and his grandmother turned up on our doorstep. She said: "Look at what your Werner did to our boy!"'[36]

The brothers were required to join the Jungvolk and, later, the Hitler Youth. Werner Baroni: 'To be honest, I enjoyed the Hitler Youth but Arno hated it. Off we went every Wednesday for physical training and to learn how to march. Arno didn't like that at all.'[36]

In April 1944 Werner became an air-raid messenger for the police and Kreisleitung (Kreisleiter Knab). 'I was one of eight messengers for this senior Nazi. It was our job to report whenever there was an air-raid alarm. I only did it as I needed new tyres for my bike. The only way to get tyres was to take a job with the Party.'[36]

The war progressed. Werner's father was badly wounded in Russia and Crete. Werner was drafted for RAD (labour service) in 1944. 'We went to Czechoslovakia and spent most of our time filling in bomb craters on airfields. I was 17 years old. After much argument I got my father's written permission to join the Navy after labour service, but it could have been the SS! Before we left for Czechoslovakia I had to report to Pforzheim Military District Headquarters. An SS sergeant told me: "You have new papers. You belong to us now." It was 20 April 1944, and they were celebrating Hitler's birthday by trawling for new SS men. They rounded up about 600 boys. I took the papers to the hospital but Father said: "I've signed once and I'm not doing it again." He refused point-blank. I got away with it by showing the SS my seamanship certificates. I said I had to join the navy as I had been in the naval branch of the Hitler Youth and had obtained my A and B seamanship certificates.'[36]

After the war Werner's father told him why he refused to sign. In Russia, some of his soldiers had seen an Einsatzkommando shooting Jewish people. 'He told them: "If what you say is true, we'd all better get rid of our uniforms. This is a crime." He wrote to his divisional commander, reporting the incident. He was summoned and the senior officer said: "Herr Baroni. I beg you to take back your message to me." Father said: "Why? What took place was a crime." The senior officer looked closely at him and said: "Do you not have a family? Two sons? Now I'm ordering you to take back the message." My father said: "After that, I decided not to sign your papers."'[36]

Werner's father eventually returned to Russia, to take command of a battlefield tank recovery unit: 'I woke up in the early hours one morning. Father had been attempting to say goodbye. Instead, he and Anna were hollering at each other. Anna said Hitler was insane. Father said Hitler was a product of Versailles. It was not a peaceful parting.'[36]

Notes

1. Harris, Air Marshal Sir Arthur (1990), *Bomber Offensive*, 242.
2. Saward, D. (1985), *Victory Denied*, 349.
3. Middlebrook, M. and Everitt, C. (1990), *The Bomber Command War Diaries*, 646.
4. Interview with Jack Harris, April 2013.
5. Administration's Report and Statistics for the Town of Pforzheim, 1945–52: City Life 1939–45.
6. Pross, M. (1995), *Die Einschläge kommen näher, Aus den Tagebüchern 1943–45 von Friedrich Adolf Katz, 1945–1947 Oberbürgermeister der Stadt Pforzheim.*
7. Interview with Dave Davidson, April 2013.
8. Newsletter No. 21, 1 November 2000, 550 Squadron and RAF North Killingholme Association.
9. Middlebrook, M. and Everitt, C. (1990), *The Bomber Command War Diaries*, 648–9.
10. Interview with Sam Lipfriend, March 2013.
11. Interview with Bill Thomas, June 2013.
12. Middlebrook, M. and Everitt, C. (1990), *The Bomber Command War Diaries*, 647–9.
13. Newsletter No. 21, 1 November 2000, 550 Squadron and RAF North Killingholme Association.
14. Administration's Report and Statistics for the Town of Pforzheim, 1945–52: City Life 1939–45.

15. Interview with Sam Lipfriend, March 2013.
16. Middlebrook, M. and Everitt, C. (1990), *The Bomber Command War Diaries*, 652.
17. Interview with Sam Lipfriend, March 2013.
18. Middlebrook, M. and Everitt, C. (1990), *The Bomber Command War Diaries*, 653.
19. Interview with Sam Lipfriend, March 2013.
20. National Archives, AIR 14/3684.
21. Pross, M. (1995), *Die Einschläge kommen näher, Aus den Tagebüchern 1943–45 von Friedrich Adolf Katz, 1945–1947 Oberbürgermeister der Stadt Pforzheim.*
22. Administration's Report and Statistics for the Town of Pforzheim, 1945–52: City Life 1939–45.
23. Interview with Doris Weber and Sigrid Kern (née Weber), November 2013.
24. Interview with Sam Lipfriend, March 2013.
25. Interview with Dave Davidson, April 2013.
26. Middlebrook, M. and Everitt, C. (1990), *The Bomber Command War Diaries*, 654.
27. Interview with Bill Thomas, June 2013.
28. Middlebrook, M. and Everitt, C. (1990), *The Bomber Command War Diaries*, 655.
29. Ibid., 656.
30. Pross, M. (1995), *Die Einschläge kommen näher, Aus den Tagebüchern 1943–45 von Friedrich Adolf Katz, 1945–1947 Oberbürgermeister der Stadt Pforzheim.*
31. Saward, D. (1985), *Victory Denied*, 349.
32. Overy, R. (1997), *Bomber Command 1939–45*, 130–1.
33. Saward, D. (1985), *Victory Denied*, 349–50.
34. Sweetman, J. (2004), *Bomber Crew*, 229.
35. Overy, R. (1997), *Bomber Command 1939–45*, 131–3.
36. Interviews with Werner Baroni, 2013.

Chapter Six

'Avenging in the Shadows'

The bombing war stretched 1940s high technology. British and German scientists fought to counter each other's moves in a complex and unceasing struggle. Failure to keep pace had deadly consequences. The British sought to increase bombing accuracy and concentration, while minimizing losses by swamping and suppressing the defences. The Germans sought to deploy their fighters to best effect, and apply technology and tactics to reduce the enemy's capacity to destroy cities and vital industrial and military targets.

In August 1943 Sir Arthur Harris developed a plan for a dedicated force to take the offensive against German air defences. This force combined radio-countermeasures (RCM) with intruder operations in enemy airspace. The intruders took the war to the night fighters and their airfields.[1] RCM's significance had been recognized as early as 1941, when a Joint Services Committee explored ways of directly supporting bomber operations over Germany.[2] Progress was slow; Harris grew impatient and called for faster action. On 1 December 1943, 100 (Special Duties) Group finally came into being. It made a major contribution to the containment of Bomber Command's losses.[3]

The role of 100 Group was to coordinate RCM activities and deploy a strong force of Mosquito intruders equipped with homers. They were to pursue German night fighters in their own skies. Home defence night fighters began flying regular intruder sorties into German airspace in June 1943. Later in the year, in 100 Group's early weeks, 141 Squadron – then flying Beaufighters – became the first unit in the force to receive Mosquitoes fitted with Serrate homers.[4]

In May 1944 the new force became known as 100 (Bomber Support) Group. Its badge was a gorgon's head and its motto was '*Sarang Tebuan Jangan Dijolok*' (Malay for 'Confound and destroy'). During 1944–5 100 Group Mosquito intruders did just that, claiming 258 German aircraft for the loss of seventy.

The 100 Group heavy aircraft carried a wide variety of RCM equipment to 'confound' the German defences. Over thirty systems were used, most of which were developed by the Telecommunications Research Establishment. They included the homers Perfectos and Serrate and the jammers Airborne Cigar, Jostle and Mandrel. Airborne Cigar (or ABC) consisted of six receiver/scanners and three transmitters to jam German VHF transmissions on 30–3 MHz and, later, 38–42 MHz.

The 100 Group fleet of around 260 aircraft operated from eight airfields. The force included 140 Mosquito intruders. The heavy aircraft included Halifaxes, Stirlings, Wellingtons, Lancasters and Fortresses.

Bomber Command's airborne RCM equipment was heavy and bulky, requiring large, four-engined aircraft. Warrant Officer Don 'Robbie' Robson, however, was not expecting a second tour on B.17 Flying Fortresses. This tour began in May 1944, but Robson's orders for Norfolk were out of date. Arriving at Sculthorpe, near Fakenham, he discovered that this airfield was virtually abandoned. His new squadron, 214, had moved to Oulton several months before.[5] The 214 Squadron badge was a nightjar *volant affrontée* and its motto was '*Ulter in umbris*' ('Avenging in the shadows').

Gunner Robson caught his first glimpse of the RCM Fortresses: 'The ball turrets had been removed and there were other modifications. The American low-pressure oxygen had been removed, replaced by the British high-pressure system. The American throat mikes had gone – 214 crews used the regular RAF flying helmet, with a microphone in the oxygen mask and earphones. Secret RCM equipment filled the bomb bays. This squadron's bombers carried no bombs! Their job was to frustrate the German defences, by jamming and issuing false orders to the enemy night fighter force.'[5]

Robson's posting came through while he was on leave. On meeting 214 Squadron's adjutant, he got off to a promising start by receiving more leave. On returning, Don joined a crew of new boys led by Pilot Officer George Wright. They were in awe of Robson: 'They had just started their first tour and had done only the one trip, whereas I had finished a first tour of twenty-nine operations. I was the expert! They asked me to pick my preferred gun position. I looked over the Fortress and selected the easiest place to jump from. That's how I became a waist gunner.'[5]

This was smart thinking. Robson was hefty for an air gunner: he was 5ft 11in, weighed 15 stone and had found it a tight fit in a Lancaster's rear turret.[5] Don

Bombers with no bombs: one of 214 Squadron's RCM Fortresses, pictured at Oulton. *Photo: Don Robson.*

The easiest place to jump from: Don Robson at the Fortress waist gun. Note the brackets limiting the arc of fire – preventing the gunner hitting the tail or mainplane. *Photo: Don Robson.*

Robson would never hear a bad word against the Lancaster but it was a death trap in an emergency. The escape rate was just 15 per cent, as against 50 per cent for a B.17.[6]

In April 1942, 214 Squadron switched from twin-engined aircraft to four-engined Short Stirlings. It became a 100 Group Fortress unit in 1944, moving to Oulton in May.[7] The first six Fortresses arriving at Oulton were fitted with Mandrel, Jostle and other RCM equipment. Within a few weeks twenty-two crews had converted to type.[8] Jostle operations became 214 Squadron's forte. They flew over 1,000 RCM sorties in the last ten months of the war.[9] Jostle was first used operationally in July 1944. It jammed HF and VHF frequencies used by German fighter controllers and could 'barrage' the whole frequency band when VHF jamming, or jam HF spot frequencies.[10]

Lancasters had a crew of seven, but 214's Fortresses had ten, including waist gunners and two wireless operators. One was the 'special operator', a fluent German speaker who tuned into enemy night fighter frequencies, operated Jostle and other RCM systems and gave German pilots false instructions whenever the opportunity arose.[11]

Don Robson got to know his Fortress crew: 'Our skipper, George Wright, was tall, slim and placid. George came from Windsor and was easy to get on with. He was married, with a young family. George survived the war and later became an air traffic controller at Heathrow.' The flight engineer, Warrant Officer Ron Williams, was the crew 'father', being a few years older than the others. The navigator was Pilot Officer Fred Mullenger, a former Metropolitan policeman who was to return to the force after the war. The wireless operator was Flight Sergeant Johnny Bates. 'He got a shock after the war. He was involved in the Methodist Church in London and was driving the Methodist bus when a police car suddenly pulled him over. It was none other than his old navigator. Fred Mullenger couldn't stop laughing.'[12]

The Canadian bomb aimer/front gunner was Pilot Officer J.R. 'Ricky' Sherbourne. Don Robson's fellow waist gunner was Flight Sergeant Robert 'Taffy' Williams, 'a shortish chap with a fine head of dark wavy hair'. The rear gunner was Flight Sergeant H.J. 'Jimmy' Southgate, from Bury St Edmunds. Robson remembers Jimmy's wife, Hazel, who was then the WAAF driver who often took them out to the aircraft: 'We would kid Jimmy, who used to get all smoothed up before an op, as he knew he would see her. Jimmy Southgate became a football referee after the war. Sadly, he died young – in his fifties. Looking back, I don't know how Jimmy stuck the rear turret position in the Fortress. It was bloody awful. I had only one flight in that position, on a fighter affiliation exercise. It was terrible. You sat on something like a motorbike seat, with your legs tucked behind you. Jimmy was quite a big bloke and he must have suffered severely in that cramped position.

'Our special operator – in charge of all the secret gear – was Sergeant Stan Bayliss. He flew on most of our operations. A perfect German speaker, he was from Birmingham, where he ran a successful business before the war. We knew absolutely nothing about his activities in the air and were forbidden to raise the subject with him. The special operators always had a separate briefing. We needed a heavy aircraft as the Jostle system alone weighed around 600lb and there were all sorts of other gadgets. I lived in the same hut as two special operators and I knew what was going on in broad terms, but didn't go into it. I never had a formal briefing on the squadron's RCM role.'[12]

Serious work: Pilot Officer George Wright with members of his crew. Standing, left to right: waist gunner Don Robson, pilot George Wright, navigator Fred Mullinger, flight engineer Ron Williams and rear gunner Jimmy Southgate. Kneeling are special operator Stan Bayliss and bomb aimer Ricky Sherbourne. *Photo: Don Robson.*

Waist gunner Don Robson flew his first operation with 214 Squadron on 2 June 1944. He did seven ops in July, five in August, four in September and five in October, making twenty-two in all. The last, of four hours' duration, was flown in Fortress Mark lll HB774 (BU-G), on 26 October. When they landed back at Oulton Don Robson had finished. He had survived fifty-one operational flights (although this was reduced officially by Bomber Command's short-lived and much-despised practice of counting sorties to French targets as only part of an operation).

Wright and crew were familiar with Fortress HB774, having flown 'G' on several occasions. This B.17 was constructed by Boeing Aircraft Co. at Dallas, Texas. It left for the UK, via the Azores, on 23 February 1944, arriving six days later. Having reached Scottish Aviation Ltd at Prestwick, it was fitted out with H_2S, Mandrel, Piperack and Jostle. It was also painted in Bomber Command colours.[13]

Robson's second tour was nearly over before it started. The first sortie supported an attack on railyards at Trappes, south-west of Paris. They were among sixteen RCM aircraft operating that night: the raid was carried out by 128 aircraft – 105 Halifaxes, 19 Lancasters and 4 Mosquitoes. Most bombs fell on the eastern half of the target. Losses were extremely high: fifteen Halifaxes and one Lancaster – 12.5 per cent of the force.[14] Robson and the rest of Wright's crew had a close call. Flight engineer Ron Williams: 'as we approached the target a huge orange flare dropped on our tail. George decided to move off track and fly a parallel course. Immediately alongside us appeared a Halifax in the full glare of the flare, exchanging fire with a Messerschmitt 210. The Halifax went down with engines on fire and the Messerschmitt following, with the rear gunner firing back, but we saw no chutes from the Halifax.

'From then on we saw many aircraft shot down, with Fred, our navigator, logging positions until he had no space to log more. We were attacked and George took evasive action by the usual corkscrewing, but we sustained a few holes from bullets which miraculously passed diagonally between the two waist gunners, Bob Williams and Don Robson.'[15] This would not be their only close call. Robson had little to say about the encounter. His logbook bears only a brief note: 'Fw190 attacked. Port waist gunner fired. No claim.'

Waist gunners: Don Robson is on the left. Fire from an attacking fighter passed diagonally between the two waist gunners. Note the ammunition belts. *Photo: Don Robson.*

The 214 Squadron Fortresses accompanied the outbound main force, climbed above the bomber stream, circled and used Jostle and other RCM to disrupt German radar. Other 100 Group squadrons specialized in Window spoofs, using clouds of foil strips to create problems for German radar operators. These aircraft often created a screen, running north–south over the North Sea and France. Then 'spoof' aircraft would break through the screen, dropping Window to simulate a large bomber force on German radar screens. The aim was to persuade German controllers to direct fighters against the spoof, so allowing the real main force to fly on unopposed. This was psychological, as well as technological, warfare. Sometimes the actual main force bombers were the first aircraft through the screen, in an attempt to fool the enemy. Were the first plots a spoof or the real thing? The Germans responded sensibly, by retaining strong fighter forces to defend the Ruhr, regardless of spoofs. Bomber Command countered by swamping the defences with vast clouds of Window, on the principle that the Germans were expecting a Ruhr attack anyway.

The first loss of a 214 Squadron aircraft came quickly, on the night of 23/4 May 1944. Pilot Officer A.J.N. 'Skipper' Hockley, RAAF, and his crew failed to return. They were in Fortress SR384 (BU-A).[16] Hockley was 27. His aircraft left Oulton just before midnight, bound for the Antwerp area. It was shot down by a night fighter flown by Oberleutnant Hermann Leube (4/NJG3) and crashed into the Oosterschelde. Two of the crew were killed, including Hockley. A fortnight later 214's crews were flying sorties in support of the D-Day landings.[16]

Jostle's first use was on the night of 4/5 July 1944. By the end of August, 214 had flown 305 operational sorties for the loss of three aircraft. This squadron had a remarkable general safety record, being free of flying accidents for a period of six months.[17]

Don Robson's second tour was very different from the first: 'On 467 Squadron we were all sergeants together, at least for the first twenty trips. I shared my accommodation with the pilot and bomb aimer. During the second tour we were officers and sergeants and, therefore, not so close. There wasn't that family atmosphere.' Robson was anxious to get on with things: 'I was a bit on edge. I just wanted to get this second tour over.' He had taken the starboard waist gunner's position, swapping the Lancaster rear turret's four .303 Brownings for a single 0.5 calibre weapon fitted with a flash eliminator for night combat. 'We had no permanent port waist gunner when I first joined. Ron "Jimmy" James [in later life the author of *Avenging in the Shadows: 214 (FMS) Squadron, Royal Air Force*] partnered me several times, although he was another pilot's gunner. Jimmy was also on his second tour, having completed his first with 90 Squadron. He jumped in whenever he could as he knew our pilot well.'[18]

Robson got used to the B.17: 'There was no bomber like the Lancaster. I had been spoilt. The Fortress certainly carried a lot of armament. We had no particular aircraft, but flew whatever B.17 was available. I didn't dislike the Fortress. It was a good aircraft – very stable – but it wasn't a Lanc and it wasn't carrying bombs. Flying as a waist gunner was different. I was very exposed. Occasionally, we operated at 30,000ft, well above the bomber stream. Yet I don't remember it being as cold as the Lanc's rear turret. I never got frostbite, although Ron James did, but there was the discomfort of standing up the entire time. Our longest trip was ten hours ten minutes, an attack on Königsberg involving a minor incursion into Swedish airspace. When we landed I got the news that my wife had had a miscarriage.'[18]

Don Robson wore woollen and silk underwear and a full body electrically heated suit, rather like an overall, controlled by a thermostat: 'This was different to my kit on a Lancaster, which consisted of an electrically heated waistcoat, with leads going to gloves and the slippers worn inside my flying boots. My preference was to wear battledress over the heated suit.' The waist guns were fitted with two brackets limiting the arc of fire and preventing the gunners hitting the tail or mainplane. Robson had no special training as a waist gunner: 'The first time I went out I cocked the gun and fired. Bang! That was it – just the one round. I cocked and fired again. Bang! Only one more. This was not encouraging! Most of our guns were well used. When I landed I took the 0.5 to the armoury, where they found the problem – a weak return spring.'[18]

Robson carried the authority of his first tour. Wright and the others listened to him. 'On one occasion, as usual, we had been briefed to fly around the perimeter of the target but George decided to cross it. I persuaded him otherwise. I rarely swore, but I did on that occasion. Why fly over a target in an RCM aircraft without bombs?'[18]

Oulton was not to everyone's taste. This airfield was 2 or 3 miles from Blickling Hall, formerly the seat of the Marquis of Lothian, Britain's ambassador in Washington. The RAF took it over for the duration. Don Robson found Oulton a curious place: 'It was a strange set-up. We were billeted on one side of Oulton and had to walk through the village to get to the flying field. Normally you would expect to be within a secure perimeter. The flying field was fenced but that didn't seem particularly secure, given what we were up to.

'There were some American aircraft on the station. We didn't have much to do with the Americans, but they were a nuisance. When they were on the piss they'd come back to their billets and start firing guns in the air. Several times we heard spent rounds pinging off the thin steel plates of our Nissen huts. On the first occasion we thought the Germans had landed, in order to disrupt D-Day. One particular memory of Oulton is the mess. It was in a very large Nissen hut and one of the men, a Canadian, had painted a mural along the wall. It was a salmon fishing scene.'[18]

Life on 214 Squadron was insular: 'We never really mixed with other crews. Frankly, we were only interested in ourselves and our own living conditions. I wasn't interested in anything other than the waist gunner's position. I saw more of the aircraft's front *after* the war, when I had a look over the preserved B.17 Sally B. This Fortress is very different from our wartime aircraft. Sally B is windowed in at the waist position.'[18]

Morale was firm on 214: 'Losses were much lighter during my second tour. It helped that we were operating after the Normandy landings. Loss rates were lower for many reasons, including the fact that only two or three RCM aircraft went out at a time. I coped very well. Compared to the first, my second tour was a piece of cake, although we still lost aircraft. One good thing about 214 was the adjutant – he always treated us fairly. If someone had been naughty and a police summons arrived, the adjutant just tore it up.'[18]

Robson got leave every six weeks. He went home and continued working at the family bakery. He then returned to Oulton, the Fortresses, operations and training.

He enjoyed the flying between operations: 'The waist gunner had an eye on the bottom of his parachute harness and this was used to attach the safety harness. When taking evasive action during fighter affiliation exercises, a quick drop of the nose would give us negative G. The waist gunners became weightless and floated up to the ceiling. I quite enjoyed that sensation.'[18]

Robson didn't enjoy his encounter with night fighters, during the 5 October 1944 attack on Saarbrücken. Three Lancasters were lost and George Wright's aircraft came close to joining them. Don Robson: 'The fighter made a firing pass. It came in from the starboard quarter down. We were struck by a single cannon shell. It entered the floor a few inches from my foot and exited through the roof without detonating. It must have been an armour-piercing round. I had no idea we had been hit until dawn broke, on our return. The sky suddenly appeared through the hole in the roof, just above my head. I never fired but the port waist gunner did.' They also attracted the attention of a Ju88 twin-engined night fighter. When they landed back, after five hours thirty minutes, Robson found time for his diary: 'Fw190 attacked. RG claims damaged. Ju88 attacked. RG and PWG claim damaged.' Robson adds: 'Several of our RCM aircraft were attacked by fighters but the Germans weren't very persistent at this time. They seemed reluctant to climb high.'[18]

Nevertheless, 214 Squadron continued to suffer losses in the final months of 1944 and into 1945. These were not always directly related to enemy action. On 17 January 1945, for example, B.17 KJ103 (BU-M), flown by Flying Officer N.T. Scott, took off from Oulton at 18.00 for a Jostle operation. It returned low on fuel and crashed near the airfield. One crew member, Flying Officer Terence McKee, was killed and six others were injured.[19]

The bellies of the B.17s continued to fill with the latest RCM equipment. In October, 'Dina' was installed in 214 Squadron aircraft. This jammed night fighter radars. As 1944 drew to a close some Fortresses carried Jostle (to jam HF and VHF communications), Carpet (to jam Würzburg radars) and Piperack (to jam SN-2 night fighter radars).[20]

Don Robson finished his second tour and left 214 Squadron during November. At the turn of the year severe winter weather took hold and vicious blizzards scoured Oulton: the base was completely snowbound at times. There were only twelve flyable nights in January 1945.

Notes

1. Probert, H. (2001), *Bomber Harris*, 234.
2. Bowman, M.W. and Cushing, T. (1996), *Confounding the Reich*, 14.
3. Probert, H. (2001), *Bomber Harris*, 234.
4. Bowman, M.W. and Cushing, T. (1996), *Confounding the Reich*, 16–22.
5. Interview with Don Robson, March 2013.
6. Nichol, J. and Rennell, T. (2004), *Tail-End Charlies*, 148.
7. Halley, James J. (1980), *The Squadrons of the Royal Air Force*, 217.

8. Bowman, M.W. and Cushing, T. (1996), *Confounding the Reich*, 85–7.
9. Ibid., 84.
10. Harris, Sir Arthur T. (1995), *Despatch on War Operations* (Appendix E, Radio-Countermeasures in Bomber Command), 143.
11. Redding, T. (2008), *Flying for Freedom*, 279–80.
12. Interview with Don Robson, March 2013.
13. 214squadron.org.uk/crews_and_losses.htm.
14. Middlebrook, M. and Everitt, C. (1990), *The Bomber Command War Diaries*, 518.
15. 214squadron.org.uk/crews_and_losses.htm.
16. Bowman, M.W. and Cushing, T. (1996), *Confounding the Reich*, 85–7.
17. Ibid., 99.
18. Interview with Don Robson, March 2013.
19. 214squadron.org.uk.
20. Bowman, M.W. (2006), *100 Group (Bomber Support)*, 24.

Chapter Seven

Dresden Destroyed

The Combined Strategic Targets Committee met at the Air Ministry on Wednesday, 7 February 1945, to consider a proposed new strategic bombing directive. A subcommittee had considered targets (in addition to Berlin, Leipzig and Dresden) associated with the movement of evacuees and military units behind Germany's Eastern Front. Seven additional cities were proposed as targets. The subcommittee also reviewed the existing (November 1944) list of 'industrial area targets', now rendered obsolete following recent successful attacks. Here, the subcommittee put forward a revised list of seventeen targets.[1]

The ten Eastern Front targets endorsed on 7 February were Berlin, Dresden, Chemnitz, Leipzig, Halle, Plauen, Dessau, Potsdam, Erfurt and Magdeburg. The seventeen on the revised industrial area list were to be attacked 'when conditions do not permit attack against priority target systems'. These towns included Pforzheim. The others were Kassel, Nuremberg, Hannover, Zwickau, Hildesheim, Flensburg, Munich, Mannheim, Gera, Würzburg, Weimar, Jena, Hanau, Bielefeld, Worms and Ludwigshafen.[1]

Those attending this meeting took account of the Russian offensive and the 2 February 'Fleece 75' signal from the Vice-Chiefs of Staff (acting on behalf of the Chiefs of Staff, then on their way to Yalta). Fleece 75 confirmed oil targets as the first priority, followed by communications, especially evacuation areas behind the Eastern Front and including the cities of Berlin, Leipzig, Dresden and Chemnitz. Lower-ranking targets included tank factories, jet aircraft plants and U-boat yards.[2]

During the Yalta plenary, Red Army Deputy Chief of Staff General Antonov called for strategic bombing to prevent the Germans moving troops from west to east: he wanted raids on communication centres, particularly Berlin and Leipzig. Fleece 75 led to the new bombing directive.[2] The key decisions on bombing were taken by the three heads of government at Yalta and the Joint Chiefs of Staff, not Bomber Command's Arthur Harris.

There were constant air-raid alarms as the Allies advanced on Pforzheim and other South German towns. Many people took up almost permanent residence in public shelters and only concerned themselves with the bare necessities of life. The loss in productive working hours was reflected in lower factory output.[3]

The public air-raid warnings (*Öffentliche Luftwarnung*) and local air alarms (*Fliegeralarm*) were supplemented from 1 February 1945 by a new warning. This was the acute alarm (*Akute Luftgefahr*).[3] On that very day, eleven American aircraft

Putting on a show: a light flak crew demonstrate their gun in Turnplatz. Goethebrücke is in the background. *Photo: Stadtarchiv Pforzheim.*

dropped 33 tons of bombs on Pforzheim's industrial area.[4] In the eight weeks to the calamity of 23 February *Fliegeralarm* or *Akute* warnings were given 106 times. Many Pforzheim schoolchildren had left for the countryside, accompanied by their teachers. On 13 January, pupils from Pforzheim's high schools were sent to reception centres at Titisee.[5]

Thursday, 1 February 1945 was significant for Flight Lieutenant 'Buzz' Burrows and crew. They flew their first operation that night, having joined 550 Squadron. Their aircraft, LM931 ('A2'), was among 382 Lancasters and 14 Mosquitoes raiding Ludwigshafen; six Lancasters were lost. Most main force aircraft bombed sky markers as the target was obscured. Nevertheless, this raid was successful. Ludwigshafen's railyards, the main target, were severely damaged. The bombers also damaged or destroyed some 900 houses.[6]

The Burrows crew followed a path trod by most Bomber Command volunteers. They joined 1662 Heavy Conversion Unit, flying Halifaxes, then progressed to Lancaster Finishing School. Ron Germain, Burrows' wireless operator: 'We reached North Killingholme in January 1945, joining 550's C Flight, commanded by Flight Lieutenant Waite. We knew this was a good squadron. Morale was high and the atmosphere calm. There were some thriving gambling schools – the Aussies were great gamblers.' The new crew logged seven hours twenty-five minutes on their first sortie. Ron Germain again: 'We were relieved to get off that night. We were briefed three or four times in late January but each op was cancelled. By the time we took off for Ludwigshafen we were chewing our nails.'[7]

Bad weather had kept 550's bombers on the ground for ten days. On 1 February North Killingholme sent thirty Lancasters to Ludwigshafen. They took off in the mid-afternoon. Cloud increased to ten-tenths on the final leg and ground markers and sky markers were dropped in difficult conditions. Nevertheless, the *Operations Record Book* commented: 'There was an encouraging incendiary glow that developed into a compact fire mass, with two explosions.' Flak was slight, later decreasing to give way to the night fighters. They were more active than usual. Flying Officer Lowrey's Lancaster failed to return to North Killingholme: 'Later, it was learned that five were safe in Allied territory after having been forced to abandon their aircraft, which had been very badly damaged through colliding with a friendly aircraft near the target area.' They jumped from Lancaster RA502 ('Z') near Nancy and the survivors were rescued by the US Army. The mid-upper gunner and wireless operator died.

Experienced 550 pilot Dave Davidson went to Ludwigshafen with a 'spare bod' navigator. His regular navigator, Flight Sergeant 'Tiny' Townsend, was on compassionate leave as his two children had gone down with pneumonia. Davidson's Lancaster returned safely after six hours thirty minutes in the air.[8]

Buzz Burrows had had a long wait for his first op but the second came within twenty-four hours. He was on 550's battle order for the Friday, 2 February raid on Wiesbaden, or, more specifically, that town's ordnance depot. Once again they climbed into 'A2' for a sortie of seven hours ten minutes. It was an eventful night. Wireless operator Ron Germain: 'A Ju88 night fighter was fired on by our mid-upper gunner, "Towse" Towson. He gave no evasive order and he didn't hit it. The squadron's gunners had been told to be aggressive.'[9] This was the only large-scale Bomber Command attack on Wiesbaden. It was carried out by 495 Lancasters and 12 Mosquitoes. Three Lancasters crashed in France; around 1,000 people died on the ground.[10]

The 550 Squadron *Operations Record Book* describes the briefing for the crews of twenty-six Lancasters sent to Wiesbaden. They were told the town was a haven for German troops refitting and preparing to move up to the Eastern Front: 'The weather, again, was our chief enemy. Cloud up to 20,000ft had been predicted over the Channel only but, in point of fact, the worst conditions were over the target, where there was layer cloud up to this height and over. Markers were completely obscured. Practically all our boys bombed by navigational aids. It was impossible to assess the impact of the raid. All aircraft returned to North Killingholme undamaged, despite the fact that three had observed and opened fire on enemy fighters.'

Jack Harris and crew had survived over thirty ops. After a well-deserved rest they took off from North Killingholme on 2 February, bound for Wiesbaden: 'This trip lasted six hours thirty minutes. We had a 4,000lb blast bomb and incendiaries. There was cloud up to 19,000ft over the target. We saw no markers so bombed on a "Gee" position.'[11]

Back in November, Harris' flight engineer, Stan Freeman, had fallen off his motorbike and broken his wrist. 'He was out of action for a month, in which time we flew six ops with a spare flight engineer. So, while the crew had done thirty ops – and the pilot thirty-one – Stan had only done twenty-four. We then volunteered to do an extra six to finish off with our flight engineer.' The only exception was Canadian mid-upper gunner Bill Barratt, a married man: 'The Canadians were always sent home immediately their tour was finished, so it was easy to understand why he was reluctant to extend.' During February, Bomber Command decided that a first tour should be extended to thirty-six for everyone.[11]

There was no peace for the new boys. Buzz Burrows was on for the Saturday, 3 February raid on the large coking plant at Bottrop, north of Essen. There was a change of mount: they were driven out to dispersal to make the acquaintance of Lancaster LM182 ('H2'). Ron Germain: 'What a contrast – a succession of scrubbed ops, followed by three in a row. We were short of sleep after Wiesbaden, but as soon as we went to bed we were told to get up: "Come on – you're on!"'[12]

Fourteen of 550's Lancasters bombed Bottrop that night. This time the weather was good – only haze or very thin cloud obscured ground detail. Jack Harris' Lancaster dropped a Cookie and sixteen 500lb bombs, and they brought back an aiming point photograph. 'It was a very concentrated attack, but there were plenty of fighters and searchlights around.'[13] Once again, 550 lost an aircraft. Luck ran out that night for Pilot Officer R.G. Nye; his Lancaster was shot down by a night fighter and there were no survivors. The rear gunner, Sergeant Taerum, RCAF, was aged just 18.

The main force of 192 Lancasters severely damaged the Prosper Works at Bottrop. Eight Lancasters were lost.[14] Burrows' crew now had a few days rest, but Bruce Potter's crew, with 153 Squadron at Scampton, were also on for the next day, Sunday, 4 February. Bottrop had been their nineteenth operation. The twentieth was a 'gardening' trip, mining waters off Heligoland.[15]

By February 1945 the behaviour of German civilians was governed as much by circumstance as by Nazi domination. Most people were too busy with daily survival to worry about the longer term: there was always the next air raid and the prospect of occupation. Those living in areas nearer the Russians than the Western Allies had just weeks to decide whether or when to join the trek westwards in appalling winter conditions.

Only two years before, Germany had seemed invincible. On Thursday, 8 October 1942, a Pforzheim schoolboy had handed in his essay, having written about a speech given the preceding Sunday by Hermann Göring in Berlin, to mark Harvest Festival. The boy wrote that the Reichsmarschall had said that attempts to blockade Germany had failed: 'Our soldiers have conquered large and fruitful territories in the east which are being farmed by German farmers and from which we will be getting large amounts of food. The sword and the plough are securing Germany's victory.' Years of indoctrination, with the planned pollution of young minds, are evident throughout this essay: 'The Reichsmarschall emphasized in his speech that Germany would have but one goal and one thought, namely to win the war; as soon as the enemy in the east is defeated, the score with England will be settled. This war is a war between the Aryan and the Jewish race. The Aryan race will win this war and all peoples who, at the moment, are still under the influence of the Jews will become anti-Semites one day.'[16]

Now the tables were turned. The conquered territories had been lost and it was the Germans' turn to live lives filled with uncertainty and fear. Old Pforzheim itself now had only a couple of weeks to live. Soon the gallows humour of pending defeat would appear on ruined walls: 'Enjoy the war! The peace will be terrible!'

Heavy bomber support for the Allied armies pushing against Germany's western frontier remained a priority. Kleve and Goch were strongpoints in the German defences blocking the advance of Lieutenant-General Horrocks' British XXX Corps into the Reichswald area. It was decided to bomb both towns on the night of 7/8 February 1945. Many years later, when presenting a television programme, Horrocks talked about the bombing of Kleve. He explained that it was a military necessity, but his face clouded with emotion. Recalling the moment, he said: 'I felt like a murderer.'

Horrocks had been asked by Canadian commander General Crerar whether he wanted Kleve taken out. 'By "taking out" he meant, of course, "totally destroyed". This is the sort of problem with which a general in war is constantly faced and from which there is no escape. I knew Kleve was a lovely old historic Rhineland town. Anne of Cleves, Henry VIII's fourth wife, came from there. No doubt a lot of civilians, plus women and children, were still living there. Their fate depended on how I answered Crerar's question and I simply hated the thought of Kleve being "taken out".

'All the same, if we were going to break out of the bottleneck into the German plain it was a race between the German reserves and the 15th (Scottish) Division and the German reserves would have to come through Kleve. If I could delay them by bombing it might make all the difference to the battle and, after all, the lives of my own troops must come first. So I said, "Yes" – the most terrible decision I had ever had to take in my life, and I can assure you that I felt almost physically sick when I saw the bombers flying overhead on their deadly mission. And yet people sometimes say to me, "As a general, surely you must like war." But then, possibly, I have too much imagination and it was fortunate for the British Army that I never rose above corps commander.

'After the war I used to suffer from nightmares and literally for years these always concerned Kleve. Unfortunately, it was even worse than I had imagined. I had specifically asked for incendiaries to be used but, through some error, 1,384 tons of high explosive had been dropped, and the huge craters in Kleve not only held up the German reserves but our own troops as well.'[17]

Buzz Burrows was among the 550 Squadron pilots briefed for Kleve. He went to the target in NG132 ('E2').[18] Eddie Edlund was also on the battle order; he took off from North Killingholme at 18.39.[19] The main force of 295 Lancasters reduced ancient Kleve to ruins. It was all in vain. As Horrocks acknowledged, instead of helping 15th (Scottish) Division break through, the sea of rubble actually hindered progress.[20]

Sam Lipfriend, Edlund's flight engineer, was matter of fact about this op. His diary note on Kleve reads: 'A tactical target five miles in front of our troops. Bombed from 5,000ft with Cookies. Very good prang.' They were back in the circuit above North Killingholme just before midnight.[21]

Dave Davidson also went to Kleve. He was among those pilots surprised at the low altitude briefed for the attack. Over sixty years on, Davidson recalled: 'The master bomber called us down below cloud but did not give the codeword. I stayed at the height I was at. I had heard stories of master bombers calling on the main force to get below cloud, only to discover that it was a German "master bomber" and then get shot to hell. However, this time he came through again, giving the correct codeword, but I had overshot the target and had to go round again before going down below cloud. At this height we could not only hear the exploding Cookies but feel them as well!'[22] Davidson's crew were veterans, having survived twenty-four operations – many against heavily defended targets.

Jack Harris also had doubts about bombing height: 'This time the master bomber brought us down to the very low height of 4,500ft. The safety height for a 4,000lb bomb was reckoned to be around 6,000ft, so there was an element of danger, in that the bombers might be hit by debris or fragments. There was a lot of cloud over the target but we could see the TIs. The bombing was very concentrated and there was virtually no flak.'[23]

Twenty-seven 550 Squadron Lancasters set out for Kleve. The briefing was uncompromising: Kleve was a road centre where six routes met. Its rail junction linked the Ruhr and those areas still held by the Germans in Holland north of the Rhine. The object was to 'blot out the town, thus denying the enemy the main route into that part of the battle area'. One aircraft, that of Flight Lieutenant Pickles, turned back owing to a defective bombsight. Oddly, another 550 Lancaster, that of Flight Lieutenant Rhude, developed the very same problem over the target. The *Operations Record Book* added that, although the target was obscured by cloud, 'the Master Bomber had the matter well-organised and brought the main force down beneath the cloud, where they found the ground marking concentrated and easy to follow. The crews were unanimous that the bombing was very concentrated, with Cookies bursting all round the markers. Flak was negligible …'

Some 550 crews were required the following night for an attack on the Pölitz synthetic oil plant. This was a powerful strike by 475 Lancasters, which hit the target in two waves. Conditions were clear and the bombing extremely accurate; fuel production ceased at this plant. Twelve Lancasters were lost.[24] This was a long trip

'Press on regardless': this phrase fits the character of ED905's pilot, Flight Lieutenant D.A. 'Jock' Shaw, DFC and Bar. This photograph was taken as 'Press on regardless' prepared to take off for her hundredth operational flight, the 2/3 November 1944 raid on Düsseldorf. *Photo: Bob Stone.*

for exhausted crews: Eddie Edlund took off at 18.57 and landed back eight hours fifty-five minutes later. Flight engineer Sam Lipfriend took up his diary: 'A long low level stooge over North Sea. Hit Denmark in cloud at 9,000ft. Down through Skagerrak towards Berlin, then turned sharply to the target. Russians 25 miles to the south. Very good prang. Flak medium. Large oil and factory fires. Travelling back via Sweden and Denmark.' Eddie Edlund had a Swedish background. Sam Lipfriend: 'Seated side by side and flying back, we turned left just by Malmö. He looked down and said: "My grandmother's down there." Edlund was very good at the controls of a Lancaster. He had trained in the United States and was so good that they kept him back as an instructor. He flew 2,000 hours instructing before returning to Britain to begin operations. He was a droll character but an excellent pilot. After the war he became the boss of Exeter Airport.'[25]

Pölitz is 3 miles north of Stettin. The 550 crews were briefed for a daylight raid, but this was cancelled owing to adverse conditions and the night raid substituted. Twenty-four Lancasters took off from North Killingholme. The weather was poor but improved on the approach to Germany, and the target was almost clear. The markers went down accurately and on time. The squadron's aircraft were in the second wave. The *Operations Record Book* included this upbeat entry: 'The target had been attacked two hours earlier and the fires started were still visible and our boys brightened them up considerably. Many explosions were seen and a particularly vicious one at 23.17 lit up the whole area and was said to have been the best ever.'

The bombing 'whirlwind' was about to strike Dresden. Pforzheim would follow a few days later. In *Bomber Offensive*, Sir Arthur Harris wrote: 'In February 1945, with the Russian army threatening the heart of Saxony, I was called upon to attack Dresden; this was considered a target of first importance for the offensive on the Eastern Front. Dresden had by this time become the main centre of communications for the defence of Germany on the southern half of the Eastern Front and it was considered that a heavy air attack would disorganise these communications and also make Dresden useless as a controlling centre for the defence. It was also by far the largest city in Germany – the pre-war population was 630,000 – which had been left intact; it had never before been bombed. As a large centre of war industry it was also of the highest importance.

'An attack on the night of February 13th–14th by just over 800 aircraft, bombing in two sections in order to get the nightfighters dispersed and grounded before the second attack, was almost as overwhelming in its effect as the Battle of Hamburg, though the area of devastation – 1,600 acres – was considerably less. There was, it appears, a fire typhoon, and the effect on German morale, not only in Dresden but in far distant parts of the country, was extremely serious. The Americans carried out two light attacks in daylight on the next two days. I know that the destruction of so large and splendid a city at this late stage of the war was considered unnecessary, even by a good many people who admit that our earlier attacks were as fully justified as any other operation of war. Here, I will only say that the attack on Dresden was at the time considered a military necessity by much more important people than myself ...'[26]

Harris also commented on a change in the distribution of bombing effort: 'In this winter of 1944–1945 we did not, as in all previous winters, use the long nights mainly for deep penetration of Germany. We attacked in the East and West with equal weight. Other important industrial centres in the East, such as Dessau and Chemnitz, were successfully attacked for the first time and, in the West, we found new targets in many of the smaller industrial towns, such as Solingen and Pforzheim. Such targets were often attacked as much for tactical as for strategic reasons, because they were not only of industrial importance but had become centres of communication for the Western Front or were occupied by troop concentrations or headquarters staffs and organisations.'[26]

Harris then explained why Bomber Command's attacks had grown so destructive: 'The application of methods developed for precision bombing to area bombing greatly increased the average area of devastation in the average successful attack.'[26] As the bombers took off for Dresden, over 40,000 people in that city had only a couple of hours to live.

Dresden's destruction by Bomber Command originated in Operation Thunderclap, a plan for ultra-heavy raids on selected German cities. The aim was to trigger the collapse of the German military and civil administration. Thunderclap was put forward in August 1944 but was deferred. It was seen as appropriate only in the final phase of the war, with Germany already approaching collapse; in the New Year it was appreciated that the new Soviet advance could create the conditions for Thunderclap. On 4 February the Russians at Yalta called for heavy air attacks on the eastern cities; and Bomber Command's chief received specific instructions for major raids on Dresden, Chemnitz and Leipzig. The Americans were to participate; in fact, the Americans were due to open the attack on Dresden but bad weather led to cancellation. This is why Bomber Command mounted the first attack.

The bombers above Dresden on the night of Tuesday, 13 February included Flight Lieutenant Buzz Burrows' Lancaster LM931 ('A2'). When they landed back home, his wireless operator, Ron Germain, wrote just one word in his logbook: 'Blitz'. They were in the second wave: 'We certainly knew where Dresden was as we approached. We could see it burning from a very long way away – much further than any other target.'[27]

Other 550 crews had no doubt about the success of this attack. It was Eddie Edlund's twentieth operation and it had been a long night – a flight of nine hours ten minutes. Later, flight engineer Sam Lipfriend wrote in his diary: 'Very little flak en route. None over target. Complete wipe-out of city. Fairly safe trip but long. Fires like that will never be seen again.' Nearly seventy years later, Lipfriend said: 'I made that comment about "complete wipe-out" the morning after. At that time I had not been exposed to any newspaper talk. It was how it looked to me then.'[28]

Dresden was Dave Davidson's twenty-fifth op. The second wave struck three hours after the first. Davidson remembers the outward flight: 'I could see Dresden burning in the distance, several hundred miles away. When I suggested to the navigator, Tiny, that I thought it was Dresden, he said: "Impossible!" I took a bearing, gave it to him and he came back: "It must be, but it's nearly two hours away!"'[29]

This sortie began in a strange manner and continued in similar vein. A few hours before, at North Killingholme, the 550 crews operating that night were issued with special vests to wear over their parachute harnesses. Davidson's wireless operator, Howell Evans: 'These vests carried a message along the lines of: "Don't shoot. We are Allies." The powers that be had been warned that we might find ourselves in the middle of trigger-happy Russian troops should we be shot down. We saw the funny side and laughed it off. However, I didn't laugh on our return from Dresden, as I stood in the astrodome and looked back. The whole city was on fire.'[30]

Dresden was Jack Harris' penultimate trip: 'That night we bombed from 15,000ft on the TIs. This was an extremely concentrated attack, with very little opposition. We dropped a 4,000lb Cookie and incendiaries. It was a difficult op. The Dresden raid had two unusual features for me. There was a very strong westerly wind of 70–80 kts, blowing at 20,000ft. Outbound it was a tailwind and we got to the target in just under three hours. Coming back, it was a headwind and the return journey took seven hours. We were in the air for ten hours twenty minutes – by far our longest trip. My own aircraft had a brake pressure problem when we started up and the ground crew could not fix it. So, at the last minute, we had to change to the reserve aircraft. This was ready to go but it was a very "tired" Lancaster. I had to flog the engines to get it up to the required height and it did not fly well – possibly a twisted airframe. Its fuel consumption was higher than usual and I had to nurse it back to the UK.

'We considered landing at an airfield in France but, with care and luck, we could just make Manston, the emergency airfield near Ramsgate in Kent. To conserve fuel in one tank for the circuit and possible overshoot, I had to run the other tanks dry, waiting until the fuel pressure warning lights came on before switching to another tank. We landed at Manston as dawn was breaking, with about fifteen minutes of fuel left. We joined forty or fifty other Lancasters and Mosquitoes that had also flopped into Manston short of fuel.'[31]

The pilots bombing Dresden that night included 153 Squadron's Bruce Potter. His crew employed unconventional defensive measures on their return. Bill Thomas was Potter's bomb aimer: 'We were flying against a headwind and making very slow progress. As we neared a turning point, I could see a searchlight dead ahead – probably a rendezvous for fighters. I went to get the empty beer bottles taken from Scampton's mess. I disconnected the bombsight – we didn't want any photos – and asked for the bomb doors to be opened. We dropped the bottles, which were supposed to scream on the way down and shake up the Germans on the ground. Some people reckoned they interfered with radar. Anyway, a moment later the searchlight went out. There had been plenty of fireworks at Dresden. The colours of the flares and explosions were fantastic. We were early and began to fly a few dog-legs, to meet our "Time Over Target", but then heard the master bomber say: "Don't worry. It's well lit. Come on in."'[32]

The first wave had a Time Over Target of 22.15, with the sports stadium as the aiming point. They crossed the city in fifteen minutes. The second wave was twice the size of the first and passed over the city in twenty-five minutes. The second wave crews gazed down on a city engulfed in flame, with huge fires swallowing the markers. The master bomber called the main force: 'No markers. Bomb visually.' As the bombers flew across Dresden, they ran into severe turbulence from the firestorm below.[33]

Twenty-six Lancasters of 550 Squadron took off for Dresden. One came to grief almost immediately: Flight Lieutenant E.S. Allen, in NF932 'B2', had just set course for Germany when his aircraft collided with another from 300 Squadron. There were no survivors. The *Operations Record Book* noted that the weather en route to Dresden was better than forecast. As the long flight entered its final phase, the target became visible from a distance of 180 miles as a dull red glow. The bombing run was clear: 'Photographs show an encouraging quantity of fire and incendiary glow ...'

Dresden, the old capital of Saxony, had been left virtually unscathed until the night of 13 February 1945. Regarding Dresden as a 'secondary target', thirty American bombers had attacked in early October 1944, killing 435 people. On 16 January 1945, 133 B.24 bombers struck, killing 376 civilians.[34]

The catastrophic raid on 13 February was delivered by 796 Lancasters and 9 Mosquitoes. They dropped 1,478 tons of high explosives and 1,182 tons of incendiaries. The first wave aircraft were hampered by cloud cover. The second wave bombed accurately in clear conditions. The result was a Hamburg-type firestorm killing over 40,000. The actual death toll has never been resolved and remains, to this day, the subject of dispute.[35]

During the following day, Wednesday, 14 February, 311 American Fortresses dropped 771 tons of bombs on the burning city, with the rail yards as the aiming point. Mustang escort fighters strafed roads around Dresden, to add to the chaos. The Americans returned the following day and again on 2 March.[35] In this last raid, 406 American aircraft bombed the ruins.

It is a wonder that anyone lived through the cataclysmic Dresden raid. By mid-February the city's population had grown to over a million, swollen by refugees from the east and evacuees from heavily bombed western cities. There were large numbers of military personnel and over 20,000 prisoners of war, conscripted workers from the occupied countries and concentration camp slave labourers.[36]

Victor Gregg, a British prisoner of war, was in Dresden on 13 February 1945. Later, he wrote: 'Dresden, to me, is remembered more as an event than a city, an event that scarred and destroyed my mind and my ability to live like a normal human being for the following forty years.'[37]

Gregg had been held at a work camp in a southern suburb of Dresden. He went out on road-sweeping work gangs and took the opportunity to admire the city's architectural beauty. The guards were easy-going and there were even occasional visits to local beer halls. Yet Gregg was not as he seemed. He was determined to escape and made two attempts in two months. There were no more beer halls for him; he was sent for hard labour in a soap factory. He joined forces with another rebellious spirit, and when they managed to burn down the place they were charged with sabotage and sentenced to death. 'To prepare for this we were both locked up, with many others, in a large red brick building that stood in the dead centre of the Altstadt. Six hours after we entered the building we found ourselves in the centre of the aiming point ...'[37]

The hall was crammed with over 200 prisoners. When the raid warning sounded no-one paid any attention until Target Indicators began to fall. They were seen through a glass pergola. What Victor Gregg experienced that night shaped his view of the raid, which he describes as 'one of the worst instances of mass genocide that life on a supposedly civilized planet had yet experienced'. He added: 'It is not my wish to elaborate further on the cruelties that ensued but I can stress it was a night's work of the very devil himself. I have described it all, in some detail, in my earlier writings, how I heard the screaming of the unlucky victims who had jumped into smooth-sided water vats to escape the overwhelming heat, only to die by being literally boiled to death (because it turned out to be impossible to climb out of the huge concrete vats), and how I saw women, holding their children, stuck in the middle of a road of bubbling tar who then, without warning, burst into flames.'[37]

Naturally, some victims of Nazi bestiality took a quite different view. Jack Myers, another British prisoner, had been locked up for five days without food in a cattle truck in Dresden's sidings. He was marched through the still burning city: 'that is one of the happiest memories that I have of three years' captivity by one of the nastiest and most poisonous nations ever to seek to rule the world'.[38]

There was also 15-year-old Ben Halfgott, held in a nearby camp. He saw the vivid red glow of the burning city: 'it was like heaven to us. We knew the end of the war must be near and our salvation was at hand. When the Russians arrived I weighed 50 kilos and you could see all my bones.'[38]

There is also the account of a Jewish woman held as a 15-year-old slave labourer south-west of Dresden in February 1945. She survived the concentration camps of Westerbork, in The Netherlands, Theresienstadt and Auschwitz. Her story was published in a Dutch newspaper in 1985. She was referred to as 'Mrs L', having demanded anonymity to protect herself from anti-Semitic phone calls or worse. A translation was made by John Carson, a navigator with 550 Squadron in February 1945, who later went to live in The Netherlands.[39]

This article gives Mrs L's answer to the question as to whether or not the bombing of Dresden was justified. It describes a 'normal' morning: 'Your emaciated body aches from lying on the wooden plank you share with another unfortunate. The top one of three, the "bed" is too narrow and you dare not move for fear of falling out. In the ice-cold barrack you suffer the pangs of hunger. Then the daily yells start ... "Get up! Get up, swine! Faster! Faster!" With difficulty you tie the strips of wood, your "shoes", to your feet and rush outside. It is pitch dark and the snow is falling. With feet and legs bare you shiver in your striped rags as the biting wind cuts through you. The march in the snow begins. In rows of five, thousands of women are marched along the road and through the town. Daylight breaks and we are overtaken by a few cars and many bicycles. Pedestrians approach and pass us and from behind curtains and from the pavements people see us being marched. They see us being marched twice a day, an hour and a half to our work and an hour and a half back to the barrack. They see us month in, month out, and later these people were to say, "We did not know."

'Fourteen hours a day we worked in a factory, starving and frequently beaten and thrashed with SS uniform belts. The work was back-breaking. The weaker we became the more difficult it was for us to control the drills and other tools we had to use, but we dared make no mistakes in the work allotted us; to do so would be regarded as sabotage and would mean being returned to the dreaded Auschwitz. To add to our tribulations was the humiliation heaped upon us, the threats and beatings carried out by German workers and members of the SS. Almost all of them came from Dresden.

'Much has been said and written about the destruction of Dresden. The area supposedly contained no military objectives. Frequently, television has shown Dresden burning after the attacks. Many have reacted with dismay and incomprehension: "How in heaven's name could the Allies do such a thing?" They have said: "It was a crime!" They have sympathized with the poor Germans of Dresden and mourned the loss of so many beautiful buildings and so many dead. Of course, there must have been innocent Dresdeners but we never made their acquaintance.' They did come into contact, however, with Jewish slaves working in an aircraft factory in the area.[39]

Those attempting to weigh the arguments for and against the Dresden raid must project their minds into the circumstances of early 1945, when no-one could be sure how long the war would continue and many still hoped that overwhelming bombing would force Germany to surrender and so shorten the war. Only a few weeks before, the Germans had surprised the Allies with a powerful armoured thrust aimed at Antwerp. This failed to achieve its goals but caused great alarm among political leaders and military commanders. What else did the Germans have up their sleeve? The enemy still talked about the 'wonder weapons' to come. Did these include nerve gases, radiological weapons or, even, an atomic bomb? We now know the truth, but that was not so in January and February 1945. Meanwhile, many thousands of innocent victims continued to die each day in the German camps. The Allies also faced an implacable enemy in the Asia–Pacific theatre. The attack on Dresden and other eastern cities has as its context a compelling need to secure victory in Europe as quickly as possible.

Neillands points out that Dresden was far from a non-military target: 'The city contained the Zeiss-Ikon optical factory and the Siemens glass factory and the immediate suburbs contained factories manufacturing radar and electronic components and fuses for anti-aircraft shells.' Around 10,000 people were engaged in war production. The grounds for attacking Dresden were as good as the grounds for attacking other German cities.[40]

Neillands argues that the Dresden controversy stemmed from myths surrounding its destruction – including the claim that it was Harris' decision and the belief that it was carried out by Bomber Command alone, with no reference to American participation. Another reason relates to the sheer extent of the loss of life, 'mainly because it seems pointless to have shattered Dresden at this stage in the war. This last is a valid point, but one that can be easily answered. The main reason for the attack in 1945 was that Dresden was a transportation target and this type of target had been under attack for months by all the Allied air forces. In January and February 1945 it was a major transportation centre and reinforcements and supplies for the Eastern Front and a large quantity of wounded men and refugees heading for the elusive safety of the West all flowed through it.

'In February 1945, therefore, Dresden was jammed with soldiers heading east to bolster the defences of the Reich against the Red Army and with tens of thousands of people fleeing west before the rape and murder that accompanied the advance of the Soviet armies into Silesia, the province to the east of Saxony. The advance had begun on January 12, 1945. A month later, many of the refugees had made their way to Dresden and the situation on the Eastern Front was critical and it was the presence of so many refugees that added so much to the death toll.'[40] Goebbels claimed 200,000 were killed in a deliberate massacre of refugees, and after the war this number was often quoted by commentators.

Large numbers of troops and prisoners of war were drafted in to recover Dresden's dead. SS men from Treblinka arrived to supervise familiar work – the burning of bodies. They arranged for street cremations at staggered times, to avoid blanketing the ruins in the smoke and stink of pyres.[41]

The reality behind the Dresden raid is that the city had long been a large military hub and, on its periphery, an important centre for optics and precision engineering. The city's *1942 Yearbook* described Dresden as 'one of the foremost industrial locations of the Reich'. The city's Chamber of Commerce declared: 'the work rhythm of Dresden is determined by the needs of our army'. Dresden was a designated defensive strongpoint but the main reason for its destruction was not war production, nor its defensive role, but, rather, its key position in the eastern rail network. Nearly thirty military transports daily passed through Dresden, bringing in reinforcements and armour to oppose the Red Army.[41] Here, Dr Alan Russell, president of The Dresden Trust, reflects: 'It was, therefore, somewhat surprising that Bomber Command's target plan focused more on the historic city centre than on the rail network. This was seriously damaged but the freight yards were only lightly touched and the lines to the east were running only a few days later.'

A couple of days after Dresden's destruction, an air commodore – an intelligence officer attached to SHAEF (Supreme Headquarters, Allied Expeditionary Forces) – handed the Germans a propaganda gift of immense proportions. While briefing the press on the new Allied bombing strategy, which was aimed at accelerating the German collapse, he made the major error of referring to German claims of 'terror raids'. An AP correspondent filed a story to American newspapers: 'Allied Air Chiefs have made the long-awaited decision to adopt deliberate terror bombing of German population centres as a ruthless expedient of hastening Hitler's doom. More raids such as those recently carried out on residential sectors of Berlin, Dresden, Chemnitz and Cottbus are in store for the Germans.' As might be expected, this caused a public storm.[42] Ever since, the Dresden raid has been interpreted, reinterpreted and misinterpreted by commentators of all persuasions and nationalities.

Far to the west, Pforzheimers aware of the Dresden catastrophe must have drawn parallels with their own city. It was still relatively intact. It was a centre for precision work. Its rail facilities had already attracted the attentions of American bombers. In the three days after Dresden, as if emphasizing the point, fighter–bombers made fresh attacks on railway targets in and around Pforzheim.[43]

During the afternoon of 19 February bombs fell at Durlacher Strasse level crossing, in Ispringer and Tunnelstrasse, Anshelm Strasse and Hohenzollernstrasse. The bombs damaged gas mains. The biggest challenge, however, was to repair the railway. Special emergency gangs were formed from military and defence reserves, together with Training Battalion 5. As this rail workforce expanded, it outgrew accommodation at Buckenberg Barracks. Schools and public buildings were taken over to house them.[43]

Meanwhile, as the catastrophic final city raids began to unfold, many senior Nazis still found time to address unfinished business relating to the 'Jewish problem'. Banker Adolf Katz had personal concerns here. There were no longer 'privileged Jews' in Pforzheim and his wife, Ruth, fell under the Nazi race laws. On 18 February 1945, he wrote in his diary: 'All Jews from mixed marriages were deported today. Anni Herrmann was taken away last week.' Anni Herrmann, a family friend from Karlsruhe, survived Theresienstadt. The sculptor Greta Budde also survived. She was responsible for the bust of Katz now in Pforzheim's town hall.[44]

Adolf Katz fell ill again in mid-February, having only just recovered from pneumonia. He went down with stomach cramps, diarrhoea and vomiting. Ruth gave him a morphine injection and he settled down, but constant anxiety was taking its toll. He had the consolation of knowing that at least some members of his family were out of harm's way, but there was now another challenge on the domestic front. On 1 February, Robert, Ruth's son from an earlier marriage, arrived home from flak service. He had two weeks' leave before beginning labour service. Stepfather and stepson didn't get on. Robert moved in with a friend after a few days, but was soon back when that arrangement didn't work out.[45]

In February 1945 a shortage of crews forced Bomber Command to increase first tours from thirty to thirty-six operations. According to Wing Commander Jack Harris, OBE, DFC, this was not the result of battle casualties but, rather, an earlier and over-optimistic forecast of the war's end: 'The crew shortage arose because long-range plans were based on the war ending in December 1944; flying training units began to close in the summer of 1944. The prolongation of the war until May 1945 found them short of crews.'[46]

The bombing of the eastern cities continued. Chemnitz was next on the list and it was raided on Wednesday, 14 February 1945. The 550 Squadron pilots flying that night included Eddie Edlund, whose aircraft joined 498 other Lancasters and 218 Halifaxes. Once again, the bombers attacked in two waves. They found the target obscured and bombed sky markers; many loads fell in open countryside. Eight

Lancasters and five Halifaxes were lost.[47] Edlund's flight engineer, Sam Lipfriend, confirmed the difficult conditions. In his diary he wrote: 'Same as Dresden but target obscured by 10/10 cloud.' He added the words: 'Good target glow.'[48]

North Killingholme sent twenty-two Lancasters to Chemnitz, described in the *Operations Record Book* as 'the Bradford of Germany'. Its important rail junctions were used by transports reinforcing the Eastern Front. The weather deteriorated on the way out and the target was cloud-covered, with tops up to 18,000ft. The markers could not be seen at times and crews were told to bomb on navigational aids. 'The consensus of opinion seemed to be that the attack was rather scattered.' All squadron aircraft returned safely.

Some people on the ground welcomed the bombing of Chemnitz, including Dutch woman Elka Schrijver, confined to a compound near the town housing some 4,000 political prisoners. The men had been told to dig a large pit for a 'reservoir'. In reality, they were digging their own mass grave – the Nazi authorities in Dresden had ordered their execution. After Dresden and Chemnitz these executions were cancelled.[49]

Dave Davidson's crew were tired. Still exhausted from the long haul to Dresden, they had been told to get ready for Chemnitz. They were in the air for eight hours thirty-five minutes. On returning, they were grateful for several days of bad weather. Davidson's name did not appear on the battle order again until Tuesday, 20 February: they were required for Bomber Command's last major attack on Dortmund. The

Good luck! 'Press on regardless' is waved off for the hundredth operational sortie. *Photo: Bob Stone.*

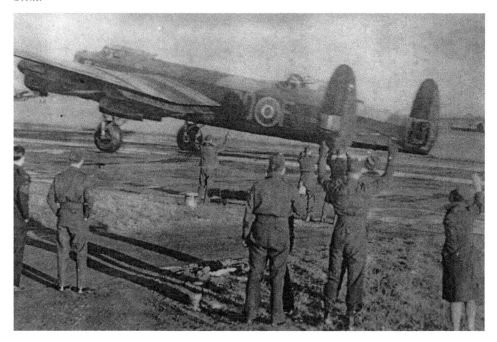

main force consisted of 514 heavy bombers; the target was the southern area of the city. Fourteen Lancasters were lost.[50] Ron Germain, Buzz Burrows' wireless operator, once again summed up an operation with one word: 'Blitz'.[51]

Twenty-seven aircraft left North Killingholme for Dortmund on a night full of engine problems for several of the Lancasters. The raid began in good weather, but Dortmund was hidden by cloud and the bombing was scattered.

On Wednesday, 21 February Bomber Command made its final raid on Duisburg. The 550 Squadron pilots operating that night included Dave Davidson, Buzz Burrows and Eddie Edlund. This was a successful raid by 362 Lancasters; seven were lost and three crashed behind Allied lines.[52] Layer cloud obscured the target. The flak was light to moderate but there were plenty of fighters around. Sam Lipfriend, Edlund's flight engineer, saw the night pierced by night fighter tracer: 'OK till over the German front line. Fighters galore. Saw six shot down. Very dicey.' At one point Lipfriend caught a glimpse of a Ju88 in the reflected glare of the aircraft it had just shot down.[53]

Twenty-four Lancasters left North Killingholme for Duisburg. The losses that night included 550 Squadron's NN715 ('A'), flown by Flight Lieutenant D.E.A. Luger. Wing Commander 'Dingle' Bell, the squadron commander, was flying with Luger. The navigator and mid-upper gunner died; the others became prisoners. Luger died shortly after his return to Britain in May 1945. The *Operations Record Book* commented: 'Everyone will be sorry to lose Wing Commander Bell, whose cheerful, forceful personality has been an inspiration to all members of the squadron and Killingholme generally.' One squadron aircraft, flown by Flying Officer Smith, reported a combat with a jet and claimed 'a suspected Me262 probably destroyed'.

Dave Davidson and crew went on leave after Duisburg. Wireless operator Howell Evans was in a cheerful mood: 'When I arrived home I told my parents my war would be over in no time at all. I had only another two to do. When I got back to North Killingholme, however, I was told the tour had been extended to thirty-six ops. I was devastated! We'd had some sticky moments and everyone was looking forward to the finish. In recent weeks we found we could laugh at almost anything. When a flak shell passed between the mid-upper gunner's legs, touching his nose on its way through the perspex roof, he recovered from the shock by laughing. We all joined in, on the intercom. Yet, it was impossible to laugh at the prospect of doing an extra six trips.'[54]

There were big smiles on the faces of Jack Harris and crew. Duisburg was their last op: 'We slapped each other on the back. There was a general feeling of euphoria. We were a mixed crew and there were celebrations in the officers' mess and sergeants' mess. We also went out as a crew to the Black Bull, at the nearby village of East Halton, for some serious drinking.'[55]

Adolf Katz tried to sleep, but the night of 21 February was full of air-raid alarms. To cap everything, the Pforzheim Volkssturm was ordered to turn out, to repel an expected landing by parachute troops on the Kieselbronn Heights. In his diary, the banker noted that 1,200 Volkssturm gathered but were unarmed. Pforzheim's citizens were fearful: 'The people are very frightened and are almost constantly sitting in the cellars and tunnels. There is something unworthy, cowardly about this crawling away to hide oneself with every alarm ...' Katz changed his habits. Now he took shelter only if bombs were falling or aircraft were confirmed heading for Pforzheim.[56]

On 12 February 1945, 13-year-old Bernhard Mauderer was busy with his last transport of child evacuees from Pforzheim. In January he became a Hitler Youth escort guard for the children: 'I carried out five transports. At Dillweissenstein station the trains were waiting, all steam. Children between 9 and 12 were taken to hotels in Titisee or Steinen. During the day the trains could move only when it was snowing or there was heavy cloud. Otherwise, we had to wait in the tunnels on account of the air raids. Our train had front- and rear-mounted anti-aircraft guns. We were attacked twice. All children and passengers had to leave the train and lie down in the fields until the bombers went. There was much panic and children cried for their parents. Two were injured.

'The children slept in dormitories in the hotels. The teachers were pensioners. My last transport was to the convalescent home at Neuenweg. The train went as far as Todtnau and, from there, it was on foot through snow and cold, about 12km. We found the home which had taken us in was full of children from Lörrach. We had to go to the hiking hostel 600 metres away. Meals and lessons were organized at the convalescent home. We were up at 6.00am daily – first the exercises, then a wash in snow. In the afternoon we trained in arms and discipline.'[57]

Bernhard Mauderer understood hardship and loss. He grew up in Wilhelmshöhe at Schulze-Delitzsch Strasse 4. His parents, Karoline and Otto, had five children. Otto had a hairdressing salon in Bergstrasse. Bernhard's father was called up in 1940; his mother kept busy looking after the family: 'Nothing got my mother down. She was up at 6.00am until late evening – always busy washing, ironing, cooking, sock-darning and mending clothes. My father was in the Air Force and served at Stalingrad. His toes became frostbitten and that was the end of his flying. He retrained in anti-aircraft defence and was posted to northern France. He returned with his battery to Merzig in Saarland, where his unit took a direct hit on 19 November 1944. They were all killed.'[57]

Notes

1. National Archives: AIR 40/1269.
2. Saward, D. (1985), *Victory Denied*, 349–52.
3. Administration's Report and Statistics for the Town of Pforzheim, 1945–52: City Life 1939–45.
4. National Archives: AIR 14/3684.
5. Administration's Report and Statistics for the Town of Pforzheim, 1945–52: City Life 1939–45.
6. Middlebrook, M. and Everitt, C. (1990), *The Bomber Command War Diaries*, 657.
7. Interview with Ron Germain, April 2013.
8. Interview with Dave Davidson, April 2013.
9. Interview with Ron Germain, April 2013.
10. Middlebrook, M. and Everitt, C. (1990), *The Bomber Command War Diaries*, 658.

11. Interview with Jack Harris, April 2013.
12. Interview with Ron Germain, April 2013.
13. Interview with Jack Harris, April 2013.
14. Middlebrook, M. and Everitt, C. (1990), *The Bomber Command War Diaries*, 659.
15. Interview with Bill Thomas, June 2013.
16. Document from Stephan Paetzold.
17. Horrocks, Sir Brian (1979) *Corps Commander*, 158–9.
18. Interview with Ron Germain, April 2013.
19. Interview with Sam Lipfriend, March 2013.
20. Middlebrook, M. and Everitt, C. (1990), *The Bomber Command War Diaries*, 661.
21. Interview with Sam Lipfriend, March 2013.
22. Interview with Dave Davidson, April 2013.
23. Interview with Jack Harris, April 2013.
24. Middlebrook, M. and Everitt, C. (1990), *The Bomber Command War Diaries*, 661.
25. Interview with Sam Lipfriend, March 2013.
26. Harris, Air Marshal Sir Arthur, *Bomber Offensive*, 242–3.
27. Interview with Ron Germain, April 2013.
28. Interview with Sam Lipfriend, March 2013.
29. Interview with Dave Davidson, April 2013.
30. Interview with Howell Evans, June 2013.
31. Interview with Jack Harris, April 2013.
32. Interview with Bill Thomas, June 2013.
33. Nichol, J. and Rennell, T. (2004), *Tail-End Charlies*, 300–1.
34. Neillands, R. (2002), *The Bomber War*, 352.
35. Middlebrook, M. and Everitt, C. (1990), *The Bomber Command War Diaries*, 663–4.
36. Neillands, R. (2002), *The Bomber War*, 365.
37. Gregg, V., *The Man who Survived in the Middle of a Firestorm*, via Dr Alan Russell, The Dresden Trust.
38. Nichol, J. and Rennell, T. (2004), *Tail-End Charlies*, 321.
39. Article in the Dutch newspaper *Het Parool*, 4 May 1985; translation by John Carson, via Wing Commander Jack Harris, OBE, DFC.
40. Neillands, R. (2002), *The Bomber War*, 352–4.
41. Nichol, J. and Rennell, T. (2004), *Tail-End Charlies*, 313–14.
42. Neillands, R. (2002), *The Bomber War*, 367–8.
43. Administration's Report and Statistics for the Town of Pforzheim, 1945–52: City Life 1939–45.
44. Pross, M. (1995), *Die Einschläge kommen näher, Aus den Tagebüchern 1943–45 von Friedrich Adolf Katz, 1945–1947 Oberbürgermeister der Stadt Pforzheim*.
45. Interview with Marianne Pross, September 2013.
46. Newsletter 39, 25 January 2008, 550 Squadron and RAF North Killingholme Association.
47. Middlebrook, M. and Everitt, C. (1990), *The Bomber Command War Diaries*, 664.
48. Interview with Sam Lipfriend, March 2013.
49. Nichol, J. and Rennell, T. (2004), *Tail-End Charlies*, 321.
50. Middlebrook, M. and Everitt, C. (1990), *The Bomber Command War Diaries*, 666.
51. Interview with Ron Germain, April 2013.
52. Middlebrook, M. and Everitt, C. (1990), *The Bomber Command War Diaries*, 667.
53. Interview with Sam Lipfriend, March 2013.
54. Interview with Howell Evans, June 2013.
55. Interview with Jack Harris, April 2013.
56. Pross, M. (1995), *Die Einschläge kommen näher, Aus den Tagebüchern 1943–45 von Friedrich Adolf Katz, 1945–1947 Oberbürgermeister der Stadt Pforzheim*.
57. Mauderer, Bernhard, personal memoir: *My Life, With Highs and Lows*.

Chapter Eight

'Goldstadt'

Pforzheim prospered in the late nineteenth century. Entrepreneurs made fortunes in the jewellery business and built fine mansions, but this deeply conservative community suffered a near fatal blow in 1930. The economic slump threw thousands of skilled men out of work. People were angry and deeply disturbed by this change in fortune, and they warmed to radical solutions. Middle-class Pforzheimers quickly showed their liking for Hitler's NSDAP.

Former Stadtarchiv Pforzheim director Christian Groh: 'Baden had liberal traditions, but Pforzheim was always a centre of conservative politics. It was receptive to National Socialism years before the Nazis took power in 1933.'[1] In the March 1933 election the National Socialists won 43.9 per cent of the vote nationally, but 57.5 per cent in Pforzheim – a city 'browner' than most.

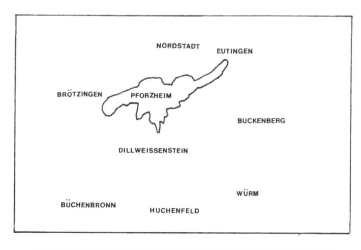

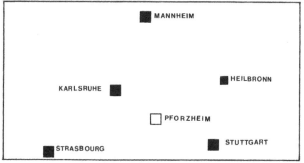

Top: Pforzheim and its outlying districts. Above: Pforzheim in relation to other cities. *Maps: Tony Redding.*

Pogrom: SA men guard the entrance to the Jewish-owned photographers Rodelsheimer. Signs warned: 'Everybody who still buys from Jews today is a scoundrel and traitor to our people.' This shop was the scene of a courageous protest by the owner. *Photo: Stadtarchiv Pforzheim.*

The Nazis began by organizing small-scale street marches. When Hitler became chancellor, however, Pforzheim's SA celebrated with a big torchlight parade. Those opposing Hitler and the Nazis were sidelined. Soon they would be oppressed. Hitler cemented his hold on power and Pforzheim's public buildings were draped in swastika banners. Hard-line Nazi Robert Wagner became Baden's Gauleiter. He took up residence in Karlsruhe and opened his reign in style, with a parade of 3,000 SA and SS men. When the initial celebrations were over, the purge began. Socialists and communists were arrested, left-wing newspapers were closed and penal camps were opened.[2]

Two of Pforzheim's newspapers (*Freie Presse* and *Pforzheimer Morgenblatt*) were shut. The mayor and left-wing councillors were pushed aside and two Jewish members of the Chamber of Commerce were told to resign. Wagner, a rabid anti-Semite, soon organized boycotts of Jewish shops. Street demonstrations took place outside Jewish homes and businesses. On the morning of 1 April 1933, SA men entered the Pforzheim department store Schocken and ordered shoppers out. They pasted large posters on the windows of the town's Jewish shops, proclaiming: 'Closed! Gone to Palestine'.[2]

Placards declared that people shopping in Jewish stores were 'traitors'. Wagner, meanwhile, began a tough crackdown on 'Jewish influence', attacking the incomes of Jewish professionals. The patients of Jewish doctors and dentists, for example, were refused reimbursement for prescription drugs.[2]

An enthusiastic crowd: Hitler parades through Pforzheim in September 1933. *Photo: Stadtarchiv Pforzheim.*

The Nazis recognized indoctrination of the young as a top priority. On Saturday, 17 June 1933, Hitler Youth members combed Pforzheim's libraries and bookshops for offending literature. That evening they set fire to a small mountain of books in the Marktplatz.[3]

Friends meeting in the street were now required to exchange the *Heil Hitler* greeting. Familiar Pforzheim street names changed: there was now an Adolf Hitler Avenue and a Goebbels School. The Führer cult reigned supreme in Pforzheim, as in every other German town. On 14 September 1933, Hitler made a personal appearance. His aircraft landed at Karlsruhe, and then, with Robert Wagner at his side, Hitler and his entourage drove through the Pfinz Valley towards Pforzheim. As they passed through the outlying villages, malcontents absent from the roadside became the subject of back-biting gossip.[4]

This was Hitler's second visit to Pforzheim. He had held a Party rally at the Saalbau back in 1928. His return, just a few months after the takeover in 1933, was connected with the misfortunes of Öschelbronn, a village just east of Pforzheim. Much of the village centre was destroyed by fire during the spring of 1933. The Nazis exploited Öschelbronn's reconstruction for propaganda purposes: it was portrayed as the rebuilding of a model Germanic agricultural community, with Hitler arriving to review the work.[5] In reality, the reconstruction still had a long way to go, but it gave Hitler a chance to play the concerned Father of the State.

Pforzheim was the home town of Fritz Todt, the future builder of the Atlantic Wall and Europe's most prolific consumer of concrete. He received the Freedom of the City. Christian Groh: 'Todt is widely regarded as the man who gave Germany its autobahn network. In reality, plans for the autobahn were progressed during the Weimar years. The National Socialists built the network because they were not too fussy about private property rights.'[5]

As Christmas 1933 approached, the Nazis launched an offensive against the festival's Christian dimension. Bibles were altered to avoid offending Nazi sensitivities. The Deutsche Christen movement of National Socialists, active within the Protestant Church, advocated a revisionist view based on 'Christ the Aryan' – or 'heroic Jesus'. Meanwhile, young children in schools were shown photographs of the bodies of ethnic Germans, said to be the victims of persecution in Russia. Hatred of communism was now part of the school curriculum.[6]

Religion was a priority for Nazi intrusion. In *Wolfram* Giles Milton describes the life of the Aichele family in Eutingen, near Pforzheim. They were part of a small religious group that followed the philosophy of Rudolf Steiner. In November 1935 Head of Reich Security Reinhard Heydrich banned the Steiner movement, as it was 'linked to Freemasonry and the Jews'. Steiner's followers became enemies of the State.[7]

Nazi oppression was applied through the close supervision of daily life. The Blockleiter was responsible for watching over some fifty households. It was his job to identify homes lacking a portrait of Hitler and those families failing to display Nazi flags on holidays. Children now threatened each other with the taunt: 'You'd better be careful, or you'll go to Dachau!'[7] National Socialism's grip on youth tightened in late 1936, when membership of the Hitler Youth became compulsory. Families of good conscience, who found National Socialism repugnant, also found life increasingly dangerous in a society where non-participation in all things Nazi was, in itself, a crime.

In National Socialist Germany, teenage girls were encouraged to get pregnant in the national interest. Wolfram Aichele's 13-year-old sister, Gunhild, was sitting on a train when she overheard a disturbing conversation between three adolescent girls. One mentioned the reason for their trip – 'to give a child to the Führer'. These were teenage volunteers for Lebensborn, the Aryan breeding programme initiated in 1935.[8] Hannelore Schöttgen, a Pforzheim schoolgirl, was in the classroom when a National Socialist speaker arrived to give a talk on the joys of Lebensborn. There were no volunteers in her class.[9]

During 1944, as victory slipped away from Nazi Germany, many people became desperate for real news as opposed to Goebbels' propaganda. Young Hans Gerstung noticed his parents and friends were talking in whispers: 'I knew they were listening to the BBC. When I wasn't around, they put a blanket over their heads and listened in. They never admitted this. They knew our teachers and Jungvolk leaders had ordered us to report our own parents if we found them listening to the BBC.

Luftschutz: an RLB (Reichsluftschutzbund) group in Stuttgart. Hans Gerstung's mother is in the middle of the group (on the rail – seven down, third from left). *Photo: Hans Gerstung.*

'Gradually, as the war continued, everyone became more concerned. Nearby Stuttgart was heavily bombed but we got no news, just a brief comment on the radio. When Pforzheim was wiped out we rated only a few sentences from the announcer. The regime was afraid of damage to morale, but it was obvious to everyone that the war was going badly.'[10]

Hans Gerstung's mother joined the NSF (NS Frauenschaft – the National Socialist Women's League) and the RLB (Reichsluftschutzbund, the State Air Protection Corps). Both organizations helped people who had been bombed out: 'She joined after the first air raid on Pforzheim. Yet her main contribution to morale was school visiting. She was a popular children's entertainer, making kids laugh at the antics of her glove puppets. No politics there!'[10]

Later in life, Gerstung learned of his mother's efforts to keep him out of the hands of Nazi zealots: 'I found out what happened only recently, when I examined our family's de-Nazification file in the Karlsruhe archives. Apparently, the local Jungvolk leader repeatedly urged my parents to send me to Napola. These were National Socialist schools for the young elite. My father agreed but mother fought hard against it and won.'[10]

War edged closer to the Gerstung family: 'My uncle – my mother's brother – served in a mountain division in Russia. He had a leg amputated because of frostbite.' Hans Gerstung had no desire to be a soldier, but he was already a runner for Pforzheim's Luftschutz: 'My friends and I put on our "uniforms". We were allowed to carry knives and were issued with Luftschutz blue steel helmets, with the silver eagle's wing motif, and armbands with a white "M" (Messenger) on a blue background. Even better, we got military issue gasmasks, not those civilian gasmasks with a green hood and a big filter on the front. We felt very grown up.'[10]

As the European war entered its final six months, Raimund Frei remained a long way from Pforzheim: he was in a prison camp in the United States. He had volunteered for the Army and took part in Barbarossa, the invasion of Russia. Frei was lucky to leave Russia before winter arrived. He was flown out for emergency surgery for appendicitis: 'While at the hospital I gave blood for a comrade about to have both legs amputated. I then developed a dangerous fever and couldn't board the hospital train due to leave the following day. The senior doctor promised to put me on the next one but this was reserved for "seated wounded". I couldn't sit up! A friendly doctor then told me to pull myself together and walk onto that train. Once on board, no-one would care if I travelled sitting or lying on the floor. The train went to Warsaw. Eventually, I travelled on to Vienna and hospital. That was in November 1941. I transferred to Karlsruhe military hospital the following month.'[11]

On the way, Raimund Frei took the opportunity to visit his family: 'My parents told me a military hospital had been set up at Osterfeld School. I knew the daughter of a doctor at the Osterfeld hospital. He fixed it with Karlsruhe and I was transferred. This allowed me to spend Christmas 1941 with my parents. I also had the family around me on 9 January 1942, my twenty-first birthday.' Hospital patients were given leave for only part of the weekend and were required to return by Saturday evening. Raimund Frei's mother had a heart condition, aggravated by worry about her son: 'One weekend I spent the Saturday at home but Mother became very ill. She died that evening. I called the hospital, asking for a few days' extra leave, but the guard commander said he had heard that story many times. I was told to report back by 24.00. When I told my doctor, I got three days' off and the other man got a dressing down.'[11]

Shortly afterwards, Frei was released from hospital and returned to his old training unit in Karlsruhe, before redeployment for frontline service. He looked for something different and applied for the Afrika Korps, but this contravened divisional orders. Transfers to other units were forbidden – soldiers had to return to their original units upon recovery. His reward for volunteering was three days' custody. The past then came to his rescue. Earlier in the war, Hermann Göring, in his role as Reichforstmeister, urged all state forest administrators to identify forest rangers interested in colonial service. Frei applied and passed the tropical service medical. The battalion adjutant was Frei's former platoon leader: 'He encouraged me to use this medical certificate in a new application. Shortly afterwards, in March 1942, I transferred to an armoured unit at Böblingen, near Stuttgart. After retraining we were issued with tropical kit on 1 June 1942. We travelled to North Africa via Yugoslavia and Greece. At the very start of this long journey, when the train stopped at Karlsruhe, I discovered that we would also stop at Pforzheim. I asked a railway official to call my father and sister. We made a brief stop and they came to the train. This was the last time I saw them alive.'[11]

The troops travelled on. They flew to Crete and on to Derna. Raimund Frei joined the staff company of the First Abteilung of Panzer Regiment 8. They fought at El Alamein and during the long retreat that followed. The Afrika Korps was pushed into a pocket in Tunisia and surrounded during the second week of May 1943. Raimund Frei began a new life as a prisoner of the Americans.[11]

Raimund Frei may have longed for home, but Roger Riblet-Buchmann felt very differently about Pforzheim. He had spent several months in the town as a 15-year-old forced labourer and loathed the place. Despite his age, he was not the youngest among 700 deportees from two Vosges villages, La Bresse and Ventron, who were now working in Pforzheim's armaments factories. In a relative sense, they were lucky: other villagers were forced to join a convoy in Strasbourg that had Dachau as its destination. The deportations from villages in the Vosges were ordered by Berlin in the second week of November 1944, and La Bresse suffered complete destruction. The women and children were driven into the woods.[12]

Roger Riblet-Buchmann was one of around 100 deportees accommodated in Pforzheim's so-called Italian camp, built to house Italian prisoners when Italy switched sides. He had company in René Guigonnat, a friend from his village. Roger and René were sent to Schaub-Werken, which, among other things, produced U-boat

War factory: the Kollmar & Jourdan building now houses a museum. It was once a 'Category A' company administered by the Upper Rhine Armaments Inspectorate in Strasbourg. It specialized in producing fuses and timers. *Photo: Tony Redding.*

radio equipment. Roger's job was to screw radio condensers into their housings: 'We were in a hall with young girls and women, together with some men who had not been called up because of their age.' The French teenagers were seen by the women as a pair of scamps and the atmosphere was not unkind. The supervisors tolerated the two boys' poor timekeeping: 'We worked as little as possible and arranged our lives such that our compulsory stay in Germany was not too unpleasant.'[12]

However, the Italian camp's timber huts were very cold in the winter weather: 'The guards were mean with the coal supplies. One bucket per day was nowhere near enough. The easiest solution was to ask for extra coal rations. Depending on the mood, sometimes this worked. Sometimes we were able to fell a tree. Occasionally, on Sundays, we organized firewood patrols.'[12]

Foreign workers played an important role in the German economy and, hence, preparations for war, well before the conflict began. There was a shortfall of over a million workers before the attack on Poland, yet 375,000 foreign workers were already working in the Reich in 1938. The employment of foreigners was seen as a relatively minor and manageable evil. The labour shortage affected production and attempts to improve matters had mixed results. In the Pforzheim 'Labour Region', 3,000 people found new work in war production. In Weimar, however, 1,250 women were asked to volunteer; 600 turned up and 120 were prepared to take a job, but most subsequently found reasons to withdraw acceptance.[13]

With labour at such a premium, the Nazis employed 'sub-humans' from the East. Pools of Polish workers were organized by General Governor Hans Frank (who was from Karlsruhe). Teams went into Polish villages and towns at night, looking for people fit to work. Those attending any sort of public gathering – such as church congregations and cinema audiences – were at risk of becoming forced labourers. In the West, the German workforce was boosted by many thousands of 'volunteers' from the occupied countries. In October 1940 around 800,000 people were out of work in the Occupied Zone of France. By May 1942 some 180,000 Frenchmen were working in the German Reich. There was also Relève, a scheme under which Vichy traded workers for the German munitions factories for the return of French POWs.[13]

The number of POWs and foreign workers employed in the German Reich in 1941–2 jumped from 3 million to 4.2 million. When Pforzheimer Fritz Todt died in February 1942, Albert Speer took over as Minister for Armaments. He teamed up with Thüringen governor Fritz Sauckel to deliver a vastly improved war production effort, heavily reliant on conscripted and slave labour. Sauckel was sentenced to death at Nuremberg and executed in October 1946. Compulsory work became the norm in the occupied territories.[13]

The Germans failed to harness the millions of Russian POWs to relieve the labour shortage. Around 3.3 million of the 5.7 million Russian prisoners died or were killed in captivity; Russian civilians were drafted for work in Germany. These 'Eastern workers' were subject to a regime of special punishment. The use of foreign labour and POWs peaked in 1944. By May of that year the German war economy employed 7.1 million foreigners – representing around 20 per cent of the labour force. By September 1944 this had risen to 28 per cent. Around 50 per cent of the armaments workforce were foreigners. At Nuremberg, Sauckel said that 10 million foreign workers had been brought to Germany during the war.[13]

In the case of Pforzheim, according to Hans-Peter Becht's well-referenced overview, the city's war production was boosted from 1941 onwards by the use of forced labourers and POWs. A Pforzheim Labour Office report on this 'work contribution', prepared in June 1942, said there were 678 POWs working in war production in the Pforzheim area.[14] They were employed in clock movements manufacturing and by Dürrwächter Refiners, then specializing in communications engineering. The POWs also built the Russian camp in Brötzingen.[15]

The major switch of Pforzheim's industry to war production took place in the second half of 1941. By the following year, the city's clock, watch and jewellery manufacturers had moved almost completely to military production. Twelve Category A companies in Pforzheim were supervised by the Upper Rhine Armaments Inspectorate in Strasbourg. At least four of the companies – Kollmar & Jourdan, Rodi & Wienenberger, Gebr. Kuttroff and Fred. Wagner – were making S30 fuses, as were the Category C companies Andreas Daub and Friedrich Speidel. As the S30 programme expanded, Pforzheim's fuse manufacturers introduced night shifts, as from the New Year 1942/3. Factories making armaments and fulfilling other military orders sucked in thousands of workers from surrounding communities. In the first

Precision work: inspection under way at a Pforzheim war factory. *Photo: Stadtarchiv Pforzheim.*

quarter of 1942 there were 7,373 workers employed in Pforzheim's armaments industry and another 6,440 in the civil sector. As from 31 May 1942, the Pforzheim jewellery industry produced only for export. It was this that freed an additional 3,000 workers for local war production.[15]

One of Pforzheim's labour camps was at Ispringer Pfad 17, according to the *1943 Pforzheim Area Directory*. The telephone number was 7585. It occupied the sports field of the Workers' Free Gymnastics Sports Club, closed by the Nazis in 1933. In 1942 it had six barrack huts and an ablutions block, together with the former 'free gymnastics' hut (which most likely housed the camp administration). The number of inmates – probably French – would have been around 250. There was accommodation for 500, and this extra space was taken up in 1941 by several hundred ethnic Germans from Bessarabia, Volenia and Bulovina. Levels of occupancy fluctuated, but in 1944 the camp probably held some 400 people.[15]

Those with good reason for feeling bitter at Nazi compulsion and control included Germans as well as foreign forced labourers. Werner Schultz had just begun his watchmaker's apprenticeship at the family shop when his Jewish father was taken into custody: 'After ten days in prison, Father was sent to Dachau and, subsequently, to Buchenwald. Altogether, he spent nine months in concentration camps. He returned in early 1939. I asked him questions but he replied: "I won't tell you anything – otherwise I go back!" He wanted to emigrate, but it was impossible, as we had no relatives abroad.

War production: examples of Pforzheim's contribution. Left to right: a military watch, a fuse and an aircraft clock. *Photo: Tony Redding.*

'When Father returned, he rarely left the house, so he wouldn't have to wear the Star of David. In addition, the word "Israel" was supposed to be added to our door plate.'[16] Werner's father was still able to earn a living by repairing watches in his workshop. He also received work from companies he knew, among them a mail order house. 'Every year he had to apply to the authorities for a work permit, since he had become a stateless person.'[16] When Posen was taken from Germany at the end of the First World War, people who had family there could choose to be Polish or German. When the Nazis came to power, those who had chosen German nationality had their citizenship revoked. 'We became stateless. That's why father had to renew his work permit every year, even though he had been living in Germany since 1904. He had known what would eventually happen to the permit that allowed him to buy from Switzerland. Before his arrest, the amount he could purchase on that permit had been progressively reduced. When a Nazi got his hands on it, of course, the amount increased immediately. This Nazi opened a new company on the strength of it. When he opened a shop on Zähringer Allee, now Heinrich-Wieland Allee, I was required to go there to continue my apprenticeship. I trained as a *remonteur* – a factory watchmaker rather than a watchmaker in the fullest sense, which is what I had wished for and what would have happened had I been apprenticed in my father's shop. Father continued with his small workshop. One of his customers was a policeman. When father asked him whether he would have problems dealing with a Jew, he replied: "I don't care."'

Concentration: work under way at Rudolf Reiling. *Photo: Stadtarchiv Pforzheim.*

'I was very angry at the way my father was treated. He had a bad leg. That's why he became a watchmaker, rather than following in his father's footsteps as a timber merchant. When in prison father was examined by a doctor, who claimed he was malingering. Yet, for all his troubles, father was a partner in a mixed marriage and, as a result, stayed safe until January 1945, when he was sent to Theresienstadt.'[16]

Werner Schultz finished his apprenticeship at the Nazi's new workshop. As a *remonteur*, he focused on assembly rather than the full range of skills required of a watchmaker. He overcame this by working in his father's shop during the evening, learning the higher skills that were required to work beyond the scope of a *remonteur*.[16]

On 28 June 1944, a US Eighth Air Force Target Information Sheet identified Pforzheim as a transportation target: 'The target is the railway traffic centre at Pforzheim ... Pforzheim lies on the main Karlsruhe-Stuttgart line, but the economic importance of the target lies in the facilities it supplies for the transportation of goods produced in the town, which before the war was one of the centres of the German jewellery and watch-making trades and is, therefore, likely to have become of considerable importance in the production of precision instruments.'

The target was described as 'long and narrow, has its main axis east–west and is 3,000 yards long and only 300 yards across at its widest point. The outstanding features within the target area are the station in the centre, the goods depot at the eastern end and the two locomotive depots at the eastern and western ends respectively.' Vital elements within the target zone included the bridges. The target assessment concluded that most of Pforzheim's factories and workshops were manufacturing precision parts for instruments, small arms components, fuses, clockwork apparatus and similar fine engineering products. The industrial facilities identified included Allgemeine Gold & Silber Scheideanstalt and Heimerle & Meule KG, two of Pforzheim's largest gold and silver refiners. The two biggest factories in Pforzheim, Rodi & Wienenberger AG and Kollmar & Jourdan AG (both on Bleichstrasse), were named as key targets. Other named establishments included: Hohmann-Moser AG, Eugen Fessler, Moritz Hausch, Andreas Daub and Wilhelm Wolff AG. These factories were all thought to be engaged in the production of precision parts for instruments, aircraft and armaments, such as fuses. There were also several hundred smaller industrial facilities and workshops, making Pforzheim's urban area an economic and military target, as well as a communications target.

This had been the position for several years. In the month of June 1941, for example, when the invasion of Russia began, Pforzheim produced at least 150,000 S30 fuses. The production target was 300,000 fuses, suggesting either gross under-performance or over-ambitious forecasting. The Pforzheim factories formed a substantial part of the large Junghans Group. By the end of 1941 Junghans plants in Pforzheim and elsewhere were producing 570,000 fuses per month.[17]

Hard at it: busy workers at Rudolf Reiling. *Photo: Stadtarchiv Pforzheim.*

The Nazi who built his business on the back of Schultz senior's import permit soon prospered. Werner Schultz: 'In 1939 we made fuses for tracer rounds. We then began producing larger fuses, for anti-aircraft and panzer shells and torpedoes. Pforzheim was a hub of war production. It was Fritz Todt's home town and he wanted Pforzheim to develop as an outstanding war production centre. This led to local industry being criticized for failing to produce enough. Pforzheim's factories and workshops no longer produced jewellery.

'As war progressed we produced fuses for larger weapons. Huge volumes of fuses were produced in Pforzheim by watch factories and jewellery businesses. That's all they did after 1940. Anyone who says otherwise is a liar. I don't know if Pforzheim was the biggest centre for fuse production, but it was certainly a major one. Many people at our company were drafted. At one point there were only two regular watchmakers left, together with a Belgian forced labourer who was also a watchmaker. Many of the original staff were now working at Junghans' large production plant at Schramberg, in the Black Forest. This was the biggest watch factory in Germany before the war. Our small workforce eventually consisted of four retired watchmakers – for fuse assembly – and four wounded men conscripted from the nearby military hospital. We also had up to eight housewives, four French POWs and five or six Russian forced labourers, who lived in really terrible conditions. Later, they were joined by three actresses (who became available when the theatre closed) and three High School girls. At full stretch we had around thirty to thirty-five people in the workshop. It was one of the smallest of Pforzheim's war factories.

'The Belgian watchmaker and I were in charge of quality control. We turned out around 150 large fuses daily. The Belgian was killed in the big raid of 23 February 1945. A couple of weeks before that attack our production of large fuses was switched to a factory down town. We concentrated, once again, on small fuses. The factory that took our share of large fuse work was badly damaged in the bombing.'[18]

Given the obvious threat of a major air attack, why wasn't more done to strengthen the defences and protect the population? Christian Groh: 'There had been minor raids before the big attack of 23 February 1945. The railway station and buildings in the north of the city suffered damage. A few areas in the south-west of the city had also been hit. Yet Pforzheim had a rather lax attitude towards air-raid precautions, despite these warnings. In the early war years Pforzheim was thought to be too far away to be under serious threat from British bombers. By the time things changed, it was much harder to find resources to undertake large-scale shelter-building. There were few public shelters of any size in the city. The largest were in the basements of two schools. It was argued that most buildings had cellars. It was in these small shelters, however, that many thousands were to suffocate only weeks before the war's end.'[19]

On Wednesday, 21 February 1945, there were air combats over Pforzheim and a few bombs were dropped. Hans Ade, then 9 years old: 'One plane flew across the town and dropped bombs that mostly fell in the fields near Hagenschiess. One hit the house behind us and demolished it. The explosion was very powerful, so powerful that the surrounding houses moved. Our house, all four floors of it, moved towards the road by about 15cm. Our house and one close by were declared unsafe, but I noticed that the cellar beams were intact. We had to move out but had nowhere to go. My sister told her boss, Prof. Dr Eberhardt. He offered to let us have his unoccupied villa in Pforzheim, at Lameystrasse 61. This solved two problems. He had someone to look after the place, which had been standing empty, and we had somewhere to live. We

Precision components: wartime fuses and timers on display at Pforzheim's Museum. *Photo: Tony Redding.*

were more secure on the outskirts of Pforzheim. I liked it better: this cellar didn't need beams.' The Ade family moved in, taking with them only bare essentials.[20]

On Thursday, 22 February 1945 – the day before Bomber Command's overwhelming attack on Pforzheim – a photo reconnaissance aircraft flew over the doomed town and railyards. This mission was flown by the 12th (Prov.) Photo Recce Group, 1st US Tactical Air Force. The mission report reads: 'M/Y [marshalling yard] at R-718336 [Pforzheim] has 305 cars at E. end of yard and 5 live locos and 7 dead locos in the vicinity of the Roundhouse. Both turntable and roundhouse are serviceable and 6 main lines are clear at this point. Activity is observed. At W. end of yard (R-710332) are 230 cars mostly box type and passenger and almost all are intact. Main lines appear almost fully serviceable at this point. Damage to the yards is slight and the centre of impact is seen to be at R-720336 and N. and S. of the M/Y in the town area. About 40% of the facilities of the M/Y are U/S [unserviceable], mostly around the E. loading area and station buildings. There is considerable activity about the Roundhouse and several trains have recently arrived. Through lines have been repaired and none appear to be out at present.'[21]

On the balance of the evidence, it seems that Pforzheim, on this date, was a legitimate target for Allied aircraft.

Notes

1. Interview with Christian Groh, April 2013.
2. Milton, G. (2011), *Wolfram*, 40–3.
3. Ibid., 45–6.
4. Ibid, 48–51.
5. Interview with Christian Groh, April 2013.
6. Milton, G. (2011), *Wolfram*, 52–5.
7. Ibid., 65–71.
8. Ibid., 107–8.
9. Ibid., 109–10.
10. Interview with Hans Gerstung, April 2013.
11. Interview with Raimund Frei, July 2013.
12. Riblet-Buchmann, R. (1993), *Unerwartete Begegnung – Als junger 'Fremdarbeiter' in Pforzheim 1944/45.*
13. Becht, Hans-Peter (1993), 'Der Arbeitseinsatz von Kriegsgefangenen und ausländischen Zivilarbeitern, in Pforzheim 1940–1945 – Ein Rekonstruktionsversuch', in: Riblet-Buchmann, R., *Unerwartete Begegnung – Als junger 'Fremdarbeiter' in Pforzheim 1944/45.*
14. General State Archive, Karlsruhe – GLA -237/28813.
15. Becht, Hans-Peter (1993), 'Der Arbeitseinsatz von Kriegsgefangenen und ausländischen Zivilarbeitern, in Pforzheim 1940-1945 – Ein Rekonstruktionsversuch', in: Riblet-Buchmann, R., *Unerwartete Begegnung – Als junger 'Fremdarbeiter' in Pforzheim 1944/45.*
16. Interview with Werner Schultz, November 2013.
17. Behner, Udo R. (1995), *Die Katastrophe kam am 4408 Tag!*
18. Interview with Werner Schultz, November 2013.
19. Interview with Christian Groh, April 2013.
20. Interview with Hans Ade, November 2013.
21. National Archives, AIR 29/287.

Chapter Nine

Courage and Depravity

Pforzheim had a dark side, shaped by Nazi persecution and murder. There was also a bright side, illuminated by the bravery of those who resisted tyranny. Researcher Gerhard Brändle has assembled information on hundreds of victims and resisters who lived in Pforzheim and the surrounding area. They included Jews, communists, socialists and trade unionists, Jehovah's Witnesses, members of other religious groups and those murdered under the National Socialists' so-called 'euthanasia' programme.

There was a sizeable pre-war Jewish population in Baden but Pforzheim's Jewish community was relatively small. Nevertheless, late nineteenth-century Pforzheim society included a number of wealthy Jewish families. Several of the town's prominent doctors and lawyers were Jewish. Giles Milton comments: 'The overt anti-semitism so prevalent in other parts of Germany was less visible in Pforzheim. Although there were sometimes tensions between the two communities, Jews played an important role in local society and several leading members of the Chamber of Commerce were Jewish. The town's two principal department stores were also owned by Jews.' When a new synagogue opened in 1892, it occupied a site in the very heart of town. 'There were occasional unpleasant incidents. In 1922 a couple of the synagogue's windows were smashed and in 1926 some tombs in the Jewish cemetery were daubed with paint. Yet these were isolated cases. In Pforzheim, the Jews had nothing to fear.'[1]

Pforzheim's Jews, however, had plenty to fear with the coming of the Nazis. The 1930 NSDAP manifesto declared: 'Only those of German blood … may be members of the nation. Accordingly, no Jew may be a member of the nation.'[2]

On 1 April 1933, SA gangs stood at the doors of Pforzheim's Jewish stores, warning shoppers not to enter. Those ignoring this intimidation had their photographs taken. That same evening, the photographs would be shown at the town's cinemas, accompanied by abusive captions: 'This man is a slave to the Jews – he still shops there.' 'This lady shows no shame. She still buys her provisions in Jewish-run stores.'[3]

National Socialism, a self-inflicted wound, rapidly festered. In 1935 Werner Becker, a pastor's son, fell in love with Margot Bloch, the daughter of a local Jewish lawyer. The banns were published on 13 May of that year. A few days later Werner turned the page of a Berlin newspaper and read that a Nazi official in Pforzheim had issued the first rejection of an Aryan's attempt to marry a Jew. He was horrified to find that he and Margot were the couple involved. A Pforzheim newspaper ran the story under the headline '*Rassenschande*' (Race-shame) and Becker was described as an 'enemy of the state and a disgusting adversary of the Nazi Party'. More stories followed,

Terror on the streets: Pforzheim's synagogue after Pogromnacht. *Photo: Stadtarchiv Pforzheim.*

praising the official for banning the marriage. Becker and his fiancée did the sensible thing – they travelled to Switzerland and then on to Argentina.[4]

Many Jewish families concluded that they could no longer live in Pforzheim or, indeed, in Germany. Dr Weill, a successful Pforzheim lawyer, decided to emigrate. The Aichele family's Jewish friends were among those leaving to forge new lives. There was no room for tolerance in National Socialist Germany. One of the Aicheles' friends, Dr Schnurmann, was imprisoned for a short period after being caught reading a book of Hitler jokes he had bought in Basle. Gerhard Brändle adds: 'Dr Schnurmann had his health insurance approval revoked on 30 March 1933 and was sentenced to twelve months in prison on 18 March 1935 for *heimtückischer Angriff auf Partei und Staat* [perfidious attack on party and nation]. After being released from prison on 18 February 1936, he emigrated to Lisbon, Portugal, in October of that year.'

Aryans and Jews were forbidden to marry as the Reich Citizenship Law sought to safeguard 'racial purity'. Gauleiter Wagner jumped on the bandwagon. The Court of Appeal in Karlsruhe had the dubious distinction of being the first German court to grant a divorce on racial grounds. Wagner allowed State courts to ask 'racial experts' to pronounce on whether or not someone was Jewish. Their approach was often less than scientific. In one instance the Karlsruhe court declared a boy to be Jewish because 'he looks like a Jew'.[5]

Hatred blossomed on 9/10 November 1938, with the organized hounding, abuse, violence and destruction of Jewish property that became known as Kristallnacht (the night of broken glass). In today's Germany, however, it is known as Pogromnacht (Kristallnacht being regarded as a euphemistic and therefore unacceptable National Socialist term). In broad daylight, Pforzheim's Nazis wrecked the synagogue in the city centre. Twenty-three Jewish men in Pforzheim were arrested on spurious charges and sent to Dachau concentration camp.[6]

Some 7,000 of Baden's Jews had already left by 1938. Giles Milton: 'Of the 800 still living in Pforzheim, 231 now decided to pack their bags and flee.' Following

Pogromnacht, Pforzheim's remaining Jews were forced to leave their homes and move into 'Jewish houses'.[7]

Nazi laws required people to complete the *Stammbuch* – a record with the names, dates and religion of family members going back several generations. When they consulted birth certificates and other records, some Pforzheimers were shocked to learn that they had Jewish ancestry. Meanwhile, the Nazi bullies were free, quite literally, to get away with murder. There are two Eberstadts in Württemberg. In the Eberstadt around 50km from Pforzheim, local NSDAP bigwig Adolf Frey shot and killed an 81-year-old Jewish woman, Susanna Stern, when she refused to give up her home. This murder was the subject of a rare court case but the 26-year-old killer got away with it. The judge branded the old lady a 'boisterous troublemaker' who provoked the attack.[7]

Jewish Pforzheimers hoping to live successfully under the National Socialists soon came to regret their optimism. Former Stadtarchiv Pforzheim director Christian Groh: 'In cities throughout Germany Jewish people were removed over a period. It happened quite differently in Baden and, thus, in Pforzheim. On Tuesday 22 October 1940, 195 Jewish people were gathered up and transported. Baden Gauleiter Robert Wagner issued orders requiring Pforzheim police to collect Jewish residents for

Deported: 195 Jewish people were rounded up and assembled at this point on 22 October 1940 for transportation to Gurs Camp. This memorial is at Pforzheim's Freight Terminal. The names of the deported are recorded on stones, beginning to the right of the picture. *Photo: Tony Redding.*

transportation to the camp at Gurs, near Navarrenx, in southern France. It took the SA and police just one day. They visited every Jewish family and informed them that they had an hour or two to pack a few things. Later, from the summer of 1942, they were transported to concentration camps in Eastern Europe and most were killed.'[8]

Around a hundred doorbells were rung on the morning of 22 October 1940. One belonged to Dr Rudolf Kuppenheim, chief physician at Pforzheim Maternity Hospital. Dr Kuppenheim had a distinguished record of service in the First World War. In his professional capacity, he had overseen the birth of 19,000 babies over a forty-year period. He was not a practising Jew, having converted to Protestantism decades before. He was a parish councillor of his local church. Nevertheless, according to the Nazis, he was a *Geltungsjude* – someone who counted as a Jew. Two SA men told Kuppenheim and his wife that they were to be deported and that they had two hours to pack. Each Jew was allowed one suitcase, a blanket and a small amount of money (100 Reichsmark). When the SA men left, Dr Kuppenheim laid out his First World War medals on a pillow placed on a table. He and his wife, Lily, then took poison.[9] They both died in Pforzheim's Städtisches Krankenhaus the following day. Lily Kuppenheim (née Ehmann) was not Jewish. Her husband had converted to Protestantism in around 1900.

Gerhard Brändle has spent years researching what happened to Pforzheim's resisters and persecuted. He says: 'Other members of the Kuppenheim family got out in 1935 and 1936, emigrating to France and the USA. The two sons went to America. They tried to get their parents out but Dr Kuppenheim refused. He believed that his background – conversion, good war record and professional contribution to Pforzheim – would keep him safe as a totally assimilated individual. He didn't recognize the Nazi view that "a Jew is a Jew". There is a memorial to Dr Kuppenheim and his wife at the entrance to Siloah Hospital, Pforzheim.'

The rest of the Jewish deportees began their journey to Gurs camp, at the foot of the Pyrenees. Baden's other Jews were also deported. Conditions at Gurs were appalling – prisoners slept on straw and had little food. Around 1,200 people died of malnourishment and dysentery.

'Madeleine' was chained up in a cell in Pforzheim prison, on Rohrstrasse. Madeleine was the codename of British agent Noor Inayat Khan, GC, a French Section wireless operator with the Special Operations Executive. Noor's father, the founder of the Sufi Movement, was a descendant of the last Muslim ruler of southern India. Her mother was an American. Noor was a remarkable young woman – cultured, musical and the author of stories for children. She began training in February 1943 and left RAF Tangmere in a Lysander aircraft on the night of 16/17 June. She was bound for a field near Angers, in north-west France. The agents landed that night were met by a traitor, the double agent Henri Dericourt. Yet 'Nora', as she was known, reached Paris and began transmitting for the Resistance. When the Germans moved against the networks and mass arrests took place, Madeleine refused to return to London

The train to hell: many Jewish deportees died at Gurs Camp. Others survived but died later in the eastern camps. *Photo: Tony Redding.*

and carried on transmitting. Eventually, she was betrayed – 'sold' for 100,000 Francs. She was arrested and taken to Gestapo headquarters in Paris, at 84 Avenue Foch, for interrogation.

In November 1943 she joined an escape party but the attempt was unsuccessful. Noor Inayat Khan refused to promise to make no further escape attempts. She was then deported as a 'Night and Fog' prisoner, a category for individuals fated to 'disappear'. She arrived at Pforzheim prison on 27 November 1943. Prison governor Wilhelm Krauss later said that the local Gestapo took a close interest in her treatment – she was kept in solitary confinement, chained hand and foot and given the lowest of rations. Krauss claimed he took pity on her and removed the chains, but the Gestapo ordered him to replace them.

In January 1944 another prisoner, Yolande Lagrave (a member of the French resistance group Réseau Alliance), was held in a cell close by. She communicated with Nora by scratching messages on mess tins. Lagrave heard Nora's cries when she was beaten in her cell. She endured this treatment for many months, before being transferred to Dachau in September 1944. Later, she was killed in the most brutal circumstances.

Throughout Baden, young minds continued to be corrupted. There were no Jews left, except Jews in mixed marriages and the '*Mischlinge*' ('half-Jews' and 'quarter-

Tyranny: Pforzheim Prison, on Rohrstrasse. *Photo: Stadtarchiv Pforzheim.*

Jews'), yet anti–Semitism retained its prominence in the school curriculum. Civilized parents could do nothing to shield their children. Giles Milton describes pupil Frithjof Rodi's lesson on creation. The teacher explained that God fashioned Adam and Eve but had a lump of clay left over. His third figure was unsuccessful and its ugliness prompted God to throw it away. This made its nose crooked and its legs bandy. 'The teacher then told them how this crippled and misshapen creature slowly came alive and started to creep towards God. God was appalled and said to it: "Go to hell, you Jew!"'[10]

Réseau Alliance mobilized over 3,000 patriots prepared to risk everything to oppose the Germans in France. Its special forte was intelligence-gathering, from troop movements to the location of V-weapon launch sites. The Germans hunted its members with great vigour and many arrests followed. The captives were often segregated from other prisoners and required to wear distinctive clothing with yellow horizontal stripes on the back and thighs. The letters 'NN' meant they were for 'Night and Fog' treatment. They were subjected to the harshest regime. Only seventy of the original batch of 180 Réseau Alliance prisoners classified NN were still alive after one month in captivity.[11] During the night of 1/2 September 1944, 107 members of Réseau Alliance were executed and cremated at Natzweiler concentration camp in Alsace.[12]

During November 1944, with the end of the war in sight, another seventy members of Réseau Alliance (held in seven prisons throughout Baden) were executed by an SS death squad, in what became known as *Schwarzwälder Blutwoche* (Black Forest blood week). The killers were led by SS officer Julius Gehrum, of Strasbourg Gestapo. Gehrum and his 'helpers' began their tour of the prisons on 23 November 1944. They were acting under the orders of SS Sturmbannführer Dr Helmut Schlierbach, Head of Strasbourg Gestapo, and other senior SS officers.

On Thursday 30 November 1944, at 5.00am, the twenty-six Réseau Alliance prisoners in Pforzheim prison were awakened and told to pack and be ready to move. One, Yolande Lagrave, was then told that she would stay. The others, eight women and seventeen men, were loaded onto trucks. They were driven to Pforzheim's Hagenschiess Forest and ordered at gunpoint to a bomb crater east of the Tiefenbronnerstrasse, near the present-day site of a wildlife park. They were killed by shots to the neck by Gehrum and his assistants.[13]

A local doctor, Dr Monoff, later reported his findings following the exhumation of the twenty-five bodies. Eight showed evidence of torture, including broken ribs, a shattered jaw and torn eyes. Two prisoners made escape attempts. One received a bullet in the head; another was caught and beaten to death with rifle butts. His spine was broken in several places.[13]

Rosa Storck had trained as a nurse. When Belgium was invaded she and her husband escaped to southern France, where she worked as a stenographer for an Army officer. Subsequently, she became involved in Réseau Alliance, working as a courier, but was betrayed to the Gestapo by her employer – a double agent. Arrested on 12 August 1943, she was incarcerated in St Michel prison, Toulouse, then transferred to Montluc prison in Lyon. Later, she and other Alliance members were moved to Fresnes prison, Paris, before transportation to Pforzheim. She was among those killed on 30 November 1944, by Julius Gehrum and his squad of SS murderers.[14]

It is uncomfortable to pick out individual examples from the hundreds of resisters and victims in Pforzheim, as each is worthy of record. Gerhard Brändle has information on 154 individuals who actively opposed the Nazis. He also has information on 232 murdered Jews from Pforzheim. The individuals discussed below represent the persecuted and those who found the courage to resist. They include Wilhelm Künzler, a unionist and communist, who was imprisoned in Ludwigsburg. He represents at least fifty local

'Black Forest Blood Week': Rosa Storck was a member of Réseau Alliance. *Photo: via Gerhard Brändle.*

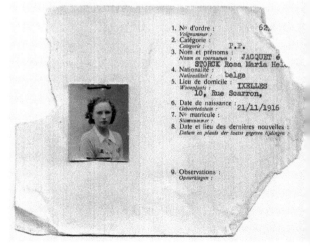

communists who engaged in active resistance and some twenty union members who worked against the worst excesses of the Nazis. Künzler came from a left-wing family. During the troubled period of 1929–30, he lost his job and was forced to accept '*Notstandsarbeiten*'. This was, in effect, forced labour in return for modest welfare support. In his own words, he was put to work 'building roads for the next war'. When Hitler came to power the KPD sent Künzler to Prague – one of many communists sent beyond Germany's borders to campaign against Nazi oppression.[14]

In October 1934 Künzler returned to Germany. He was arrested by the Gestapo on 26 January 1935, and tortured. On 2 August 1935, he was convicted by the People's Court in Berlin of 'conspiracy to commit high treason' and sentenced to twelve years. He spent his days making bags and basketry in Ludwigsburg prison, while awaiting the next letter from his wife. He was allowed one letter every six weeks. Ironically, his status as an 'ordinary prisoner' kept him safe. There were virtually no transfers of such inmates between prisons and concentration camps.[14]

The SAP (Sozialistische Arbeiterpartei Deutschlands), a small left-wing breakaway from the SPD (Sozialdemokratische Partei Deutschlands), was closely associated with resistance. Karl Schroth represents around twenty individuals from SAP resistance circles who were persecuted. Gerhard Brändle: 'Karl Schroth was a steel engraver who lived in Pforzheim. When the Nazis took power in 1933, SAP ran an underground press. They printed and distributed leaflets and the illegal publication *Beacon*, which warned against a war of aggression. They were also responsible for graffiti on walls. They helped the persecuted escape, usually to France or Switzerland. South German towns, including Stuttgart and Pforzheim, were waystations on the road to safety. The persecuted often made for Basle.'[14]

Schroth became known to the Nazis and was detained and interrogated in 1935. On 5 May 1938, he was arrested by the Gestapo and held in solitary at Pforzheim prison until March 1939. In September of that year he was sentenced by the People's Court to another term in prison. He had to join the work gangs draining marshland and breaking stones. Life brightened in the spring of 1940, on his release from Dieburg work camp. He married his fiancée, Clara, a few months later. Schroth was required to report daily to the Gestapo until May 1941, when he was drafted into the Wehrmacht. The invasion of Russia was imminent. The German Army needed more soldiers, and special 'penal battalions' were formed – sinkholes for criminals and those judged guilty of political offences. Schroth was fated to end up in custody yet again. He served in France and then in Italy, where he became a prisoner of the Americans in May 1944. He had the misfortune to be transferred to a French POW cage in the Algerian desert and by April 1945 was in a Saharan labour camp.[14]

Another SAP resister, Karl Otto Bührer, did not survive. He died in jail in Brandenburg, in unknown circumstances, on 27 December 1942. Bührer was a teacher and an SPD member. He joined SAP in 1931, as he supported its platform for an alliance between workers' parties and unions opposed to National Socialism. He was an active fundraiser, helping families leave Germany. Karl Bührer was arrested in

1935 but there was insufficient evidence to secure a conviction. He was arrested again in 1938, along with Schroth and others, and sentenced in 1939 to ten years for 'conspiracy to commit high treason'.[14]

Adolf Baier survived, despite being wounded three times in Spain while fighting with the International Brigade against Franco. Baier was a locksmith, a member of the Metalworkers' Union in Pforzheim and a communist prepared to put his life on the line. The Nazis were soon on his trail. He fled to France in July 1933, from where he organized the printing of anti-Nazi literature and helped organizations in Baden opposing the National Socialists. He went to fight in Spain in 1936 and, later, managed to escape to France. Subsequently, he operated in Sweden, organizing the sabotage of transports to Germany. He was caught by the Germans in 1941 and imprisoned for three and a half years. Gerhard Brändle adds: 'He lived, and his signature is on the first labour agreement in Pforzheim after twelve years of dictatorship.'[14]

Arrested, imprisoned, tortured: Wilhelm Künzler was convicted of 'conspiracy to commit high treason'. *Photo: Mrs Perplies (Wilhelm Künzler's daughter), via Gerhard Brändle.*

Edgar Ginsberger was another of the four Pforzheimers who fought with the International Brigade. Edgar was a Jewish member of the KPD (Kommunistische Partei Deutschlands). Gerhard Brändle: 'Every time I looked out of the windows of my school, I saw the house at Osterfeldstrasse 33, where he had lived in 1933. When the Nazis took power, Edgar was deported to Heuberg concentration camp for producing communist pamphlets. He was released later in 1933 and fled to Britain. In 1936 he went to Spain and was killed on 7 January 1937, in the defence of Madrid. In 1939, the International Brigade cemetery in Madrid was desecrated. The graves were destroyed and the site bulldozed. As for Arnold, Edgar's father, he was deported in October 1940 and died in Gurs camp in 1942.'[14]

The Weiss family – father, mother and daughter – lived in the same house as the Ginsbergers, at Osterfeldstrasse 33. They were denounced for listening to the BBC. The father, Emil, distributed BBC news in leaflets. He received four years and was locked away in Bruchsal prison, between Karlsruhe and Heidelberg. His wife, Emma, was also imprisoned, firstly in Karlsruhe, then in Haguenau in the Alsace and, finally, the women's prison at Ingolstadt. She was killed in an American air raid a few weeks before the end of the war. The daughter, Margarete, was also arrested but released after a couple of days.[14]

There were also the victims of the Nazis' so-called 'euthanasia' programme, including the mentally and physically handicapped. Gerhard Brändle has information on 232 people murdered at Grafeneck Castle, a schloss near Ulm then run as a 'care and nursing home': 'The Nazis labelled certain people for "treatment", a euphemism for killing.' The victims included Mathäus Seitz, who had travelled extensively in Africa and India, living hand to mouth. Mathäus was not ill, just a non-conformist. That was enough to get him into Grafeneck, where people were killed in a small gas chamber in the garage. This was preferred to other alternatives, such as the carbon dioxide injections trialled at Brandenburg prison. In 2013 a memorial was dedicated to 'euthanasia' victims at Pforzheim's main cemetery.[14] Another victim was Wilhelmine Argast. She was the widow of SPD city councillor Emil Argast. She was murdered at Grafeneck on 10 July 1940, at the age of 63.

Max Rödelsheimer is one of nine Pforzheim Jews whose resistance is documented. Rödelsheimer had fought in the First World War. He was a photographer at Schlossberg 11, next to the town hall. On 1 April 1933 – when the Nazis were on the streets, ordering people not to buy at Jewish-owned shops – Max Rödelsheimer was defiant. He sat in his shop window, wearing his First World War medals in protest. The National Socialists took revenge. His shop was targeted under the Aryanization programme. It became the subject of a forced sale and went for next to nothing. Afterwards, Max was forced out of his apartment and went to live in the *Judenhäus* (ghetto house) at Erbprinzenstrasse 20. He was rounded up on 22 October 1940 and sent to Gurs camp. In August 1942 he was moved from Gurs camp to Drancy, near Paris. Subsequently, he was transported to Auschwitz. After the war he was declared dead.[14]

A memorial at Pforzheim's Güterbahnhof (freight terminal) commemorates the deportation of the city's Jewish community on Tuesday, 22 October 1940, to Gurs.

Stolpersteine (stumbling stones) is a pan-European project to remember victims of all backgrounds. Stolpersteine are reminders of the expulsion and murder of Jewish people, Romanies, political opponents, Jehovah's Witnesses, homosexuals and, indeed, all who were unwanted or seen as a threat in Hitler's Third Reich. Cologne artist Gunter Demnig launched the Stolpersteine project, in the belief that a human being is forgotten only when his or her name is forgotten. Victims are remembered by brass plaques set in the pavement, usually at the last residence of the victim's own choice.[15]

As at August 2013 there were 125 such plaques in Pforzheim; many more have yet to be laid. All but one bears an engraved name, biographical details and the fate of the victim (No. 125 is a memorial to forced labourers). Over 37,000 Stolpersteine have been laid at more than 650 locations in Germany and a further 100 locations in The Netherlands, Belgium, Italy, Norway, Austria, Poland, Slovakia, the Czech Republic, Hungary and the Ukraine. Each location represents a local initiative, sponsored by individuals and groups.[15]

A review of the 124 Stolpersteine in Pforzheim dedicated to individuals shows that all but eighteen commemorate Jewish victims. One individual (Hedwig David) is commemorated twice – one plaque is in front of what was the Bertholdstrasse 4 ghetto house and another at what is now Osterfeldschule, where she was made to work. She was banned from her professional role as a teacher when the Nazis came to power in 1933.

Of the 123 individuals, 70 died or are unaccounted for (10 are described as 'missing' and 4 are declared 'fate unknown'). All fifty-three survivors were Jewish and all but three were children or teenagers at the time. The young adult survivors were two 20 year olds and one aged 21.[15]

Fifty-six dead are accounted for. Twenty-five died in Auschwitz, twenty-five died elsewhere (primarily in other Nazi camps) and six died during internment at Gurs. The dead included three teachers, two factory owners, two teenage schoolchildren, a gynaecologist, a pharmacist, an engraver, an engineer, a wine merchant and a rabbi. The dead included thirty-nine Jewish people, forced labourers (two were shot and five died of 'malnutrition or TB'), the children of forced labourers, two 'opponents of the regime' and two Jehovah's Witnesses. The dead children were a 6-year-old boy, a 3-year-old girl, a 10-month-old boy, a 9-month-old boy and an infant girl. Her name was Julia Singaewska (Stolperstein 124), the daughter of a female forced labourer from the Soviet Union. She was born on 9 March 1943, and died on 29 April, probably owing to malnutrition.[15]

Babies were victims: Julia Singaewska is remembered. The daughter of a Russian forced labourer, she died when just under two months old, probably because of malnutrition. *Photo: Tony Redding.*

Friedrich Burger, manager of the Pfannkuch store, was one of at least fifteen Jehovah's Witnesses who refused to bend to the Nazis and, thus, were persecuted. In National Socialist eyes, Burger was guilty of many sins. He was sent to prison in October 1937 and was subsequently held in '*Schutzhaft*' (protective custody) at Dachau. He was deported to Mauthausen in March 1940, where he died, aged 44, from starvation and abuse by camp guards.[16] His wife, Ernestine, was held in a women's prison at Gotteszell. Gerhard Brändle adds: 'The Bibelforscher were known as "*Unbelehrbare*" [obstinate/unteachable] by the Nazis. The Jehovah's Witnesses refused military service, refused the oath of loyalty to the Führer and continued to "missionize" – to spread the Word.'

Of all their opponents, the National Socialists were often hardest on Jehovah's Witnesses, who rejected everything Nazi. They were pacifists and refused to

Resisters and victims: top (left) Pastor Heinz Kappes, who protested against Nazi persecution, and Friedrich Burger (right), persecuted as a Jehovah's Witness. Bottom (left): Dr Rudolf Kuppenheim – he and his wife committed suicide. Julius Moser (centre), who was deported to Theresienstadt, and Fred Josef, imprisoned for his involvement in the Scout Movement. *Photos: Gerhard Brändle/ Stadtarchiv Pforzheim.*

Med.-Rat Dr. Kuppenheim,
Stabsarzt d. L.

vote. Their children were not in the Hitler Youth and they regarded all forms of government as godless. Jehovah's Witnesses refused to serve in the Luftschutz air-raid defence units. They refused to work in factories making components that could be put to military use. Jehovah's Witnesses imprisoned in Ravensbrück refused to mend Wehrmacht uniforms. According to the Jehovah's Witness archive, there were around 25,000 Jehovah's Witnesses in Germany in 1933 and around half were persecuted by the National Socialists (8,800 were imprisoned, some 2,800 ended up in concentration camps and 950 lost their lives).

Burger was a friend of the Facoltosi family, who were also Jehovah's Witnesses. Irma Baroni (née Facoltosi) remembers: 'Friedrich Burger was the manager of a large store in town. My grandmother shopped there for years.'[17]

Klara Müssle, Jehovah's Witness and mother of two young children, was unyielding. Her opposition to all things Nazi came to notice. She worked at Schmidt u. Bruckmann and her feelings were obvious when she refused to listen to Hitler's speeches on the radio. She also refused to turn up for Luftschutz training. Klara was imprisoned in 1940 and held in a cell without light. Attempts were made to get her to sign a paper recanting her beliefs. She refused and stayed in prison until 1942, when she was transferred to Ravensbrück and then to Auschwitz, where she was murdered on 24 September 1942. She was 40 years old when she died. There was much discussion within Pforzheim's small community of Jehovah's Witnesses. Some felt it wrong for a mother of young children to take such a stand. They argued that she should have put the children first and that she should have been encouraged to relent for their sake. Clearly, however, Klara Müssle made her own choice.[18]

Jewish couple Albert and Felicitas Eckstein are remembered by the first Stolpersteine in Pforzheim (Nos 1 and 2). They were both 49 when deported to Gurs in October 1940. They were transported to Auschwitz on 10 August 1942, and subsequently declared dead. Another Jewish couple, living at Erbprinzenstrasse 20, were separated following deportation. Setty Michelson (Stolperstein 18) was 60 and her husband, Otto (Stolperstein 19), was 61. Otto died in December 1941, having been moved from Gurs to Les Milles. Setty was transported to Auschwitz a week after Albert and Felicitas Eckstein. She died in the camp.[19]

Julius Moser studied civil engineering and was an artillery officer in the First World War. He had a distinguished war record, winning the Iron Cross First Class and the Iron Cross Second Class. Afterwards, he took over his father's successful textile and clothing company, but the Nazis forced him out because of his Jewish origins. On 14 February 1945, he and his brother Emil, together with eleven others from Pforzheim who had lived in mixed marriages, were deported to Theresienstadt. There were around thirty deportations of this type in all. Moser survived and witnessed the camp's liberation by the Red Army on 8 May 1945.[20]

How much did people know about the reality behind Nazi anti-Semitism? Over the decades, historians and commentators have visited this question repeatedly and have delivered many verdicts. The truth must surely embrace all levels of knowledge and include those who did their best not to know. As for Pforzheim banker Adolf Katz, his diary entry for 12 July 1944 clearly shows that he understood that Nazi policy towards the Jews was based on the 'final solution', extermination: 'The Jews from Hungary are taken to special camps in Poland and are murdered there by the thousands. I have to think a lot about the mentality of the people giving and carrying out such orders. All the words one would like to use in order to describe such terrible deeds come from a world in which something like this was not even possible.'[21]

Two days later he recorded another example of Nazi brutality: 'I have just heard that a couple of days ago a freight train with captured French terrorists on board passed through. The train came from Paris and had already been on the road for eight days. Throughout the entire time the captives had nothing to eat and drink and were not even allowed to leave the wagons in order to relieve themselves. What inhumane, senseless cruelty.'[21]

Yet Katz was among the majority who could see no alternative future. On 22 July 1944, he made a diary entry about the failed attempt to assassinate Hitler. He wrote that, had the attempt succeeded, the result would have been chaos: 'the conviction that our enemies want to annihilate us, no matter what government is at the top, is deeply rooted among the majority of the population. Thus a change of government would only increase the difficulties instead of reducing them.'[21]

A sense of helplessness became evident in Katz's diary. On 25 July 1944, he referred to the devastating air attacks on Stuttgart and the extreme pressures faced by German troops on the Eastern Front. He then wrote: 'Today, I heard of a man who gave a revolver to his wife when he said goodbye, to go to the Russian Front, so she could kill herself and the children. There are many imaginable situations nowadays in which that solution might be best!' As for propaganda about 'wonder weapons', the public had heard it all before: 'The people are already starting to call the V1 *Versager 1* [Failure 1].'[21]

Opposition to Nazism took root in various religious groups. Researcher Gerhard Brändle has information on six resisters from the Protestant Church and four from the Catholic Church. The Protestant pastor Heinz Kappes is one of five 'religious socialists' persecuted despite his distinguished First World War record. His decorations included the Iron Cross First Class, the Iron Cross Second Class and the Black Badge for Wounded (only 182 of which were awarded during the First World War).[22]

He began his theological studies after the First World War, worked within the SPD as a pacifist and became a left-wing organizer. He was a pastor in Brötzingen. Kappes was outspoken and unbowed. In 1933 he protested against the ban on Jewish children attending secondary schools. He delivered a sermon in Büchenbronn attacking the Nazis for locking up 26,000 opponents in prisons and labour camps. It wasn't long before Heinz Kappes joined them. The pastor was arrested on 21 August 1933, and spent ten days in Pforzheim prison. He was dismissed by the Church on 1 December of that year. In a highly unusual move, the authorities banished him from Baden. His answer was to take his whole family to Palestine, where he found work as a German teacher. In 1939, however, he was interned by the British for nine months. There were no hard feelings as he soon began working for the agency British Food Control. Eventually, he returned from exile.[22]

Ludwig Pfältzer represents a group of over ten Adventists (mostly women). Gerhard Brändle describes him as 'an opponent of war'. He adds: 'When called up for Wehrmacht service Ludwig Pfältzer went underground for ten months. Eventually, however, he was arrested and imprisoned in the Brandenburg Zuchthaus. He was murdered there on 1 September 1942.'[22]

Fred Josef (Stolperstein 10) was a Catholic but also a 'half-Jew', according to the Nazis. A pharmacist, he was much involved in the Scout movement, and in 1941 he received a twelve-month prison sentence for continued involvement in a banned youth organization. Upon release he returned to his home town of Würzburg, but was rearrested and sent to Auschwitz. He died in the camp on 21 January 1943.[22]

Some opponents of the regime became early, pre-war casualties. They included Eugen Weidle (Stolperstein 13), who lived at Grosse Gerbergasse 5. He was 'shot on the run' by SA men in 1936. Many of the Jewish people deported from Pforzheim in October 1940 were dead by the end of 1942. Amalie Nachmann and her husband Ludwig (Stolpersteine 22 and 23) were rounded up by the Nazis. They had been living at the ghetto house at Bertholdstrasse 4. Ludwig, aged 53, was a factory owner. In 1941 he was sent from Gurs to Noé, a camp for the sick and disabled, where he died on 2 March 1942. Amalie, five years Ludwig's junior, was also deported to Noé. Later in 1942, after her husband's death, she was transported to Auschwitz, where she died.[23]

Those transported to Gurs in 1940 included Jewish steel engraver Isidor Lazarus Jeremias (Stolperstein 15), who lived at Östliche Karl-Friedrich-Strasse 103. He died in August 1941 aged 62. At the other end of the age range was 13-year-old Jewish boy Erich Reutlinger (Stolperstein 100), murdered after being transported to Auschwitz on 13 October 1942. The parents had sent one son, Michael, to Britain in 1938. Later, he travelled on to the USA. Brothers Erich and Fritz went to Belgium in February 1939. Erich was caught up in the deportations following the end of the campaign in the West in 1940. Fritz escaped to Palestine.[23]

Ernst Wilhelm Hildinger (Stolperstein 116) was jailed several times for 'notorious complaining' and 'supposed membership' of the KPD. He was deported to Dachau on 22 July 1942, and to Neuengamme on 5 January 1943. He was murdered on 31 March of that year, at the age of 48.[23]

Most deaths of forced labourers were attributed to 'malnutrition or TB'. The deaths of five of the seven forced labourers commemorated by Pforzheim's Stolpersteine were so registered. After the big raid, in February 1945, the other two Russians, known only as Kossi (Stolperstein 117) and Meteschewski (Stolperstein 118), were arrested for allegedly stealing food from a broken down freight train at Brötzingen. They were shot in front of the Russian camp on 27 February. Stolperstein 125 commemorates all victims of the Zwangsarbeiterlager (forced labour camp) in the Brötzingen valley.[23]

The survivors among the 123 individuals commemorated included thirty-four children: nineteen boys up to the age of 15 and fifteen girls in the same age range. The boys included Martin Eckstein (Stolperstein 4), just 11 when deported to Gurs. Later, he was held in a children's camp. He survived as an 'illegal' and subsequently went to live in New York. His sister Lore (Stolperstein 3) was also deported to Gurs and, subsequently, Auschwitz. She is listed as 'missing'. As mentioned earlier, their parents were declared dead.[23]

From 1936 Jewish schoolchildren and teachers were concentrated in the 'Ghetto School' at Hindenburgschule (Osterfeldschule, pre-1933 and post-war). The Ghetto School closed in November 1938. The young victims are commemorated by Stolpersteine in front of the Osterfeldschule and Osterfeld Kulturhaus (arts centre), together with Stolpersteine in front of their original schools in Pforzheim: Nordstadtschule, Calwerschule, Hebel Gymnasium and Hilda Gymnasium.[23]

Hans Isaak Bensinger (Stolperstein 46) was 11 when he got out of Germany in 1939, escaping to Bolivia – as did his 19-year-old sister, Ida Irma Bensinger (Stolperstein 59). Bernd Kahn (Stolperstein 48) was the same age when he arrived in the USA that year. Franz Mayer (Stolperstein 56) was 14 in 1939. He went to England. The Ghetto School survivors also included Hans-Dieter Weinschel (Stolperstein 96), who was deported to Poland in 1939 at the age of 12, yet, somehow, managed to survive the blood-soaked events in that country.[23]

Ghetto School girls who survived included Edith Furchheimer (Stolperstein 47) – just nine when she escaped to the USA via Britain. An older girl, Klara Stein (Stolperstein 54), escaped to Palestine in 1939. Lieselotte Krieg (Stolperstein 61) got out to Australia in 1938, at the age of 14. Nineteen-year-old Herta Levy (Stolperstein 62) made it to Belgium and travelled on to the USA in 1940. Lore Hirsch (Stolperstein 77) was 15 in 1939; she got away to Switzerland.[23]

Ursula Nathan (Stolperstein 84) survived. She was deported to Theresienstadt on 14 February 1945. Later, she emigrated to the USA. The fortunate ones also included Amalie Meier (Stolperstein 53) and Lily Braun (Stolperstein 60), who were 18 and 15 respectively when deported to Gurs. Amalie was hidden in France and emigrated to New York in September 1946. Lily was also hidden in France and survived the war.[23]

Additional Stolpersteine memorials continue to be sponsored. Werner Baroni, for example, was preparing to sponsor Pforzheim Stolpersteine as this book was in preparation. They are for his aunt Eliese ('Lisel'), grandmother Anna and the Gabriels, Jewish friends of the Baroni family.[23]

Survival did not always mean that a family remained intact. Gerhard Brändle knows of a woman who was one of two young siblings in Gurs camp. She was smuggled out and eventually got away to America. She never returned to Europe. The first family reunion took place in the USA during the 1960s. The two infant prisoners in Gurs were reunited but were strangers. The family bond had been lost.[24]

Notes

1. Milton, G. (2011), *Wolfram*, 18.
2. Ibid., 22.
3. Ibid., 56.
4. Ibid., 58.
5. Ibid., 57–60.
6. Ibid., 91–2.
7. Ibid., 93–4.
8. Interview with Christian Groh, April 2013.
9. Milton, G. (2011), *Wolfram*, 110–15.
10. Ibid., 128–9.
11. http.//www.pfenz.de/wiki/ Erschiessung_ französischer_Widerstandskämpfer
12. Fr.wikipedia.org/wiki/Alliance_(réseau)
13. www. pfenz.de/wiki/Alliance_(réseau); Zentralle Stelle der Landesjustizverwaltungen Ludwigsburg, file Dr. Schlierbach, Helmut- KLNatzweiler Bd 111 Bl.402 (BA B162 …), (See also F. Bouchard (law clerk of the military court in Paris), Service de Renseignements 'Alliance', Strasbourg, 1946, S. 18f; Souvenir Francais, archive, file Pforzheim, S.58.
14. Interviews with Gerhard Brändle, 2013.
15. *Stolpersteine in Pforzheim* (pamphlet).
16. Interviews with Gerhard Brändle, 2013.
17. Interviews with Irma Baroni, August 2013.
18. Interviews with Gerhard Brändle, 2013.
19. *Stolpersteine in Pforzheim* (pamphlet).
20. Interviews with Gerhard Brändle, 2013.
21. Pross, M. (1995), *Die Einschläge kommen näher, Aus den Tagebüchern 1943–45 von Friedrich Adolf Katz, 1945–1947 Oberbürgermeister der Stadt Pforzheim.*
22. Interviews with Gerhard Brändle, 2013.
23. *Stolpersteine in Pforzheim* (pamphlet).
24. Interviews with Gerhard Brändle, 2013.

Chapter Ten

Obliterated

Air Vice-Marshal Sir Robert Saundby was Arthur Harris' Deputy Air Officer Commanding. He had been a Royal Flying Corps pilot during the First World War. Saundby was a keen fisherman and this influenced his choice of codenames for German cities. Berlin was 'Whitebait'. Hamburg was 'Weaverfish'. Munich was 'Catfish'. Pforzheim was 'Yellowfin' (a tuna).[1] It was decided that an attack on Pforzheim would assist the Allied advance into southern Germany. It would contribute to intensified attacks on the German railways. This concentrated campaign began on Thursday, 22 February 1945, with Allied aircraft striking some eighty rail targets throughout Germany.

Friday, 23 February 1945 was a fine morning in Pforzheim. It was mild for the time of year. Old Pforzheim's last day unfolded. Schoolboy Hans Gerstung: 'We had three or four alarms during the morning. On the last occasion we were dismissed from school and told to go home. I headed for our apartment in the northern part of the city. We lived on the second floor of Philippstrasse 4, on the corner of Hohenzollernstrasse. On reaching home I sat down to my usual good soup and bread.'[2]

The air-raid alarms that morning were nothing special. The *Akute* began at 10.10 and lasted until 10.50. It began again five minutes later and lasted until 11.10. This set the pattern for the day. There was another *Akute* at 11.45 which lasted until 14.10 and yet again from 16.45 to 17.45. The public shelters were occupied throughout the day. Single aircraft circled Pforzheim. With the early evening all-clear, workers headed for home and the trams and buses ran.[3]

Those with the time and inclination scanned *Pforzheimer Anzeiger*. This newspaper was now a single sheet, printed both sides. It contained no good news: there were stories about the Soviet attack on East Prussia, heavy fighting between the Moselle and Saar and air raids on Worms and Nuremberg. Yet there was also room for more pedestrian matters. For example, a German Shepherd dog with an illustrious pedigree was for sale at an address in Theaterstrasse.[4]

More interesting (at least until readers took in the details) was the announcement of a special food bonus for people with bomb-damaged homes. This consisted of 250g of *Kleinstfische*, an anchovy-like fish. Those who qualified could collect this windfall from Cuxhavener Fischhalle at Dillsteiner Strasse 5, Nordsee-Fischhalle at Hafnergasse 2, the Pfannkuch store at Westliche Karl-Friedrich-Strasse 265 and other locations. Another newspaper item offered useful tips for looking after the 'emergency suitcase'. Most people held their valuables in small suitcases when sheltering during

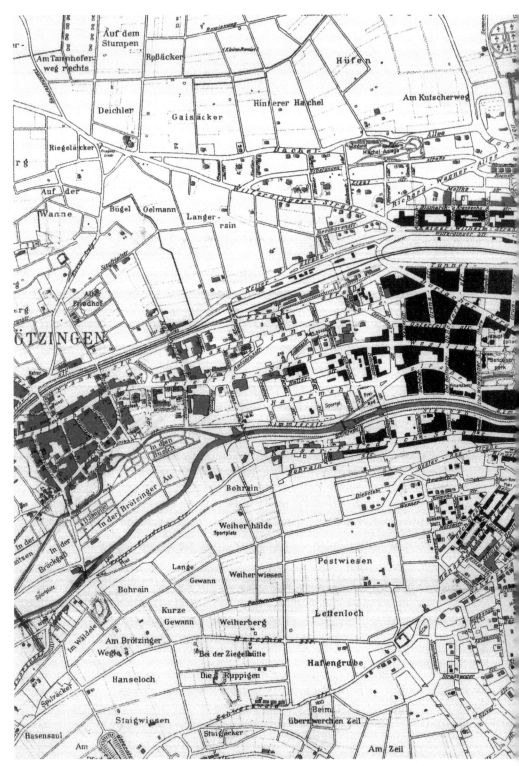

Obliterated: the central area of Pforzheim, with the destroyed areas shown in black. *Graphic: Stadtarchiv Pforzheim.*

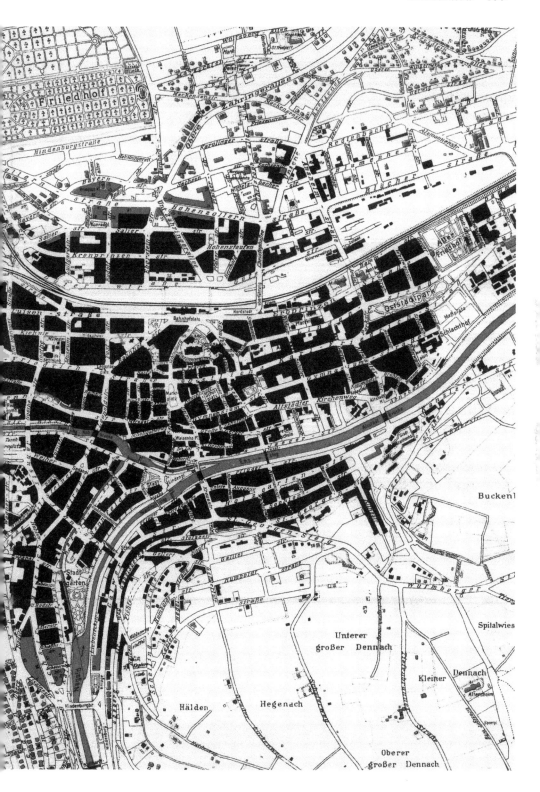

an alarm. There was also a piece from Professor J.H. Schulz, who pontificated about 'Life and performance – work makes you stronger' – a rather sinister echo of another claim: '*Arbeit macht frei*'. Indeed, this single sheet was crammed with advice. Another story was headed 'Budgeting to be more important than ever!' This was absolutely true: food ration cards now had to last nine weeks instead of eight – in effect, a cut of over 11 per cent. There were also the long lists of obituaries to scan: 'They died for Führer and Fatherland.' 'They fell victim to enemy air terror.'[4]

Ellen Eberle and her mother alternated between Pforzheim and Dobel, in the Black Forest. Ellen: 'We learned on 20 February 1945 that my uncle had been killed by fighter-bombers while driving his truck. They strafed him. Mother got the news in a telephone call. We had our usual lunch at the hotel in Dobel, where you could eat without ration cards. A group of Wehrmacht staff officers were resident. They were friendly enough and when mother said she had to go to Pforzheim for the funeral, they warned her against going, suggesting that it would be attacked.

'We went regardless. We set out by truck on Thursday, 22 February 1945. We spent the night in Pforzheim and we were due at the main cemetery at 11 o'clock the next day, 23 February, but there were constant alarms. In the end we had to leave. We took shelter at Bayernstrasse 2, where one of my mother's friends had lived many years before. She had died in the 1919 flu epidemic. Subsequently, the widower, Karl Weber, became my stepfather. Later that day we went to the apartment, where Grandmother had prepared tea and sandwiches. Finally, at four o'clock in the afternoon, we were able to go to the cemetery and bury Uncle, everyone clutching their small emergency suitcases.'[5]

Waffen SS soldier Gerd Fleig remained in Room 35 of Pforzheim's Hindenburg Lazarett, a military hospital established in the Osterfeld School. His recovery had progressed. He had been transferred to an artillery regiment, but remained in hospital at this time. Friday, 23 February began much as usual. His temperature was taken and he went to the hospital lab for a blood count and other tests. Then the alarms began: 'Time and again we went into the shelter. Each time I returned to bed and continued to read. By 5pm I was writing up my diary, before dinner and an early night.'[6]

Six-year-old Dieter Essig also had an unremarkable Friday: 'During the afternoon we visited Grandmother. Her grocery shop was on the Marktplatz, roughly where Pforzheim's theatre now stands. I believe mothers have protective intuition, a sort of sixth sense. My mother *knew* something was wrong when the preliminary alarm sounded and we entered the large public shelter near the Marktplatz. After a short while she said we had to get out. The shelter wardens were reluctant to let us go but finally relented. On the way back to our apartment we saw *Christbäume* [Christmas tree flares] dropping. We reached home just as the main alarm went.'[7]

Many people had premonitions that day. Later, some insisted that they owed their lives to a sixth sense. Three art students at the Meisterschule (now the Hochschule

Transportation target: Pforzheim's railyards today, looking east. The railway was Werner Schultz's salvation – he was deported by train two hours before the bombing began. *Photo: Tony Redding.*

für Gestaltung, Technik und Wirtschaft) had plans. Twenty-four-year-old Gisela Bär: 'We had prepared a little birthday party for 23 February. It was supposed to be celebrated at two locations in the city. In the afternoon we made our first stop in Hohenzollernstrasse, together with our teacher. Here, we spent most of the time sitting in the cellar and, after the all-clear, we strolled leisurely towards our second stop, the Hotel Post on Leopoldstrasse.

'Eva lived in an apartment on the fourth floor and we stood waiting in the entrance hall, in front of the elevator. When the elevator arrived I found it physically impossible to get in. It felt like a superior power had paralysed me, holding me back. I told the others and we decided to continue the birthday party the next day. We ambled over to Bohnenberger Schlössle and stood chatting at the corner of Goethestrasse. Suddenly, I became restless and said we should leave. I just reached my parents' home on Durlacherstrasse when the sky and the city were illuminated as bright as day by the Christmas trees.'[8]

There was some hesitation over the alerts. Karlsruhe Luftschutzwarnstelle (Air Defence Headquarters) announced the approach of a few planes, revised the warning to a group of aircraft heading towards Stuttgart, then upgraded it to '*Starke Verbände*' (a strong force) making for Stuttgart. Pforzheim's sirens went at 19.45 and loud engine noise was then heard all over the city. The bombing started just five minutes later.[9]

After the burial of her uncle, Ellen Eberle and her mother were returning home: 'Mother had a strange feeling that something was going to happen. There was an alarm and we went into the half-finished tunnel shelter on what is now Heinrich-Wieland-Allee. As we went inside I saw Christmas trees in the sky. We didn't go home as mother felt the tunnel was safer. Grandmother reached the tunnel just before they shut the door. I remember the explosions as muffled noise. The atmosphere inside was tense. I heard my mother tell the woman next to her to stop praying out loud, as it used too much oxygen. Everyone just sat there, holding hands or hugging each other. I squeezed between Mother and Grandmother.'[10]

Helmut Watter and his brother played in a slit trench at his grandfather's market garden on Eutinger Strasse. Three slit trenches had been dug along a row of large pear trees, to provide cover from fighter-bomber attacks: 'there was a lot going on overhead. Mother told us to come inside, rather than sit in a trench only 1.5m deep.' His mother had spent that afternoon visiting her husband at the Hindenburg Lazarett, in the Osterfeld School. He had been seriously wounded on the Western Front in September 1944. She took 2-year-old Gudrun and Lieselotte, a *Pflichtjahrmädchen* (a girl doing her compulsory year of work in a household). That afternoon Lieselotte decided to go to the cinema and stayed in the city. She was never seen again.[11]

In Eutingen village, Marie Charlotte Aichele was in the kitchen, preparing supper. She served potato pie to her husband Erwin, daughter Gunhild and her friend Frau Weber. It had been a tense twenty-four hours. American forces had advanced the previous morning and the enemy was now 90 miles from Pforzheim. The day had been full of alerts and people in Eutingen had spent hours in the cellars. As the Aicheles sat down to eat they heard aircraft noise but no sirens sounded. Erwin went outside. In the moonlight he gazed south-west across the valley, towards Pforzheim, and froze. He ran inside and shouted: '*Christbäume*! There are *Christbäume* all over Pforzheim.' Then the siren went.[12]

Sigrid Kern (née Weber) left work and began the 4km walk home. 'When I arrived the table was set for a meal. Suddenly, the Army officer billeted in our attic came in, wearing just underpants and a uniform top. He said: "Get into the cellar, right now." He had seen the Christmas trees over Pforzheim.'[13]

Sigrid's younger sister, Doris: 'I heard bombs dropping. I snuggled against Mother. Sigrid was standing against a wall. I looked at my father and my aunt (my mother's sister) and her husband. I felt this was the end. My aunt cried throughout the attack. We were all petrified. When the bombing stopped Mother set out for town, taking Hannelore, our eldest sister. They reached the outskirts but were told to go back. Everything was burning. Bombs were going off and it was too hot to bear. There were dead people everywhere.'[13]

Teenager Roger Riblet-Buchmann, a forced labourer from Pforzheim's Italian camp in the Eutingen valley, was in town that Friday evening. He turned into the Marktplatz just after 7.00pm. He and his friend, René, often went to the Beckh Inn, where deportees from the Vosges were regulars. On this occasion, however, Roger had other things on his mind. He was looking for a man known simply as 'The Belgian', to pay off a debt in white bread stamps. Afterwards, he called in at the Komet, his and René's local. René had been too tired to accompany him. He had had to get up for work at 5.00am, helping in the preparations to relocate deportees in the Italian camp, with its inadequate sanitary arrangements, to the Russian camp at Brötzingen, at the other end of town, where facilities were said to be better.[14]

Roger went into the Komet: 'The usual, pleasant atmosphere prevailed.' Shortly afterwards, the teenager took the decision that saved his life. He decided not to move on to the Beckh but rather return directly to the camp. He walked past the Schaub factory, feeling anger rise within him. He had been treated well, but he hated that factory, Pforzheim and Nazi Germany. He had been forced to work in Pforzheim and, as far as he was concerned, 'the Flying Fortresses could blow Germany to bits'.[14]

He and René talked about escape. They hatched a plan to get to Switzerland and, naively, asked two policemen for directions to the Swiss consulate. They were told to follow the officers and soon discovered that their destination was the police station – rather than the consulate – where they faced some stiff questioning.[14]

British Lancasters, rather than the Fortresses, blew Pforzheim to bits. Roger Riblet-Buchmann: 'The Marktplatz was a single area of fire, the Beckh had buried hundreds of unfortunate victims within it; the Lindenstrasse and the Komet had sunk under a sea of flames and the Schaub factory was ablaze.' Roger was still alive at the end of the raid, but thirty-nine Vosges deportees were not. Some of the surviving forced labourers took their opportunity and had a few days off, hiding in the ruins.[14]

Friday morning began routinely for Flying Officer W.E. 'Monty' Monteith. There was a knock at the door and Batman 'Jimmy' entered with a welcome cuppa: 'It was his usual strong brew, guaranteed to sustain body and soul against the penetrating chill of the North Lincolnshire climate.' The rear gunner got up, had a wash and shave and decided yesterday's shirt would do for another day. He heard his skipper, Squadron Leader Ken Butler, shout 'Ready!' from the next room. The two men set out on a brisk, half-mile walk to Elsham Wolds' mess. Monty Monteith: 'As always, I devoured all placed before me: porridge, bacon, egg, sausage and fried bread – followed by toast, marmalade and lashings of hot, sweet tea.'[15]

With breakfast over, Monteith visited 103 Squadron's gunnery section, where Gunnery Leader Flight Lieutenant Johnny Whymark, DSO, DFC presided. He and other crew members then headed for the Red Shield canteen. Aircrew and ground staff chatted as they drank their mid-morning tea and kept watch on two telephone boxes just outside the station guardroom. If service police padlocked those kiosks, they could be flying that night. The kiosks were secured and the watchers reacted in two ways. Some men left their tea and hurried away; others lingered, as if reluctant to leave the haven of Red Shield.[15]

Butler and his crew were new to the squadron. Their first trip, to Munich on 7 January 1945, was aborted owing to navigational problems. Monteith flew as a 'spare bod' on a minelaying operation to Heligoland Bight on 5 February. The pending operation might be their first opportunity to join a 103 Squadron attack on a German target. Sure enough, they were on the battle order for that night. The regular mid-upper gunner, Bill Treen, was away on a course and Monty recommended Sergeant Walford to take his place. Later, the WAAF corporal in the armoury made the usual show of embarrassment as thick issue contraceptives were rolled over the muzzleflash of each gun, to keep out moisture which would otherwise freeze as soon as they took off for Germany. The guns were installed in 'I-Item'.[15]

Ken Butler wanted a game of snooker. This was followed by lunch: Brown Windsor soup and liver and bacon, potatoes and carrots, followed by Bakewell tart and custard. In an idle moment, Monty Monteith had calculated that he consumed around 90 gallons of custard a year while in the RAF. Later, the crew made their way to the briefing room. The station commander and squadron commander entered. The former said: 'Tonight, gentlemen, you are privileged to strike deep into the heart of Germany. Your target has never been attacked before and, though you will be part of a comparatively small force, I am confident you will destroy your objective in tonight's attack. Your target is Pforzheim. Hit hard and good luck.'[15]

A main force of 362 Lancasters, supported by thirteen Mosquitoes, was fuelled and bombed up to attack Pforzheim. Most aircraft were provided by 1 Group, with others from 5 Group, 6 Group and 8 Group (the Pathfinders). A Crown Film Unit Lancaster filmed the attack. This dramatic footage shows the glare of the firestorm below and is probably the most frequently used film sequence in television programmes dealing with night bombing in the Second World War. During that night, Horten Fjord in Norway was also attacked, by seventy-three Lancasters and ten Mosquitoes of 5 Group (with one Lancaster lost), and seventy Mosquitoes attacked Berlin (again with one aircraft lost). Darmstadt, Essen and Frankfurt each received nuisance raids from groups of four Mosquitoes. Twenty-two aircraft from 5 and 6 Groups were sent to lay mines in Oslo Fjord and off Fredrikstad.[16]

A major bomber support effort was organized by 100 Group. Eight four-engined Stirlings provided a Mandrel screen and fourteen Halifaxes, nine Fortresses and three Liberators provided a feint on Neuss, dropping Window. Neuss was actually bombed from 19.49 to 20.02 by a small force of Halifaxes and American Liberators. Specific radio countermeasures for Pforzheim were provided by three Liberators, a Fortress and a Mosquito. Jostle and Piperack RCM were in use that night. Support was also provided by twenty-four heavily armed Mosquito intruders – eighteen at high level (these aircraft reporting three chases) and six uneventful patrols at low level.[16]

During the Friday, the bombers were fuelled – the minimum load was 1,940 gallons. Pforzheim is some 430 miles from the Wash, on the east coast of England. Most heavy aircraft were bombed up with 4,000lb Cookie high-capacity blast bombs and incendiaries. Ten per cent of all incendiaries were of the X type (explosive).[17]

Fourteen 1 Group squadrons sent Lancasters to Pforzheim; 550 Squadron provided twenty-seven – the greatest number from a single squadron. One of the 259 1 Group aircraft scheduled was cancelled. Of the 258 that took off, 247 are known to have bombed the target. Eleven failed to return; nothing was heard from them after take-off.[17] The Lancasters were briefed to attack in waves, methodically destroying Yellowfin's built-up areas, industry and rail facilities. Crews were briefed on bombing heights. The 1 Group aircraft had bombing heights of between 5,000ft and 11,000ft, with a Time Over Target of 19.58–20.11. The weather was forecast clear over southern Germany, with a three-quarter moon above the horizon all night and local ground haze.[18]

Main force crews were briefed to aim bombs in the following order of preference: (a) on the master bomber's instructions, (b) the centre of mixed red and green TIs, (c) the centre of red TIs and (d) the centre of green TIs. Had the target been obscured, the aircraft would have bombed on sky markers (red with green stars).[19]

The attack opened at 19.42, when a Mosquito meteorological reconnaissance aircraft informed the master bomber that Pforzheim was free of low or medium cloud. The weather over the target was excellent; conditions were clear and visibility good, with the city bathed in bright moonlight. The first mixed load of red and green TIs went down at 19.57. These were assessed as short and to port by about 500yd. Two loads then fell on top of each other. The South African master bomber, Captain Edwin 'Ted' Swales, then dropped markers which were assessed as accurate. He gave instructions to bomb cascading red and green TIs as a second load fell on the aiming point. The post-raid report from Swales' crew added: 'We then ran over the target and, on orbiting, greens were seen cascading accurately into TIs and smoke. We gave orders to bomb cascading green TIs and then, later, to bomb the centre of smoke. Considered a very concentrated and accurate attack.' The immediate raid appraisal, unlike the marking, was of mixed accuracy: 'Do not think south of town hit very much. One large explosion in west of town at 20.02 hrs. Very good fires.'[20]

Many brightly coloured pyrotechnics were hooded, to protect the night vision of the crews above. Lancaster pilot Bill Manifold described how TIs appeared when looking down from bombing height: 'A red TI, cascading down to form its characteristic shimmering pool, looked just like a cigarette carelessly knocked against somebody's trouser leg in the dark …'[21]

The marking sequence continued to unfold. The 8 Group (Pathfinders) *Operations Record Book* commented: 'The marking was then augmented by the red and green TIs dropped by the Primary Visual Markers and the Deputy Master Bomber. The initial accuracy was maintained and thenceforward concentrated marking lasted throughout the attack, providing a satisfactory basis for subsequent bombing instructions. No difficulty was encountered in identifying ground features and it was seen that the marker concentration covered the aiming point. Bombing was generally very good and the fires started early in the attack soon increased until the target was covered by much smoke rising to several thousand feet and with a glow that was visible for 100 miles on the return journey. Several large explosions are reported and a successful attack appears to have been achieved.'[22]

Over 2,500 aircrew bombed Pforzheim that evening, and virtually all had never heard of the place. Some sources in Pforzheim and the author Mel Rolfe (*To Hell and Back*, 179, 186) suggest the aircrew were briefed to bomb Pforzheim forty-eight hours before, on Wednesday 21 February 1945, but the operation was scrubbed. Research at the National Archives has failed to substantiate these claims. Rear Gunner Monty Monteith, with 103 Squadron at Elsham Wolds, recalled the moment on the Friday when the curtain was pulled back from the briefing room's map of Europe: 'Glancing about, I could see I was not alone in my ignorance. No-one had ever heard of, or seen, the name "Pforzheim" before that moment. Squadron Leader Green, the intelligence officer, began his briefing by painting a word picture of Pforzheim – size, population, historical background, and what I remember most was that the town housed a great number of small workshops – even some homes – engaged in the manufacture of intricate time fuses, aircraft instrumentation and small parts for high technology weapons, including V weapons.'[23]

Green then gave the crews a round-up of the latest intelligence on the German defences, adding that flak was expected to be 'light'.[23] Everyone feared the 88mm flak; each shell was designed to burst into 1,500 pieces of red-hot shrapnel.[24] As for the fighters, 103 Squadron Gunnery Leader Johnny Whymark began by urging his gunners to maintain a constant vigil. He gave the usual warning: switch guns from 'Safe' to 'Fire' as soon as the aircraft turns onto the runway. He reminded them to set the correct wingspan on the gunsight and told them to be aggressive.[25]

With the briefing over, crews downed their pre-flight meal and began dressing in the aircrew locker room. Monteith stripped down to his 'shreddies' (underpants): 'I donned a pair of my girlfriend's (now my wife) discarded, laddered silk stockings, then my aircrew-issue silk/wool set of long-johns, a pair of black everyday socks, followed by electric socks. Next came my electric suit – pressing in the sock connectors. Then, shirt minus collar, battledress trousers, white sea-boot stockings with trousers tucked in, fleece-lined flying boots, long, thick white aircrew sweater and battledress top.' He put on his 'Mae West' life vest, carefully tying the cords. Next came the parachute harness: 'I am testing a back-type chute and, fully kitted out, I look like the Hunchback of Notre Dame. Having to don this mass of clothing, I am always the one the rest of the crew have to wait for. I grab four pairs of gloves, helmet with attached oxygen mask and intercom cord, my lucky mascot (a polka-dot silk scarf given to me by my mother), which I never flew without, and waddle out to the crew bus.'[25]

Monteith climbed into 'Item' and slithered, feet first, down the slope to the rear turret doors, wriggled into the turret and had a quick look round: 'Guns on "Safe", load and cock each gun in turn, switch on the gunsight, set wingspan to 60ft (representing a twin-engined German night fighter) and unlock the turret to check the manual traverse, then return to fore and aft position and lock for take-off.'

Monty then levered himself out of the rear turret, onto the sloping way, rolled over and crawled up to the rear door. He joined the rest of the crew for a 'last fag' before start-up. Then it was time to board again. Monteith wriggled into his turret, settled into the seat, plugged in the intercom lead and connected up to the oxygen supply. With the intercom live, skipper Ken Butler checked each crew position. Monteith confirmed he was on full oxygen – gunners and pilots were on oxygen from the ground, the others from 10,000ft.[25]

With the engines running, Monteith tested the turret hydraulics, moving his guns from side to side and up and down, checking for full function. It was time to 'glove up': the first pair of fine silk, followed by electric (Monty always struggled with the connecting studs at the wrists), woollen gloves and, finally, leather gauntlets. 'I flex my fingers to assure myself that I will be able to carry out all my required tasks with the confined digits …' The Lancaster moved forward on the perimeter track. As each aircraft turned onto the runway the gunners switched guns to 'Fire'. On receiving the green light from the control caravan, I-Item's 66,000lb bulk began to roll. When they took off, Monteith immediately started his 180 degree square search pattern: 'I can feel butterflies in my stomach. This feeling of apprehension was with me for the first and last thirty minutes of every operational flight. I made peace with God. I was at peace with myself and the rest of the world, until thirty minutes before touch-down. I presume that feeling was fear …'[25]

They climbed through 10,000ft and Butler warned everyone to switch to full oxygen: 'At last we attained our operational height and we pressed on towards an unsuspecting, doomed Pforzheim.' Suddenly, Monteith felt a burning sensation in his right foot. His electric suit was malfunctioning. He switched it off and wondered if he could do without it for the next five and a half hours.[25]

The aircrew flying towards Pforzheim saw this operation as nothing special. Ron Germain, wireless operator with Flight Lieutenant 'Buzz' Burrows' crew on 550 Squadron, found the entire round trip of seven hours fifty minutes unremarkable: 'I just thought Pforzheim was a small market town.'[26] Ken Sidwell and his crew flew six operations in February 1945 and Pforzheim was the last. Mid-upper gunner Frank Woodley remembers that they bombed from just 7,000ft. The next day the BBC announced that Pforzheim had been 'obliterated'.[27] Eddie Edlund's Lancaster bombed from 8,000ft. Later, flight engineer Sam Lipfriend wrote in his diary: 'Very good results. Fighters again from over front line. Saw seven shot down. Saw Me109. Glittering diamonds.' Pforzheim was a milestone in Lipfriend's war. Edlund and the rest of the crew had completed a number of ops before Sam joined them. They were now tour-expired and it was time to say goodbye. Lipfriend had more to do, and he became a 'spare bod' flight engineer.[28]

Pforzheim had been bombed by 550 Squadron before, albeit in a minor way. On an earlier occasion a 550 pilot, Flying Officer Smith, had a 'hang-up'. He got rid of the rogue bomb over Pforzheim. Another 550 skipper, Dave Davidson, told his wife that the seven hours thirty-five minutes Pforzheim operation had been 'quite an enjoyable trip'. Later, however, he confessed to Babs that it had been 'dreadful'.[29] It was the Davidson crew's twenty-ninth operation. Wireless operator Howell Evans: 'We were told by the master bomber to come down low. I remember standing in the astrodome, looking out for fighters. We were so low I could see flak positions on the ground.'[30]

There were three main types of *Fliegeralarm*. Hans Gerstung: 'A very slow "up and down" sound from the siren made everyone aware of a threat. The main alarm was a fast rising and falling siren signal. A continuous note signalled the all-clear. Warnings were also broadcast on the wireless. The programme would be interrupted, to be replaced by a slow beat like a metronome. The wireless made a special announcement about the air threat; everyone then listened for more warnings.'[31]

Hans and his mother sat down to dinner that Friday evening when the radio suddenly broadcast the initial warning: 'I don't recall sirens, but I do remember the urgency in the announcer's voice. We abandoned the meal, grabbed our suitcases and made for the cellar. Seven other families lived in our block and we all used the cellar. Everyone seemed to be running downstairs at the same time. We were used to alarms so there was no panic at first, but it became crowded down there. The cellar had four bunk beds. About twenty people were sheltering when we closed the heavy door protecting us from blast. Then there was an urgent knock on the door. We opened it and a soldier and his girlfriend pleaded to be let in. As he entered the soldier said: "I can already see the Christmas trees." Flares were dropping.

'There was a dim electric light in the shelter. The little children were placed on top of the bunk beds. Some grown-ups sat on the bottom beds; others sat on chairs brought down to the cellar. Everyone clutched a glass – there was always a barrel of something in the cellar and some of the adults began to help themselves. A small window provided a little light during the day, but was now sealed off by a steel shutter. I heard bombs detonating in the distance. They were coming closer. The ground vibrated and I was afraid. Still the bombs came and the ground shook violently. Dust fell from the ceiling and little kids began crying. Women prayed. My mother threw herself on top of me, almost suffocating me in the process. I saw Mr Abele, the big, strong man in charge of our cellar, reach for a large, white-painted pick-axe. These cellars were built next to each other. One area of dividing wall was made of thin brickwork. It would be easy to break through if our cellar entrance was blocked and we had to escape by moving next door. Mr Abele would have no difficulty knocking through if he had to. I heard a loud humming sound. It might have been the bombers or the firestorm developing outside. The explosions were all around us. The ground was heaving then, suddenly, the bombing stopped.'[31]

Helmut Watter's mother put his little sister to bed, then the sirens sounded and everyone went into the cellar: 'We sat on a bench. Then my uncle came in. He was in the military and on leave from Buckenberg barracks.' The attack began: 'The little storm lantern on the wall started to swing back and forth menacingly. We sat in a row, with our backs towards the heavy sandstone wall. There was my grandfather and grandmother, my aunt and uncle, me and my brother and mother, who had my little sister in her arms. We held hands and kept our mouths wide open – as the *Luftschutzverordnung* [air-raid protection regulations] recommended – and trembled with fear.

'Grandfather bravely went over to the little cellar window and said the whole city was burning. After a while the grown-ups decided to go to help and to save a few things. They took my brother along. I was to stay and look after my sister, in the bassinet. I stood on a little box and could see the inferno through the cellar window. I saw the nearby gas plant burn. The roof of the office building with the siren collapsed. I was terribly afraid that my mother, brother and all the others might never come back and that I would be left by myself, with my little sister.'[32]

Ellen Eberle, her mother and grandmother left their shelter at around 10pm. Ellen: 'I had to go to the bathroom. Outside, there were flames everywhere. Everything was smashed and burning. We went back to the tunnel and talked about what to do next. Finally, at around midnight, we went to the apartment. We were lucky – it was still intact. All the buildings were down in the southern and eastern districts but the houses looked OK in our area. Ebersteinstrasse wasn't burning. Mother put me straight to bed. We set out for Dobel the next morning; it is 25km away and I don't remember how we got there. Anyway, the Wehrmacht officers at the hotel were pleased to see us.'[33]

The Rodi family lived close to the town centre. Martha Luise Rodi heard the 'ticking metronome' on her wireless just after 7.30pm. A group of thirty aircraft was said to have crossed the Rhine, west of Pforzheim. She telephoned her mother and sister, to make sure they took shelter. Then came the warning that planes were making for Pforzheim. The last words were: 'Bombs are being dropped.' Then silence. Martha and the three children at home at the time went into the shelter, with the kids putting their hands over their ears. Then the lights went out and they were left with just a small torch.

Some people ignored the sirens. They sounded daily and, invariably, Pforzheim was not the target. Hannelore Schöttgen was cycling home from labour service duty when the sirens went. A warden ordered her into a public shelter. She stayed only briefly, argued her way out and carried on. She reached the town centre, where another warden also told her to get into a shelter.[34]

In the cellar of the Aicheles' hillside villa at Eutingen, the ground thumped and shook from the detonations in the nearby city. At one point, Erwin and Marie Charlotte went upstairs to look and found themselves struggling for breath. The firestorm in the valley below was sucking oxygen from the air.[34]

Klaus P. Feucht was only four. The family lived on Pflügerstrasse, west of the Auer Brücke: 'My brother, a year older, and I were sent into the cellar ahead of the others that evening. My mother and father came down later. I could sense the fear in the dark cellar. A woman constantly cried out: "Mrs Feucht, please pray!"'[35]

Lancasters over Pforzheim: the aircraft are surrounded by flak bursts and silhouetted against dense smoke by a photoflash bomb. Target indicators cascade down at the lower left. *Photo: Trustees of the Imperial War Museum.*

Deutsche Bank director Adolf Katz's last diary note before the 23 February 1945 attack was made forty-eight hours earlier. Ironically, in contrast to his oft-repeated expectation of a catastrophic raid, he wrote: 'You can hear so clearly, especially at night, how they run in droves into the tunnel with their children, yet there has never been a major attack on the city at night and it would be improbable, because Pforzheim is way too small and unimportant.'[36]

Later, Katz recalled the moment the sirens began: 'We only ran into the cellar when we heard the first explosions. The heavy blasts came closer and closer; the house was shaking. The plaster came down from the ceiling; the blast tore the door open and slammed it shut again. The red glow of fire shone in. We sat next to each other, Ruth and me hand in hand, quiet and waiting for the end. Robert and Traudel ducked, Mrs Müller lay on the floor and one of the children cried. Then the explosions gradually stopped.'[36]

Teenager Irma Facoltosi was with her family that evening. The wireless programme was interrupted by the tick-tock of an alert. Then it became the fast tick of an *Akute*. Her friend, Arno Baroni, had been called up for military service but was on leave that Friday: 'He told me he was at his grandmother's when the alarm went. His granny had bad arthritis and refused to go down to the shelter. In the end he carried her down on his shoulders.'[37]

The Mössner family were friends of the Facoltosis, who were Jehovah's Witnesses. Tina Facoltosi occasionally helped out in the Mössners' butcher's shop. Teenager Karl Mössner's father had come to the attention of the local Nazis as he refused to vote and, therefore, was 'a traitor to our people'. He had supported the National Socialists until he read *Mein Kampf* and realized that it meant war. Karl Mössner was at Niefern, 8km east of Pforzheim, on the night of the attack. For the past fortnight he had been undergoing Volkssturm training: 'Friday, 23 February had been a still day – no wind. When the first aircraft flew over and dropped flares, a north-west wind came up and blew the Christmas trees south-east. That's why the northern part of town and Brötzingen was spared. Niefern, however, was in the south-east.'

Random factors determined life or death. Karl Mössner's parents were working in another butcher's shop, with Karl's sister, Lore, busy preparing orders for collection the following morning. His father and sister went home, leaving the mother with the shop owner's wife, who insisted that she, also, called it a day. She told her three times to finish and go home. Karl's mother caught the last train to Brötzingen and saw the attack begin. The butcher's wife died in the raid. She was among forty dead found in a shelter on Sedanplatz. Karl Mössner: 'Sedanplatz was flattened. All I could find was bones.'

Rainer Luppold was 12 years old. The family had been bombed out and now lived in a small, two-roomed apartment at Bleichstrasse 17. Rainer's school was closed that Friday owing to air-raid warnings. It had been some time since the family had sat down together for dinner. Usually, his father was on night duty with the Heimatflak. They had just finished the meal when the main alarm went and flares appeared in the sky: 'We immediately grabbed our bags. We had just closed the cellar door when we heard bombs detonating. Then the explosions came closer and closer.'[38]

Art student Gisela Bär was late getting into the shelter and was blown down the cellar stairs by a near miss: 'What followed was hell. I laid on the floor near the lintel. I couldn't find my gas mask in the dark. I covered my eyes with my hands and heard mother praying next to me, over the dreadful roar of exploding bombs.'[39]

Young Hans Ade remembers that Friday as a bright day, with fighter-bombers constantly overhead. Their home had been damaged and they had relocated: 'Mother and I made three trips back to our house, with a handcart, to collect more possessions. There were constant alarms owing to fighter-bomber activity. We were repeatedly told to take shelter but carried on. Back at our new home we were sitting down to dinner and waiting for my sister to return from the hospital when the alarms went. I had just finished my meal as my sister came in. I went outside, looked down and could see lights. I shouted: "Everyone in the cellar!" This was the first time I had seen the Christmas trees. Everything was illuminated, as bright as daylight.

'When we got into the shelter the bombing felt like an earthquake. Everything was shaking. We got out as soon as the planes had gone and looked down on the city. Everything was ablaze and we could feel the wind gather strength and turn into a firestorm. There were lots of explosions after the planes had gone, with delayed action bombs going off.'[40]

Beyond learning how to fire a machine gun and Panzerfaust, school had also taught 9-year-old Hans how to defuse incendiary bombs – a highly dangerous procedure, given that one in ten carried an explosive charge: 'It was simply a question of unscrewing the fuse. It was harmless without the fuse. If it was already burning, it could be covered with sand or beaten out. When we left the cellar I saw an incendiary burning in the empty house next door. I broke in and put it out.'[40]

The Nazis came as close as they ever did to doing young watchmaker Werner Schultz a favour on Friday, 23 February 1945. As a *Mischling*, he was finally being deported – despite his status as a valuable craftsman engaged in vital war work, assembling fuses. He was told to report to the railway station at 6pm. That was barely two hours before the bombers arrived. 'I have often asked myself this question. Did they do me a favour? I'm not sure. I could have been in the factory that evening, but the factory survived. I could have been at home but that building also survived.[41]

'It wasn't unusual to be told to report. Two months before we had to work on fortifications in Alsace. When I went to the station, however, the six or eight others in the group were all *Mischlinge*. I can't remember being guarded. Anyway, we were put on a train for Dresden. At one point we heard on the radio that Pforzheim had been bombed. Eventually, we arrived at Hirschfelde and a camp for Italian workers that was now a labour camp for *Mischlinge*. They were needed to work on the sites of new synthetic oil plants, which were to be constructed nearby.'[41]

Some men were already under cover well before the alarm. Max Gaupp was working on a tunnel shelter in the north of town, in the Bayernstrasse area. When the sirens went, the workers found themselves surrounded by people attempting to escape the bombs: 'Wham! Wham! Wham! One every second. Wham! The air was compressed into the tunnel, then sucked out.' Gaupp feared for his wife. When the lights went out, more people crowded in as he and others attempted to get out. Then all the men were ordered out. Bayernstrasse was enveloped in fire. Gaupp's house was still standing and he asked a neighbour if she had seen his wife. She replied: 'We all made it. She must be over there, carrying things out of the apartment.'[42]

They were reunited and worked together to save what they could. The roof was on fire. At around 9.30pm a fire engine appeared. Max Gaupp stopped the vehicle. He told them that they would save the apartments of nine families if they could put out the roof fire. They responded, and Gaupp began to think about his father in Rennfeldstrasse and sister-in-law in Schwarzwaldstrasse, but it was impossible to get through in the firestorm.[42]

Erika Christmann-Schmidt's family grabbed their *Luftschutzgepäck* (air-raid suitcases) when the alert came, joining the neighbours in the cellar. The steel door was closed but they could still hear the bombers' engines. Then it began: 'The light went out. A terrible crashing … I lay flat and felt the blast in my ears. The neighbour's daughter had thrown herself over me.' A woman nearby moaned 'Dear saviour. Dear saviour'. Erika: 'An enormous explosion burst the steel bars of the cellar door. It swung open. Smoke came in. A flickering glow was reflected on the walls. Someone yelled: "Outside! We're running out of air in here."'[42]

The exit was blocked and fire seemed to flow down the cellar stairs. The occupants escaped through a laundry room window; luckily, the window grating had been removed just a few days before. 'I think it was my aunt who yelled: "Into the pond. Let's go!" This little pond, home to a couple of goldfish, became our life-saver. We were sitting in there, five people including my 75-year-old grandmother, bent forward to the water's surface, to be able to breathe. We splashed ourselves with water for protection against flying sparks.'[42]

A neighbour eventually led them to the river: 'On the banks of the Enz people were surrounded by household goods, furniture and bed linen.' There was a police officer at the scene: 'A woman came up and said her husband was dead, on the riverbank. The policeman told her to put a name tag on the body.'[42]

On 17 February Heinrich Külmann had been told that his youngest son had been killed in an air crash. On 23 February he was returning from the funeral. The truck giving him a lift stopped near Bauschlott as flares burst over Pforzheim. Külmann's only thoughts were for his wife and eldest son, who was in the Lazarett at Osterfeld School. He left the truck at Mackensenstrasse: 'The entire city was a gigantic sea of flames. I ran down the burning Obere Zähringerallee. At Ebersteinstrasse firemen tried to hold me back because of collapsing houses.' He reached his home at Güterstrasse 24. It had burnt out and collapsed: his wife was buried in the cellar. He crossed the railway to get help from the police department, but their building was also a pile of rubble: 'Since the air was scorching, I could hardly breathe. I looked for sanctuary in the public shelter of the Hotel Sauter, on Bahnhofstrasse, but we had to leave the cellar after a short while, as burning phosphorous flowed in through the ventilation shafts. We ran to the western railway underpass with wet cloths over our faces.'[42]

Külmann was found by his surviving son at some time after 10.00pm. He had been on a visit home. Heinrich learnt that his wife and seventy others were trapped in their cellar. The son said: 'They will suffocate without help! I'm the only one who made it out of there.' This multi-roomed cellar belonged to Güterstrasse 22 and 24 and Rudolfstrasse 8, 8a and 8b. These buildings had once been a brewery and the cellars were vaulted and connected by shafts. It was robust, but those trapped inside were suffering from dust, smoke and low oxygen levels. All emergency exits were buried, although one blast had ripped open a corner of the cellar. Father and son sought help from a police post but they were too busy. They returned to the underpass and found five volunteer helpers, two medics and three soldiers.[42]

Heinrich Külmann: 'In Güterstrasse the heat was overwhelming. The three soldiers turned back. My son collapsed several times. We reached the bomb crater and crawled into the upper air-raid shelter. We saved four unconscious people. The others, in the cellars further down, no longer had the strength to climb the ladders in the shafts. We had to get ropes. One man who was still conscious begged me not to abandon them.'[42]

They returned to the police bunker and got two more volunteers. They were then joined by a Fire Department rescue squad from Karlsruhe. An SS Oberscharführer then ordered some French conscripted workers to join the rescue effort. They got over ninety people out: 'Almost all were unconscious and five were dead. My wife was among the people rescued.'[42]

In the Benckiserpark area, Johanna Stöber had just finished dinner when the sirens went. She and two elderly ladies went into the cellar and the steel door was shut: 'A thunderous roar broke loose – a floodtide of blows, noise and smashing glass. The lights went out. The ceiling caved in. The chimney door burst open and we were showered with a hail of stones, dust, soot and sand. Mouths, eyes and noses were immediately bunged up with dirt. I moaned: "Jesus. Jesus." Another woman cried: "Dear God, help us!"'[42]

The bombing eased, then raged again with the arrival of the second wave: 'We were sitting in chaos, up to our necks in rubble. After the second tempest passed above us, there were flames on all sides. The south side of the house was open, doors and windows torn out.' The steel shutters at the exit shook in the blast and more rubble fell on them. Then it ceased: 'With the noise ebbing away we heard a hail of brief, dull thuds. Thousands of incendiary bombs were pattering down.'[42]

They now heard the roar of the fires as they struggled to get out of the narrow shelter. Johanna Stöber: 'I crawled ahead and tried to climb out. The small stepladder had gone. I climbed up over a potato crate and then crawled on my stomach through the window. The women pushed from behind. The bright light outside, on the street, was dazzling. White hot sparks pattered on the cobbles like rain.'[42]

Somehow she extracted the two elderly ladies, then ran up the hill to look for an escape route: 'A huge burning plane tree straddled the road. A maze of electric wires hindered my progress. The way was blocked by walls of flame. An incredible firestorm and whirlwind raged in all directions, sometimes towards me, sometimes away from me. My coat flapped like a flag and the ground was scorching hot. At that moment a large incendiary went off 5 or 6m in front of me. I entered a dazzling, greenish-white hell. I screamed!'[42]

Johanna's legs were burning. A lump of phosphorous fell into her bag, which caught fire. Somehow she reached the park and took shelter from the sparks behind a big tree. The other side of the trunk and the branches were alight. The pain from her burns became intolerable. She found some woollen spats in her damaged bag and they protected the wounds from radiated heat. The park was full of slit trenches and bomb craters. Johanna got into a crater, to shelter from the sparks. 'A man and a

Firestorm: Flying Officer Bruce Potter's aiming point photo, taken over Pforzheim, showing a rapidly developing tidal wave of fire. *Photo: Bill Thomas.*

woman crouched in my crater. Next to them was a dead woman. The man struggled to get up, tripped over my legs and ripped off the skin.'[42]

Houses around Benckiserpark were ablaze, including an orphanage. There was a continuous rumbling noise as walls collapsed. It was impossible to get out of the park. 'We had to hold out here until the flames retreated. Someone said the air would be better down at the Mühlkanal.' She reached the canal, then staggered on, exhausted, half-blind and almost unconscious. Suddenly Johanna ran into a friend with three small children, and she was heartened to see that they had survived. Then she moved on, looking for the two elderly ladies. Instead, she found the general manager of the company she worked for. He was in a crater with his wife and children: 'I was so exhausted I broke down. The wife held me in her arms for a while.'[42]

Johanna Stöber had reached the park at about 8.15pm. She moved out of the area at around 1.00am and made for Brötzingen, where she arrived two hours later. Her legs were dressed at an aid post at Brötzingen School. Later, she discovered her relatives were unharmed and the two old ladies she had rescued had also survived.[42]

At Luisenplatz, Agnes and Alfons Fischer took shelter at the Hildaschule. The large cellars were crowded. The occupants included 360 Volkssturm men, mobilized earlier that day; they also included refugees from Alsace. When the attack began the school building was shaken, as if by a gigantic fist. The Luisenplatz wing took a direct hit. Agnes and Alfons heard someone shout: 'Get out! Everything is ablaze!'[42]

The entrance was passable although partially blocked by burning beams. Most people backed away: they stayed in the cellars and waited for rescue later. Agnes and Alfons left the shelter but had to find refuge from a blizzard of firestorm sparks. They watched two teenage girls run down Museumstrasse in their pleated skirts. The Museum Society clubhouse collapsed on them. Agnes and Alfons were helped over a wall. They were joined by others in the museum garden and grabbed sheets of corrugated iron to use as shields against the heat. A woman from Goethestrasse arrived. Her hands were badly burnt and she passed out. Then a Luftschutzwart (air-raid warden) appeared and found a way out across Luisenplatz. Climbing over red-hot rubble, they reached the Luitgardstrasse underpass.[42]

Agnes and Alfons soon realized that most people in the underpass were dead, their lungs torn by blast. The terribly mutilated body of a woman lay face down. They were hoping to get to the cemetery through Luitgardstrasse, but those in front of them were suddenly buried in rubble. The couple turned, climbed the railway embankment and made their way towards the Ispringer Tunnel, where survivors were crammed together, moaning and sobbing.[42]

There were desperate scenes at the Luftschutzrettungsstation (air-raid rescue centre) at Reuchlin Gymnasium that night. Dr Karl Hillenbrand had finished with his last patient and was cycling along in the Sedanplatz area when the sirens went. He was close to Schwarzwaldschule when he saw the first markers burst in the sky. On Bleichstrasse he got up speed, trying to reach the tunnel shelter at Kupferhammer. He saw that many others were panicking and heading towards the centre of town.[42]

'I wasn't able to make it over Kallhardtbrücke because the first bombs were dropping. So I dropped my bike at Davosweg and ran into the tunnel there …' Women knelt down and prayed and children screamed with the concussion of the big bombs. When it was over, Dr Hillenbrand set out for home. It was still standing and his family was unharmed. He soon set off again, to do what he could to help in the city. Houses in Friedenstrasse, beyond the Rodstrasse junction, were burning. All the houses towards Schwarzwaldstrasse seemed to be destroyed. It was impossible to negotiate Dillsteinerstrasse, a narrow canyon filled with fire. He tried a different way, via Nebeniusstrasse, Bunsenstrasse and Gustav-Rau-Strasse. The city was a bowl of fire. Hillenbrand reached Rossbrücke via Turnplatz, but again found his way blocked by fire: 'A young man stood in the middle of the bridge, talking madly, with only a shirt on.' Hillenbrand was joined by a friend who agreed to take the distressed man to the bunker at Gustav-Rau-Strasse. The doctor failed to reach the city centre via Goethestrasse – the road was blocked by burning debris. He went to the rescue centre in the Gymnasium's cellars: 'The roof was burning and gigantic blocks of stone obstructed the cellar's stairs. I squeezed through. Downstairs, the emergency lighting was working.'[42]

The doctor was joined by a medic and a teenage assistant. They had medical instruments and supplies, but no patients. Hillenbrand knew why: he had seen a stream of wounded and burns victims making for the Gustav-Rau-Strasse bunker. He knocked out the windows of the instrument cabinet, opened the supplies and set out for the bunker, to establish a new aid centre: 'It was impossible. That tunnel was too crowded. You couldn't make enough space.' There was no choice but to return to the Gymnasium. They cleared the cellar stairs as far as possible and set to work. Two more doctors arrived, and they were soon dealing with a large number of casualties. 'Rescue teams, soldiers, firefighters from Büchenbronn, medics and volunteer helpers hauled the half-burned people in on stretchers, boards, doors or on their backs. Many had only a black crust instead of skin on their body parts. During the escape through the fire extensive burns developed – especially on the legs – from which many people died days later. Many suffered damage to the eyes, smoke poisoning and broken bones.'[42]

The doctors and assistants continued to splint broken bones, treat burns, administer eye drops and give morphine as the Gymnasium above burnt down. Conditions became more difficult when the cellar ceiling became hot and oxygen levels fell in the overcrowded rooms. Later, Hillenbrand paid tribute to his team, especially a nurse from Siloah Hospital who worked until she reached the point of collapse.[42]

Many Pforzheimers became confused when the sirens went: they were not sure which shelter to go to. Friedrich Wagner was on Bahnhofstrasse and his first thought was to get away from the station. He moved as fast as he could along Schlossberg as the bombers' engines became audible. An officer in charge of a group of fifty soldiers asked him the way to the nearest shelter. Wagner said he would take them. The flares burst in the sky and it took time for the soldiers to file into the shelter. When bombs fell, Wagner shouted to those still waiting to go in to follow him, but they wanted to stay together. Wagner then abandoned his plan to make for the town hall and, instead, ran through Barfüssergasse towards the Barfüsserkirche. He banged hard on the shelter door. It opened and he squeezed through. He threaded his way through the overcrowded front rooms and eventually found a place. The shelter shook from near misses and the men shouted to the women and children on the floor, telling them to don smoke masks or press wet handkerchiefs over their faces.[42]

Within a few minutes the wall of the next room was pushed in, bringing fire, smoke and dust. There was panic as the room's door jammed. It was impossible to open the emergency exits. They tried the opening to the cellar of the next building, the health office, but fire, smoke and gas blocked the way. Friedrich Wagner: 'A woman lay at my feet with her child and cried for help. We tried to calm the people. We told them to stay on the ground and breathe as calmly as possible, so the air would not be used up too quickly.' Wagner then attempted to get out, squeezing through the damaged door. At that point the front rooms were almost empty. He searched for the Barfüssergasse exit. It was blocked by rubble. There was an opening, however, and Wagner – covering his upper body and face with a wet coat and handkerchief – jumped. He found himself in Barfüssergasse: 'to my horror I was standing in the middle of a terrible sea of flames; debris crashed down on all sides. I was forced to abandon my plan to help the trapped people. I tried to run towards Blumenhof. Impossible. My path was blocked by a burning mountain of rubble.' Westliche Karl-Friedrich-Strasse was also impassable, filled with 'ramparts of rubble'. Wagner's face and hands were singed and he was afraid his clothes would burst into flame. In desperation, he jumped onto a pile of burning rubble and 'took a header into the unknown'. He landed in the Blumenhof compound, also a sea of fire. He escaped by taking a run through a smoke- and flame-filled passage and took shelter in a hole in Bahnhofstrasse. He was bombarded by sparks and had no choice but to try for the railway underpass. Finding it increasingly difficult to breathe, he ran across Bahnhofplatz. He was joined by two others, but one fell behind and was never seen again. Eventually, they reached the northern part of town and Wagner set out for home.[42]

Friedrich Wagner: 'My goal was Brettener Strasse. The houses were burning there as well. The gale-force westerly storm carried the flames across the street. I tried to get through but had to give up.' He turned back and tried Wittelsbacher Strasse, but this was a wall of flame. Finally he reached a clear area north of Hohenzollernstrasse, alongside Pfälzerstrasse. His way home was clear. He found the building intact and his family unharmed. He then decided to return to the maelstrom and do what he could to help. He reached Osterfeldschule via Wolfsbergallee and the cemetery. One wing of the building was on fire. He went in and came close to dying when a ceiling collapsed. He helped recover wounded from the military hospital.[42]

Many survivors suffered smoke poisoning. Emmi Nagel was in the cellar at Gymnasiumstrasse 46 when the bombs fell. The blast door was blown in, fire followed and they failed to put out the flames. There was a moment of panic when a neighbour's axe broke as he attempted to open up an escape hole to the next cellar. Desperation spurred them on and they squeezed through into the cellar of Gymnasiumstrasse 52 – a public shelter holding around eighty people.[42]

Emmi Nagel: 'My mother and I sat next to one another. We tied cloths over our mouths, for protection against smoke. Some people wore gas masks. The firestorm sounded like screaming cats.' Then they began to pass out. A young, fit-looking woman next to Emmi suddenly slumped against her. 'At that very moment, my heart started to throb, my ears started to buzz and I said: "I'm feeling very ill." Then I passed out as well.'[42]

Meta Stanger went into her cellar with her two children and made a show of putting them to bed. She was alone with them when a deluge of bombs fell. Fire came down the chimney and they crawled through a hole into the next cellar. It was dark, full of dust and people were screaming. The cellar was part of the Arcades near Rossbrücke, and someone said the only hope was to jump into the river. Meta and her children couldn't swim. Meta jumped and found she could stand up. Then her daughter jumped and she caught her, but there was no sign of Karl-Heinz, the boy. There was no way back into the cellar. Burning debris fell on the girl and she shrieked. Meta Stanger: 'I realized that we couldn't stay here and that I would have to escort the child to safety. We needed cover or else we would be crushed. To save the girl I had to abandon my boy to his fate in the cellar.'[42]

Van driver and janitor Artur Kühn was on his delivery round that Friday. His company made munitions, specializing in incendiary grenades. It was Friday at 6.00pm and Artur was driving back. On the way he stopped to look over a branch of Rodi & Wienenberger, which had been destroyed in an earlier bombing. He had almost reached the Café Hasenmayer when flares appeared in the night sky. He stopped on Wartberg. Later, after the raid, he and his company's general manager went into the city: the manager feared for his wife and daughter. His home on Friedrich-Ebert-Strasse was intact, however, and the wife and daughter were unhurt. Artur then went on alone to the company's building at Luisenstrasse 32, where he had an apartment. He knew his wife, 20-year-old daughter and the entire night shift would be in the cellar. As he fought his way towards Luisenstrasse, he began to appreciate the scale of the destruction. He sheltered in a railway underpass, cold and shivering despite the firestorm all around. Suddenly, he knew his wife and daughter were dead.[42]

Marie Lupus, her husband and two of her three children were still alive. The Friday had been busy in the shop: Metzgerstrasse was full of people taking advantage of a fine day and there were plenty of customers. When they closed, her mother provided a meal of fish and potatoes. The siren sounded and her mother went to her flat next door, to get her air-raid case. That was the last time Marie saw her alive. 'They found her in next door's cellar as a charred corpse …'[42]

When the bombing stopped, Marie's husband and a soldier managed to dig out a hole leading into the street. Marie handed the 11-month-old girl to the soldier, then squeezed through herself, followed by her 9-year-old son. Marie suffered burns on the way to the canal. She had the two children, but was now separated from her husband and 6-year-old daughter. They got into the canal as the firestorm rapidly consumed the oxygen. Then the boy found his father, also in the water. He had failed in his attempt to save his mother from the flames. The 6-year-old girl was missing. They found her later, dead in front of the cellar exit. Other family members also died and were buried in a mass grave. Marie's husband had severe phosphorous burns on his hands, face and neck.[42]

Many people were now in agony from severe burns. Anneliese Vestewig-Fischer was with her family in the cellar of their home, on Sedanplatz, when a bomb blew away half the house and fire took hold. The cellar stairs were blocked: 'Suddenly I saw a glowing snake crawl towards me. "Back! Phosphorous!"' Anneliese lost contact with her sister and got no answer when she shouted for her and for her mother. She then squeezed through a hole into the cellar next door and shouted again, but there was no response. The shelterers next door were transfixed, speechless with horror. Anneliese began to despair: 'I was only 22 and had married at Christmas. Was my life over already?'[42]

She joined forces with a young man and made it out into the open. He stopped her going back in to help the others: the house was collapsing and the way back inside was buried. The man disappeared and Anneliese clambered towards the centre of Sedanplatz. 'More people came into the square. It was getting hotter and hotter. The firestorm broke loose. You couldn't stand upright any more. The five large chestnut trees in the square caught fire and became blazing torches …' People fought to get away from the flames: 'I tried to protect my face with my hands. Some prayed. Some screamed. Some ran directly into the fire. Someone next to me said: "She's burning." He was talking about me. It was so hot that you couldn't tell whether you were burning or not.'[42]

She found refuge behind a toppled advertising column, but there was a sudden wave of blazing heat and Anneliese pressed her face into the ground. Then a man took charge and led them to the banks of the Enz. She slipped into the water: 'I was in terrible pain and almost unconscious. Then somebody stumbled over me and said to his companion: "She's still alive."'[42]

Ottmar Hess was with Buckenberg barracks' Discharge Company. They sent home invalids who had been badly wounded and were no longer fit for service. In his room he heard the bombers, rather than a siren, and looked out and saw the flares as the Christmas trees burst over Buckenberg. He ran for shelter as bombs began to fall. The lights went out and Hess called for emergency lighting, but blast pressure immediately returned them to darkness. Sticky hot smoke, mixed with sand and dust, blew through the cellar, and the walls shook. When it was over, Hess went upstairs and saw the city ablaze.[42]

Gertrude Fass-Winkler was in the Städtisches Krankenhaus (municipal hospital): she had recently given birth to a daughter. Now in the cellar, she held the baby, resting on a pillow, as the room shook from the explosions. She watched the steel doors quiver, then a folding screen fell on her and smoke and dust filled the space. She spat repeatedly into a diaper and put it over the baby's face, then stuck the corners of a handkerchief up her nose and waited for the ceiling to collapse. Scalding water entered the cellar when boiler pipes burst. The light went out, the emergency lighting failed and the atmosphere went from relative calm to panic. A Catholic nurse went past. Gertrude grabbed her clothes and followed her out, into another cellar room with lighting. All the mothers and babies were saved by the nurses, who repeatedly went back and forth between the cellar rooms.[42]

Later, the maternity patients were taken to Buckenberg barracks. When they were halfway up the hill, the soldiers came down to meet them. The babies seemed unaware of the events of the night: 'Or were they? My Karin wasn't able to sleep through a single night without crying over the next three years. The doctors put it down to the attack.'[42]

Notes

1. Longmate, N. (1988), *The Bombers*, 148.
2. Interview with Hans Gerstung, April 2013.
3. Administration's Report and Statistics for the Town of Pforzheim, 1945–1952: City Life 1939–1945.
4. *Pforzheimer Zeitung*, 23 February 2005.
5. Interview with Ellen Eberle, November 2013.
6. Interview with Gerd Fleig, July 2013.
7. Interview with Dieter Essig, April 2013.
8. Schmalacker-Wyrich, Esther (Ed.), (1980), 'Pforzheim 23. Februar 1945, der Untergang einer Stadt', in: *Bildern und Augenzeugenberichten* (third edition).
9. Administration's Report and Statistics for the Town of Pforzheim, 1945–1952: City Life 1939–1945.
10. Interview with Ellen Eberle, November 2013.
11. Watter, Helmut, written account, February 2013.
12. Milton, G. (2011), *Wolfram*, 236–8.
13. Interview with Doris Weber and Sigrid Kern (née Weber), November 2013.
14. Riblet-Buchmann, R. (1993), *Unerwartete Begegnung – Als junger 'Fremdarbeiter' in Pforzheim 1944/45*.
15. Monteith, W.E., 'An Account of the 103 Squadron Air Raid on Pforzheim', via R.J. Whymark.
16. National Archives, AIR 14/3378 ('Headquarters, Bomber Command, Air Staff Intelligence BC/S. 27876/Int. 3, issued at 18.00 hrs 27th February, 1945').
17. National Archives, Air 25/3,16 (appendices), '1 Group, Royal Air Force, Operations Record Book, 23rd/24th February, 1945'.
18. National Archives, AIR 14/3378 ('Headquarters, Bomber Command, Air Staff Intelligence BC/S. 27876/Int. 3, issued at 18.00 hrs 27th February, 1945').
19. National Archives, Air 25/3,16 (appendices), '1 Group, Royal Air Force, Operations Record Book, 23rd/24th February, 1945'.
20. Operations Record Book, 582 Squadron, 8 Group, February 1945.
21. Redding, T. (2008), *Flying for Freedom*, 61.
22. National Archives, AIR 25/154, 171 (appendices), Operations Record Book, No. 8 (PFF) Group.
23. Monteith, W.E., 'An Account of the 103 Squadron Air Raid on Pforzheim', via R.J. Whymark.
24. Redding, T. (2008), *Flying for Freedom*, 61.
25. Monteith, W.E., 'An Account of the 103 Squadron Air Raid on Pforzheim', via R.J. Whymark.
26. Interview with Ron Germain, April 2013.
27. Interview with Frank Woodley, March 2013.
28. Interview with Sam Lipfriend, March 2013.
29. Interview with Dave Davidson, April 2013.
30. Interview with Howell Evans, June 2013.
31. Interview with Hans Gerstung, April 2013.
32. Watter, Helmut, written account, February 2013.
33. Interview with Ellen Eberle, November 2013.
34. Milton, G. (2011), *Wolfram*, 241–5.
35. *Pforzheimer Zeitung*, 23 February 2005.
36. Pross, M. (1995), *Die Einschläge kommen näher, Aus den Tagebüchern 1943–45 von Friedrich Adolf Katz, 1945–1947 Oberbürgermeister der Stadt Pforzheim*.
37. Interviews with Irma Baroni (née Facoltosi), August 2013.
38. *Pforzheimer Zeitung*, 11 February 2005.

39. Schmalacker-Wyrich, Esther (Ed.), (1980), 'Pforzheim 23. Februar 1945, der Untergang einer Stadt', in: *Bildern und Augenzeugenberichten* (third edition).
40. Interview with Hans Ade, November 2013.
41. Interview with Werner Schultz, November 2013.
42. Schmalacker-Wyrich, Esther (Ed.), (1980), 'Pforzheim 23. Februar 1945, der Untergang einer Stadt', in: *Bildern und Augenzeugenberichten* (third edition).

Chapter Eleven

Leaving the Cellars

Lancaster captain Ken Butler announced 'target dead ahead'. The R/T was tuned to the master bomber's frequency. Squadron Leader Butler's rear gunner, Monty Monteith, heard the master bomber calmly give instructions for bombing his selected TIs from among those now spread across central Pforzheim. Still some minutes from 'bombs away', Butler's Lancaster continued as bomb aimer Flight Sergeant Nobby Clark took up his prone position. Monteith re-set the gunsight wingspan selector to 40ft, as the target area was the hunting ground of single-engined fighters. He searched the night sky: 'Almost immediately there was a movement on the starboard quarter, slightly higher than ourselves, at about 800yd range. A Fw190 was stalking us. He maintained position and range. I calmly reported to the skipper. He replied: "Roger". I continued to report as the mid-upper gunner confirmed the sighting and swung his turret over to port, just in case fighters were hunting as a pair.'[1]

Monty Monteith: 'As we commenced our bombing run the 190 maintained his position and range and I began to wonder if, in fact, he had spotted us. I couldn't believe he hadn't, as we must have stood out against the glow of the target ahead. It flashed through my mind that, when fired on, German pilots were discouraged and usually left wide-awake crews to search for the less vigilant. He started to close the range without committing himself to a "curve of pursuit" attack. I alerted the skipper to prepare to "corkscrew – starboard" and, remembering Johnny Whymark's brief to be aggressive, I decided to open fire at 400yd if he had not committed himself to a curve of pursuit. The skipper concurred and I let loose with two short, sharp bursts of around three seconds each. A stream of tracer passed all around the enemy aircraft and a very startled fighter pilot immediately dived to port.[1]

'He levelled out on our port quarter, at about 800yd range. I kept a beady eye on him then, seconds later, his port wing dropped. He began a curve of pursuit to lay off deflection for another target. I spotted his prey low on our port beam – it was another Lancaster. Closing to 200yd, the 190 levelled off dead astern, to give himself a zero deflection shot. He loosed off a deadly stream of shells into an unsuspecting prey. The Lancaster rolled over, plunged down to earth and to her doom.'[1]

On the ground, a torrent of bombs tore Pforzheim apart, devastating an area 3km by 1.5km. The fire bombs had a wider spread and many houses surrounding the main area of destruction burnt down. Huge surface fires developed in the inner city, producing a firestorm.[2]

Young Hans Gerstung was in the cellar, watching Mr Abele, who was in charge of the shelter. He opened the door and took a look outside, accompanied by the other men: 'Immediately in front of the door they found two dud incendiaries, stuck in the sidewalk. They went into the apartment block. Most windows had gone and some doors had been blown out. A burning incendiary was lodged in the roof. Mr Abele climbed up and used a shovel to knock it to the ground, where it was extinguished. The roof was burning, but not too badly. We were told to come out and help.

'Every apartment kept the bathtub full of water and had a couple of sandbags for their own use. Galvanized tubs filled with water were kept on the stairs between floors, for common use. I carried a sandbag to the roof, to help put out the fire. Mr Abele used a special tool – a heavy mop soaked with water – to put out the blaze. We were fortunate to live in the north of the city, which escaped the worst of the bombing. As it was, we were only 150m away from the fringe of the devastated area, now burning fiercely.'[3]

As an air-raid runner, Hans had to report to his post in nearby Kronprinzenstrasse: 'Mother warned me to be careful. I set out about twenty minutes after the bombing ended and headed down Rudolfstrasse, as far as the beginning of Kronprinzenstrasse, but could go no further. Ahead of me, buildings on both sides of Kronprinzenstrasse were burning and collapsing. There was fire and falling walls everywhere. I turned

Where people fought for their lives: Hans Gerstung pictured nearly seventy years after the raid. He helped extract people from this cellar chute. *Photo: Tony Redding.*

and looked for a safer way. Then I heard shouts from a butcher's across the road. A woman screamed: "We need help. People are burning in the cellar!" The fire had reached stores of fat and people were trying to climb out through a small chute. They extended their arms and I helped pull them free.

'Then someone grabbed me on the shoulder. I turned and saw a young mother carrying a baby wrapped in a blanket. She was also carrying a small suitcase. She looked directly into my eyes and said: "Can you help us? We'll burn if we stay here." I took her suitcase and began to lead her back towards our home at Philippstrasse 4. On the way there was a large garden belonging to the Vogel family, who were wealthy jewellers. We would be safe there from the fires and falling debris. We walked through total chaos. Bombs that had yet to explode were now detonating in the fires. The noise of the fires and collapsing buildings was terrific. People shouted orders or simply screamed for help. This was a complete catastrophe – physically and mentally overwhelming. Everyone was afraid of dying.

'All I recall was confusion and the need to avoid buildings that looked as if they might collapse. We were about 200m along Luitgardstrasse when I caught sight of the Vogels' garden. I remember thinking: "We'll be safe now." Then, that was that! I felt a heavy blow on my steel helmet and remember nothing else. When I came to, I found I had been moved around 20m. I was in an area, right outside the garden,

'That was that!' This is where Hans Gerstung was struck on the head and knocked unconscious. When he awoke, he found himself laid out in a row of bodies, approximately where the three bollards are, at the end of the street. *Photo: Tony Redding.*

where bodies were being collected. There were dead people all around me. There was no sign of the mother and baby. I never saw them again.'[3]

During the attack the fire brigade and other emergency services were virtually powerless to intervene. When the bombing stopped, firefighting was hampered by the lack of water. The reservoirs soon drained. Firefighting vehicles trying to get into the city found their way blocked by bomb craters and collapsed buildings. The rubble was up to 3m high. The only successful firefighting took place on the outskirts – mainly by local volunteer fire services and helpers. They saved the gasworks and the military hospital at Osterfeld School from total destruction.[4] However, an area totalling 237ha, stretching from the gasworks in the east to Wildergrundallee in the west, was destroyed.[5]

Waffen SS soldier Gerd Fleig had been on his hospital bed, reading, when the alarm went shortly before 8.00pm: 'I went down into the cellar with Max, my room-mate. Then the bombing began. One wall caved in and we had to get out. We climbed over the rubble. I believe everyone got out of the shelter but the entire hospital block, although still largely intact, was ablaze. Yet we went back inside to save our few personal belongings. I told Max he could come with me to my parents' home in Weissenburgstrasse.'[6]

The fires took a firm hold in the hospital behind them. Gerd Fleig again: 'Following the false alarms many had decided not to go into the cellars. They were now trapped in the building. Ahead of us, I could see that much of the town was on fire. The houses on the opposite side of Osterfeldstrasse were in ruins. Usually, the shortest way to get to Rodrücken was via Turnplatz and Schwarzwaldstrasse, but that way was blocked. I told Max we should try to reach the railway underpass via Maximilianstrasse, Grenzstrasse and Tunnelstrasse. On every side the houses were burning. There were mountains of rubble everywhere.

'I told Max I needed to check whether my grandparents were OK. They lived on Bleichstrasse. I could see that most of the damage was in the southern part of town, so this was my priority. We tried to get over the tracks, via the railway station, to reach Lindenstrasse. I could see that the NSDAP's Kreisleitung building (now the site of the District Court) had been bombed out. The Oststadtpark was devastated and the gasworks was burning. We kept doubling back on ourselves, as roads were blocked by fire and rubble.'[6]

The two men turned round, waded the river Enz near Reitturnierplatz and progressed through Gesellstrasse, St Georgen-Steige, Schoferweg and Schellingstrasse to Kupferhammer, where the Würm and Nagold rivers meet. The Hindenburg Bridge (Kallhardtbrücke today) was still intact. On reaching Bleichstrasse, Gerd Fleig saw that his grandparents' home had been totally destroyed: 'All the houses higher than 74 were gone. They lived at 76.'[6]

Fortunately, his grandparents were not at home, having wisely decided to spend time at a quieter location. Gerd and Max continued, and finally reached

Weissenburgstrasse, via Lisainestrasse and Strassburgerstrasse, after a struggle lasting three hours: 'I saw the house next door was well alight. Our house had also been hit by incendiaries. My brother, Dieter, was alive. My mother had gone to Neuenbürg. Thirteen-year-old Dieter was inside, trying to put out incendiaries. I went in to help him. He was attempting to throw a burning sofa out of the window into the garden.'[6]

According to the city authorities, a firestorm developed within ten minutes of the start of the attack; hundreds of thousands of incendiaries did their work. The firestorm's hurricane winds swept up light debris and deposited ash and paper many miles from Pforzheim. A Pforzheim doctor's letter-headed paper was found in Stuttgart-Degerloch.[7]

Former Stadtarchiv Pforzheim director Christian Groh: 'This catastrophic attack killed over 17,000 people – approaching one quarter of Pforzheim's population. This estimate is as accurate as we are likely to get. The blazing city created a bright glow in the sky, visible for many miles around. Many bodies were never recovered. Thousands were totally incinerated – reduced to ash. There were many thousands of wounded. The city's main hospital, Städtisches Krankenhaus, was destroyed, but the Church-run Siloah Hospital was left largely intact.

'On that night the survivors found it difficult to leave the central area, as it was consumed by the firestorm. They had to climb uphill, to the north or south, in order to save themselves. Most of those who couldn't get out burnt to death or were asphyxiated. Some jumped into the rivers to escape the flames. Many drowned as a result. Those who didn't drown became hypothermic – it was February and cold.'[8]

Ken Butler's Lancaster was on its way back to Elsham Wolds; Pforzheim and their close brush with a German fighter were behind them. They had just started the long return flight, with well over three hours to go. Rear gunner Monty Monteith worried about his ability to withstand the cold without his electric suit, which had developed a fault earlier on: 'I had been without the heat of my suit for nearly two hours and I started to feel the effects. My hands, feet, legs and upper body were not too bad but there was a distinct feeling of numbness elsewhere. I wondered what effect frostbite would have on the "family jewels". This was on my mind constantly over the next three hours or so. I said a few prayers against frostbite. When "Item" finally kissed the tarmac and turned starboard off the runway, I busied myself with selecting guns to "safe", peeling off my gloves and turning off the oxygen as we taxied slowly to dispersal.' When out of his turret Monty tried to rub some feeling back into his numb buttocks. He joined the others climbing down from the rear door: 'I waddled out into the darkness with only one thought – I had to relieve myself. That was sheer bliss.'[9]

Ken and his crew arrived at the Intelligence section and entered the room: 'In the immediate right-hand corner, the doctor and padre dispensed coffee, Horlicks or cocoa laced with Navy rum. The skipper had a quick word with Doc Henderson,

who poured a double rum into a mug and ordered me to "Drink, as prescribed".'
The near-frozen gunner then received a steaming mug of Horlicks, laced with
another rum. The Butler crew sat down with Flying Officer 'Buster' Brown for the
debriefing. Monteith described the encounter with the Fw190. Bomb aimer Nobby
Clark described the target and the aiming point used, under the instructions of the
master bomber.[9]

When viewed from the surrounding heights, it seemed that a cloud of fire had
descended on Pforzheim. The city's official account described the scene: 'The red
sky, coloured by the fires, was visible as far as Tübingen and beyond.' Many died in
a state of utter confusion – disorientated by the bombing, the detonation of delayed
action bombs and the fear of being caught by the firestorm. 'People stayed in their
bunkers and cellars and suffocated as the flames consumed all oxygen ...' Many died
of carbon monoxide poisoning. Others died in 'fire-waves', leaving their horribly
deformed bodies sprawled on the rubble heaps. Some people fighting for life sought
refuge in the rivers. Along the Enz, bomb damage led to the flooding of the arcades.
Pforzheimers who might otherwise have survived drowned in this area and in the
flooded cellars of Zerrennerstrasse and at Waisenhausplatz. Bombs exploding in
Grosse Gerbergasse damaged an underground canal. The casualties included twelve
firemen, who drowned in their fire station on Waisenhausplatz. Pforzheim's volunteer
fire service lost seventy men that night.[10]

Hans Gerstung was in shock after waking up in a line of dead bodies. He was
quite close to home: 'Instinctively, I made for the door of our apartment block. Some
neighbours were there. The women screamed when they saw me – my face was
covered in blood. Whatever hit me had caved in my steel helmet, forcing the rim of
the leather liner into my forehead. I still have the scar, although it is now covered by
wrinkles!'[11]

The women carried Hans into the building, laid him on the floor and found a first
aid kit to dress his wounds: 'I suppose it must have been about 9.00pm – around
forty-five minutes after the end of the bombing. Mother decided we had to leave,
as firestorm winds were sweeping the area. Pforzheim suffered damage from a freak
tornado in 1968 but that was nothing. The firestorm winds were many times stronger
and lasted for hours. Everything in the devastated area was incinerated. The heat
was intense but bearable if we kept our distance from burning buildings. Everything
was lit up. We escaped by heading west towards Arlinger, where we had relatives. My
memory of these events is as vivid as a movie. I can see us setting out, choking with
fumes and the smell of burning timber and hot cement dust.'[11] They sought shelter
with his mother's cousin, a married woman with three sons in the Wehrmacht.

Over 90 per cent of central Pforzheim's buildings were on fire. The flames ate
through supporting timbers and roofs and walls collapsed. Temperatures in some
areas approached 1,600 degrees C, hot enough to melt metal beams. In the middle of
this maelstrom teenager Hannelore Schöttgen was still alive: 'We were sitting there,

huddled together. All we could hear was bomb after bomb, screaming and screeching and noises of things falling down. The whole house seemed to be moving. A section of ceiling fell down. There was disgusting dust everywhere. More things fell in. Was the house going to collapse on top of us? Was it going to bury us alive?'[12]

The shelter wireless was still on and the announcer said the raid was ending. Suddenly, he warned that a second, larger formation of bombers was nearing Pforzheim. Then the lights went out and the wireless went dead. Hannelore Schöttgen was one of thousands trapped underground; her shelter door was blocked by fallen masonry. Those inside were alive. They covered their mouths and noses with wet cloths, to protect against the thick dust. The shelter warden began tapping the wall with a hammer, looking for the best location to break through to the cellar next door. Then smoke began to fill the space and he gave up, turned to the girls and asked them to pray.[12]

Martha Luise Rodi's mother and sister had acted on her warning and were sheltering. As the firestorm developed, poisonous fumes crept into the cellar. The building owner told them they had to leave and take their chances on the street. The elderly woman had bad feet and found it hard going climbing the small ladder, then crawling through the burning house. Once out, they found the entire neighbourhood on fire. Fortunately, the apartment was next to the river Nagold and this offered some protection from the flames. They made their way along the bank and eventually reached the Rodi house.[12]

Hannelore Schöttgen, still trapped, had given up hope. Then the shelter warden made a new attempt to break into the adjoining cellar. This time he succeeded, helped by shelterers on the other side. It was a narrow escape. As they scrambled through, their cellar collapsed with the weight of rubble above. Now the danger was lack of oxygen. The city was burning from end to end and, in this ocean of fire, walls and piles of rubble glowed red hot. The warden told them to cover their faces, rush the barrier of fire and burst through to the river. They succeeded, but were left gasping for oxygen.[12]

By this time the Aichele family had emerged from their cellar in Eutingen. They stared across to Pforzheim. Marie Charlotte Aichele: 'We could see the entire town in flames. A gigantic black cloud of smoke was drifting along the Enz valley. The sky was completely red.' They could hear a rumbling noise; it was the sound of Pforzheim's buildings collapsing.[12]

On Pflügerstrasse, near Auer Brücke, Klaus Feucht's father opened the shelter window and the 4-year-old caught a glimpse of the inferno. His father shut the window, paced around, went outside, returned and ordered everyone out. 'When we climbed up the basement stairs the door frame was burning. Outside I felt cool air. People were rushing away. My father grabbed my brother. My mother took me by the hand and pulled me away. Something hit my left ear and burnt into my skin, causing me pain. My mother removed the piece of phosphorous. She fell through some debris with one foot, got stuck and wasn't able to free herself. I was handed to a soldier, who took me across the bridge, ignoring my cries of "Mama! Mama!" On the other side the man took me down to the river, over a narrow stairway by a wall. He carried me on his shoulders. The firestorm then whipped me into the water. I must have lost consciousness. Later, I was told that I had been carried downriver for about a kilometre. Somebody pulled me out just before the weir.'[13]

Meta Stanger, who had to abandon her son to save her daughter, was still in the Enz river with the girl, sheltering under the Rossbrücke. She grabbed a blanket as it floated past and held it over their heads, to protect them from flying sparks. The firestorm was making it difficult to breathe. 'We had felt our way along the side wall until we were under the bridge. Other people were also glued to the wall.'[14]

Eventually, Meta crawled up the riverbank and moved along it, towards Brötzingen. On reaching their friends' home, she faced the dreadful question: 'Where's Karl-Heinz?' Later, she returned to the cellar and searched for the missing boy. There was no sign of him: 'I couldn't face living in Pforzheim any more. I never had the feeling that my child was dead, rather that he would live on without me, with strangers.'[14]

Over time, having contacted survivors from the cellar, Meta Stanger came to believe that two soldiers in the shelter might have saved Karl-Heinz. In her account of that night she made a plea: 'Is there anybody in this world who can tell me whether that's what happened? Are the soldiers still alive? Did they drop the child off somewhere, or did they all perish eventually, somewhere? One thing I am sure of: the child did not die in the cellar, otherwise he would have been found. The hope that Karl-Heinz is still alive today is what keeps me searching and will never let me rest.'[14]

The soldiers at Buckenberg barracks went into the city to help. Ottmar Hess: 'When the fire company eventually came back, most couldn't report as their voices had gone.' A dressing station was established at the barracks as blood-stained wounded started to arrive on farm carts. Hess remembered one in particular: 'an exhausted woman trudged apathetically across the barrack yard. She wore a torn skirt. Her upper body was draped in a horse blanket. Barefoot and shaggy-haired, she tottered about.' More wounded arrived by the minute: 'There was no end in sight and we had almost nothing to help them.'[14]

The banker Adolf Katz and his family emerged from their cellar when the bombing stopped. Later, he wrote in his diary: 'What a sight! Doors, windows torn out, cupboards knocked over, a shambles. We ran up to the attic and extinguished five incendiary bombs.' Two phosphorous bombs remained, however, and the entire building was overwhelmed by fire: 'When we saw we could not save the house, we carried our belongings into the garden.' Beds, paintings, carpets, linen, a couch and groceries were saved. The books were lost. At 3.00am they rested in the garden, sitting on the rescued green sofa. Then people came for Katz's wife. Ruth was wanted, to help care for the wounded.[15]

The bright moonlight offered near-ideal night-fighting conditions. One combat that night involved a 419 Squadron aircraft of the Royal Canadian Air Force. This squadron sent thirteen aircraft to Pforzheim, including rear gunner Flying Officer M. Charbonneau's bomber. This was KB866 ('M'), captained by Flight Lieutenant M.W. McLaughlin. Charbonneau claimed an enemy fighter destroyed.[16]

The 550 Squadron *Operations Record Book* noted that the Lancasters sent to Pforzheim began taking off from North Killingholme at 16.00. Conditions at base were poor – ten-tenths cloud down to 600ft – but soon improved as the flight progressed. Then the problem was 'dangerous moonlight'. It added: 'The markers were accurately placed and the bombing was correspondingly concentrated and the attack has every appearance of being a highly successful one. Fires could still be seen 150 miles away on the homeward journey. Very slight light flak was encountered over the target and nightfighters were much in evidence.' The squadron lost an aircraft that night. It was the Lancaster flown by Flying Officer D.H. Grundy, RCAF. The crew were experienced: Pforzheim was their twenty-first operation. Three were killed and four (including Grundy) became prisoners.

In later years, 550 Squadron's newsletter said the Pforzheim raid did 'enormous damage'. It added: 'On a percentage scale, this was probably more destructive than those on Hamburg and Dresden.'[17] Conditions over Pforzheim were extremely dangerous for the bomber crews. Added to the usual hazards of flak and fighters was the risk of being hit by bombs falling from aircraft above, as tight waves of Lancasters crossed the target. A number of aircraft flew into clouds of incendiaries. Of fifteen aircraft dispatched by 100 Squadron, two were hit by incendiaries, although all made it back.[18] The crew of an aircraft from 431 Squadron, RCAF, also had this unpleasant experience. The squadron sent twelve Lancasters to Pforzheim; all bombed and got back, but one had to divert to Manston, having been hit by incendiaries from a friendly aircraft.[19]

Flying Officer R.D. Harris, RCAF, and crew joined 550 Squadron on 8 January 1945. Pforzheim, their fifth operation, was very nearly their last. Douglas Hicks was rear gunner. They took off in NF998 ('D-Dog') at 15.58. In his turret, Hicks was excited by the prospect of an unusually low-level flight across France as night closed in. When approaching the target, they listened to the master bomber's commentary and instructions and aligned themselves for the bombing run. The bomb doors opened and they entered the final minute. Fifteen seconds after bombing from 8,000ft they ran into near disaster. Doug Hicks: 'All of a sudden the aircraft lurched violently to the left and started a downward spiral. Sparks and flames were visible, streaming past my turret, and my intercom went dead. The hydraulic power to my turret was cut. At that time I noticed tracer bullets arcing some 20ft behind the aircraft. I partially stood up in the turret and returned fire in the direction of the tracer. I did not see where they originated from.

'Looking round, the whole target area was transformed into daylight conditions. The fire-lit sky was filled with dozens of Lancasters, all with the same intent – to bomb the target and head for home. With the aircraft still seemingly out of control, the thought crossed my mind that perhaps I should bale out. I took one look at the burning inferno beneath me and with no hesitation at all decided I would rather ride the aircraft into the ground than jump into the burning hell that was Pforzheim.'[20]

Suddenly, 'D-Dog' righted itself and appeared to be back under control. They then discovered that, although a fighter had fired on them, their problems had a different cause. They had flown into another Lancaster's bombload and had been struck by around sixty 4lb incendiaries: 'Up front, in the cockpit, the pilot had a fire warning from No. 1 engine and feathered it. This was the engine that supplied hydraulic power to my turret. With the engine feathered, the aircraft wanted to turn left. With help from the engineer, the rudder pedals were lashed into the fully right position. The pilot was not aware, at the time, that the left rudder control rod had been burned through, just as if an acetylene torch had been used ...'[20]

Another incendiary punched through the perspex of the mid-upper turret, fracturing the shoulder of Sergeant M.T. Ditson, RCAF, the gunner. He was now on the floor and in agony. Other incendiaries hit both mainplanes, the tailplane and rudders and about ten had fallen inside the fuselage; most failed to ignite. Doug Hicks: 'Back at my end of the aircraft I could see the two main horizontal tailplane assemblies. I counted six holes on the left side and another five on the right side. At this time I was still ignorant of what had happened.'[20]

Harris asked for a course for Manston. The Lancaster's IFF (Identification, Friend or Foe) was set to emergency. Doug Hicks: 'All the crew took up emergency landing positions. We were cleared to land and could feel the aircraft descending on Manston. We touched down and the landing was really smooth. We jumped up and cheered and clapped.' Their elation was premature. 'D-Dog's' left main wheel tyre blew and the bomber sheared off the runway to the left. 'As luck would have it, they were installing new sewer pipes along the side of the runway. The aircraft came into contact with these pipes and the undercarriage collapsed and was flung up through the wing. "D-Dog" came to an abrupt halt. There was no fire and everyone managed to scramble out. No harm done, apart from the mid-upper gunner's broken shoulder.'[20]

They were debriefed, had breakfast and got to bed. Later, they took a ride out to 'D-Dog': 'We counted over sixty holes in all parts of the aircraft. There were holes that revealed the sides of the tanks - a shift of 1in either way would have no doubt set the aircraft on fire. Some incendiaries had hit the aircraft, caught fire, then with their immense heat burned through, falling out of the bottom and continuing their downward trip. One had fallen behind the firewall of No. 1 engine, then started to burn and fall through. This caused the pilot to feather the engine. There were many holes in the tailplane and we could now see where one of the incendiaries had burned through the main operating control rod, some 2in in diameter, effectively causing the left rudder to malfunction. There were ten incendiaries still embedded in various parts of the interior of the aircraft that, luckily, had not ignited. The aircraft was written off on the spot.'[20]

Harris and crew hoped the squadron would send an aircraft south, to pick them up: 'No such luck. We were given vouchers and the bus timetable. Still in our flying gear, we headed for home. We were more than disappointed. After all, we had not only written off an aircraft, but had come very close to buying it.' After their ordeal, they had a crew conference and discussed what to do if another bomber suddenly appeared beneath them during the bombing run. Doug Hicks: 'Our conclusion, to a man, was that no way would we go round again … if he was underneath, too bad.'[20] Harris' aircraft failed to return from an attack on Dessau, on 7 March.

Others had similar, terrifying experiences over Pforzheim, including the crew of Lancaster 'O' of 625 Squadron, from RAF Kelstern, in Lincolnshire. The pilot was 22-year-old Flying Officer Derrell Paige, RCAF. They took a 4,000lb Cookie and a full load of incendiaries to Pforzheim. They lost their Lancaster yet were back in England just three days later, very lucky to be alive. This crew were briefed for the first wave, with a Time Over Target of 20.00–20.03. They took off at 16.29, reached the target and bombed at 20.02 from 7,400ft. As they turned, the target was well alight. There was no flak or searchlights. A large oil tank had just burst into flames. About thirty seconds after release Paige saw a shower of incendiaries immediately ahead and could do nothing to avoid them. The Lancaster flew straight through them, still on a heading of 084 degrees true, completing the photo run following release.[21]

Fifteen to twenty 4lb incendiaries entered the fuselage from above, just astern of the main spar. Three burning incendiaries fell directly behind the wireless operator, who immediately threw them out through a hole in the fuselage made by other incendiaries. One entered in front of the wireless operator, on the starboard side of the fuselage, and this he stamped out with his foot. One bomblet struck the rear turret, coming down behind the rear gunner. It hit to starboard and exploded inside, going out through the bottom of the turret. The turret was jammed and one door would not open, but it left no fire.[21]

Incendiaries destroyed the intercom link to the gunners. Much damage was caused near the rest bed. All wiring was ripped from the main spar astern. There was an incendiary in each wing, in the proximity of each No. 3 tank, almost behind the outboard engines. There was another incendiary in the wing, inboard of the starboard inner engine, which probably did some damage to the coolant system. This caused the starboard inner to vibrate. It caught fire about sixty seconds after the aircraft was hit. The engine was feathered and the fire went out.[21]

Paige had an instinctive desire to get as far away from the target as the condition of his aircraft would allow. He altered course south, onto the next leg, then almost immediately turned west, making for Allied lines. The Lancaster flew on this westerly heading for around five minutes, at which point the incendiary by the No. 3 starboard tank blew up and the starboard outer caught fire. This engine was feathered and the flight engineer managed to put out the fire with the Gravener extinguisher almost immediately. Two minutes later, at around 20.10, Paige asked his navigator for a southerly course, to allow them to regain the protection of the bomber stream.

Gradually losing height, they flew on until they crossed the Rhine at the bend east of Bischweiler, east of Haguenau. They flew over the river at around 4,000ft and the navigator gave a course for Juvincourt, north of Reims, for an emergency landing.[21]

A higher power, however, had decided that this Lancaster was finished. Around two minutes after crossing the Rhine, at around 20.22, the incendiary by the port outer blazed up furiously and Paige gave the order to bale out. The wireless operator went back to tell the gunners. All three then left by the rear door. The wireless operator used the spare parachute, as his own became caught up in broken wiring when he threw out burning incendiaries. It had opened and was useless. The rest of the crew left from the front escape hatch: the bomb aimer went first, followed by the flight engineer, navigator and, finally, the pilot. The port wing was now a mass of flames but Paige had managed to keep control. With everyone out, he made a dash for it, as 'George' – the automatic pilot – was out of action. The abandoned Lancaster turned to starboard, entered a steep dive and the port wing exploded just before it hit the ground.[21]

Dieter Essig was accustomed to alarms and wasn't frightened. He and his mother reached home and just got into the cellar as the bombing began. He sensed the tension among the mothers as the heavy door was shut: 'Our big fear was being trapped. Every shelter had its Blockwart. If the exit was blocked, it was his job to use the pick-axe, smash a hole in the wall and allow us to escape into the cellar next door. My sister and I curled up on a carpet and hugged each other. People around us started to pray.[22]

'As soon as we entered the cellar we put on our gas masks. I hated my mask. It was very hard to breathe – I felt I was suffocating. I have no particular memory of the bombing.' It was different, however, when they opened the door. As it swung back Dieter heard someone mutter: 'Thank God we are alive.' They took in the scene. It was obvious that this was no ordinary raid but something quite exceptional: 'Mother said we had to go down town to find her parents. We made for Nordstadtbrücke. Before we reached it, however, someone coming the other way yelled that it was pointless going on, as the bridge had been destroyed. We tried another way, using the underpass to cross the railway. This underpass had built-in air-raid shelters. We never got beyond the front of the station – there was fire everywhere. A small boy passed us, lost and crying for his mother. Everything was ablaze. We turned back.'[22]

Art student Gisela Bär heard only fragments of words above the noise of bombs. Then a huge blast crushed the cellar: 'The beams gave way like matches. I saw fire flowing into our cellar and Father, uncannily illuminated by the glow of fire, standing against the wall with arms outspread, as if he was crucified …' In a split second the cellar collapsed in a second tremendous explosion. 'Then we were free. Our house had been blasted away. In front of us the street, above us the sky, around us fire. Delayed action bombs went off everywhere. We had to get out. The three of us made it to the nearby railway. The only thing that saved us was our house being blasted

After the raid: the wrecked Nordstadtbrücke. *Photo: Stadtarchiv Pforzheim.*

away! Nobody survived the inferno in the houses next door. Wounded, with singed clothes and hair, we made it to our garden, where we had a little shed that took us for the night.'[23]

Irma Facoltosi also knew this raid was different: 'When the bombing started everything shook, even as far out as Arlinger.' In her future husband's shelter, the near misses forced soot out of the chimneys and turned everyone black: 'Arno knew he had to get everyone out. They just about squeezed through a hole knocked through to the next cellar. Only his Aunt Lizzie was hurt. When scrambling to get out, phosphorous dropped onto her arm. At first she felt no pain, as her skin was protected by a soaked cloth. Then there was contact with her flesh and she started to scream. She bore the scars for the rest of her life. Our shelter withstood the bombing. We came out and saw the city on fire. We went to the top floor and just stared. The entire city had become Hell. That scene is imprinted on my brain; I will never forget it. I can still see it.'[24]

Twelve-year-old Rainer Luppold's shelter was struck by blast from a large bomb. Benches and shelves tumbled and pressure sucked caps and hats from the heads of those inside. The light went out, the cellar door was torn away and people were thrown from one wall to the other. They were trapped as the cellar stairs were blocked by debris: 'We could hear cries for help from the next cellar. We managed to clear the safety door of rubble and we and our ten fellow shelterers were saved.'[25]

They got out just in time as phosphorous was trickling down the stairs. They found Bleichstrasse completely ablaze. The heat was terrific and they could hear desperate cries for help. They broke through the ring of fire by running across open ground towards the Metzelgraben canal. 'We jumped into the water. It almost reached our necks. This saved our lives, but our fellow shelterers didn't make it. They either burnt or were suffocated.'[25]

As people on the ground struggled to leave the cellars and escape the flames, Derrell Paige and his crew left their crippled bomber, on fire after colliding with incendiaries over Pforzheim. They had sent no message, as the wireless was destroyed when the incendiaries struck. Everyone baled out successfully after crossing the Rhine, but both the rear gunner and navigator had to pull the covers from their parachutes in mid-air, as the rip-cords failed. The navigator made a heavy landing and injured his ankle.[26]

Paige landed about half a mile from the crash site. American troops reunited him with his navigator and bomb aimer. The flight engineer landed in a ploughed field and was also picked up by the Americans. The wireless operator dropped into a field and could see his aircraft burning to the west of him. Uncertain of his location, he buried his parachute, saw lights and skirted round them. Two Americans then pounced on him and took him back to their unit. He joined the rest of the crew the next morning. The two gunners landed in a field a quarter of a mile apart and 6 miles east of the crash site. They hid their chutes and set out in a westerly direction. They sat in a road ditch for half an hour, watching passing traffic. Three jeeps went by, then two large vehicles definitely identified as American. They hailed the next jeep and were taken to Hagenau, where they learnt that everyone else was safe. They went to Lunéville by jeep, Paris by train and to England by Dakota, arriving at Croydon on 26 February.[26]

When Squadron Leader Ken Butler's gunner fired on a Fw190 and saw the fighter go on to destroy another bomber, the Lancaster continued its bombing run over Pforzheim. Flight Sergeant Nobby Clark, the bomb aimer, took control and gave instructions: 'Left, left. Steady … steady.' Suddenly, they heard the master bomber announce that he was handing over to his deputy.[27]

In preparing for Pforzheim, 8 Group (Pathfinders) ordered 582 Squadron to provide the master bomber. South African Edwin 'Ted' Swales was selected. Seven supporting aircraft were then added to the battle order. This squadron's motto was '*Praecolamus Designantes*' ('We fly before marking').

Ted Swales was a big man in every sense of the word; he stood out from the crowd in his South African khaki uniform. Swales was destined to win a posthumous Victoria Cross – Bomber Command's last VC of the war – that night. *The Bomber Command War Diaries*, in its entry for the Pforzheim raid, states: 'The Master Bomber was Captain Edwin Swales, DFC … his Lancaster was twice attacked over the target by a German fighter. Captain Swales could not hear the evasion directions given by his gunners because he was broadcasting his own instructions to the main force. Two engines and the rear turret of the Lancaster were put out of action. Captain Swales continued to control the bombing until the end of the raid and must take some credit for the accuracy of the attack. He set out on the return flight but encountered turbulent cloud and ordered his crew to bale out. This they all did successfully but Captain Swales had no opportunity to leave the aircraft and was killed when it crashed. He is buried at the Leopold War Cemetery at Limburg in Belgium.' His aircraft crashed near Valenciennes, some 350 miles from Pforzheim.[28]

Swales' aircraft, PB538, was first hit at a position around 5km north of Pforzheim. He continued to orbit the city perimeter, directing the attack. His luck had held on previous occasions. He got away with it on 23/4 July 1944, as Lancaster JB417 was returning from a raid on Kiel. He was very short of fuel and attempted an emergency landing at Handley Page's Radlett site in Hertfordshire. The aircraft crashed at 03.40 but all survived this misadventure.[29]

Twenty-nine-year-old Ted Swales was a man of unusual character. On leaving school he went to work at Barclays Bank DC & O, Durban. He loved rugby and other sports, and joined the Natal Mounted Rifles before the outbreak of war. He transferred to the South African Air Force, gained his wings in June 1943 and arrived at 582 Squadron, RAF Little Staughton, in June 1944. He flew his first operation on 12 July. It was very unusual for a pilot with no prior operational experience to join the Pathfinders. Towards the end of the year he was flying as deputy for the master bomber, his close friend Squadron Leader Robert Palmer, DFC. Palmer was a Mosquito pilot seconded to 582 from 109 Squadron, also based at Little Staughton.[29]

In a strange echo of what was to come, Palmer's aircraft was damaged over Cologne's Gremberg railyards and the master bomber died, winning a posthumous VC. Swales received the DFC for his part – he took over from Palmer. Swales' citation read: 'This officer was pilot and captain of an aircraft detailed to attack Cologne in December 1944. When approaching the target, intense anti-aircraft fire was encountered. Despite this, a good bombing attack was executed. Soon afterwards the aircraft was attacked by five enemy aircraft. In the ensuing fights, Captain Swales manoeuvred with great skill. As a result, his gunners were able to bring effective fire to bear upon the attackers, one of which is believed to have been shot down.' His DFC was gazetted on the very day he died.[29]

Swales fought hard for a safe return from Pforzheim. He held on until his aircraft was over friendly territory, but he had lost most of his instruments. It is thought that, by the time the others had jumped, the aircraft was too low for Swales to bale out. He died attempting a crash landing. According to Feast: 'The following morning Swales' charred remains were still at the controls, a booted foot jammed in a rudder pedal.'[30]

Swales' last flight was his forty-third operation with 582 Squadron. His VC citation reads: 'Soon after he reached the target area he was engaged by an enemy aircraft and one of his engines was put out of action. His rear guns failed. His crippled aircraft was an easy prey for fighter attacks. Unperturbed, he carried on with his allotted task; clearly and precisely he issued aiming instructions to the main force. Meanwhile, the enemy fighter closed the range and fired again. A second engine of Captain Swales' aircraft was put out of action. Almost defenceless, he stayed over the target area, issuing his aiming instructions until he was satisfied that the attack had achieved its purpose.'[31]

This citation – published in *The London Gazette* of 24 April 1945 – adds that the Pforzheim attack was 'one of the most concentrated and successful of the war'. The final comment on Swales summed up his actions: 'Intrepid in the attack, courageous in the face of danger, he did his duty to the last, giving his life that his comrades might live.'[31]

Some idea of Swales' great courage and determination over Pforzheim is conveyed by the account of Pilot Officer Al Bourne, RCAF, his rear gunner on the 23 February raid. At 20.06 Bourne spotted an aircraft low, to starboard, and he kept a close watch. Unfortunately, he was out of communication with the pilot, who was then broadcasting to the main force: 'At that moment, an enemy aircraft dropped rapidly astern of us and seemed to rise slightly at approximately 20 degrees low on our starboard quarter at a range of less than 400yd. "Fighter. Starboard! Go!" I called on the intercom, then realized there was no response to my call for a corkscrew to starboard because the pilot could not hear me when transmitting. Immediately, I began flashing my starboard "fighter call light", to warn Ted visually of our plight. At no more than 200yd, I opened fire with all four guns. At the same time I felt the aircraft shudder and go into a starboard corkscrew as the fighter opened up with his cannon. As we levelled, with the Me410 still close on our tail, cannon shells straddled each side of my turret, scoring hits on both rudders and inner engines. As the rudder surfaces disintegrated, they looked for all the world like washing on a line on a windy day.'[32]

Bourne's guns were useless without hydraulic power, although he hit the fighter with his last burst. The Lancaster lost height as the master bomber made his last broadcast to the main force. Swales' first plan was to make for Switzerland, but changed his mind when he found he could keep the Lancaster on a steady course. They turned for home. Swales struggled for an hour, with both arms wrapped around the control column, but the aircraft's behaviour deteriorated and they were at around 2,000ft when he confirmed with his navigator that they were over France. He told his crew: 'Jump! Jump! I can't hold her any longer.'[32]

More information on the last flight of 'M-Mike' is contained in a report on the debrief of Swales' crew. The master bomber was due over Pforzheim at 19.58 and he arrived exactly on time and at the right height. They had approached at 5,000ft and then climbed to 8,000 ft. The H₂S radar was off, to avoid early detection. However, this also meant that the Lancaster's Fishpond tail-warner was also off.[33]

Al Bourne fired around 300 rounds until all four guns jammed in quick succession. These were link stoppages and could not be cleared in time to make a difference. The mid-upper gunner, Flight Sergeant B. Leach, saw the fighter when it pulled up to close. He fired a hundred rounds as it broke to port and claimed hits at 300yd range. The fighter fell away vertically and was claimed as 'damaged'.[33]

The debriefing revealed the extent of Swales' difficulties. They had found themselves flying in cloud and Swales had no artificial horizon. The aircraft's behaviour became increasingly erratic and the pilot made constant use of the elevator trim. The Lancaster repeatedly switchbacked, stalled several times and progressively lost height. When they were down to 3,000ft, Swales ordered his crew to don their parachutes. The front hatch was removed and Bourne was given permission to leave the rear turret. On receiving the OK from everyone, Swales told them to jump. Bomb aimer Clive Dodson went first, jumping from 2,200ft. He stood on the rear edge of the front hatch and did a forward roll. He landed safely. Dodson was followed by the flight engineer, C.W. Bennington. He sat on the rear edge, dropped straight down and made a heavy landing, striking his head and shoulder. Pilot Officer A.V Goodacre, RAAF, the wireless operator, dived out of the rear door head first and Al Bourne followed him. It was important to go head first from the rear door, to avoid being struck by the tail. Bourne's chute opened as he left the door and part of it blew back inside, but this was immediately thrust out by Bryn Leach, the mid-upper gunner, who followed him.[33]

Navigator (Nav. 1) Squadron Leader D.P.D. Archer plugged into the flight engineer's position and Swales told him: 'Hurry up. I can't hold her much longer.' Archer dived head first from the rear edge of the front hatchway. He had baled out twice before but still forgot to remove his flying helmet. When the chute opened, the shrouds ripped the helmet off. Pilot Officer R.A. Wheaton, RAAF (Nav. 2), was the last man to leave. He baled out at around 800ft. Before jumping he went forward and gave Swales a 'thumbs up', indicating that everyone had jumped. Later, he said he thought the pilot had understood him. It seems the aircraft, at that moment, was recovering from a dive, as Wheaton had to fight against 'G' to get out. He landed hard, feet together, on soft ground. A foot penetrated some 18in and he twisted his ankle as he rolled over.[33]

Everyone landed within a mile of the burning wreck – the fuel tanks had exploded when it crashed. Wheaton and Bennington came down within 300yd of the aircraft. They were joined by some of the others and went to the Lancaster, but the searing heat made it impossible to approach. There was no sign of Swales. The survivors called at a nearby farm and used the telephone to contact the Americans. Before leaving the area they visited the wreck and found Swales' body. It was unrecognizable, but in a position that suggested he had made no attempt to bale out. The report states: 'The general opinion of the crew is that the captain attempted a belly landing, but that the aircraft was not sufficiently under control.' This report recommended that VHF equipment be modified, to permit any crew member to cut in on the intercom in an emergency.[33]

Notes

1. Monteith, W.E., 'An Account of the 103 Squadron Air Raid on Pforzheim', via R.J. Whymark.
2. Administration's Report and Statistics for the Town of Pforzheim, 1945–1952: City Life 1939–1945.
3. Interview with Hans Gerstung, April 2013.
4. Administration's Report and Statistics for the Town of Pforzheim, 1945–1952: City Life 1939–1945.

5. *Pforzheimer Zeitung*, 23 February 2005.
6. Interview with Gerd Fleig, July 2013.
7. Administration's Report and Statistics for the Town of Pforzheim, 1945–1952: City Life 1939–1945.
8. Interview with Christian Groh, April 2013.
9. Monteith, W.E., 'An Account of the 103 Squadron Air Raid on Pforzheim', via R.J. Whymark.
10. Administration's Report and Statistics for the Town of Pforzheim, 1945–1952: City Life 1939–1945.
11. Interview with Hans Gerstung, April 2013.
12. Milton, G. (2011), *Wolfram*, 247–53.
13. *Pforzheimer Zeitung*, 23 February 2005.
14. Schmalacker-Wyrich, Esther (Ed.), (1980), 'Pforzheim 23. Februar 1945, der Untergang einer Stadt', in: *Bildern und Augenzeugenberichten* (third edition).
15. Pross, M. (1995), *Die Einschläge kommen näher, Aus den Tagebüchern 1943–45 von Friedrich Adolf Katz, 1945–1947 Oberbürgermeister der Stadt Pforzheim*.
16. Operations Record Book entries, 419 Squadron, forwarded 17 April 2013 by German Air Force Flying Instructor Jan Schluetter, an exchange pilot attached to 419 Squadron, a unit training future fighter pilots.
17. Newsletter 44, 26 October 2009, 550 Squadron and RAF North Killingholme Association.
18. Letter from Air Commodore Norman Bonnor, 100 Squadron Association, 23 March 2013.
19. Letter from Chief Warrant Officer Alan R. Blakney, 431 Squadron, RCAF, 18 March 2013.
20. Account by Douglas Hicks, written May 1998, and Newsletter 20, 5 May 2000, 550 Squadron and RAF North Killingholme Association.
21. National Archives, Air 14/314, Report into loss of Lancaster Mk. I (625/O) on Pforzheim raid, 27 February 1945, RAF Kelstern (completed on the crew's return to England following the loss of the aircraft).
22. Interview with Dieter Essig, April 2013.
23. Schmalacker-Wyrich, Esther (Ed.), (1980), 'Pforzheim 23. Februar 1945, der Untergang einer Stadt', in: *Bildern und Augenzeugenberichten* (third edition).
24. Interviews with Irma Baroni (neé Facoltosi), August 2013.
25. *Pforzheimer Zeitung*, 11 February 2005.
26. National Archives, Air 14/314, Report into loss of Lancaster Mk. I (625/O) on Pforzheim raid, February 27, 1945, RAF Kelstern (completed on the crew's return to England following the loss of the aircraft).
27. Monteith, W.E., 'An Account of the 103 Squadron Air Raid on Pforzheim', via R.J. Whymark.
28. Middlebrook, M. and Everitt, C. (1990), *The Bomber Command War Diaries*, 669.
29. Redding, T. (2008), *Flying for Freedom*, 218–20.
30. Feast, S. (2008), *Master Bombers*, 152.
31. Redding, T. (2008), *Flying for Freedom*, 218–20.
32. Feast, S. (2008), *Master Bombers*, 174–6.
33. National Archives, AIR 14/309, Interrogation of aircrew returning from Allied occupied territory: Report No. 8G/K.4.

Chapter Twelve

The Morning After

The Pforzheim death toll, at over 17,000, is cited as the third heaviest in Germany after Hamburg and Dresden.[1] The first local report to the Reich Propaganda Ministry stated: 'Pforzheim, 23 February 1945: 4–500 fast four-engined tactical aircraft; duration twenty minutes; 2–3,000 high explosive bombs, 92 of which were duds; 100 mines, one of which was a dud; 55 long term time-delays; 100,000 stick-type incendiary bombs, 1,500 of which were duds; 20,000 stick-type incendiary bombs with explosive charges, 500 of which were duds; 6–7,000 flame jet incendiary bombs and liquid incendiary bombs; 6–7,000 dead; 35,000 injured; 45,000 homeless.' The Wehrmacht report for 24 February 1945 gave this catastrophe the briefest mention: 'In the early evening hours, a heavy British attack was directed towards Pforzheim.'[2] The first figure for the dead was a gross underestimate. The number of incendiaries dropped was far higher than reported. The number of high explosive bombs was overstated.

At dawn on Saturday, 24 February Waffen SS soldier Gerd Fleig watched the house next door burn down for lack of firefighting water: 'We were lucky. Our house was hit by ten stick incendiaries and some penetrated through to the ground floor. Part of the roof had gone and the windows were out. In the morning I saw the full extent of the devastation. It was almost impossible to get into the city. Dead bodies were all around, sprawled in the debris. Desperate people were looking for relatives.'[3]

In the coming weeks Fleig sought to impose order on chaos. The family set to work: 'The upper floor of our house was soon made fit to live in. The ground floor, rented to another family, was more difficult. We were reunited at Weissenburgstrasse about four weeks after the raid. It took a year to complete the repairs.'[3]

Gerd Fleig was still under the military hospital: 'I went to the officer in charge, explained the position and he told me to take all the time I needed to sort things out. The town itself was in a catastrophic state. I was always extremely fond of Pforzheim and was deeply affected by its destruction. When I looked round, I felt sure the place was too far gone – beyond rebuilding.[3]

In the western suburb of Arlinger, the Facoltosi home was undamaged beyond some broken windows. Teenager Irma Facoltosi: 'During the next day bombed-out friends – including some Jehovah's Witnesses – arrived at our apartment. Within a day or two we had sixteen people living under our roof. On that first morning Mum said we had to start looking for people. Her sister, Amelia Mokel, lived in eastern Pforzhcim. She and her husband escaped along the river and then went into the forest. We tried to get into town but the smoke and flames were too fierce and we

Gutted: a vertical aerial reconnaissance photograph showing the devastated centre of Pforzheim.
Photo: Trustees of the Imperial War Museum.

had to turn back. We were afraid for George and Anna Heiley, friends of the family for many years. George, a retired goldsmith, played the piano. He was an asthma sufferer but often managed the tram ride to visit us. They lived in the city centre, close to the Enz. Had they survived, safe in their cellar? Mum was also worried about Franz and Ida Schlong, friends and fellow Jehovah's Witnesses. Franz was the caretaker at the fine metals company Degussa. They also lived in the town centre, on Zerrennerstrasse.

'George and Anna survived the bombing and went to a reception centre. Their daughter told us they were alive. George and Anna then moved to the spa village of Bad Liebenzell, some 20km away. Mum and I eventually reached their apartment in town. The building was in ruins. We found their small sausage dog sitting in the rubble. We took the dog home. Every time there was an air-raid alert it did something on the carpet.'[4]

Young Rainer Luppold and his family lost their home but escaped the flames and eventually reached Büchenbronn. They found refuge in the attic of the home of a woman apprenticed to his father, Franz. They had no idea they would stay there until mid-1947. Rainer's mother had third-degree burns and was unable to walk for weeks. His father had second-degree burns but, nonetheless, was drafted into the Wehrmacht for the last-ditch defence of the Rhine near Offenburg. Within a couple of weeks he was a prisoner and was held by the French until 1947. Rainer also had burns and suffered smoke inhalation. These injuries soon cleared up but later in life, even in his seventies, the mental scars remained.[5]

Christian Groh, Stadtarchiv Pforzheim's former director: 'Survivors were billeted in nearby villages or stayed with relatives on the city outskirts or just beyond. The main area of devastation, in the centre, was cordoned off. Notices warned that looters would be shot, although there is no record of executions. There was very little looting, but there was total confusion. Inside the wrecked city, work went on to recover and identify bodies. The dead were buried in several mass graves; the biggest were at the main cemetery, Hauptfriedhof. Fearful of disease, the authorities were in a hurry. Many corpses were cremated. Later, during the decades of reconstruction, the bodies of the missing continued to be found. Yet, despite the overwhelming scale of the damage and the terrible human loss, morale in Pforzheim did not collapse. People were very disciplined.'[6]

In the early morning of 24 February art student Gisela Bär tried to reach the Hotel Post on Leopoldsplatz. 'I wanted to find Eva. I found my way to the Luisen underpass, where many people lay sleeping on both sides. At first I was surprised, until I realized with sudden horror that these were dead people.' She was unable to walk on, but recovered as two people approached the underpass from Luisenplatz. 'They were parents looking for their son. They found him dead in the underpass. The father picked up the boy, hit his head against the wall again and again and yelled: "Wake up! Come on, wake up!" and then repeated "Thank you very much, Adolf Hitler!" The mother had a screaming fit and started to spin round. This was too much for me. I felt terribly sick and fainted. When I came to everything was quiet. I lay

Recovering Pforzheim's dead: bodies laid out for collection. *Photo: Stadtarchiv Pforzheim.*

face down on a corpse, my hands in the charred hair. Something broke inside me. I was no longer able to feel any kind of emotion. I continued as a different human being. I imagine the instinct of self-preservation wrapped a protective wall around me. I would need that over the coming days and weeks.'[7]

Gisela reached the heap of debris that was once the Hotel Post: 'Eva stood in front of it, crying but safe! We hugged without speaking.' Rescuers were trying to reach people trapped in the cellar. They entered the shelter through Blumenstrasse and found people tightly packed on the stairs: 'They were all dead, suffocated. We carried several of them outside until we were exhausted. Then we crawled downstairs over the dead bodies. I can't and don't want to describe the images that presented themselves to us down there! It was terrible; nobody could be saved.'[7]

Four-year-old Klaus Feucht was safe, having been rescued from the river Enz by an elderly man and his wife. 'They had a tiny house and kitchen garden with geese and hens running about and washing on a wire. They took good care of me.' Feucht had yet to tell anyone his name. He was taken to a woman in Eutingen who also treated him with kindness and understanding. With much patience, she finally learnt that his address was Pflügerstrasse 24. A postman was consulted, to find his family name. At that point he said he was Klaus Feucht: 'After some time my father came on a bicycle to pick me up. The nice woman offered me a toy as a farewell present. I could choose between a kitten and a puppy dog. After hesitating for a long time I chose the dog. Unfortunately, it was lost during the turmoil that followed.'[8]

The immediate post-raid Bomber Command intelligence reports may vary in detail and statistics but all have no doubt about the outcome for Pforzheim. The results were summed up in three words: 'large scale destruction'. A document issued four weeks after the attack – *Night Raid Report No. 846* – comments: 'The intention was to destroy the built-up area and associated industries and rail facilities. This was an outstanding attack with destruction on a scale as complete as any target ever attacked. There was hardly a single building left intact throughout the whole area and, apart from the tremendous gutting by fires, many acres of buildings were levelled to the ground. Damage to railway facilities was also heavy, the goods yard was completely burnt out, rolling stock destroyed, two of the river bridges had collapsed and the road-over-rail bridge spanning the marshalling yard was hit and rendered unserviceable.'[9]

The Pforzheim *Night Raid Report* had this to say about the enemy defences: 'Bombers flew south of Paris at a low altitude (below 5,000ft) to attack Pforzheim, preserving signals silence and having only 60 miles of enemy territory to cross. At the same time a "Window" feint was directed towards Neuss, strengthened by a "Mandrel" screen moving up with it, while "Oboe" Mosquitoes bombed Essen. The enemy put up locally based fighters, about the time our bombers reached the battle line, and an order was received three minutes after zero hour instructing them to fly towards the flares, which must have been visible in the clear conditions prevailing.

There was heavy and light flak at Pforzheim and visual targets were accurately engaged.'[9]

Another Bomber Command report, made the day after the attack, summarized the raid on the basis of aircrew debriefing: 'Markers were concentrated, well placed and strongly backed up. Ground detail was identified without difficulty and bombing is reported to have been very good. Fires started early in the attack and spread rapidly. By the end of the attack almost the entire town north of the river was a mass of flames. Smoke rose to several thousand feet and a number of large explosions were reported.'[10]

The bombers released 820.2 tons of incendiaries (including markers) and 727.5 tons of high explosive bombs over Pforzheim: 327 4,000lb high capacity blast bombs (Cookies); 52 2,000lb high capacity bombs; 48 1,000lb medium capacity bombs; 60 1,000lb American bombs; 170 500lb medium capacity bombs; 15 500lb general purpose bombs and 34 500lb American bombs.[10] At this stage in the war, with the intensity of bombing reaching unprecedented levels, Bomber Command occasionally ran short of bombs and its heavy aircraft were loaded with whatever was available, including American bombs.

The majority of Lancasters bombing Pforzheim that night came from 1 Group squadrons. This Group's summary of the Yellowfin raid offers a vivid impression of how events unfolded: 'The target was quite clear of cloud and ground detail was clearly visible through thin ground haze in the brilliant moonlight. At 19.54 hrs the first red TIs went down, quickly followed by illuminating flares and salvoes of mixed red and green TIs. The markers were all very concentrated and in the excellent visibility could be seen to be accurately placed. The whole marking effort was first rate and, following the Master Bomber's instructions, the bombing was extremely concentrated and accurate. Fires got a very quick hold and almost the whole of the town north of the river appeared a mass of flames. By 20.06 hrs no TIs could be seen owing to the brilliance of the fires, whereupon the Master Bomber ordered bombing on the centre of the smoke. Several large explosions were observed, continuing to 20.30 hrs, and fires could be seen for 150 miles on the return. Very slight light flak was encountered over the target. Two aircraft were hit by flak and two more were damaged by falling incendiaries. There was considerable fighter activity over the target and along the first two legs of the homeward trip. Thirteen aircraft were engaged in combat and there were five claims of enemy aircraft destroyed and one probably destroyed.' The report added: 'Photographs show the whole of the town burning furiously and the attack would appear to have been a marked success.'[11]

Another report, from 6 Group (RCAF), echoes other official accounts: 'The target area was described as a blazing inferno, with smoke rising to 12,000ft …' It comments on the opposition: 'Defences over the target were surprisingly accurate, especially towards the end of the attack, with light and slight to moderate heavy flak bursting between 6,000ft and 9,000ft in barrage form. There was considerable fighter activity, mostly at a higher altitude in the target area and as far as the battle line on the homeward route. Four combats were reported …'[12] Canadian aircraft dropped 89.3 tons of high explosive and 99.8 tons of incendiaries on Pforzheim.

How effective were the British radio-countermeasures? The post-raid Signals Intelligence report commented: 'The raid was carried out at low level – below 5,000ft as far as 07 deg. East and bombing below 10,000ft … Signals silence was observed until 07 deg. East and, except for the PFF, no H_2S was switched on. These precautions effectively concealed the approach of the bombers and the first indication of their presence was given by reports of bombing from 19.50 onwards.'[13]

On the night fighter effort, this report stated that three fighter groups were involved (probably I, II and IV NJG6). 'One unidentified unit was ordered to the target at 20.04. The reaction was very late but these three units, based in the Stuttgart area, could have been on the spot within a very few minutes. Plots on the return route were passed as far as the Rhine.'[13] The fighters took their toll over the first 50 miles of the return, when around eight of the casualties occurred.[14]

According to Bomber Command's *Interception Tactics Report*, there were twelve losses on the Pforzheim raid: ten Lancasters and two other aircraft (carrying out signals patrols with the main force). These casualties were attributed as follows: eight to fighters, three to flak (two to light flak) and one classified 'unknown'. The fighter bases providing opposition were probably Tailfingen (25 miles from target), Grosssachsenheim (20 miles) and Schwäbisch Hall (50 miles).[14]

Thirteen-year-old Bernhard Mauderer had lost his father only a couple of months before the raid. Now he had lost his mother and two of his four siblings. Their house and the family's hairdressing salon were destroyed on 23 February 1945. He had stayed with the evacuees on completing the final escort trip for children who were fortunate enough to leave Pforzheim before the big attack: 'We were twenty-eight children evacuated to Neuenweg. All except two received news from Pforzheim that their relatives had survived. The two were my friend Herbert Kuhn and myself. We got permission to go by train to Pforzheim, to find out what had happened. Pforzheim was still shrouded in smoke and fire. We struggled through the debris to Leopoldplatz. Herbert and I agreed that we would go to our respective homes, but would meet up at midday to exchange news. This didn't happen. I waited until 2pm. I never heard anything more of Herbert.

'I struggled over mountains of debris to reach Schulze-Delitzsch-Strasse. When I got there, all I found was parts of the cellar walls. In chalk on a wall were thirteen crosses with the names of those who had died in the cellar. Among these were my mother, my younger brother and my sister. Two bombed houses along, soldiers were busy searching for survivors. I asked them if they had taken the dead from No. 4. They said yes and that the bodies were all at the cemetery. My first thoughts were: "What now?" I realized that, at the age of 13, I was an orphan. I returned to the crosses on the wall, to make sure and to say farewell to the house. I couldn't cry. We children were so influenced by the war. We all believed victory would come. The Hitler Jugend taught us that, after victory, everything would be better.'[15]

'All alive': chalked messages among the ruins. *Photo: Stadtarchiv Pforzheim.*

Bernhard went to his Aunt Louise's house: 'I knew immediately I wasn't welcome. I told them about the death of my mother and the two kids. Nobody knew what had happened to the others, Hans and Rosemarie. My brother Hans was apprenticed to a baker who had lost a leg at the beginning of the war. When the bombing began Hans carried his employer across the street to a trench. He survived the raid, along with the other occupants of the house. The baker was from Nagold. He and his wife took Hans in.'[15]

Bernhard Mauderer was left with nothing except his Hitler Jugend uniform, two pairs of pants and two pairs of socks: 'My aunt and uncle in Hamberg village had a small farm – two cows, a calf, pigs, hens and rabbits. There was a small carpenter's workshop. I had to share a room with my grandmother, who was well into her seventies. My grandmother and I were not allowed to sit at the same table with them. I had to feed the cows and pigs, muck out and do a lot more. After two weeks Hans turned up, looking for me. We hugged each other and cried. He stayed four days and then returned to Nagold.'[15]

In preparation for a major attack, the city had established a series of first aid centres manned by doctors and support staff. Four were located in town and three (Nordstadtschule, the museum and Schwarzwaldschule) were now in ruins. Only the one located in the Gymnasium remained. This aid post functioned in the surviving cellars. There were people with phosphorous burns, others suffering from smoke poisoning and some with broken limbs. People arrived on stretchers or doors. The official report described the scene as 'an image of misery and pain'. A nursing home was used as a hospital, but this overflowed and the injured were taken to Herrenalb, Neuenbürg, Bad Liebenzell, Mühlacker, Maulbronn and Bretten.[16]

During the first twenty-four hours survivors sheltered wherever they could, from barracks to garden sheds. Many found shelter in the outlying districts. The Seehaus emergency feeding station came into use during that Saturday. Soon, other feeding centres were set up, in Würm, Eutingen, Dietlingen and behind the Dillweissenstein paper mill. Field kitchens served survivors who had reached Büchenbronn and Huchenfeld. Initially, food was given free. The feeding stations provided breakfast, stew or soup for lunch and a cold dinner. Trucks took food to fifteen distribution points across town and around 30,000 people received emergency meals.[16]

This response worked reasonably well. Food stored in warehouses was destroyed in the bombing, but the Ernährungsamt (municipal food office) had stored sufficient food out of town to cover the first days. Buckenberg barracks survived the bombing and now housed a food and reception centre. Karlsruhe supplied bread for Pforzheimers until emergency bakeries began operating. The authorities arranged for restocks of food and a generous ration of tobacco and brandy. Two major emergency response teams arrived. One set up a catering facility in Dietlingen, serving bombed-out people. The second, at Eutingen, distributed clothing and household goods. A third distribution centre then opened next to Dillweissenstein's open air swimming pool. Banking points were also established and each bombed out individual received an emergency allowance of 100 Reichsmark.[16]

Soup kitchen: Hans Gerstung's mother serving a meal at the Brauhauskeller. This photograph was taken before the February 1945 raid. Soup kitchens fed troops in transit and soldiers on leave. They were a lifeline for bombed out families. Other soup kitchens were established at Saalbau and, subsequently, Nordstadtschule (then known as Adolf Hitler Schule). *Photo: Hans Gerstung.*

Dieter Essig, his mother and his sister continued their search at first light that Saturday: 'We tried to reach the city to find Grandma. We climbed over rubble and bodies. Many people were sprawled in the streets where they had died, their bodies shrunk in the extreme heat. My mother had me and my sister firmly by the hand.

When we finally reached Grandma's, we saw only huge hills of burning rubble. Days later Mother was told that burning people, in their agony, jumped into the Nonnenmühlwehr reservoir. Grandma jumped into the water to escape the flames and survived, unlike many others. She was rescued and taken to the improvised hospital at Öschelbronn. At first we thought she was dead but then heard she was alive and at the hospital. My grandfather was never seen again; I don't know where he died. As for the Marktplatz shelter, it received a direct hit and there were no survivors.

'My aunt and uncle lived elsewhere in the city. My uncle was never found. My aunt survived – she also ended up in hospital at Öschelbronn. She had a broken leg.' [17] Interestingly, Essig described his aunt as 'uninjured' – which was true, in a relative sense: a broken leg didn't count in the face of total catastrophe. The Essig apartment was damaged, with the windows blown out, yet they still had a home: 'I don't remember crying. This was wartime and part of everyday life. I didn't have any toys to lose. My sister told me I could have toys when the war was over. Following the attack our feelings were numbed. There was numbness everywhere. I am now in my seventies and never have nightmares. I have memories and sometimes I think of it, but I was not traumatized.' Essig has no memory of what they did later that morning: 'I know we spent the afternoon and most of the evening outside, with my mother turning over bodies, looking for her mother.'[17]

Hans Gerstung stayed two days with his aunt, on the city outskirts. He remembers the morning after: 'When dawn came, my aunt made coffee and shared out her bread ration. After breakfast, Mother and I made our way back to our apartment. It was still pretty much intact but we couldn't live there in winter without windows and doors. Father had missed the bombing – he was away in Alsace. He came back as soon as he heard. As an architect, he knew plenty of tradesmen living in the largely undamaged city outskirts. He organized them to come in and shutter the windows. Many were sealed by cutting internal doors in half and nailing them into place.'[18]

Hans Gerstung's father had six sisters. One was missing. Anna and her husband, Richard Salé, lived near Leopoldsplatz, at Westliche Karl-Friedrich-Strasse 48. Their bodies were thought to be in the cellar but the building was still too hot to enter, even three days after the bombing: 'We clambered over rubble and bodies and managed to enter the cellar but we could get only halfway in. The extreme heat forced us back. We returned a few days later; neighbours said the building had cooled. We went into the cellar and found seven bodies. They were tiny – shrunk by the heat. We took a closer look and noticed that two bodies were pressed together, as though hugging each other when overcome by death. We had to use a lot of force to separate them. Their heads and other extremities were tiny, shrunken by heat. They were unrecognizable but Mother said: "That's Anna!" She recognized her dress. The dress material was intact where the bodies had been squeezed together and she recognized the pattern. That's how we identified them.'[18]

Young Bernhard Mauderer was ordered back for duty with Pforzheim's Hitler Jugend on 27 February: 'I helped with the mountains of dead bodies. I had to report to Eutingen. Failure to report within two days meant no ration cards. Sedanplatz was the assembly point for working parties.' He rose at 6.00am, walked through the woods to Pforzheim and, upon arrival, received hot tea and two slices of coarse rye bread with artificial honey. Lunch came in large containers from Buckenberg barracks: 'Mostly it was soup or stew with rye bread. Once I remember there was soup with a sausage. At 5.00pm I had to walk back to Hamberg village.

'Those ten days have stayed with me all my life. I had to take dead bodies on a wheelbarrow or by handcart to Sedanplatz. There, farmers with horses and carts were taking the bodies to the cemetery. Dead bodies were stacked like logs. When each layer of bodies was loaded, they were spread with lime and off they went. One body I shall never forget. He must have been an SS man. Somebody had placed the body in a child's bath tub. In the heat, the body had shrivelled. Burnt into the forehead was an imprint of his cap badge. This picture will remain with me to my death.'[19]

A photo reconnaissance sortie flown two days after the raid was timed to allow smoke to clear. The camera aircraft crossed the ruins at 13.20 hrs on Sunday 25 February 1945. The photo interpretation report stated: 'The attack on the night of February 23/24 has reduced the buildings in the greater part of the town to hollow shells or heaps of rubble. Most of the identifiable factories, including seven of priority 3 rating, have been destroyed or severely damaged. The passenger station is now completely gutted; further damage has been caused to buildings associated with the goods depot and marshalling yard and the road bridge spanning the yard has been cut. The Goethe Bridge over the river Enz has been demolished … the electricity works has been destroyed, the gasworks severely damaged and many public buildings destroyed.'

The report concluded: 'scarcely a building remains intact south of the railway, between the river and the goods stations on the east and west sides of town. A further area of devastation is seen in the built-up area between the Enz and Nagold rivers and in the small suburb lying south of the Enz. It is known that almost every house in this town was a small workshop engaged in the production of precision parts for instruments, small arms and fuses and, in consequence, it is not possible to identify individual concerns among the closely packed dwellings, many of which are now demolished almost down to ground level, with isolated fires still burning among the ruins. However, the majority of the identifiable factories … are either severely damaged or totally destroyed. Damage to transportation facilities is confined chiefly to buildings connected with the marshalling yard and the main passenger station. In addition, the road–over–rail bridge spanning the marshalling yard has been hit and is unserviceable and two of the river bridges are collapsed and unserviceable.'[20]

Some survivors recalled the strange silence that Saturday morning. Martha Luise Rodi: 'Everything is deathly quiet. Everyone is paralysed, speechless and dumb.'

From time to time the silence was broken by rumbling, as another building collapsed.[21] Thousands of survivors were leaving the stricken city. Hannelore Schöttgen had survived by moving away from the firestorm and following the riverbank. She was surprised to find her parents' house intact, and they were soon reunited.[22]

Captain Max Rodi was in Stuttgart at the time of the bombing. He saw the orange glow over Pforzheim. It then began to rain ash, deposited up to 30 miles from the fires. He tried to telephone his family but all lines were dead and he was then given leave to find them. On the way into Pforzheim he passed groups of shocked survivors going in the opposite direction. He finally reached Martha Luise and their undamaged home.[23]

Soot-blackened survivors began to reach Eutingen. Marie Charlotte Aichele prepared food for the refugees. Hannelore Schöttgen's mother made hot drinks. Friends turned up grasping tokens of past lives, including ski boots and a violin. Then a family friend, Ferdinand von der Sanden, arrived at the Schöttgens' kitchen door. Hannelore asked where his wife was. The man was distraught. He pointed to the bag he had carried in: 'What's left of her is here.' He opened the bag. The woman's face and shoulders had been cut off by a timber beam: 'That's probably what stopped her burning completely. It must have fallen on her.' He asked them to go with him to the cemetery, but then collapsed.[23]

Hannelore Schöttgen saw people digging frantically, trying to reach family members and friends buried under the rubble: 'On the roadside there were bodies, put there so people could identify them.' She and her mother went along the remains of Durlacherstrasse and came across Gretel, a family friend: 'There were two tiny blackened corpses lying on the street, like bits of burnt wood. Gretel pointed to one of them and said: "That's what's left of my mother." A nearby Nazi Blockleiter then abused her for being unpatriotic. People filled carts and wheelbarrows with the dead.'[23]

Leaving Eutingen, Marie Charlotte Aichele walked down the hill and into the devastation: 'Climbing over rubble, walking over corpses – there is no end to the horror. All the people in the Marktplatz, Lammstrasse, Schlossberg, Leopoldstrasse and Sedanplatz died in their cellars.'[23]

Marie Charlotte began to learn of the deaths of people she knew. She walked up the hillside to Spichernstrasse, to check whether the Rodis had survived. She found them, and the two women began talking as Max Rodi recorded his experiences. He had used a pick-axe to break into a close friend's cellar: 'the stones got hotter and hotter the deeper I dug. No-one could possibly be alive under there.' He ran into a cousin looking for his family: 'The two of us clambered over heaps of rubble and managed to get into one of the cellars, where we found what was left of his family. We didn't stay to identify them because Walter couldn't cope with it.'[23]

Sigrid Kern (née Weber), who had been a home-help at the Aicheles' home, saw a terrible thing: shrunken bodies recovered from a public shelter were stacked on the pavement. 'We worried about grandmother and my friends. It was impossible to get into Pforzheim. The next day I climbed over debris and saw the shrunken bodies of those who had burnt to death trying to get into the Enz. There was still intense heat, a strong wind and an awful stench. I made it to the Kunstgewerbeschule, where Professor Aichele taught. I tried to get through via Leopoldplatz. Then I tried to find my aunt's house at Westliche and went past the large air-raid shelter at Bohnenberger Schlössle. The bodies from this shelter had been laid out on the pavement. Helpers were wiping the faces of the corpses with wet rags, to make identification easier. I didn't recognize anyone. There were carts there, stacked with bodies. They were taking the dead to the cemetery. In the physical sense I was petrified, but I wasn't panicking. I could still think straight. As terrible as it was, it was expected – everyone had been talking about such a raid for so long. I had a habit of talking to myself. I told myself that I could do nothing about these terrible things. But I also told myself that I would survive and play my part in recovery and reconstruction.

'I had to give up my search for Gran. I couldn't get through. Later, we discovered that she was dead. There was no body, just a blue purse with her house keys. Some French POWs were ordered to help clear the streets. My father struck up a good relationship with these men. He gave them schnapps to clear the area around our home. It wasn't a bribe; it was a gesture, to help them cope with the stench and the mangled bodies. The stench stayed in my nose and in my hair. You couldn't wash it out.'[24]

Sigrid saw soot-covered survivors arriving at Eutingen: 'It was difficult to accommodate so many refugees. They were not just from Pforzheim but also from nearby cities such as Karlsruhe. We already had the Bartel family from Karlsruhe billeted with us. Five people now lived in our apartment. It seemed like the end of the world - no schools, no place of work, no city.'[24]

Burying thousands of dead was a major challenge as no working excavator could be found. A machine had to be brought in from Heilbronn, 45 miles away. Mass graves were excavated and corpses were covered with quicklime. The soldiers undertaking the mass burials were issued with cognac. There were no formal funerals. Priests stood by the grave pits for days, blessing newly arrived corpses. Many remains were carried to the cemetery by surviving family members. A solitary figure worked in the stench, trying to register bodies.[25]

The banker Adolf Katz had feared this day for so long. He watched the swirling dust and smoke in the subdued light of dawn: 'Around us nothing but rubble. I went through buried streets to the bank; it was heavily damaged by two direct hits. The basement was burning but the safe was still intact, although the doors can't be opened owing to heat and blast. In the streets, many dead people are lying around, horribly disfigured or half-charred. Sixty BDM girls suffocated in a cellar. Not a single inhabitable house in the entire city. Only half of Brötzingen and a narrow rim of villas on the heights are still intact. Other than that, there is only rubble and many thousands buried underneath it.'[26]

Max Gaupp was still trying to discover if his father, in Rennfeldstrasse, and sister-in-law, in Schwarzwaldstrasse, were still alive. He had been forced to retreat from the fires during the night, but tried again and made more progress during the morning. It was a 'climbing tour' of rubble mounds and, slowly, Gaupp came to appreciate the scale of the disaster that had overwhelmed Pforzheim. He began in Zähringerallee and ended up in Schwarzwaldstrasse: 'the smoke burnt my eyes and the smell of scorched corpses took my breath away. People who hardly knew each other called out: "You're still alive!" "Yes, but that's it. Everything is gone!"'[27]

The station had burnt out and it was impossible to reach the post office via Luisenstrasse. 'I climbed up to the railway tracks and walked until I was right across from the post office. There I climbed down rubble that was metres high. In Leopoldplatz there was a deep bomb crater in the middle of the square. No more houses. It took me over half an hour to get from Leopoldplatz to Rossbrücke. Scorched bodies everywhere. From Rossbrücke to Herz-Jesu-Kirche – dozens of corpses. The same in Sedanplatz. All burnt.'[27]

Gaupp's father's house was destroyed. His usual shelter was now a pile of rubble 2m high: 'I didn't have to look for survivors and went on to Saalbau ... the debris field ended only beyond Lameystrasse. My brother's house was still standing ...'[27]

When Gaupp made his way back he saw the destruction in Dillsteiner Strasse, Jahnstrasse and Turnplatz: 'Over the little bridge at Reichsbank. No more Reichsbank. No more Oberrealschule, no more Gymnasium. It was impossible to get through at Emilienstrasse, so I went past the northern bank of the Enz to Goethestrasse. There were dead bodies floating in the water. After I had climbed up Goethestrasse, I made a turn to Westliche Karl-Friedrich-Strasse. Bohnenberger Schlössle, with its large air-raid shelter underneath, had taken several direct hits. A dozen dead people were in front of the entrance. Down in the shelter there were almost another hundred victims. All the dead had foam at the mouth. They were killed by blast.'[27]

There were no intact houses in Museumstrasse and Max Gaupp could hardly recognize Luisenplatz. 'There were bodies in the passage to Luitgardstrasse, among them two children.' He had been walking for four hours. He noticed how the public shelters had failed to withstand hits: 'There was a cellar filled with 900 dead at Schlossberg. A company of soldiers among them had been on their way to the station.'[27]

In the Gymnasium cellars, military rescue teams arrived and began removing the badly injured. Dr Karl Hillenbrand stood in a largely emptied space by 16.00 that Saturday. The flood of injured had been treated and moved on. 'A little girl of around 3 years of age still lay on the straw. She had third-degree burns. I took the child in with me for a couple of days, until she was picked up by relatives.' Later he discovered that her parents and siblings had all died in their home in Leopoldstrasse.[27]

The recovery of bodies and the burials continued for many weeks. Foreign workers were drafted in to dig out the victims. At the main cemetery, burials in family crypts and grave plots were allowed, but families had to dig the graves themselves. In many cases this task was not demanding, as the remains consisted of just a few bones, brought to the cemetery in a cardboard box.[28]

Helmut Watter's mother and small sister had been to the military hospital – set up at Osterfeld School – that day. They visited Helmut's soldier father, who was recovering from wounds. In the evening, when the bombing stopped, Helmut was left to watch over his sister, while the adults went out to help: 'the next morning they came back tired, full of despair and with black hands and faces. They sat on the bench, underneath the apple tree in the yard. Nobody slept. My brother told me about men and women running into burning houses to save what they could: small items of furniture, mattresses, sewing machines and so on. All these things were piled up in the streets. Men drank schnapps to give themselves courage to go back into burning houses. One or two days after the attack my mother told me she had to go to the municipal hospital in order to help. She was a certified nurse and had worked there before she got married.'[29]

The day after the attack Hans Ade's father tried to go downtown, to Sophienstrasse, to check the apartment. 'He took me but we never made it – we couldn't get through. It was a week before we could reach our home. On the way we passed the butcher's, now a pile of rubble. We had to clamber over debris. Much of the rubble was still very hot after a week. We had to keep moving, otherwise our feet would burn. We reached the Kunstgewerbeschule. It was burnt out, although the outer shell was still standing. Then we got to the apartment. Everything was flattened. The only recognizable thing was the big bakery oven, on the ground floor. It rose above the pile of rubble. We started digging, trying to reach the cellar. The temperature had been so high that jars of preserved fruit had become small glass balls. Father had several barrels of apple wine down there. All we found were the iron hoops of the barrels. We found some dishes. In the extreme heat they had been fired again! The only things we recovered were ceramic jars that had held pickled foods. We used one as an umbrella stand for years. One day, without warning, it shattered into pieces. I remember returning from our first visit to the apartment. Near the Stadtkirche I saw slit trenches full of dead people. They had burnt to death. They had been hit by phosphorous.'[30]

Hans Ade was not in shock, but, rather, overwhelmed with helplessness. He felt hatred: 'The pictures in my mind never went away. I can remember exactly what the bodies looked like. I thought the fifty or sixty people in the slit trenches were all children. In fact, they were mostly adults but their bodies had shrunk to the size of kids in the intense heat. A terrible stench hung over the ruins. The clean-up *kommandos* got to work. They excavated a big shelter at Sedanplatz that was really deep. Everyone inside had suffocated. There were hundreds of bodies lined up on Marktplatz. They looked as if they were asleep. I joined other boys scavenging in the rubble for food and anything else that might be useful. At least we still had somewhere to live. The doctor's villa belonged to the city. When the French took over, we were told we could stay there until a new administration started up later in the year.'[30]

When dawn broke Friedrich Wagner paused from his rescue work at the Osterfeldschule military hospital. He headed for Schlossberg and the Barfüsserkirche shelter: 'A terrible scene at Bohnenberger Schlössle. A large number of dead, partly mangled, lay in front of the building – many children among them. Several charred corpses lay in front of the air-raid shelter at Schlossberg, shrunk to doll size. They crumbled away to ash at the slightest touch. You could tell from the remains of clothes lying around that these were the corpses of the soldiers I had guided the evening before. Inside the shelter everyone was dead.' He then found a rescue team working at the Barfüsserkirche shelter: 'Most of the occupants were dead.' Later, he joined an attempt to enter the town hall shelter, but intense heat forced them back.[31]

Emmi Nagel came close to asphyxiation in the public shelter of Gymnasiumstrasse 52. When she came to it was daylight: 'I lay in a slit trench on Theaterplatz, on a bench between dead people. To my right was a little boy. To my left was an old lady. A man was walking up and down, repeating to himself: "I won't allow them to pick up the body!" I got up slowly, climbed over debris into the open and all I could see were destroyed houses and dead bodies. Two Red Cross nurses came along. When they saw me they threw up their hands in horror. When one of them shouted: "You're still alive?", the other gave her a thump.'[31]

Emmi was taken to a first aid post on Forststrasse: 'I had a blue face and my teeth were chattering.' Still dazed by smoke poisoning, she was put on a truck full of seriously injured people. The military hospital was too full to take them and they ended up on straw in a nearby church. Emmi didn't ask about her mother. She didn't utter a word.[31]

Artur Kühn, the delivery driver who knew instinctively that his wife and daughter were dead, had taken shelter in a room on Ludwig-Wilhelm-Strasse. He couldn't sleep and got moving at 5am. He headed for the factory, in the company of the husband of one of the female workers. They found the works completely destroyed, although the cellar looked intact. They cut through the steel blind and saw someone on the exit ladder. It was Joachim, the boss' son. His mother stood behind him. Both were dead. 'Two men climbed down. They all sat peacefully down there, on cane chairs and benches. My wife and daughter as well. They had froth bubbles under their noses. All had been killed by tremendous pressure. A heavy aerial mine had exploded right next to the cellar. All life down there had been snuffed out abruptly …'[31]

The dead were recovered and taken to Ispringer underpass, where Artur's van was parked. He drove the dead to the cemetery and attached labels around their necks, identifying the corpses. His wife, Lydia, was the third name on the list of dead. His daughter, Anneliese, was the fourth. The wife of a nightshift worker asked Artur to drive her husband's body to Eutingen. He went to the Hauptfriedhof (the main cemetery) to pick up the body: 'the entire building was crowded with dead. Outside lay a couple of hundred mutilated, half-burned, half-charred bodies.' He decided to take the bodies of his wife and daughter to Eutingen, 'away from this dead city'.[31]

Artur Kühn continued to recover bodies and drive them to the cemetery. He held onto the knowledge that his son was alive, as a POW. People around him were confused and in shock. He helped one old man recover his son's body, pushing it along in a handcart. When he got home his wife told him that it was not their son.[31]

Anneliese Vestewig-Fischer had got into the river Enz to escape the flames. She passed out. When she came to, she was in a bed in Brötzingen. During the morning, her rescuers took her to a first aid post. She was moved again and heard a doctor say: 'She'll probably die. Try to get her name.' Four days later her husband arrived: 'He looked at me for a moment and then left the room again. When outside, he asked the doctor if it really was me. He couldn't recognize me. My hair was burnt frizzles, my skin scorched. I was disfigured by burns ...'[31]

Notes

1. Middlebrook, M. and Everitt, C. (1990), *The Bomber Command War Diaries*, 669–70.
2. *Pforzheimer Zeitung*, 23 February 2005.
3. Interview with Gerd Fleig, July 2013.
4. Interviews with Irma Baroni (neé Facoltosi), August 2013.
5. *Pforzheimer Zeitung*, 11 February 2005.
6. Interview with Christian Groh, April 2013.
7. Schmalacker-Wyrich, Esther (Ed.), (1980), 'Pforzheim 23. Februar 1945, der Untergang einer Stadt', in: *Bildern und Augenzeugenberichten* (third edition).
8. *Pforzheimer Zeitung*, 23 February 2005.
9. National Archives, AIR 14/3412: Pforzheim: 23/24 February: Night Raid Report No. 846, 25 March 1945.
10. National Archives, AIR 14/3422, Bomber Command Intelligence Narrative of Operations, No. 1015.
11. National Archives, AIR 25/3, 16 (Appendices), No. 1 Group, Summary of Operations, Night 23/24 February 1945.
12. National Archives, AIR 25/131, 145 (Appendices), HQ, No. 6 (RCAF) Group, Operations Record Book.
13. National Archives, AIR 14/309, Bomber Command Signals Intelligence and RCM Report No. 53, Night 23/24 February, 1945.
14. National Archives, AIR 14/3378, Interception Tactics Report, Part II – Night, HQ BC, Air Staff Intelligence BC/S.27876/Int.3.
15. Mauderer, B., memoir.
16. Administration's Report and Statistics for the Town of Pforzheim, 1945–1952: City Life 1939–1945.
17. Interview with Dieter Essig, April 2013.
18. Interview with Hans Gerstung, April 2013.
19. Mauderer, B., memoir.
20. National Archives, AIR 21/288, Immediate Interpretation Report No. K 3838: Pforzheim: Provisional Statement of Damage, 26 February 1945.
21. Milton, G. (2011), *Wolfram*, 258.
22. Ibid., 254–5.
23. Ibid., 255–62.

24. Interview with Doris Weber and Sigrid Kern, November 2013.
25. Milton, G. (2011), *Wolfram*, 264.
26. Pross, M. (1995), *Die Einschläge kommen näher, Aus den Tagebüchern 1943–45 von Friedrich Adolf Katz, 1945–1947 Oberbürgermeister der Stadt Pforzheim.*
27. Schmalacker-Wyrich, Esther (Ed.), (1980), 'Pforzheim 23. Februar 1945, der Untergang einer Stadt', in: *Bildern und Augenzeugenberichten* (third edition).
28. Administration's Report and Statistics for the Town of Pforzheim, 1945–1952: City Life 1939–1945.
29. Watter, Helmut, written account, February 2013.
30. Interview with Hans Ade, November, 2013.
31. Schmalacker-Wyrich, Esther (Ed.), (1980), 'Pforzheim 23. Februar 1945, der Untergang einer Stadt', in: *Bildern und Augenzeugenberichten* (third edition).

Chapter Thirteen

The Bombing Continues

The Rhine was crossed in March 1945 and the Ruhr encircled on 1 April. Berlin fell on 2 May. As winter became spring the war dragged on for millions, soldiers and civilians alike. The British aircrew continued to assemble in their briefing rooms. Bomber Command dropped 181,740 tons of bombs in the 1 January to 7/8 May period.[1]

In the second week of March the heavy bombers targeted German defences in preparation for the Rhine crossing. The aim was to disrupt German efforts to move up reinforcements. Many targets were in the Ruhr. Essen received 4,738 tons of bombs on 11 March. Dortmund received 4,889 tons the next day. Field Marshal Montgomery's 21st Army Group crossed the Rhine at Wesel. Seventeen raids were mounted in direct support, hitting marshalling yards, bridges and troop concentrations.[2]

City bombing and attacks on the German rail network added to the general disintegration of the enemy's ability to resist ground forces on both fronts. On the ground and in the air, however, the Germans remained resolute opponents. Bomber Command's young volunteers continued to die. At North Killingholme, March 1945 was 550 Squadron's worst month for losses. The squadron flew a record number of 321 operational sorties and lost eight aircraft. The attackers now had many advantages but, at the same time, the German night fighters had a smaller area of Germany to defend and they took opportunities to concentrate and inflict serious losses.[3]

The Lancasters had no reason to return to the wasteland that was Pforzheim, but eight American bombers appeared overhead on Sunday, 4 March and dropped 19 tons of bombs on the railyards. This was Pforzheim's last blow from heavy bombers.[4] Banker Adolf Katz returned to his diary on 1 March: 'Only gradually was I able to realize the horrible dimensions of the catastrophe. The entire city is a complete field of rubble, the streets are buried, many corpses are lined up in the squares. Some of them look peaceful, as if they had a quick, easy death. Others are dreadfully rigid, disfigured by the heat, partially or almost entirely charred. There is a man lying in the entrance of the bank with his head torn off. Terrible stories are emerging. Fritz Soellner survived but his wife and his only son are dead, the factory entirely smashed. Our landlord lies under the debris of the Ratskeller [a restaurant on Marktplatz]. Mr Osswald, whose wife had been deported as a Jew a couple of days earlier, is dead, as is Reichsbankdirektor Blume.' According to Brigitte and Gerhard Brändle's records, Mrs Osswald was deported to Theresienstadt concentration camp. She survived. 'Where Reichsbank used to be, there is a large bomb crater. The entire family of Richard Kraft, with whom I often talked to about the hopelessness of the situation, is dead … In the past I used to be surprised that the bomb terror didn't undermine the people's morale. Now I experienced myself how an enormous will to live rises from death and destruction. While the attack lasted you sat there crouching, with your chest clenched up. However, as soon as it is over, you feel relieved from an enormous pressure, full of energy and drive. Certainly, I met many entirely broken people who were completely distraught over the loss of their relatives and their property and who could only weep or moan, but I talked to just as many who were making determined plans for reconstruction.'[5]

The Katz home was burnt out. The family now rented two small rooms from a shoemaker in Mönsheim, a move suggested by one of Ruth's patients. On the day after the bombing the family rescued some possessions. Robert came into his own. Adolf Katz: 'Robert, who is as strong as an ox, proved his worth indeed.' With the entrance cleared and the basement intact, items saved from the fire were taken down into the cellar.[5]

In 2013, nearly seventy years on, Marianne Pross' stepbrother, Robert, finally told her what had happened to him during the raid: 'He was 16 and had gone to the movies with a girlfriend. When he took her home, he was invited to stay for dinner but declined and headed back to Schwarzwaldstrasse. When the bombing was over he made his way back to his girlfriend's house, struggling through burning streets. When he got there it was all gone. There was just a big hole in the ground. He would have died, too, had he stayed for dinner.'[6]

The bad news about the Katz home caused distress in Überlingen, Lake Constance, where Annina and Marianne had been evacuated. Annina cried over her burnt piano in far away Pforzheim. Marianne grieved for her doll's house. On the other hand, her two dolls and the white bear remained. Life in Mönsheim, meanwhile, soon lost its edge for her parents.[6] On top of this, Adolf Katz, confronted by the horror of total war, still found time to be irritated by a teenager. Robert was out of favour again. Katz's diary entry for 11 March 1945 reads: 'I am so fed up sitting together in the kitchen with the Bauer family. Robert can't stand sitting with us. He always goes down to the kitchen to play cards and fool around with the girls. He sleeps upstairs in the attic, together with his friend, Wolfram, in the large beds that don't fit into our little bedroom. And they begin their Sundays by [playing] dance records on the gramophone. It hurts me to see how he is entirely thoughtless and lives life superficially in such hard times.'[7]

Nerves were on edge as Dave Davidson and crew approached the end of their long tour: 'We had been hit by flak several times. We had been coned by searchlights and escaped by diving through. On one occasion the rear gunner sprayed a night fighter that came too close.'[8] Davidson's long run of luck was now fully extended. A week after Pforzheim – on Thursday, 1 March – they were briefed for a daylight area raid on Mannheim. The main force of 372 Lancasters and 90 Halifaxes found the city obscured by cloud and they bombed sky markers. Three Lancasters were lost.[9] This was the last big attack on Mannheim, and Davidson and his crew were extremely fortunate to get away with it. North Killingholme contributed twenty-six Lancasters, taking off from 11.30. The target was German troop concentrations near the Rhine bridgeheads, close to Mannheim. Davidson, flying Lancaster 'K', lost an engine on the way out but pressed on and bombed the target. According to 550's *Operations Record Book*, the problem was a fire in the starboard outer engine. Their aircraft, an hour and a quarter overdue, was presumed lost, but they landed back after seven hours twenty-five minutes. The skipper was awarded the DFC.[10]

Wing Commander J.C. McWalters, 550's commander, made his recommendation for Davidson's DFC within forty-eight hours: 'On the day of 1 March, Flying Officer Davidson was pilot and captain of a Lancaster bomber detailed to attack an important target in the heavily defended area of Mannheim. Forty-one minutes before reaching the target, at a height of 17,000ft, the starboard outer engine of the aircraft failed. Despite this handicap, with an aircraft carrying a full load of bombs and with the mid-upper turret unserviceable, this pilot immediately made the decision to press home his attack. This meant there was little chance of maintaining his position in the bomber stream and that the target would have to be attacked from a height considerably below the main force. Nothing daunted, this gallant pilot flew for 160 miles with a full bomb load on three engines, to make a determined attack on the target, and flew for a further 575 miles to bring his aircraft and crew safely back to base.'[11]

Davidson's wireless operator, Howell Evans, describes what actually happened: 'Dave gave us the option of continuing to the target or returning. We "voted" over the intercom. The vote was 4–3 in favour of going on. I voted to go back, as did the navigator, who had two kids. There was some banter on the intercom, but no argument once the decision was made. I wasn't really scared, but I don't know why not. I think I'd reached the point where I had complete faith in the idea we would come through. After all, we were very experienced at that point.'[12]

The 550 Squadron aircraft over Mannheim that day included Buzz Burrows' Lancaster. They took off at 11.39 and landed back at 18.14.[13] Ken Sidwell's crew found Mannheim a novel experience – they had an escort of Mustang fighters. Sidwell's mid-upper gunner, Frank Woodley: 'This was our first experience of fighter escort and I was impressed. The American fighter pilots were black and they were a very welcome sight over Germany!'[14]

Davidson made no mention in his logbook of the events of 1 March leading to his DFC. Of more immediate concern was the Friday, 2 March briefing for another daylight, the last big attack on Cologne. It was an early start for 550 Squadron crews and thousands of other airmen manning the 858 participating aircraft. The Lancasters began leaving North Killingholme at 06.45, taking off in good weather. The target was also clear. American troops entered Cologne just four days later. One of their first tasks was to clear the bodies of at least 400 air-raid victims from the streets.[15]

Frank Woodley thought it strange that Cologne was bombed so close to its occupation. On 2 March, however, the natives remained hostile. Their aircraft was hit by flak during the attack.[16] According to the *Operations Record Book*, they were bombing the approaches to the Rhine bridges at Cologne, to prevent German troops escaping to the east of the river.

The Germans may have been close to defeat, yet they were still prepared to take the war back to British airspace. Germany's leading night fighter ace, Major Heinz-Wolfgang Schnaufer, was Kommodore of NJG4. He came up with Operation Gisela. Schnaufer, who ended the war with 121 victories, proposed the deployment of German night fighters en masse as intruders, to catch the British bombers as they landed back at their bases.[17]

On the night of 3/4 March 1945, around 200 German aircraft attacked airfields and aircraft across eastern England. The bombers were returning from raids against a synthetic oil plant at Kamen and the Dortmund-Ems Canal at Ladbergen.[18] The intruders shot down twenty returning aircraft and another five on training flights. More aircraft were destroyed or damaged on the ground.

Pilot Officer Bennett, in a 214 Squadron radio-countermeasures Fortress, was about to land at Oulton when told to go round again, as A Flight's commander, Squadron Leader Bob Davies, was coming in on three engines. Davies saw Bennett climb away, then a long burst of cannon fire from a Ju88 hit the aircraft. Leutnant Arnold Döring, of 10/NJG3, based at Jever, gained his twentieth victory.[18]

In January 1945 Ron James had returned to operations and was posted to 214 Squadron. He had a crew of second tour veterans and new boys fresh from training. The veterans were keen to fly again, but 'some showed visible signs of mental stress, which we called "flak happy" or, more commonly, "the twitch".'[19] Ron James described what happened to the squadron's Gisela casualty: 'Harry Bennett, returning from patrol, was making his landing approach when he was caught by an intruder's cannon fire and crashed on the runway in flames, killing eight of the crew, among whom was one of my best friends, flight engineer Les Billington. After shooting down the Fortress, the fighter came in again for another attack, this time shooting up the operations block, station headquarters and squadron offices.' Leutnant Döring, flying a Ju88 G-6, had shot down Bennett's Fortress and then went on to destroy a Lancaster. He was recommended for the Knight's Cross but never received it. Later, the documents were found and Döring received his decoration in 1965. He was credited with thirteen victories.[20]

Gisela did little to encourage the Germans; they lost twenty-five Ju88s.[21] Nevertheless, this was a reminder that the Luftwaffe still had teeth. Much later, Bob Davies gave his account of how 'Benny' Bennett, aged 24, died in Fortress HB815, BU-J. The story is rich in terror, tragedy and farce. He heard Bennett call up Oulton at 20 miles – the usual procedure. He was cleared to land. Bob Davies: 'When I subsequently announced my arrival "on three", I was given priority to land first. Bennett was told to go round again.

'I continued my approach, turning left onto finals as normal, with all navigation and identity lights on. When I looked forward, to satisfy myself that Bennett was overshooting and not in my way, I saw his port, starboard and white light quite clearly but, at the same time, I saw the flash of tracer from an unseen aircraft hit the Fortress in the port wing root and the wing started to burn. I looked away then, to better concentrate on landing my own aircraft on the still fully illuminated runway. At about the same time I heard the tower call 'Bandits! Bandits!' and the runway lights went out just as I came to a quick stop, thus better able to switch off my own lights. I thought my flight engineer and I did this in double quick time, only to be contradicted by the tail gunner, who said a white light still burned brightly high above him on the aircraft's fin. By this time I felt very, very exposed and I am sure the nine crew felt the same but, despite checking with my flight engineer from left to right in the cockpit, we still heard the rear gunner entreating us to "turn that ******* light off!"

'I can still remember the feeling of utter panic, expecting to be shot up at any time. Trying to compose myself, in desperation, I very reluctantly used my torch to search the cockpit for the final, elusive key to our survival. After what seemed an eternity, I found what I was looking for, a small, unmarked switch that controlled, of all things, a lone white light at the very top of the fin. This was fitted not for operational use but as an aid to night formation flying. With this switch in the off position, and in the glow of Bennett's burning aircraft, I was able to clear the runway and taxi back to dispersal. We were all very relieved to be safely on the ground, especially when we realized we were the last aircraft to make it back to Oulton – the remaining Fortresses and Liberators having the dubious privilege of facing an extra two hours flying to their diversions …'[22]

Bob Davies saw his crew into the bus, then told Jack Fitzsimmonds, his flight engineer on that occasion, to get into his Hillman Utility. They drove out to Bennett's burning Fortress, close to the station's sick quarters. 'There, wonder of wonders, we saw the two apparently uninjured waist gunners (Alistair McDermid and Bill Church), who had miraculously walked out of the half shell of the rear fuselage, the only sizeable part of the wreck which looked as if it had once been an aeroplane. We didn't hang around the burning wreck.'[22]

After debriefing and coffee with powdered milk and Navy rum, they had a quick breakfast, took their leave and returned to the Hillman, passing the station commander, Group Captain Dickens. He had parked his Humber Hawk but had left the fog lamps on – illuminating the tower and briefing room. Bob Davies: 'Fitz and I each opened a door of the car to find the switch controlling the offending lights. However, as we searched, with our backsides high in the air, we both became aware of the sound of aircraft engines at very high revs, approaching us at speed. We quickly dropped onto the concrete in the lee of the staff car as the Ju88 (yes, the same one!) opened up on the Humber. How he missed I don't know. Cannon shells bounced off the tarmac all around us, some finding the corner of the briefing room which, fortunately, was fairly empty by then. If I remember correctly, the panic inside was considerable but only one or two WAAF intelligence officers were slightly injured.' And the car lights? Jack Fitzsimmonds had a simple remedy. 'He quickly and expertly kicked both into darkness.'[22]

Bob Davies added: 'I have discovered that on Bennett's previous operation, about four days before his last, he was returning from the target when a Ju88 night fighter attacked them. Although the rear gunner shot it down, its cannon fire severely damaged Bennett's aircraft and wounded the navigator so badly that he was not able to carry on with his duties. These were taken over by the bomb aimer, who got them back to Manston in Kent, where the navigator died in the sick quarters. Bennett was awarded an immediate DFC and his bomb aimer the DFM.' Bennett, now short of a navigator for his next op, took with him the navigator of a newly arrived crew who had yet to make a trip. Now this unfortunate had flown his first and last sortie.[22] According to Ron James, Bennett's operation resulting in the loss of his regular navigator also resulted in injuries to the special operator and a waist gunner.[23] March was a bad patch for 214 Squadron, with the loss of seven aircraft. This led to speculation that the Germans had a new detection device, capable of homing onto the jamming and other special equipment on board the Fortresses.[24]

'Failed to return' is a bald phrase, papering over the sudden trauma, pain and death that were the realities of being shot down. Thousands escaped with their lives but most were gone forever. One survivor, Stan Keirle, was a 550 Squadron wireless operator in Flight Sergeant A.H. Jefferies' crew. They were in Lancaster LM455 (BN-Q) when shot down during the costly Nuremberg raid of 30/1 March 1944. Jefferies' aircraft was one of over ninety bombers that failed to return. His aircraft was outbound when hit by flak 12 miles south of Aachen. Three survivors, including Keirle, were thrown clear when their bomber blew up. Keirle suffered serious stomach, rib and leg injuries. The four dead, including the pilot, were buried in Heverlee War Cemetery.[25]

Keirle had an extraordinary escape. He had seen the starboard outer engine catch fire; it quickly reignited after the extinguisher was used. He then watched in amazement as the starboard outer fell off, taking with it the wing beyond the engine. The aircraft was uncontrollable and spiralled down. 'The G forces inside the aircraft became enormous and I was propelled forward in a flash, sailing past the navigator's station in mid-air and finishing up against the pilot's instrument panel.' He passed out and came to falling clear of the aircraft: 'I tried to find the parachute ripcord. My harness was loose, the chute pack was not on my chest but down towards my feet. Somehow I readjusted my harness, found the chute and pulled the D-ring. Something hit me under the chin and knocked me out again. I woke to find myself tumbling through trees, sensing that my right arm was entangled in a bulky object. I passed out again.' When he came to once more, he removed his right arm from a

The human cost: Flight Sergeant Arthur Jefferies, CGM, and five of his crew. Left to right: Sergeant J. Whitley, killed in action during the 30/1 March 1944 Nuremberg raid; Sergeant Stan Keirle, who became a prisoner; Flying Officer W. Bull; Flight Sergeant Jefferies, killed in action; Sergeant G. Upton; and Sergeant H. Simpson, killed in action. *Photo: Bob Stone.*

10ft section of cockpit canopy. When the Lancaster blew up, he had been propelled through the cockpit roof.[25]

While Keirle was in hospital in Aachen, on 11–12 April 1944, 341 Lancasters attacked the town's marshalling yards. Keirle was now on the receiving end of a Bomber Command raid. A 4lb incendiary crashed through the roof and landed by his bed. He got up, threw it out of a window and got under the bed. This saved him when the roof collapsed. Later, he discovered that his pilot, Flight Sergeant Jefferies, had been awarded the Conspicuous Gallantry Medal. He was still struggling at the controls when his Lancaster exploded.[25]

The odds were heavily stacked against them, but all operational aircrew were provided with two small packs for use if shot down. One was a survival kit, to help a downed airman in the first forty-eight hours, when he needed to put distance between himself and the crash site. This lightweight acetate box was stowed in the inside pocket of the battledress blouse. It contained malted milk tablets, boiled sweets, toffee, chewing gum, water purifying tablets, rubber water bottle, matches, compass, fishing line, needle and thread, razor and soap and Benzedrine tablets (to help the evader stay awake at critical periods). There was also a small, sealed pack containing foreign currency, silk maps of Western Europe and a small chain that could be used as a hacksaw. The two packs had to be handed in immediately upon return. Lancaster pilot Jack Harris recalls the briefings on behaviour to adopt if shot down: remove wristwatches, ties, moustaches and beards; cut down flying boots to appear as walking shoes; avoid walking in a military manner (adopt a slouch); acquire a rake or hoe to look like a farmworker; and acquire a beret, to look more like a local.[26]

Warrant Officer Sidney Knott, DFC, a Lancaster rear gunner who survived two tours totalling sixty-four operations, always took a 'Tammy hat' with him – a beret tucked into his battledress blouse. Knott became close friends with fellow gunner Don Robson on 467 Squadron. On completing their first tours they became instructors before returning to operations. Robson joined 214 RCM Squadron as a waist gunner. Sidney Knott joined 582 Squadron, the Pathfinder unit Swales flew with until shot down during the Pforzheim attack. Knott had no illusions about what might happen if he baled out over or near a German target that had just been bombed: 'Both my crews knew that, whatever happened, the idea was to keep the aircraft flying away from the target.'[27]

Many aircrew, including Knott, believed that the people of Hamburg, Bremen and other cities in North Germany would be 'harder to cope with' than their counterparts in South Germany. Events on the ground suggest that this was not necessarily so. Sidney Knott: 'Under the Geneva Convention POWs were required to give only their name, rank and number. We needed no telling that the Gestapo and SS were brutal. We were warned to make sure that, if captured, we were taken into custody by Luftwaffe or regular Wehrmacht personnel. Equally, we were cautioned that German Air Force interrogators were skilled at extracting information in an atmosphere of kindness and consideration.'[27]

There was always the possibility of evasion, although this was an unlikely prospect if baling out over Germany. Yet it could be done. Sidney Knott: 'On successfully abandoning the aircraft, it was "every man for himself". We had lectures on how to evade capture. One talk was given by a sergeant who had done the impossible – he had evaded after baling out over Germany. He made his way into France by keeping to the fields, avoiding roads and staying out of sight during daylight hours. On one occasion, in a starved condition, he came across a crop of carrots and ate so many that his skin turned orange for a while. Later, he continued to serve his country by acting as a model for those cultivating survival and evasion skills. He made a lecture tour of the bomber stations, having shown that a "home run" from Germany was possible without fluent German. In fact, he didn't speak a word of German.'[28] During his trek to safety this evader had to cross a major river. Sidney Knott: 'There was no question of swimming it. The bridge was heavily guarded but he decided to brazen it out. He walked across and a guard wished him good luck. He certainly had plenty of that.'[28]

Evading Germans on the ground – especially vengeful civilians – was just one of many concerns for crews determined to stay alive. Knott was a member of two highly professional crews: 'In our billet we sat on beds and had our "crew talks", to go over emergency situations such as abandoning the aircraft or ditching. My second tour was in the spring and summer and we had our meetings in a quiet place outside. We were convinced that the more you talk about a situation, the more chance you have of successful escape in an emergency. The fact was, however, that no-one in my two crews spoke German. It would be a matter of blending in and keeping low – hence the Tammy!'[29]

Twenty-six Lancasters of 550 Squadron took off on Monday, 5 March 1945, to attack Chemnitz. One aircraft ('E2'), flown by Flight Lieutenant Dale, aborted when the port outer engine failed. The long flight east to Chemnitz was uneventful – for the most part over ten-tenths cloud – and the aircraft bombed on sky markers. The *Operations Record Book* noted: 'The first release point flares went down three minutes before "H" Hour; they were plentiful and well grouped but fell into the cloud tops rather quickly and later there was a gap when no flares were seen. Detailed results could not be seen but, judging from the incendiary glow and the bursts of the cookies, bombing appeared to be concentrated. There was slight heavy flak over the target, but the Leipzig defences were active and the night fighters attentive, both over the target and on the first two legs of the homeward flight.' Three 550 aircraft reported combats but no night fighters were claimed destroyed. Twenty-two of the twenty-five made North Killingholme. Lancaster 'J' (Pilot Officer Findlay) landed at Benson, 'O' (Flying Officer Harris) got down at Carnaby with unserviceable flaps and 'F' (Flight Sergeant Wilson) reached Tempsford with combat damage but no casualties. They returned to base the following day.

Chemnitz involved a nine-hour flight, less five minutes, for Dave Davidson and crew.[30] North Killingholme suffered no losses but it was a bad night for Bomber Command. The attack was made by 760 aircraft – 498 Lancasters, 256 Halifaxes and six Mosquitoes. Twenty-two aircraft (fourteen Lancasters and eight Halifaxes) were lost, but the true picture was much worse, as nine 6 Group aircraft crashed shortly after take-off owing to severe icing. There was heavy damage to the central and southern districts of Chemnitz.[31] Buzz Burrows spent even longer in the air than Davidson, logging nine hours twenty-eight minutes in 'A2'.[32]

On the night of 7/8 March 1945, Bomber Command attacked Dessau and North Killingholme sent twenty-seven Lancasters. They began taking off at 17.00. One Lancaster, with Warrant Officer Lukies at the controls, lost the starboard outer engine on take-off. The *Operations Record Book* commented: 'The aircraft swung dangerously but the pilot, by masterly handling, avoided a hangar and other obstacles, proceeded to the jettison area and returned safely. The other aircraft set course on the long route to Dessau.' The opposition was described as 'lively'. Some crews got a clear view of the town and the Elbe; others found it obscured and bombed on sky markers: 'General opinion was that the attack was well concentrated and that the target was set well and truly ablaze.'

Lancaster 'M' (Squadron Leader Pickles) had an unserviceable 'Gee' box from the first, yet reached the target and bombed the concentration of fires. Two crews reported inconclusive combats with night fighters. It was a bad night for 550 Squadron, with three losses. Veteran Lancaster PA995 ('K', later 'V') – 'Vulture Strikes' – was lost to a night fighter during the Dessau raid. The pilot, Flying Officer C.J. Jones, RCAF, the navigator and the bomb aimer died. Four others became prisoners, but the rear gunner escaped and was back in the UK by the end of the month.[33] The 550 losses that night also included ME503 ('R'). Pilot Officer S.W. Nielsen, RAAF, and four others were killed. The flight engineer and rear gunner survived and returned to the UK on 3 April 1945. Lancaster ME428 ('O') also failed to return. Flying Officer R.D. Harris, RCAF, was the pilot, with Canadian gunner Doug Hicks in the rear turret; 7/8 March was the night their luck ran out.[34] The target was 35 miles south-west of Berlin. Dessau cost Bomber Command eighteen Lancasters – 3.4 per cent of the main force.[35] The outbound leg, across France, gave no encouragement. From his rear turret, Doug Hicks reported two bombers crashing as they flew low over France. The display of red, green and yellow pyrotechnics on the ground suggested that two Pathfinder aircraft had collided. Hicks saw another aircraft go in, and this crash produced only burning incendiaries, indicating the loss of a main force aircraft.[36]

Veteran: a 550 Squadron photograph to mark the hundredth operation of PA995 (BQ-V), 'Vulture strikes'. Shortly afterwards, this aircraft was lost on the 7/8 March 1945 Dessau raid. The Lancaster was shot down by a night fighter. The pilot, Flying Officer C.J. Jones, RCAF, and his navigator and bomb aimer were killed. *Photo: Bob Stone.*

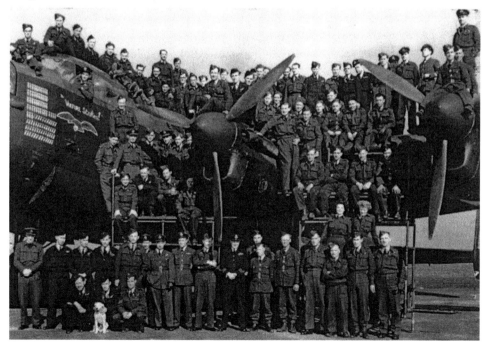

Flying at 20,000ft and around 100 miles short of the target, Harris' Lancaster suddenly shook violently. Sparks and smoke streamed past Hicks' turret as tracer rounds came up from below. They were under attack by a night fighter with Schräge Musik upward-firing 20mm cannon. The wings were on fire and Harris gave the order: 'Jump! Jump! Jump!' Doug Hicks began disconnecting his oxygen and intercom leads, an awkward task with heavily gloved hands. He pulled off the gloves from his left hand but still struggled as the aircraft was now flying very erratically. Hicks felt the heat from the fire and redoubled his efforts. He rotated his turret to port, opened both turret doors and, wearing a seat-type parachute, pushed his behind through the open doors and fell backwards into the slipstream. He was out but, unfortunately, one foot caught in the turret and he found himself being towed along by the burning aircraft. He had just decided that his only hope was to pull the ripcord when there was a sudden, blinding flash. Lancaster ME428 blew up and the rear gunner found himself floating free with his parachute open. He landed safely and became a prisoner, along with the navigator, bomb aimer and wireless operator. The flight engineer and mid-upper gunner are buried in Berlin War Cemetery. The pilot's body was never found and his name, Flying Officer R.D. Harris, RCAF, appears on

Remembered at Runnymede: Flying Officer R.D. Harris, RCAF, and crew. His Lancaster was lost to a Schräge Musik night fighter on their eighth operation, the 7/8 March raid on Dessau. Harris, his flight engineer and the mid-upper gunner were killed. Harris' body was never found and his name appears on the Runnymede Memorial to the missing. *Photo: Bob Stone.*

the Runnymede Memorial to the missing. Four weeks later, Doug Hicks and the three others were liberated by American troops and flown back to England, where Hicks' burns were treated in hospital.[36]

With 550 Squadron pilot Eddie Edlund and five of his crew now tour-expired, flight engineer Sam Lipfriend joined Flying Officer Haynes' crew for the long round trip to Dessau, logged at nine hours thirty minutes. Afterwards, Sam found a quiet moment and wrote a few words in his diary: 'Will be a decent crew with more experience. Flak medium. Two shot down. Very dicey.'[37]

Afrika Korps soldier Raimund Frei became accustomed to life as an American prisoner. He had been captured nearly two years before in Tunisia. He was now in Texas. When first captured, Frei refused to accept his lot. He joined forces with three like-minded prisoners, a translator attached to the Arab Legion and two Arab legionnaires: 'We had the ambitious idea of taking a jeep and driving to Algeria and eventually reaching friendly lines. Unfortunately, the French stepped up their border patrols. There was a bounty on our heads. It was pointless so we turned ourselves in, boarded a train with other prisoners and arrived at Casablanca.

'We boarded a ship bound for Gibraltar and then Glasgow. We sailed in the company of other ships carrying POWs. During the voyage we were warned by an American lieutenant that we would be under Polish control when we reached the UK. He said the Poles would steal everything. He offered to act as the custodian of our valuables, to be returned later at our new address. Since he gave us his word of honour as an officer, I did what he asked and the others also fell for it. Later, when we arrived at a British camp, the American failed to put in an appearance.

'When we disembarked I suddenly remembered that I didn't know the name of the ship. The guards made us run, rather than march. I looked back at the ship, to get the name, but the guards screamed at me in German: '*Vorne spielt die Musik!*' [The front is where the music plays]. I looked up and saw the word "Poland" on a sleeve. Another man also looked back and was struck with rifle butts. The Polish guards were very harsh and humiliated us at every opportunity. We were taken to the prison camp by train. We were then in British custody. Our Scottish escorts were elderly men who occasionally offered a cigarette. One in particular was not without humour. He tapped me on the shoulder and said: "You should have come earlier, in 1940, when you had the chance. We would have helped you!"

'Subsequently, we boarded another ship at Glasgow. I made sure I got the name this time: it was the *Ile de France*. We sailed without escort to New York and went on by train to the Swift and Brady POW camps, near Austin, Texas. There was certainly nothing to complain about when it came to food in America. We even had turkey for Christmas lunch! The surprising thing was the sheer variety of foods. It was really great. We weren't used to such choice.'[38]

Stan Keirle had a very different experience, as a prisoner of the Germans. The 550 Squadron wireless operator was resident in Stalag Luft 7 at Bankau, just east of Breslau (Wroclaw). In January 1945 the Germans began a hurried evacuation of aircrew prison camps in Upper Silesia as the Red Army rapidly advanced westwards. The prisoners were expecting the move, as daily news was received by a hidden wireless. On Wednesday, 17 January 1945, Bankau's camp commandant warned all prisoners to be ready to move at one hour's notice. The Red Cross parcel store was opened and the prisoners took whatever they wanted for the journey. The camp theatre was stripped of wood and fabric, to make sledges and backpacks for the coming trek. The men would soon be tested by terrible winter weather. Both sides were nervous and had conflicting intentions on the road. The POWs wanted to go slow, to give the Russians a chance to catch up. The Germans wanted to move fast, to cross the Oder before the bridges were blown.[39]

Bankau was the first camp to be emptied. The main gate opened at 3.30am on Friday, 19 January. Heavy snow was falling and normal walking was almost impossible. Feet had to be lifted vertically out of the snow and advanced 18in at a time. The air was so cold that breathing was difficult. No transport was provided for sick or injured prisoners. Keirle had injuries to his spine and left leg and needed help from time to time.[39]

When the Bankau prisoners reached the main road, they joined the floodtide of civilians moving west, all terrified of being overwhelmed by vengeful Soviet troops. The marchers soon realized that weighty possessions had to be abandoned. Belongings were repacked, with clothing and lightweight tradable items – such as tea, coffee, cigarettes and soap – retained. These could be exchanged for milk, bread and potatoes from farms along the line of march. They covered 20 miles in ten hours on the first day, with fifteen minutes' rest every ninety minutes. That night they sheltered in barns and haylofts. They covered 7 miles of very difficult going on the second day, finishing in a filthy, abandoned brick factory which at least offered shelter. Two field kitchens provided food for 1,500 men. The only warm drink was a cup of *Ersatz kaffee*. The medical officer was given a horse and cart to take six of the worst cases.[39]

On the third day they set off in sub-zero temperatures for a walk of 26 miles, including the crossing of the Oder. The bridge was blown the day after they crossed. Fog reduced visibility to less than 30yd. A group of thirty men, too exhausted to continue, were left in roadside houses, to be picked up by the Russians. Most of this twelve-hour walk was completed in darkness. When they reached the barns and cowsheds allocated to them, the prisoners received half a cup of *Ersatz kaffee* and three biscuits each. Stan Keirle: 'The next day involved a march of 15 miles in snow drifts reaching up to 10ft high. The roads were choked with civilians. The POW column could be a mile long and the guards found it difficult to control. Each day brought a march of about 15 miles. A meal consisted of two slices of black bread and half a cup of watery soup. The intense cold was a huge problem. Boots got very wet but if you took them off overnight they were frozen stiff by the morning. The medical officer had to amputate frostbitten toes in a stable, presumably without any anaesthetic.'[39]

At Prausnitz they had a five-day break on a farm, where they received one-third of a loaf and some tinned meat each day. The next stage in this ordeal was a 5 mile march to Goldberg, where they entrained. They were crammed into cattle trucks, fifty-five to sixty men to each wagon. The train eventually arrived during the morning of Thursday, 8 February at Luckenwalde, around 30 miles south of Berlin. The prisoners had been on the move for twenty-one days. They had walked about 160 miles in extreme conditions.[39]

Stan Keirle became detached from the main Bankau group – his injuries prevented him from keeping pace with the column. On the seventh day, the medical officer pulled Keirle and twenty-one others out of the main party and diverted them to Sagan camp, now empty and in the hands of a German care and maintenance unit. After one night at Sagan, the injured and sick were put on a goods train and sent to Luckenwalde, where they arrived well before the main group. Luckenwalde eventually held 15,000 prisoners. The daily ration was a bowl of weak, dirty soup and a 53oz loaf shared between seven men. Stan Keirle: 'A representative of the Swiss Protecting Power visited the camp on 17 February and was appalled. A strong complaint was lodged with the German authorities. On 2 March a delivery of American Red Cross parcels arrived – the first for two months – followed by regular deliveries.'[39]

On 153 Squadron, Bruce Potter and crew were exhausted after the ten-hour round trip to Dessau on the night of 7/8 March. After a few hours' sleep they were called to a briefing for Kassel. Bill Thomas and other members of Potter's crew, however, had already flown the last operation with their skipper. Bill Thomas: 'Potter lost it when we took off for Kassel. We began the ground run and I was doing my usual – guarding the fuel cocks – when I peeped out and saw the runway in the wrong place! Bruce had fainted over the controls and the aircraft, fully laden with bombs and fuel, began a ground loop. Gordon, the flight engineer, acted swiftly and wiped the throttles back. He grabbed the control column and pulled back but Bruce's foot had fouled the controls. Gordon was still struggling when our aircraft completed its ground loop.

'After a quick check, the aircraft was found to be undamaged. In fact, it was fit to fly and we were told to get in and have another go. Our response was: "Not likely". We explained that we were not refusing to fly, but we were done for that night. Anyway, our wireless operator, Digger Askew, had legged it as soon as the Lanc came to a stop. Convinced that the bombs were about to go up, he ran like hell. We were told we could be on a charge for refusing a second attempt, but we were content with that. Everything was hushed up and we were stood down. Another crew took that aircraft.'[40]

Bruce Potter needed just three more trips to complete his tour. It wasn't to be. Bill Thomas: 'He was taken off to sick bay and didn't return to the room. Later, the doctor visited us but gave little away. He asked whether Bruce had ever shown any signs of breathing difficulties when in the air. It was impossible to say, due to the high noise level and the fact that we all wore oxygen masks. Doc seemed to think Bruce might have had a fit.

'Shortly afterwards, our skipper reappeared. Later on he told me: "I'm all right, but they think I've gone mad." We were taking a walk. Suddenly, he turned towards the hangar housing the Spitfire Fighter Affiliation Flight. There was a Spitfire in front of us, trolley accumulator alongside. Bruce suddenly turned and said: "I'm going to fly that. They're grounding me but we can start her up. I can fly this." Needless to say, Bruce went to hospital and we never saw him again. His kit was collected the following morning and there was an empty bed in our billet. We completed our tour with another pilot.'[40]

Sam Lipfriend, meanwhile, was reunited with Eddie Edlund and the boys, having done one trip as a 'spare bod'. Edlund's 550 Squadron crew, with the exception of Lipfriend, thought they were finished but were caught by the extension of the first tour, from thirty to thirty-six trips.[41] They were together in North Killingholme's briefing room on Thursday, 8 March for the Kassel briefing. This was the first major raid on Kassel since October 1943. The main force consisted of 262 Lancasters. Bomber Command also sent 303 heavy bombers to Hamburg that night, to hit shipyards assembling new, Schnorchel-equipped U-boats.[42] Eddie Edlund took off at 17.15. They found Kassel obscured. The medium flak was moderate but Lipfriend

Engaging the enemy: a battery of German flak guns – at that time the best in the world. *Photo: Trustees of the Imperial War Museum.*

saw one bomber half a mile ahead go down after being hit. Later, he wrote in his diary: 'We had to climb to miss the flak. The casualty went down in a vertical spin, with fire from both wings.' They got back to North Killingholme at 00.45. Lipfriend, unlike so many of his comrades, had survived twenty-five operations.[43]

North Killingholme sent twenty-three aircraft to Kassel and all bombed the primary TIs. They included Lancaster 'H', captained by Flying Officer Cowper. This aircraft's port inner engine caught fire and was feathered some 200 miles short of the target. Cowper pressed on. It was ten-tenths cloud all the way to the target area, where conditions cleared. The *Operations Record Book* noted: 'Bombing was highly concentrated, the incendiaries took a firm hold and the resultant fire glow could still be seen when aircraft were crossing the Rhine over 100 miles away.' There was little opposition; all squadron aircraft returned safely.

Edlund and crew were also among the 550 Squadron aircrew briefed on Sunday, 11 March 1945 for what would be the largest raid of the war to date. The target was Essen and 1,079 aircraft made this daylight attack. The main force consisted of 750 Lancasters and 293 Halifaxes. They dropped 4,661 tons of bombs on Oboe-positioned sky markers, as the target was totally obscured. The bombing was accurate and around 900 people died. This was the last of the many Bomber Command raids on Essen; three Lancasters were lost.[44]

As far as Eddie Edlund's flight engineer was concerned, this was the end of Essen. Sam Lipfriend's diary read: 'Wonderful sight. Essen was 14 miles ahead of our troops. Cloud obscured target. Tops 6,000. Cloud and smoke up to 7,000. No fighters. Nil flak. Target a complete write-off.'[45] The *Operations Record Book* commented: 'It was considered that the bombing was quite concentrated and very soon a protuberance, in the shape of mushrooming fire smoke, agitated the top layers of the cloud – evidently something was burning "down under". Opposition was negligible and all aircraft returned safely.'

The pace was relentless. Another raid was on for Monday, 12 March. North Killingholme sent twenty-three aircraft to Dortmund. This raid demonstrated Bomber Command's ability to mount devastating 1,000 bomber attacks on successive nights. This meant that many men, including Edlund, had to fly again the day after Essen. The Dortmund attack broke records: it involved 1,108 aircraft: 748 Lancasters, 292 Halifaxes and 68 Mosquitoes. Bomber Command had triumphed over the German defences. Two Lancasters were lost. The tonnage of bombs dropped was a record: Dortmund received 4,851 tons.[46]

This was Eddie Edlund's last trip. The tour requirement had been adjusted once again, this time in favour of aircrew. When Sam Lipfriend arrived back at North Killingholme he was a 'spare bod' once more, as Edlund and the others were deemed finished. Lipfriend took up his diary and recorded his impressions of Dortmund: 'Slight flak at first over the target and then none. 10/10 cloud. Tops 7,000. Clouds of smoke to 8,000. Another complete write-off.'[47]

Twenty-three Lancasters took off from North Killingholme in the early afternoon, bound for Dortmund. The *Operations Record Book* confirmed Lipfriend's comments: 'As over Essen, a large mushroom cloud of dark smoke appeared through the cloud tops. There was virtually no opposition and all aircraft returned safely.'

Tuesday's task was a night raid on the Erin Benzole plant at Herne, in the north central Ruhr. Some crews saw jets over the target area. There were boozy celebrations afterwards at North Killingholme – three crews had completed their tours.

Ken Sidwell and crew joined 126 other men assembling in 550 Squadron's briefing room on Thursday, 15 March. If they could survive the next trip they would have completed thirty-three operations. Once again, however, this raid reminded everyone that there were no grounds for complacency. Sidwell's mid-upper gunner, Frank Woodley: 'This was a long night flight to Misburg, near Hannover, to attack the Deurag refinery. The round trip was eight hours thirty minutes. We lost the starboard inner to flak fifteen minutes after bombing and returned on three. Then the port outer caught fire as we joined the circuit above North Killingholme. We landed on two.'[48]

The raiding force included nineteen Lancasters from 550 Squadron. As they took off in the late afternoon, many aircrew were smiling at the spectacle of the squadron CO using his car to chase away a horse that strayed onto the runway. Flying conditions were good, with some ground haze over the target. The marking was accurate and well-concentrated. The *Operations Record Book* stated: 'Almost immediately after the first bombs had dropped, the target was enveloped in flames and smoke which rose to 10,000ft from a particularly big explosion. An excellent, concentrated attack developed, large fires became established and two further large explosions occurred.'

Buzz Burrows, a 550 Lancaster captain, joined the attack. He and his crew were back after a ten-day break following Chemnitz. They took 'A2' and logged seven hours fifty-eight minutes.[49] A main force of 257 Lancasters, supported by eight Mosquitoes, attacked the refinery. Four Lancasters were lost.[50] It had been a long six weeks for Burrows' wireless operator, Ron Germain. There was still two-thirds of the tour to do. He and the others had no way of knowing that the next op would be their last. Ron Germain was always aware of the possibility of personal disaster: 'I hoped, rather than believed, that I would live. I just carried on and went down the pub with the boys for a few beers.'[51]

Germain and the others had already had a close call: 'On one op we had just flown over the target when the rear gunner spotted a fighter coming in. He ordered a corkscrew. Our bomb doors were still open! I stood up in the astrodome to keep watch when it suddenly blew off. It was bloody cold on the way home. I nursed my feet, warming them against the heater pipe.'[51]

North Killingholme's hard-working ground crews were busy the next day, Friday, 16 March 1945. They were bombing up and fuelling nineteen aircraft for a night raid on Nuremberg. Ken Sidwell was operating as a flight lieutenant for the first time, having been made up from flying officer. Mid-upper gunner Frank Woodley remembers the bright moonlight over Germany: 'Rotating the turret, I spotted a Ju88 night fighter come over the skyline towards us, on a converging course. On the intercom I said: "He's very close. Don't fire." The Ju88 flew past us, no more than 20ft above. He didn't see us. It was a test of nerve. Then our nerves were overstretched when, with a loud "whoosh", an Me262 jet fighter jumped over our wing. He had come in head on. Within a second I was looking at the bright lights of his jet exhausts. We lost twenty-four Lancasters that night, within a few weeks of the end of the war.'[52]

Dave Davidson's Lancaster was over Nuremberg that night. His comments on this operation were recorded in his wife's diary: 'Worst trip ever. Opposition all round. Very shaky do.'[53] Davidson's views were justified. One 550 Lancaster failed to return and others reported night fighter combats. The attack was delivered by 231 Lancasters of 1 Group and 46 Lancasters and 16 Mosquitoes of 8 Group. Casualties were very heavy, a loss equivalent to an entire heavy bomber squadron. The twenty-four Lancasters shot down were all from 1 Group. They amounted to 10.4 per cent of all 1 Group aircraft committed and 8.7 per cent of the entire Lancaster force. Most fell to night fighters. The casualties on the ground included 529 dead.[54]

The 550 Squadron strength totalled fifty-two crews at this time. Eighteen 550 aircraft took off from North Killingholme in the late afternoon to bomb Nuremberg. The nineteenth, Flying Officer Luder's Lancaster, had an unserviceable rear turret. Over Nuremberg, a large gap in the cloud gave a good view of ground markers. The *Operations Record Book* noted: 'The Master Bomber's instructions came through clearly. Fires got going quickly, outlining the street patterns, finally merging into one large conflagration, the glow from which could be seen for 150 miles on the return journey.' Flak was slight but there was intense fighter activity: 'Many combats were reported; "L" (Flight Sergeant Wilson) claimed to have damaged a Ju88. "K" (Pilot Officer Findlay) saw strikes on another. "D" (Flight Sergeant Jamieson) landed at Manston with the rear gunner, Sergeant Klementoski, wounded so seriously that he has since died.' Lancaster NG336 ('B') also failed to return. The pilot, Flight Lieutenant R.J. Liefooghe, became a POW. He was the sole survivor.[55]

German intruders returned on the night of Friday, 16 March 1945. During March 550 Squadron participated in seventeen raids and flew the record number of 2,069 operational hours (roughly equally divided between day and night trips). In the same period the squadron lost seven aircraft over enemy territory, but another was claimed by an intruder during the night of 16/17 March. The victim, Flight Sergeant Lockyer, RNZAF, was on his first training flight with the squadron. Lancaster captain Jack Harris: 'They were halfway through a practice bombing exercise when the range instructed them to return to North Killingholme. There was no intruder warning. The aircraft still had its navigation lights on when it reached North Killingholme, to find the runway and circuit lights out. North Killingholme tower told the captain to douse his lights, which he did, and the rear gunner immediately reported a twin-engined aircraft closing rapidly. The gunner ordered "corkscrew port", which the pilot initiated.' The night fighter pilot was highly skilled. He was able to follow two corkscrews, firing each time. On the third corkscrew the Lanc was hit badly in the tail area, damaging elevators or trim-tabs. 'This caused severe control problems and set fire to the central fuselage. The pilot told the crew to bale out and the bomb aimer was first to go through the front escape hatch. The flight engineer followed but only after a delay – he got stuck in the hatch. Sergeant Drawbridge freed himself and, realizing the aircraft was very low, pulled the ripcord immediately and landed 1 mile east of Patrington. He was the sole survivor. The aircraft crashed near Withernsea. Coastguards heard calls for help from the Humber Estuary but the lifeboat and other craft could not find either the bomb aimer or any of the other crew members who might have jumped from the rear door.'[56]

The vicious final weeks unfolded. On Sunday, 18 March, 550 Squadron readied eighteen aircraft for a raid on Hanau, but 'M2' had engine trouble and stayed at the dispersal. The others took off just before midnight. This raid laid waste Hanau's Altstadt and killed around 2,000 people.[57]

This was Flight Lieutenant Buzz Burrows' last op. Wireless operator Ron Germain: 'We had to bale out around 12 miles south-west of Mainz. There was nothing special about this op. We dropped on the target, turned away and headed for home. Then we were hit. I was sitting at my station and there was a sudden, violent WHOOSH. I looked back and saw we were on fire through the fuselage. One wing was also on fire. I had been on the wireless and missed the bale-out order. The navigator turned to me and gave me the sign to jump. I went forward, towards the hatch in the floor. Our usual bomb aimer was sick and we had a spare bod New Zealander with us. He was very unlucky that night – he had only this trip to do to complete his tour! Anyway, he had a problem with the hatch. It jammed firm. Finally, he got out and disappeared. The flight engineer went next, followed by the navigator. It was my turn. The two gunners were behind me. The aircraft was in level flight, with Buzz still at the controls.

'I tumbled out. It was pitch black. Thankfully, I had remembered to clip on the parachute harness leg straps and tighten them. I had a habit of flying with the leg straps loose or undone, for comfort. The chute deployed and my right flying boot came off. I didn't see the ground coming and landed sideways, on my face. My only injury was a facial cut. I had landed in the middle of a field, on top of a hill. I buried the chute under a bush and settled down to wait for dawn. I could already see that I was looking down into a valley. As it grew light I could see a flat area extending away from me, towards what looked like a river. When the sun came up, however, I realized that the "river" was just mist in the fields. There was no-one around and I began to walk down, into the valley. There was a wide road running along the valley bottom. There was a lot of waste paper scattered about and I was disappointed to see that the text was in German. Eventually, I came to a stream and washed the blood off my face. I dried myself with my silk scarf. There was no sign of the others. I then looked to the right and watched a road that stretched into the distance and eventually spiralled down the other side of the valley to meet the road at the bottom. I could just see vehicles at the top, including some trucks with red crosses on them.

'I spent the rest of that day walking, heading west towards the traffic in the far distance. I was making for a forested area close to the road, from where I could observe the vehicles. I kept watch under cover, looking down on a stretch of road. I glimpsed two helmets which looked German, but then saw a jeep with a large white star on it. Americans! I ran over and shouted: "Wait for me!" A sergeant and an officer stared at me and one said: "Who the hell are you?" I reached for my identification, in my battledress pocket, but one of them pushed my hand away and got it himself.

'I said: "I'm glad to see you!" He replied: "Don't be too glad – there's nothing in front of us!" I was sitting in the back of a jeep that was, in effect, the American spearhead – a reconnaissance unit of General Patton's Third Army. We drove on and came to a village. There was no-one around as we arrived in the square, but white sheets were draped from the windows. I had no idea where I was. My companions were nervous; the officer told his sergeant: "Turn round and get the hell out of here!"

'We didn't come under fire and pressed on to the next village. It was obvious that there had been fighting here earlier, when a tank unit went through. One GI noticed I was minus a boot. He went into a house and ordered an old guy to surrender his boots to me. I rather lamely handed over one flying boot in return. I then noticed a big pile of weapons outside the village church. A soldier saw me look and told me: "The bodies are inside."

'Arrangements were made to take me back. Once again I boarded the jeep, rejoining the officer and sergeant. We drove through the night into Luxembourg and finally entered a camp for American and British troops. Earlier, I had been reunited with the flight engineer and navigator. I found them in the village where the Germans had put up some resistance. Happily, they were none the worse for the experience. We found the radio tent and informed the Air Ministry that we were still alive. Sadly, I discovered later that Burrows, who was married, and Towson had died that night. Curly Miles and the New Zealand bomb aimer had survived. I met up with Curly later and he gave me his account of what happened: "Something came at us from the rear port quarter. My turret was damaged and my feet were injured. I managed to open the turret doors and found Towse looking for his chute. He tried to open the side door, but it was buckled. We had no choice. We went forward, clambered over the main spar and went out through the forward hatch."'[58]

Ron Germain and his comrades flew back to the UK in a Dakota. They landed at the American base at Mount Farm, near Oxford. Another aircraft ferried them to North Killingholme. They arrived back from their four-day adventure on Thursday, 22 March. Ron Germain: 'When I returned to my billet, my bed was gone. My kit was also missing. When we joined the next pay parade, we received no money. Our names had been crossed off.'[58]

Teenage forced labourer Roger Riblet-Buchmann, together with friend René and other Vosges deportees, finally moved from Pforzheim's Italian camp to the Russian camp on 19 March 1945: 'The sanitary arrangements were somewhat better but we had to familiarize ourselves with the bugs which were comfortably established in the mattresses and the fleas which became active at night.'[59]

The Russian camp was on the edge of Brötzingen, between the railway lines, the Enz railway bridge, a power station and flak batteries – 'enough to draw the bombers like wasps to a jar of jam. We were continually under air-raid warning conditions. Some of us refused to sleep there and joined the locals in the railway tunnel, or anywhere else providing shelter.'[59]

Roger had a new job. Every day, at 7am, he set out with a shovel, to clear debris at what had once been the Schaub factory. This was never an easy trip. The 'Jabos' (fighter-bombers) patrolled overhead, looking for targets. On one occasion he pushed himself into the earth and survived a series of four strafing runs. When it was over he was uninjured but found he couldn't control his shaking legs. On that morning it took him two hours to reach Schaub, as he was repeatedly forced to take shelter.[59]

On Wednesday, 21 March North Killingholme's briefing room began to fill. The early briefing was for an attack on the Deutsche Vacuum refinery, north-west of Bremen. This raid was flown in clear conditions, with a hot reception from the flak defences. Flight engineer Sam Lipfriend joined Pilot Officer Screen's crew for this operation. The raid involved 133 Lancasters and six Mosquitoes.[60] No aircraft were lost, but it was not without incident for Lipfriend. His diary reads: 'Nice crew. 7/10 cloud. Clear over target. Some very good hits ...' They had a lucky escape. Screen's Lancaster took a flak hit in the port outer's radiator. The damaged engine was feathered: 'We came out over Holland with a fighter escort. We met another Lanc over the North Sea. They had two engines out and our escort joined them. We went on alone.'[61]

Fifteen 550 Squadron Lancasters attacked the refinery. The *Operations Record Book* described the raid: 'Marking was very accurate and the Master Bomber had a firm and clear control of the attack. Very quickly, a pall of smoke of varying shades enveloped the target.' It also made an observation on the flak that had cost Screen an engine: 'Along the bombing run the aircraft had to fly through a lane of hot, quite accurate heavy flak and several aircraft were hit ...'

On Thursday, 22 March it was the turn of Hildesheim. Until then the town had escaped a major raid, but it now suffered a saturation attack by 227 Lancasters and eight Mosquitoes; four Lancasters failed to return. This was a devastating raid. British bombing assessors later reported that 263 acres (70 per cent of the town) had been destroyed and that 1,645 people had died. Over 10,000 apartments were destroyed or seriously damaged.[62]

Sam Lipfriend flew with Screen on this daylight. The flight engineer noted in his diary: 'Hildesheim. Went in via Dutch coast. Met little opposition. Fair amount of flak over the target. Met quite a bit of flak in the Cologne–Düsseldorf gap. Five flak holes. Nothing serious.'[63]

North Killingholme sent sixteen Lancasters to Hildesheim. The formation flew in almost perfect weather. The *Operations Record Book* commented: 'crews had no difficulty visually identifying the aiming point. Marking was accurate and concentrated … within a few minutes the whole of the built-up area was a mass of smoke and dust. The smoke, rising to 15,000ft, could be seen for 200 miles. All Lancs landed back safely.' Lancaster 'C2', flown by Flight Lieutenant Parsons, was hit by heavy flak and had two fuel tanks holed. Lancaster 'L', Flight Sergeant Wilson's aircraft, was hit by incendiaries over the target. There was damage to the port wing tip and aileron.

Hildesheim completed Dave Davidson's tour. After the war, he acquired a copy of the March 1945 pages of 550's *Operations Record Book*. In the margin, against 22 March, he wrote: 'Hallelujah. End of tour. Amen.'[64]

Howell Evans, Davidson's wireless operator, said the end came quickly: 'On 21 March we went to Bremen in daylight. The following day we bombed Hildesheim. When we got back we went to debriefing, then returned to our billets, dumped our kit and headed for the pub. We drank as if there was no tomorrow. I telephoned my parents from the pub. I just said: "I've finished!" I told my father I intended to get plastered. He replied: "I think I will too!" I knew he would soon be in the Green Dragon, Hendy's village pub. When the war started, we had a strictly father-son relationship. Later, when I came home on leave, we were more like pals – equals. Father would have his evening snooze in the chair, stir himself at exactly 8.45, consult his pocket watch and announce his intention to visit the pub, as though it was a rare event rather than a nightly occurrence. I realized things had changed when, on one leave, he put his coat on to go to the Green Dragon, then suddenly turned to me and said: "Do you drink an occasional pint? Would you like to come with me?"

'I joined his pals in their special room at the Green Dragon. Everyone had his own chair. All conversation was in Welsh. This "conversation" consisted of arguments – mainly about rugby, gardening and politics. At the end of the evening, when we got outside, the cold suddenly hit him. Father was almost legless. I got him back and tucked him into his chair. It was the first time he had arrived home the worse for drink. The next morning he greeted me with the words: "Occasional pint be damned!"'[65]

It had been a long, eventful tour. Davidson's crew had their idiosyncrasies. Dave tolerated no photography. He had noticed that many crews were lost very shortly after having their photographs taken. Howell Evans wasn't superstitious until his close friend, Jim, died in an air accident during training: 'I was the sort of chap who deliberately walked under ladders, just to prove a point. After Jim was lost I carried a lucky charm – a pair of miniature Dutch clogs. I can't remember who gave them to me. My aunt gave me a prayer book, which I stowed in my kit. I also had a little ritual. On returning from an op I would cut another small notch in my comb. I used to pray a lot – especially in the aircraft.

'Sometimes a crew member missed a sortie. Dick spent a few days in hospital and missed a trip. Paddy was badly beaten in a fight and also missed one. He claimed he had gone to the aid of a girl who was being assaulted, but that story lacked conviction. Tiny missed one or two trips when his kids were ill. We covered the absences by flying with "spare bods".'[65]

Others had yet to finish. Flight engineer Sam Lipfriend joined Flight Lieutenant Reg Franklin's crew for a precision daylight attack on a benzol plant at Dortmund on Saturday, 24 March 1945. In fact, the force of 173 Lancasters and 12 Mosquitoes attacked this works and the Mathias Stinnes plant at Bottrop. Three Lancasters were lost from the Dortmund force.[66] Visibility was excellent and crews visually acquired the targets. One of the losses was 550 Squadron Lancaster 'H', piloted by Flight Lieutenant J.B. Barnes, RCAF. He and his crew were killed.[67]

Much decorated: a 550 Squadron crew's mascot – George Bear, DSO, DFC, AFC, Croix de Guerre, American Air Force Medal, Canadian Operational Medal and British campaign medals. George flew thirty-two operations. *Photo: Bob Stone.*

North Killingholme sent fourteen Lancasters. Franklin took off at 12.52 and arrived back at 18.10. Sam Lipfriend took up his diary for the thirtieth time and wrote: 'Very small target, 700ft long. Only 80 Lancs on it. Flew with Reg – good crew. Got some flak going in. Good prang. Quite a bit of flak on the way out. A few flak holes. Mid-upper nearly bought it. Reg's face cut by splintered perspex.' The excitement followed them back to base: 'Flight Lieutenant Parsons nearly pranged us on landing – he came in very quickly after us.'[68]

Sam Lipfriend partnered Reg Franklin again early the next morning. Their Lancaster was one of six prepared at North Killingholme to attack Hannover. 'M2' had engine problems; the other five took off, to join 262 other Lancasters and eight Mosquitoes for the raid. Three towns – Hannover, Münster and Osnabrück – were attacked, to disrupt the movement of reinforcements for the Rhine battlefront. One Lancaster was lost.[69]

Hannover was Reg Franklin's last trip. It was an early start; they took off at 06.50 and were back at 11.58. The Franklin crew had completed their tour, leaving Lipfriend as a 'spare bod' once more. Lipfriend made a diary entry for Hannover:

'Very little flak over the target. Collected some more flak on the way out.' It seems that Franklin's mid-upper gunner had finished just in time. He had a near miss from shrapnel during the Dortmund benzol plant attack. Only a few hours later he had a second narrow escape, over Hannover. A red hot chunk of flak penetrated the fuselage only 12in away from him. Lipfriend was also reminded of his mortality: 'A lump of flak hit just behind my head.'[70]

March 1945 was a black month for 550 Squadron. There were also losses among 214 Squadron's radio-countermeasures Fortresses. On 7 March Fortress KJ106 ('BU-G') left Oulton at 18.14 with 22-year-old Flying Officer George Stewart at the controls. They were briefed for a Jostle patrol to support an attack on Harburg. Their aircraft crashed near Buxtehude. Five of the crew died and five became prisoners. Stewart, a New Zealander, was among those killed in action.[71]

The crews of two more Fortresses of 214 Squadron ran out of luck on 14 March, when supporting a raid on the Lützkendorf oil refinery, Leipzig. Flight Lieutenant Norman Rix, DFC and crew successfully baled out and became prisoners. Some of the crew of the second Fortress, however, were much less fortunate. Flight Lieutenant Johnny Wynne, DFC brought back HB799 after a long struggle; his crew had baled out, and subsequently five of them were murdered. Then, on 15 March, Flying Officer Anderson was returning from Misburg when shot down by a Ju88 using its Schräge Musik cannon. The crew baled out. Four were injured and two were killed. On 20 March, Flying Officer Kingdom, RCAF, failed to return in HB803. This aircraft was supporting an attack on an oil target.[71]

The squadron's last war loss was on 22 March. Flight Lieutenant Bill Allies, aged 30, was the pilot of KJ112 ('BU-P'), making a Jostle patrol to support a raid on Hamburg. This aircraft was lost without trace. It is thought to have gone down in the Heligoland Bight.[71] Flying Officer M. 'Bing' Crosbie had a lucky escape a few weeks later. On 17 April his aircraft was damaged by flak. He overshot and crashed on landing at Florennes-Juzaine, Belgium. The Fortress was a write-off.

North Killingholme's Lancasters flew two more raids in March. On Tuesday, 27 March 550 sent eighteen Lancasters against Paderborn. The target was obscured but a large mushroom of smoke, 12,000ft high, appeared through the cloud tops. There was no flak or fighter opposition but one aircraft, Flying Officer Percival's 'J', was struck by incendiaries from an aircraft above. A few days later, on Saturday, 31 March, the squadron sent sixteen aircraft for an early morning attack on Hamburg. The weather was bad and there was ten-tenths cloud over the target. The bombing, on sky markers, lacked concentration. Two of 550's Lancasters received flak damage but all returned safely.

The long bombing war against Germany reached its final days. The Lancasters of 550 Squadron flew eight raids in April, four by day and four by night. On Tuesday, 3 April Frank Woodley flew his thirty-fifth operation, joining New Zealander Flying Officer Lohrey. Frank had said goodbye to Ken Sidwell and the boys, who had finished. He settled into the mid-upper turret of Lohrey's Lancaster for an attack on

Nordhausen.[72] There was thought to be a large concentration of German troops at this location. Unfortunately, the barracks housed slave labourers and concentration camp prisoners, kept like animals as the workforce of this underground V-weapons plant.

Sam Lipfriend had enjoyed a breather of just over a week. He joined Flight Lieutenant Mitchell's crew for the next day's attack on Lützkendorf oil refinery. Their aircraft was one of 258 Lancasters dispatched.[73] Six were lost, including 550's last war casualty. This was ME301 ('X', later 'K'), flown by 20-year-old Flying Officer M.D. Hayes, who had completed twenty-two operations. They crashed near Berlin and all seven were killed.[74]

Mitchell's aircraft took off for Lützkendorf at 21.02 and arrived back eight hours twenty minutes later. Lipfriend wrote in his diary: 'Ops have changed considerably. Flew over our troops most of the way. Pretty good prang. It was nice to see the old fire glow after the recent daylights.' Lipfriend had finished his tour, after thirty-two trips. He pointed wryly to the injustice of his situation: 'They made the first tour of thirty trips into thirty-six, then reduced it to thirty-three. That meant I had one more to do after Lützkendorf. Then they reduced it again, from thirty-three to thirty. That meant they got two extra out of me.'[75]

There was a late loss for 153 Squadron at Scampton. Bill Thomas, who had been Lancaster captain Bruce Potter's bomb aimer: 'We lost Wing Commander Francis Powley on the night of the Lützkendorf raid. He joined a minelaying crew. I hated those "gardening" trips. We did three of them; there was no bomber stream to shelter in when minelaying.'[76]

Bill Thomas' last op, his twenty-ninth, was an attack on Kiel's naval yards and facilities, on the night of 9/10 April. The raiders capsized the pocket battleship *Admiral Scheer* and severely damaged the heavy cruisers *Admiral Hipper* and *Emden*. With that trip over, Thomas became a screened bomb aimer. He had joined a lucky crew: 'We were never attacked by fighters and we took no serious flak damage – just two or three holes.'[76]

The real challenges for this crew were mechanical failures. After one op Bill Thomas was accused of dropping his bombs unfused: 'I was always extremely careful with fusing. I was able to show that I had done my job but that there had been a mechanical problem. I always followed my routines. When flying with a full load – including a 4,000lb Cookie – the Lanc had a rather nose-up attitude. The big Cookie was suspended from a single station. When it dropped you felt the aircraft shudder. The rest of the bombs released in a few seconds. I always looked into the bomb bay to check for any hang-ups. Bruce also opened the bomb doors and gave the Lanc a "shake" when we were over the North Sea. We didn't want to land with incendiaries jammed in the small bomb containers.

'We had a problem one night when Scampton was fogged in. We diverted to another airfield but began to struggle when the altimeter and ASI started to play up. Suddenly, we lost the altimeter. I said to Bruce: "That's great. We're flying into a strange airfield, in poor visibility and with no altimeter." After a chat, we decided to land at Woodbridge, one of Bomber Command's three emergency landing grounds. On landing, we found the copper pitot head had been squashed. Later, on returning to Scampton, we discovered that the squadron diversion had involved a visit to a Yankee airbase. Everyone came back laden with cigarettes, chocolate and other PX goodies. We got nothing!'[76]

Kiel was Frank Woodley's last op. He joined Flight Lieutenant Fleming's crew for the night attack. He felt a little chastened when told, on his return from his thirty-sixth operation, that the length of the tour had been reduced. His feelings were coloured by the events of that night. Kiel was a disturbing experience. Woodley was accustomed to flying with an experienced crew: 'It was absolute mayhem over the target. Kiel was Fleming's first operation. They had no R/T discipline whatsoever. I got fed up in the end and told them to shut up. I didn't think much of flying as a spare bod.' His consolation was an overwhelming feeling of relief. It was over and he was still in one piece.[77]

Among the lucky Lancasters on 550 Squadron was EE139 ('B'), otherwise known as 'Phantom of the Ruhr'. It sported some lurid nose art. This aircraft joined the squadron in November 1943. During the course of the following twelve months it reached a total of 121 operations (thirty-two with 100 Squadron before moving to 550). The Phantom was retired to a Heavy Conversion Unit. Two other 550 Squadron aircraft completed over a hundred operations: ED905 ('BQ-F'), known as 'Press on regardless', and PA995 ('BQ-V'), 'Vulture strikes' (lost during the 7/8 March raid on Dessau).[78]

Veteran: Lancaster EE139 (BQ-B), 'Phantom of the Ruhr' – the survivor of 121 operations. *Photo: Bob Stone.*

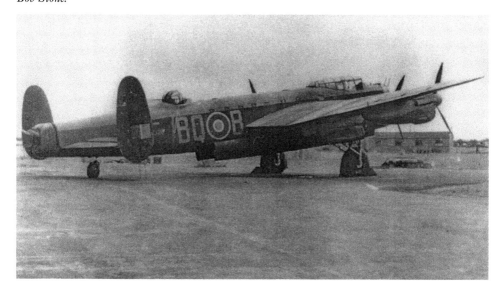

D-Day debut: Lancaster LL811 (J-Jig), 'Bad Penny II', opened D-Day at 23.34 on 5 June 1944. Lined up alongside Bad Penny are Flying Officer Harry Manley and crew. *Photo: Bob Stone.*

These are 550 Squadron's vital statistics: participation in 194 raids; 3,485 take-offs and 3,175 successful sorties; 9,259 operational hours flown (4,271 hours at night); and 16,195 tons of bombs dropped. Lancaster LL811 ('J-Jig'), known as 'Bad Penny II', opened D-Day, dropping bombs at 23.34 on 5 June 1944. This was recognized with the award of the *Croix de Guerre*.[78]

Notes

1. Middlebrook, M. and Everitt, C. (1990), *The Bomber Command War Diaries*, 704.
2. Saward, D. (1985), *Victory Denied*, 353–5.
3. Newsletter 21, 1 November 2000, 550 Squadron and RAF North Killingholme Association.
4. National Archives, AIR 14/3684.
5. Pross, M. (1995), *Die Einschläge kommen näher, Aus den Tagebüchern 1943–45 von Friedrich Adolf Katz, 1945–1947 Oberbürgermeister der Stadt Pforzheim.*
6. Interview with Marianne Pross, September 2013.
7. Pross, M. (1995), *Die Einschläge kommen näher, Aus den Tagebüchern 1943–45 von Friedrich Adolf Katz, 1945–1947 Oberbürgermeister der Stadt Pforzheim.*
8. Interview with Dave Davidson, April 2013.
9. Middlebrook, M. and Everitt, C. (1990), *The Bomber Command War Diaries*, 672–3.
10. Interview with Dave Davidson, April 2013.
11. Papers provided by the Davidson family.
12. Interview with Howell Evans, June 2013.
13. Interview with Ron Germain, April 2013.

14. Interview with Frank Woodley, March 2013.
15. Middlebrook, M. and Everitt, C. (1990), *The Bomber Command War Diaries*, 673.
16. Interview with Frank Woodley, March 2013.
17. Bowman, M.W. (2006), *100 Group (Bomber Support)*, 26.
18. Bowman, M.W. and Cushing, T. (1996), *Confounding the Reich*, 176–7.
19. James, R. (1989), *214 (FMS) Squadron, RAF: Avenging in the Shadows*, 163.
20. Ibid., 165.
21. Newsletter 32, 23 May 2005, 550 Squadron and RAF North Killingholme Association.
22. 214squadron.org.uk; Nightjar Newsletter, Spring 2003.
23. James, R. (1989), *214 (FMS) Squadron, RAF: Avenging in the Shadows*, 163.
24. Ibid., 165.
25. Papers provided by Wing Commander Jack Harris, OBE, DFC.
26. Newsletter 43, 20 May 2009, 550 Squadron and RAF North Killingholme Association.
27. Interview with Sidney Knott, March 2013.
28. Redding, T. (2008), *Flying for Freedom*, 130.
29. Interview with Sidney Knott, March 2013.
30. Interview with Dave Davidson, April 2013.
31. Middlebrook, M. and Everitt, C. (1990), *The Bomber Command War Diaries*, 675.
32. Interview with Ron Germain, April 2013.
33. Newsletter 21, 1 November 2000, 550 Squadron and RAF North Killingholme Association.
34. Newsletter 20, 5 May 2000, 550 Squadron and RAF North Killingholme Association.
35. Middlebrook, M. and Everitt, C. (1990), *The Bomber Command War Diaries*, 676.
36. Newsletter 20, 5 May 2000, 550 Squadron and RAF North Killingholme Association.
37. Interview with Sam Lipfriend, March 2013.
38. Interview with Raimund Frei, July 2013.
39. Keirle, Stan and other aircrew POWs, 'A Winter's Tale'; papers via Wing Commander Jack Harris, OBE, DFC.
40. Interview with Bill Thomas, June 2013.
41. Interview with Sam Lipfriend, March 2013.
42. Middlebrook, M. and Everitt, C. (1990), *The Bomber Command War Diaries*, 677.
43. Interview with Sam Lipfriend, March 2013.
44. Middlebrook, M. and Everitt, C. (1990), *The Bomber Command War Diaries*, 678.
45. Interview with Sam Lipfriend, March 2013.
46. Middlebrook, M. and Everitt, C. (1990), *The Bomber Command War Diaries*, 679.
47. Interview with Sam Lipfriend, March 2013.
48. Interview with Frank Woodley, March 2013.
49. Interview with Ron Germain, April 2013.
50. Middlebrook, M. and Everitt, C. (1990), *The Bomber Command War Diaries*, 681.
51. Interview with Ron Germain, April 2013.
52. Interview with Frank Woodley, March 2013.
53. Interview with Dave Davidson, April 2013.
54. Middlebrook, M. and Everitt, C. (1990), *The Bomber Command War Diaries*, 682.
55. Newsletter 21, 1 November 2000, 550 Squadron and RAF North Killingholme Association.
56. Newsletter 32, 23 May 2005, 550 Squadron and RAF North Killingholme Association.
57. Middlebrook, M. and Everitt, C. (1990), *The Bomber Command War Diaries*, 683.
58. Interview with Ron Germain, April 2013.
59. Riblet-Buchmann, R. (1993), *Unerwartete Begegnung – Als junger 'Fremdarbeiter' in Pforzheim 1944/45*.
60. Middlebrook, M. and Everitt, C. (1990), *The Bomber Command War Diaries*, 685.
61. Interview with Sam Lipfriend, March 2013.
62. Middlebrook, M. and Everitt, C. (1990), *The Bomber Command War Diaries*, 685.
63. Interview with Sam Lipfriend, March 2013.

64. Interview with Dave Davidson, April 2013.
65. Interview with Howell Evans, June 2013.
66. Middlebrook, M. and Everitt, C. (1990), *The Bomber Command War Diaries*, 687.
67. Newsletter 21, 1 November 2000, 550 Squadron and RAF North Killingholme Association.
68. Interview with Sam Lipfriend, March 2013.
69. Middlebrook, M. and Everitt, C. (1990), *The Bomber Command War Diaries*, 688.
70. Interview with Sam Lipfriend, March 2013.
71. James, R. (1989), *214 (FMS) Squadron, RAF: Avenging in the Shadows*, 165–9; 214squadron. org.uk
72. Interview with Frank Woodley, March 2013.
73. Middlebrook, M. and Everitt, C. (1990), *The Bomber Command War Diaries*, 691.
74. Newsletter 21, 1 November 2000, 550 Squadron and RAF North Killingholme Association.
75. Interview with Sam Lipfriend, March 2013.
76. Interview with Bill Thomas, June 2013.
77. Interview with Frank Woodley, March 2013.
78. Papers provided by Wing Commander Jack Harris, OBE, DFC.

Chapter Fourteen

Living in the Ruins

Life continued in the ruins. Surviving Pforzheimers slowly drew together the basics of daily existence. In an assessment of German civilian morale, the British Bombing Survey Unit commented: 'The hardships to which the German population were put were born stoically in the face of what must have been a growing realization, from the beginning of 1944 onwards, that, short of a miracle, Germany was bound to lose the war. Even the mounting toll of casualties failed to break the hold which the Nazi Party had over the German population. As Speer said: "the outlook of the people was often poor, but their behaviour was almost always excellent".'[1]

Helmut Watter remembers the long hunt for bodies in the ruins: 'The search for close family members, relatives and friends continued after the burning city had cooled down and the smoke decreased. The smell of burning remained and the dead bodies were laid in lines on Marktplatz and Schlossberg. We searched in Rohrstrasse, Grosse Gerbergasse, Untere Ispringer Strasse and in the western part of the city, unable to find anybody. Later, we heard that an uncle presumably perished in Zerrennerstrasse, when the water from the Metzelgraben [an inner city canal] flooded cellars.'[2]

Bodies were laid out in the road, to be picked up and taken to the cemetery. Helmut Watter: 'Men, women and children – some charred and mangled, some absolutely peaceful – were on the roadside by the dozens. An old man with a pipe in his mouth lay there as if he were asleep. Right next to him the horrible sight of charred people that were burned beyond recognition.'[2] Later on, there were wooden crosses all over the ruins, bearing the names of the dead.

On Sunday, 25 February 1945, ruined Pforzheim was under martial law. Max Gaupp, the van driver who found his wife and daughter dead, heard talk of around 20,000 dead. 'There is no bread, no water, no light, no gas, no candles, only the NSV [NS People's Welfare] soup brought in from the surrounding area.' He added: 'Pillagers and grumblers are to be shot – not in the city but in the cemetery. They say they have to march up there so they won't have to carry the bodies up afterwards. The people who have lost their families and all their belongings don't mince words any more. Everywhere you go there are groups cursing Adolf Hitler as the reason for this disaster: "All because of this maniac … the damned dog … if only he had croaked back then, on 20 July … sacrificing the entire German people … he has no right to do this."'[3]

The Gerstung family remained in Pforzheim after the attack. Hans Gerstung: 'Our home was still standing and habitable. The roof was soon fixed. In fact, we took in two bombed-out families. We had five rooms in the apartment and two were given over to these families. There was grammar school professor Martin Reichmann and his wife, Elizabeth, who were friends of my parents. There was also Dr Schnorr's wife and three children. Dr Schnorr, a radiologist, was a prisoner at that time.'[4]

Apartments housing bombed-out families had priority when scarce building materials were distributed for repairs: 'The rooms we provided had been used by Father for his work as an architect. Our apartment now housed nine people – three Gerstungs, four Schnorrs and two Reichmanns. We all shared the bathroom and separate toilet. There was one stove for cooking. Some careful planning was required, from first thing in the morning, to ensure everyone had an opportunity to use the facilities. I found this particularly unpleasant.'[4]

Dieter Essig, then six years old, remembers searching for food in the immediate aftermath of the attack: 'During the following days we were issued with stamps and began to queue at improvised food distribution points run by the Red Cross. Farmers in the surrounding countryside also helped, bringing in food for the city's stricken population. Mother took us on a long hike to a farm, to get milk and potatoes. It was 12km there and back. This farm was near relatives who lived in Tiefenbronn. We pushed a pram laden with provisions. We met a couple of soldiers who had been separated from their unit. One helped Mother push the pram. At one point he shoved us into a ditch and opened fire on an aircraft with his machine gun.'[5]

On Tuesday 27 February fires were still burning and many corpses still awaited collection. Max Gaupp noticed how everyone asked the same question: 'Where are you living?' On Thursday, 1 March Gaupp was back in the ruins, renewing the search for his father. Seven men joined him. They climbed the rubble and saw holes blasted into each end of the arched cellar. The front wall had been torn away. 'The rubble was piled up a metre high in the cellar. The heat was still unbearable. There was nothing to find. No remains. No bones. Nothing.

'The whole city was shrouded in a sweetish smell. The smell of corpses. They were still excavating cellars and recovering bodies. On the bank of the Enz lay the bodies of 117 women workers.' Again and again he saw pushcarts with bodies: 'Today, they buried one foot belonging to my sister-in-law's brother. On Leopoldplatz, in front of the Hogg shop, a madman yelled: "Come here now, Mr Goebbels, and take a look at this, but you have to come very close so you can see all of it."'[6]

The police established a missing persons list at the Café Epple. Later in the year, in October, the city's registry office stated that 7,200 victims of the bombing had been buried; 2,432 were unnamed. At that time it was seen as impossible to give any reliable estimate of those still buried under the debris. The generally accepted total of 17,600 air-raid dead (including the relatively low losses before the main attack) was not arrived at until 1948. Human remains continued to be found for many years, as debris was removed. Wooden crosses dotted the wide expanse of ruins. They were decorated with flowers at Christmas and other special days. Slowly, the crosses disappeared as more bodies were found and taken for burial.[7]

Allied assessment teams used aerial photographic survey techniques to arrive at their estimates of bomb damage. The official sources, including the report of the British Bombing Survey Unit (see Appendix A, Report on the effects of strategic bombing on German towns, Towns Panel, British Bombing Survey Unit), show that of seventy cities attacked by Bomber Command, forty-six were approximately half-destroyed and, of these, twenty-three were more than 60 per cent destroyed in terms of built-up area. Thirty-one of the seventy cities had over 500 acres destroyed. Wuppertal/Elberfeld topped the list, with 870 acres (94 per cent of the targeted built-up area) destroyed, followed by Würzburg, with 422 acres (89 per cent). Pforzheim, with 304 acres (83 per cent) destroyed, shared third place in percentage terms with Bochum (532 acres) and Remscheid (281 acres). By way of contrast, Berlin had 6,427 acres destroyed (33 per cent of the built-up area), Hamburg had 6,200 acres destroyed (75 per cent) and Dresden 1,681 acres (59 per cent).

As for Pforzheim, photo reconnaissance sorties flown after the raid allowed a preliminary assessment of damage to industrial premises. The Interpretation Report (K.3838) lists seven priority industrial plants destroyed or severely damaged. Eugen Fessler (Ostl. Karl-Friedrich-Strasse), Moritz Hausch (Durlacherstrasse) and Andreas Daub (Luisenstrasse) were assessed as 'A' – total losses. Allgemeine

Sea of rubble: the wasteland that was once the city of Pforzheim. *Photo: Stadtarchiv Pforzheim.*

Gold und Silber Scheideanstalt (Altstädter Kirchenweg), Rodi und Wienenberger AG (Bleichstrasse) and Heimerle und Meule (a precious metals refinery on Ostl. Karl-Friedrich-Strasse) were ranked as 'B' – 'entire works 95 per cent–75 per cent devastated.' Kollmar und Jourdan AG (Bleichstrasse) was ranked as 'C' – 'major damage to important buildings and subsidiary damage elsewhere'. With the exception of the gold and silver refineries, all were listed as manufacturers of precision parts and fuses.

The electricity works was assessed in the report as 'A', totally destroyed. The gasworks (Eutinger Strasse) was ranked 'C' (major damage). The passenger station was 'gutted' and there was severe damage to the goods depot, warehousing and sheds. The Goethebrücke over the Enz and the Werderbrücke over the Nagold were destroyed, and a long section of the road bridge over the marshalling yards had collapsed.

Stan Keirle, a 550 Squadron wireless operator, was still held at Luckenwalde, near Berlin. For some time the prisoners had watched aircraft raid Berlin, the 'Big City' to Bomber Command crews. As March became April, the war crept closer to Luckenwalde. The POWs took cover when the camp was strafed by Russian aircraft. An artillery duel followed, with shells flying overhead in both directions. One day in mid-April the German guards fled the camp, mingling with refugees heading west, away from the Russians.[8]

Control of the camp fell into the hands of senior British, American and Norwegian officers. They received a delegation from Luckenwalde town, headed by the Bürgermeister. He wanted to surrender to the British, rather than the Russians. Things were not straightforward: scouts sent into the town reported the presence of about 100 SS troops and around 1,000 Hitler Youth, all under arms. The latter were trigger happy and occasionally wore civilian clothes. Indeed, German civilians began to seek sanctuary in the POW camp. It was too late for Luckenwalde: on 22 April a Russian tank and motorized infantry arrived. The prisoners were fascinated by the tough, heavily armed women soldiers. The tank symbolically destroyed the camp's main gates and 4,000 Russian prisoners in Luckenwalde were released. They went into town to loot shops and attack women: they had scores to settle following their abominable treatment in the camp. With the arrival of the Russians, the British prisoners assumed they would soon be repatriated, but they were in for a shock. The Russians were in no hurry, and stalled for weeks as they compiled detailed rolls of the POWs.[8]

Conditions in Pforzheim were appalling. Families struggled to get on their feet. Four-year-old Klaus Feucht's family squeezed into one room of a Stuttgart apartment. It became even more crowded when his eldest brother, evacuated to Titisee, returned to the family.[9]

Thirteen-year-old Bernhard Mauderer had escorted schoolchildren during their evacuation. He was ordered to return on 27 February. The Pforzheim Hitler Jugend wanted him to help recover the dead. He had lost his mother in the raid and his father had been killed a few months before. After ten days collecting corpses, he went back to the frosty atmosphere of Aunt Louise's farm. He had a ration card but no money to buy food. Bernhard got up early every morning to feed hay to the chopping machine. His uncle stopped him kicking a football around, reminding him that he had just the one pair of shoes. He and his grandmother were still not permitted to eat at the same table as the others. 'We had to sit next to the kitchen sink. Mostly, we were given sour milk and unpeeled potatoes – all home produced. Sauerkraut with bacon rinds – Uncle said this was best for us. Aunt and Uncle always had a nice piece of bacon in their sauerkraut. In the mornings there was fresh warm milk, old, hard bread and an infrequent egg or two. I had not used my food ration card, so Uncle used it for me. He gave me work in the barn, chopping wood in the backyard and stacking logs.'[10]

When the French arrived, the takeover left three corpses in the village. Bernhard and his uncle were required to bury them; his uncle made the coffins. With the arrival of spring, Bernhard accompanied his aunt to the meadow, to mow and bring in green fodder. 'My uncle always grumbled at me and I toyed with the idea of running away.'

By July 1945 the first hay harvest was in, and then came the second cut. When his uncle moaned at him for taking too much time on an errand, Bernhard had had enough. Before going to bed that night, he packed his meagre possessions. 'It was just my uniform and clothing the soldiers had thrown out: army shoes (two sizes too big), socks, shirts, blankets, overalls and trousers. It all went into an air force kitbag that weighed about 35 kilos.' He rose early on 10 August, had something to eat and told his aunt and uncle that he was leaving for good. 'I had 10 Reichsmark and I demanded my ration card. I grabbed my bag and went to the door leading to the outside stairs. My uncle called after me: "I don't want to see you again. You won't get far. If you come back, I'll throw you down the stairs." I headed south. I slept in the forest next to a logpile and washed myself in a stream. I ate wild berries growing at the edge of the forest.'[10]

The 23 February raid destroyed the offices of Pforzheim's power utility on Enzstrasse, together with the water power plant at Rennfeld and various distribution sites. There was no power to the inner city and in Nordstadt. Work was under way to restore overhead power lines serving Nordstadt and to restart the pumping stations. The power supply to Brötzingen and Dillweissenstein was uninterrupted. The town's gasworks had been hit and badly damaged, but some critical installations remained intact. The supply infrastructure was severely mauled, though, and gas supply was not reinstated until April 1946, and then only partially.[11]

The town's water supply, largely undamaged, was reinstated the next day in areas beyond the inner zone of devastation. The surviving eastern and western districts were served separately and water trucks were needed in the damaged northern districts for some time. The trams were badly affected. Much of the overhead cable system had gone. Before the attack Pforzheim was served by three tram routes with a total track length of 12.8km, 10.2km of which suffered loss of overhead cables and much of the track. Only the forest route from Kupferhammer to Dillweissenstein was largely unscathed, as was the narrow gauge railway connecting Pforzheim to Ittersbach. As for other city infrastructure, the Goethebrücke had collapsed and other bridges were damaged. The northern town train overpass was destroyed and the Ispringer Strasse underpass suffered damage. Both the Mühlkanal and Metzelgraben canals were seriously damaged.[11]

Pforzheim had 24,175 flats before the bombing; two-thirds had been destroyed. The level of destruction of factories and other business and commercial premises was even higher. As for public buildings, most had been swept away by high explosive bombs and fire. The losses included the offices of health, police, customs, employment, forestry, district court, revenue and highways. The town hall on Marktplatz was destroyed, as were many schools, including Schwarzwaldschule and Calwerschule. The Nordstadtschule, Brötzingerschule, Klingschule, Oberrealschule, Hildaschule and Handelsschule were among those very badly damaged or burnt out. The surviving school, in Dillweissenstein, was taken over by the Military Government following occupation.[11]

Desolation: the ruins surrounding Pforzheim's Stadtkirche. The crosses in the rubble – visible in the foreground, just right of centre – mark the location of bodies yet to be recovered. *Photo: Stadtarchiv Pforzheim.*

Of the three hospitals, only St Trudpert was unharmed. The City Hospital had been damaged by bombs on 21 January 1945. Now seventeen of its twenty-four buildings were totally destroyed and the remainder severely damaged. The Siloah Hospital was damaged. The churches destroyed included the Stadtkirche, Schlosskirche and Altstadtkirche.[11]

Early efforts to respond to civil needs after 23 February were hampered by the large number of casualties among council staff. Mayor Karl Mohrenstein died in an air attack on 4 March and town building director Ludwig Seibel died a week later. He was an experienced hand, having been the Oberbürgermeister's deputy for most of the war. The town hall's administrative framework had been consumed by fire; yet the lower basement was spared and the council pay office and treasury infrastructure survived. This was a platform for reviving a basic level of council administration. Council departments were set up in outlying villages. The head office and personnel department were established at Brötzingen Town Hall. The food and economics bureau was housed in Dillweissenstein school and the city treasury was located in the old town hall.[11]

People continued to dig in the ruins for household goods and other possessions. Efforts were made to retrieve equipment from ruined factories and workshops. Intact or lightly damaged premises on the outskirts attempted to open for work. The banks set up emergency offices at accessible locations. The Reichsbank opened at Ersinger Strasse 7, Adolf Katz's Deutsche Bank opened in the Maihäldenhof pub, at Kelterstrasse 62, while the Volksbank opened at Westl. Karl-Friedrich-Strasse 273. The Sparkasse operated two branches, in Niefern and Arlinger, with additional offices in the Hoheneck pub and in the Café Davos.[11]

Key local government functions were organized. Police offices were located on Frankstrasse and the notary's office and probate court operated from Nebeniusstrasse 1. Basic postal services were provided from a motor vehicle yard at Zeppelinstrasse 16. The Brötzingen mail offices relocated to accommodation nearby, but post office branches at Dillweissenstein, Buckenberg, Ispringer Pfad and Hagenschiess were unscathed. There were also mobile post offices on Messplatz, at pubs serving the eastern and northern districts and at Kupferhammer, for the southern area. Mail deliveries were impossible in the inner and southern districts. People were told to collect their mail from mobile offices. Locations and times were announced by loudspeaker.[11]

A BDM girl took Emmi Nagel home and gave her a bed. Emmi had come close to death in the public shelter at Gymnasiumstrasse 52. In a few days she recovered sufficiently to search for her missing mother. 'I stood by the side of the country road at around six or seven in the morning and waved at passing cars. It snowed and was very dark.' She got a lift to the northern town and climbed over rubble until reaching the corner of Östl.-Karl-Friedrich-Strasse and Schulberg, when she met a neighbour who shouted: 'My son must shoot me when he comes home!' She had lost fourteen family members – her husband, daughter, grandchildren and, elsewhere, her mother and siblings.[12]

Grim task: nurses and volunteers at Siloah Hospital help ready the dead for transport to the cemetery. *Photo: Stadtarchiv Pforzheim.*

When Emmi asked about her mother, the woman sent her towards Theaterplatz: 'Sixty people lay there in a row, among them my mother. I stood there for a long time. Then I climbed down into the cellar. I felt my way to the place where we had sat and pulled out our woollen blanket. I used this to cover my mother. A soldier was walking past. I asked him for a pencil. I wrote a note and pinned it to the blanket with a hairpin: "Please not into the mass grave. Will be buried privately!"' Emmi Nagel then went to her sister-in-law's, on Pflügerstrasse: 'Nothing but ruins here, too. On a fragment of wall it said in chalk: "We're living in Eutingen, Adolf Hitler Strasse, at W's."' In fact, the sister-in-law had travelled on to Emmi's sister in Ulm. Emmi took a room at 'W's'.[12]

Permission was needed for private burials. Emmi made her request to the cemetery administration, which had set up an open-air post to the east of the cemetery building. The smell was terrible: 'Hundreds and hundreds of dead were piled up where, today, the roses grow.' The bodies had been sprinkled with lime. Everyone was under strain. When a woman next to Emmi held her nose, the man at the desk snapped at her, pointing out that he and his team would be sitting there all day, breathing in the stench.[12]

She was then told that her mother could be buried privately, but she would have to find a coffin and dig the grave herself. Her new landlady helped obtain a coffin and two soldiers helped her dig the grave in the family plot. Then her sister turned up. At Theaterplatz they put the mother in her coffin: 'Clean-up teams next to us were loading corpses onto hay carts. The men were shouting loudly as they had been "treated" with schnapps. Most wore rubber gloves for protection against contagion. Others dipped their arms into chlorinated lime and looked like millers. On the way to the cemetery we saw many carts and wheelbarrows with dead people. Most didn't have a coffin. Hands and feet stuck out from under blankets or paper.'[12]

Before reaching the cemetery there was an alarm and the two women were forced to leave the coffin and take shelter. Eventually, her mother was buried and Emmi decided to go to Ulm with her sister. When they arrived they found the town still burning after a raid the previous night, 28 February/1 March. Her sister's apartment was ablaze. Now they were both homeless.[12]

On Tuesday 27 February Artur Kühn dug a double grave for his wife and daughter at Eutingen. During the graveside service they sheltered behind gravestones as fighter-bombers swooped over the village. On returning to Pforzheim a woman asked him to take her dead parents to the cemetery: 'Near the cemetery we had to put cloths over our mouths and noses, as the smell was unbearable.'[12]

Deep burial pits had been excavated: 'About 3,500 dead went into each pit, ten to fourteen on top of each other.' At one point, a Red Cross nurse asked Artur if he wanted a bowl of soup. It was his first hot meal for days. He remembers soldiers shooting themselves on the rubble of their homes.[12]

Some people had no remains to bury. Anneliese Vestewig-Fischer's husband searched for her missing family in a cellar on Sedanplatz. When he arrived, the house was still burning. Anneliese: 'Later, I had our cellar excavated. I searched everywhere to find a trace of my mother and sister. Nothing.' They found a couple of bones, but there had been fifteen people in that cellar. It was impossible, at that time, to attribute the remains. Years later, she discovered that her father had lost his life at Schlossberg, trying to rescue others.[12]

The army and other specialists moved in to deal with unexploded bombs and organize road clearance. Meanwhile, people queuing at food distribution points were exposed to attacks by Allied fighter-bombers. Queues were strafed by low-flying aircraft on Sunday, 4 March. There were attacks on local railway targets on Wednesday, 14 March and Friday, 16 March. The autobahn was hit on 17 March, the rail line from Brötzingen to Birkenfeld on Sunday the 18th and Pforzheim's goods station on the 19th. The Mühlacker–Karlsruhe rail line was attacked on Tuesday 20 March. On that day all males aged 16 were required to register with the police for compulsory service. On Saturday, 24 March there were repeated air attacks on the Enztal rail viaduct and the power station was seriously damaged. The fighter-bomber attacks continued into early April.[13]

Kreisleiter Knab and his Nazi bosses were not prepared to give up the fight – at least in public. The newspapers for Saturday, 31 March published 'Order 1' from the Gauleiter and Reich Defence commissioner. It declared: 'Party Leaders and Party Officers to remain wherever the enemy attacks, in the combat zone. They will fight within the Volkssturm, in support of the Army. Withdrawal from the enemy is only permitted if ordered by high-ranking Army officers or the Gauleiter.'[13] Kreisleiter Knab, for one, had no intention of obeying this order.

In contrast, Werner Baroni and his fellow naval cadets were expected to fight to the last. Baroni had arrived at the Naval Academy, Flensburg, in November 1944. A few months later, while on guard at the academy's main gate, he was suddenly relieved. His father had sent a telegram saying that the family had been bombed out. 'Later, in a British prison camp, I heard a rumour that Pforzheim had been so badly bombed that one could stand on the west side of town and see all the way through to the east. From the academy we were posted to the island of Sylt. We were told the British were about to invade north Germany.'[14]

Werner Baroni took part in the final weeks of fighting, but not on the German coast. The naval cadets received orders to fight their way east and 'liberate' Berlin.

Bad news: Werner Baroni (right), pictured with a comrade at the Naval Academy, Flensburg, in November 1944. He was on guard at the Academy's main gate when told of the bombing of Pforzheim. *Photo: Werner Baroni.*

'We kids were expected to defeat the Red Army! We reached the front line in the area of Teterow-Sukow. We prepared for an attack by Russian T-34 tanks. Our company commander told us: "Well, men. We have to deal with the Red Army – a bunch of cowards!" I said: "If they are such cowards, how have they managed to come so deep into Germany?" The officer replied: "Don't worry. We have an SS artillery regiment behind us." That was a big lie. The tanks came in and all we had were hand-held Panzerfausts. We then realized that we would not be liberating Berlin. This battle, at Warin, killed many of us. We had set out with 198 cadets. When we were captured by the British there were eighteen left. The rest were dead, seriously wounded or missing.

'I became a prisoner of the British following a "democratic" decision. In early May we held positions defending a railway line just outside Bad Kleinen, in the Schwerin-Wismar area. Our officer said: "We have the Red Army 300 metres in front of us and Canadian paratroops behind us in Bad Kleinen. I leave it up to you as to which direction we should go." We all said: 'West!' In Bad Kleinen a Canadian captain approached and our officer told us to put down our weapons. I walked to Gadebusch and a POW cage holding around 9,000 prisoners. The British couldn't feed us – we were too many. We were worried that we would be handed over to the Russians, to end our days in a Siberian camp.'[14]

Plans were made to find new and happier employment for the British heavy bomber fleet. Between 29 April and 7 May 1945, 550 Squadron Lancasters from North Killingholme joined hundreds of other Bomber Command aircraft dropping food to the starving Dutch. The so-called 'Cook's Tour' flights began in late May. The idea was to allow non-flying personnel at the bomber bases to see the results of the campaign. The Lancasters flew low over Germany's ruined cities; many aircrew, as well as ground staff, were shocked at what they saw. On Thursday, 26 July, 550 Squadron began flights to bring back British troops from Italy. The 550 Squadron disbandment parade was held on Wednesday, 24 October 1945, and the unit ceased to exist the following Wednesday, 31 October. During November the last of its aircraft arrived back from Italy. It was all over.[15]

The end of the war couldn't come quickly enough for 550 Squadron wireless operator Stan Keirle, one of many thousands of British prisoners who had suffered on long forced marches in bitter winter weather. In April the Russians reached Luckenwalde camp, then took measures to block the repatriation of prisoners. When Russian troops fired into the air over American trucks on Saturday, 5 May – forcing the POWs' motor transport to retire – Keirle and five friends had had enough. They were also fired on as they slipped away and headed west, aiming to link up with the Americans. They avoided roads, keeping to the forest. They had every reason to be nervous. There were plenty of heavily armed Russian troops around, together with German troops dressed in civilian clothes but armed nonetheless.[16]

They spent the first night in the forest, then fell in with crowds of civilians heading west on the main road. Their map, provided by the camp's escape committee, suggested that they were near Jüterbog. They had some money and managed to buy fresh bread in a small village. They shared vodka with a Russian, in return for cigarettes. On reaching Wittenberg that afternoon they found all the bridges over the Elbe had been blown. There were no American troops on the far bank. They spent the night in an empty apartment and travelled on the next morning, eventually finding a blown bridge that still had enough girders above water to allow pedestrians to cross. In another village a woman offered them refreshment and then asked them to stay the night, to protect her two daughters. Her fears were well founded. During the night three drunken Russians tried to enter, only to find their way blocked by the POWs.[16]

Later that day the group reached Bitterfeld and met up with the Americans. A jeep took them to a camp near Halle, where they rested for two days. They were then flown to Reims and on to another airfield for the repatriation flight. They landed at RAF Benson, Oxfordshire. Stan was allowed one free phone call, to announce his safe return. It was over.[16]

The number of dead resulting from the 23 February 1945 Pforzheim raid was exceptionally high. In the early post-war years the city authorities addressed this issue. An official publication suggested that people had failed to take air-raid defence seriously enough. Pforzheim had been regarded as a second order priority for funds from the central air-raid defence budget. Bigger cities, such as Stuttgart, Karlsruhe and Mannheim, had priority and Pforzheim was left to its own devices: 'The lack of workforce and materials set tight limits on local efforts.' The report added: 'In 1940/41 the Town Council had already drawn up plans for tunnels at the Schwarzwaldschule and by the sports field and station, but permission was refused – based on the fact that, apparently, it was too expensive and also because Pforzheim was a second order air defence priority … Only towards the end of the war, when the danger became more widely recognized, [did] the Luftgaukommando fund tunnel construction.'[17]

According to the city authorities, in the final year of the war there were sixty-four public shelters available, with a total of 6,600 spaces. There were twenty partially constructed shelter tunnels, four of which were centrally funded. Improvements to residential shelters were held back by lack of materials, labour and time.[17] It was too late for many thousands of Pforzheimers.

Adolf Katz spent much of March 1945 trying to reorganize his battered bank in Pforzheim. Two of the girls, Marianne and Annina, together with Aunt Friederike, had returned safely from Lake Constance. They arrived in Mönsheim during the first days of April, with Robert as escort. On 2 April, Katz described the panic in the village the day before. People were told to prepare for evacuation. Even at this point 'wonder weapon' fantasies persisted. The village Ortsgruppenleiter told Katz that they had been informed that a terrible new weapon was going to be used 'which would exterminate all life in a wide area.' Katz wrote: 'The real reason, however, seems to be that Stuttgart is to be defended as a stronghold and, because of that, everyone has to be evacuated within a 30km radius.'[18]

The fuss died away, but those who had just returned from Überlingen had more pressing domestic problems. Marianne Pross (née Katz): 'I can see the Bauers' house before my eyes – the wooden stairs inside, leading upstairs to the first floor. There are two little rooms. The parents are sleeping in one of them, but what about Tanti, Annina and me? I can't place myself anywhere – no bed, no nook, maybe mattresses on the floor in the second room? Or in the attic with Robert? And where do we eat?' Adolf Katz talked over the immediate food problem with the Bauers. They bought a pig, which was accommodated in the laundry room before its dispatch. The butcher failed to turn up – he was too busy slaughtering other 'illegals'. Mr Bauer killed the animal.[18]

The Nazis were still working hard to stamp out any signs of disloyalty to the regime. One day the doorbell rang at the Weber home. Doris Weber: 'Mother was out. It was a Gestapo man. He asked us: "What does your father say about Hitler?" We knew

Father had come to hate Hitler and the whole system. I said Father couldn't bear Hitler's screaming voice and had taken his photograph from the wall and smashed it.' Her older sisters, Hannelore and Sigrid, knew enough to keep their mouths shut.[19]

Some wartime memories are indelible. Sigrid Kern: 'I remember a freight train stopping at Eutingen. It had very small windows but I could see people peeking out. No-one said who they were. Father saw one of those trains of deportees at Pforzheim station. He could hear people crying out for water.'[19]

Notes

1. The strategic air war against Germany (The official report of the British Bombing Survey Unit), (1998), 77.
2. Watter, Helmut, written account, February 2013.
3. Schmalacker-Wyrich, Esther (Ed.), (1980), 'Pforzheim 23. Februar 1945, der Untergang einer Stadt', in: *Bildern und Augenzeugenberichten* (third edition).
4. Interview with Hans Gerstung, April 2013.
5. Interview with Dieter Essig, April 2013.
6. Schmalacker-Wyrich, Esther (Ed.), (1980), 'Pforzheim 23. Februar 1945, der Untergang einer Stadt', in: *Bildern und Augenzeugenberichten* (third edition).
7. Administration's Report and Statistics for the Town of Pforzheim, 1945–1952: City Life 1939–1945.
8. Keirle, Stan and other aircrew POWs, 'A Winter's Tale'; papers via Wing Commander Jack Harris, OBE, DFC.
9. *Pforzheimer Zeitung*, 23 February 2005.
10. Mauderer, B., memoir.
11. Administration's Report and Statistics for the Town of Pforzheim, 1945–1952: City Life 1939–1945.
12. Schmalacker-Wyrich, Esther (Ed.), (1980), 'Pforzheim 23. Februar 1945, der Untergang einer Stadt', in: *Bildern und Augenzeugenberichten* (third edition).
13. Administration's Report and Statistics for the Town of Pforzheim, 1945–1952: City Life 1939–1945.
14. Interviews with Werner Baroni, 2013.
15. Documents provided by Wing Commander Jack Harris, OBE, DFC.
16. Keirle, Stan and other aircrew POWs, 'A Winter's Tale'; papers via Wing Commander Jack Harris, OBE, DFC.
17. Administration's Report and Statistics for the Town of Pforzheim, 1945–1952: City Life 1939–1945.
18. Unpublished entries from the diary of Adolf Katz and information provided by Marianne Pross.
19. Interview with Doris Weber and Sigrid Kern, November 2013.

Chapter Fifteen

Murder on the Ground

'Prisoners must at all times be treated with humanity and protected particularly against acts of violence.'

(The Geneva Convention)

'it is expressly forbidden to kill or wound an enemy who, having laid down his arms, or having no longer any means of defence, has surrendered at discretion'.

(The Hague Convention)

Following Dresden, Propaganda Minister Josef Goebbels proposed the mass execution of several thousand aircrew prisoners, an idea supported by Hitler, Jodl and Keitel but strongly opposed by Göring. The Luftwaffe and Wehrmacht had little involvement in 'reprisal actions' and, for the most part, did their best to protect downed airmen from Nazi officials and the mob. Neillands cites comments from Hitler Jugend leader Richard Braun, of Ludwigshafen: 'I do not know of violence against shot-down Allied aircrew taking place in our towns and cities. What I do know is that such outrages seemed to happen relatively often in the open countryside, committed by villagers and NSDAP officials. By contrast, shot-down crew were almost always safe when captured by soldiers, particularly by the Luftwaffe.'[1]

Neillands records the experience of an American, Quinton V. Brown, who baled out near Berlin on 18 April 1944. He spent ten weeks in hospital and described his German nurse, Sister Maria Lorenzen, as a Florence Nightingale. After the war he returned to Germany on six occasions to visit her.[2] The other extreme is the *Kugel Erlass*, or Bullet Decree, introduced in 1944. This provided for the execution of aircrew in certain circumstances, such as attempted escape.[3] Public opinion on the treatment of captured aircrew hardened as the bombing intensified during 1944. In Ludwigshafen, Richard Braun saw the change in his own father, a Social Democrat. After one raid the son heard him say: 'If I come across one of them, I shall beat him to death.'[4]

Another Ludwigshafen resident, Peter Menges, saw two German soldiers murder Sergeant Cyril Sibley, a 158 Squadron pilot, on the night of 21/2 February 1945. He baled out safely, landed in a back garden and a woman began treating his wounds. Then a soldier, Adolf Wilfert, arrived and rounded on the woman. He was joined by Volkssturm member Georg Hartleb. They took Sibley away; the woman then heard three shots. The next morning she saw Sibley's body, dumped on a handcart. The two men paid for this crime: they were hanged on 11 October 1946.[4]

There are many accounts of the murder of Allied aircrew. Many perpetrators went unpunished for lack of evidence. Others simply disappeared in the confusion following surrender. One case came about when Flight Sergeant J.P. Doyle baled out over Germany in July 1943. Police handed him over to a nearby military unit. He was beaten and shot by guards at the Veddel Russian POW camp at Harburg, near Hamburg: they broke up a chair and beat him with the legs. He was buried as 'an unknown airman'. There was no trial as those responsible could not be traced. An investigation after the war indicated that the three perpetrators – unusually – were punished after the killing. They were sent to the Russian Front. There is doubt over the fate of the guards involved, and even over whether a body examined in March 1946 was that of Doyle.[5]

Records are more precise concerning the murder of Sergeant C.J. Ludlow, the flight engineer of Lancaster ME864. The aircraft crashed near Eutingen, on the outskirts of Pforzheim. Ludlow, who had a broken leg, was murdered in Eutingen Town Hall on 29 July 1944. Pforzheim Kreisleiter Hans Knab was implicated in this killing.[6]

Fifteen-year-old Werner Rothfuss was called in to translate during Ludlow's interrogation. His father, Erwin (a dentist and head of the Red Cross in Eutingen), tended the airman's injured leg. Then local Nazi hardliner Julius Zorn arrived with his cronies. Zorn began to abuse the injured man and Erwin and his son left the room.[7] The helpless airman was murdered by Zorn and his accomplices.

This crime brought the horrors of war home to young Doris Weber: 'I was coming back from the playground with Hildegard, Mr Rothfuss' daughter. There were lots of people in the street, including some French POWs. Someone told us to go home.' They lived next door to the town hall. Doris had a shock the following morning: 'Looking out of the window I saw a long wooden box in the town hall yard. Inside was the murdered airman's body.' Later, Erwin and Werner testified before a war crimes court in Hamburg.[8] Zorn, who came from a long-established family in Eutingen, lacked the courage to face justice. He committed suicide.

A navigator with 550 Squadron at North Killingholme was murdered by the Gestapo just before the Pforzheim attack. He was a member of Flight Lieutenant D.E. Luger's crew. They were shot down by a night fighter on the night of 20/1 February 1945, during an attack on Duisburg. Wing Commander 'Dingle' Bell, 550's commanding officer, had joined this crew for the night. Six men became POWs. The rear gunner, Sergeant F.G. Jones, was killed in the attack. The navigator, Sergeant G. Hancock, was shot by the Gestapo. The pilot, Flight Lieutenant Luger, was repatriated to the UK on 8 May but died in a Manchester hospital at the end of that month.[9]

At least one British airman was murdered after being shot down during the Pforzheim raid. He was a member of Pilot Officer Pierre Gérard 'Gerry' Ythier's crew, with 150 Squadron at RAF Hemswell. Their Lancaster, PB780 ('T') was attacked by a Ju88 night fighter just a few minutes after leaving the target. Ythier gave the order to jump as the port wing became a mass of flames. Bomb aimer Flying Officer Bert Delieu – married just two weeks before – went first, followed by the flight engineer, Sergeant 'Nobby' Clarke, and the navigator, Flight Sergeant Leo Horrax. Rear gunner Sergeant Ted Buckley also succeeded in leaving the doomed bomber. Ythier, the wireless operator Sergeant Ron Lewis and the mid-upper gunner Bob Conning failed to jump. Their bodies were recovered from the wreck.[10]

This case is a reminder of the fragility of memory. According to Horrax, Nobby Clarke and Bert Delieu faced the wrath of farm labourers at Neuhausen, near Pforzheim. Clarke's parachute failed, then fully deployed at around 500ft. He landed heavily, breaking an ankle. Delieu had landed close by and walked towards him, but was suddenly surrounded by farmworkers armed with pitchforks. Clarke saw his crewmate stabbed to death. The mob then began to torment him with pitchforks. German soldiers arrived and fired into the air to stop the mob killing Clarke, who was taken to hospital. Leo Horrax was picked up early the next morning. He was taken to a Luftwaffe base near Stuttgart and breakfasted on thin soup. He then heard a shout – 'Is this all we're fucking getting?' – and realized that rear gunner Ted Buckley was alive.[10]

This account, based on Horrax's recollection of Clarke's story, suggests that three of the four survivors could have been murdered. Delieu may have been killed in cold blood, Clarke had a narrow escape and Leo Horrax's life was in the balance while in police custody. He remembers a Canadian bomb aimer brought into Neuhausen police station and, at that point, there was a threat to shoot them both.[10]

During the 1990s Hermann Bogner, Neuhausen's Bürgermeister at the time of the crash, was interviewed, and said that one of the two men seen to jump had his parachute lines wrapped round his legs. That could have been Clarke, but this may have been an attempt to suggest that this was how Delieu died. Anyway, he remembered how the man with the injured leg (Clarke) was immediately taken to the town hall on a wheelbarrow. He said the survivor was trembling, sitting on a bench and constantly kissing the crucifix around his neck. He added that an angry mob was out for blood and one man wanted to cut the airman's throat. Bogner claimed he had protected Clarke, who was taken to the military hospital at Bad Liebenzell the next day. He said the four dead were buried, but made no specific mention of Delieu. It should be said that the primary purpose of this interview was to determine the location of the crash site, rather than to explore the fate of the crew.[11]

A newspaper story about this incident, published a few days before the sixtieth anniversary of the Pforzheim raid, quotes an unnamed eyewitness who was then a wounded soldier on convalescent leave in Neuhausen. He put the crash site at about 800m east of the edge of Neuhausen, near the road to Lehningen. He recalled the terrible 'rumbling and roaring' that came from Pforzheim as the raid unfolded: 'the sky turned into a flaming red and yellow inferno'.[12]

Neuhausen is 15km south of Pforzheim. Perhaps Delieu's death was a genuine expression of 'the fury of the people', as they watched catastrophe overwhelm Pforzheim. The newspaper story made no mention of the killing, only that the body of an airman, whose parachute had failed to open, had been discovered. After the war, in July 1948, the four bodies were recovered and laid to rest in Durnbach Military Cemetery. Bert Delieu was 24 years old at the time of his death. Ironically, he had been born in Germany.

The account of Delieu's death, as told by Horrax on the basis of what he remembered of what Clarke had told him many years before, may well be broadly accurate, but the fact is that *no-one really knows*. Clarke did not actually see what happened to Delieu. Furthermore, Clarke was not threatened with pitchforks. Clarke did help launch a war crimes investigation. In a letter to the war crimes investigators in late 1946, he made it clear he was unsure of what happened to the bomb aimer, other than the fact that he was alive when he last saw him. Clarke added that he had been suffering from shock and his impressions were 'vague'. In contrast to the account later relayed by Horrax (who had been busy trying to evade capture at the time), Clarke told a different story in 1946. He said that he and Delieu had landed close together, about 500yd from the nearest houses: 'Flying Officer Delieu immediately stood up and snapped off his harness. He then started to run to the nearest hedge when a crowd of people appeared and intercepted him. The last I saw he appeared to be fighting with them and my attention was then diverted by the approach of two soldiers who searched me and carried me off to prison.'[13]

In his 1946 letter, Clarke added: 'Next day I was taken out in an ox cart and Flying Officer Delieu's uniform was dumped on top. During the drive to Pforzheim I inspected the uniform and found it covered in blood and the uniform itself had large cuts in various places. I attempted to question my guards but, owing to the difficulty of language, I could elicit no information.'[13]

The case investigating officer, Flying Officer B. Parsons, produced a preliminary report dated 6 March 1947. By this time, Neuhausen had a new Bürgermeister. Bogner, the former Bürgermeister, was in custody at Ludwigsburg. In his report Parsons wrote: 'Investigations at this place (Neuhausen) lead me to suspect that the Bürgermeister, Mr Harn, was trying to conceal some information concerning the crash from me, but, as is only to be expected, I was unable to glean any information concerning any atrocities which may have been committed ...'[13]

Harn's demeanour under questioning was described as 'excited and nervous'. Parsons noted: 'He reported that three of the airmen were recovered from the wreckage by French POWs and were burned beyond recognition.' Another was found dead with a leg caught in the parachute lines. He hit the ground head first. When I asked who found this man the Bürgermeister became worried, saying to his secretary: "I don't know and you don't know either."' When pressed, the secretary admitted he had found the man, but records suggest he said little else. Parsons visited the graves of the four airmen, still in Neuhausen Cemetery at that time. He found the plot planted out and well kept. The man responsible for tending the cemetery was most anxious that Parsons should inspect his handiwork.[13]

In summary, there should have been four survivors from Lancaster PB780. The four baled out at 20.10 – the exact time nearby Pforzheim went up in a firestorm. It may have been that Delieu was murdered and the cover story was that his parachute fouled – although this is supposition. In any event, the war crimes investigation lacked vigour. Months went by. On 2 July 1947, Lieutenant-Colonel R.A. Nightingale, Officer in Charge of Field Investigations, pressed for news of progress in the Delieu case. In February 1948, however, the case was closed. It had been recognized from the first that it would have to be dropped unless the perpetrators were identified.[13]

If Delieu's death was the result of 'people's fury', another and better documented case linked to the Pforzheim raid was exactly the opposite. It was a matter of premeditated, cold-blooded murder, and on this occasion the perpetrators (or at least most of them) paid for their crimes.

On the night of Wednesday, 14 March 1945, Bomber Command mounted three major raids. One targeted the Wintershall synthetic oil plant at Lützkendorf, near Leipzig. The others hit the towns of Zweibrücken and Homberg. The Lützkendorf raid caused only moderate damage but losses were high, totalling eighteen Lancasters (7.4 per cent of the main force). A further five aircraft were lost that night: two Halifaxes attacking Homberg, together with two Mosquitoes and a Fortress.[14] A second Fortress came very close to being lost. This was 'BU-L', captained by Flight Lieutenant Johnny Wynne. This 214 Squadron aircraft took off for a radio-countermeasures sortie in the Leipzig area. Wynne and crew were flying into a nightmare. There were ten men on board the Fortress when it left Oulton; half never saw England again.

The Wynne crew had joined 214 Squadron in January 1945. Some were decorated second tour veterans. Wynne had completed his first tour in the Middle East. His flight engineer was Flying Officer Jimmy Vinall, DFM. At 40 years old, he was rather mature for aircrew duties. Vinall had flown operationally with 9 Squadron. The recommendation for his DFM stated: 'His devotion to duty and his technical efficiency have been an example to all …'. Vinall's first tour involved thirty-one operations.

Wynne's special operator was responsible for the aircraft's secret jamming equipment. He was 22-year-old Flying Officer G.A. Hall. The navigator was Flying Officer Dudley Heal and the bomb aimer was Flight Lieutenant G. Pow. The wireless operator, Flight Lieutenant T.H. Tate, had completed a first tour. The four gunners were Flight Sergeant N.J. Bradley, DFM, Flying Officer Harold Frost, DFM, Flight Lieutenant S.C. Matthews, DFC, and Flight Sergeant Edward Arthur Percival, DFM. Matthews was 25 years old. Frost had previously flown as a rear gunner with

The victims: Johnny Wynne and members of his 214 Squadron RCM Fortress crew. Standing, left to right: Tom Tate, Johnny Wynne, Sidney Matthews, Dudley Heal and Jimmy Vinall. Front: Harold Frost, G. Pow and Gordon Hall. Bradley and Percival are not in the photograph. *Photo: via Stephan Paetzold.*

49 Squadron. His DFM was gazetted on 13 July 1943. It said: 'His cool direction when attacked by a night fighter over Holland resulted in the safe return of his aircraft.' Percival, aged 30, had flown as a rear gunner with 12 Squadron. His award was gazetted on 19 September 1944. The recommendation stated: 'On one occasion the aircraft in which he was operating received five attacks from enemy fighters, shortly before reaching the target. By skilful directions to the pilot, he enabled the aircraft to defeat the fighters, receiving only slight damage, at the same time handling his turret and guns with such dexterity that he succeeded in shooting down one fighter. By his prompt action, he enabled the pilot to continue and bomb the target successfully.' His station commander commented on his 'magnificent fighting spirit' and the base commander noted his 'exceptional fighting qualities'. Johnny Wynne had the honour to lead a very fine crew.

Ron James, another 214 Squadron pilot, described what happened to Wynne's aircraft when it was picked up by searchlights: 'At some point near Baden the aircraft was caught by light flak and No. 2 engine caught fire. Wynne ordered the crew to stand by to bale out.' This was a serious engine fire and the vibration was very severe. Given the danger of fire enveloping the whole wing, Wynne ordered the crew to abandon, which they did in good order.[15]

Vinall's efforts to put out the port inner engine fire had failed and they lost height. The navigator, Heal, calculated that they were only 20 miles from the French border. In fact, however, they were still some way east of that position. Wynne gave the order to jump and Heal got out, landed on the roof of a large warehouse and was soon taken prisoner. Heal's parents had to wait months – until just after VE Day – for news. They received a telegram from a repatriated POW. It read: 'Dudley safe and well Germany awaiting transport home.' Heal was back within forty-eight hours.[16]

Wireless operator Tom Tate and special operator Gordon Hall were together when the order to abandon was given. Tate saw the look of despair on Hall's face. The gunners had jettisoned the escape hatch door. Tate recalled: 'I just had to dive through. I shook Gordon's hand and off he went.' Later, Tate regretted not saying a few words to Hall, as he was among those who did not survive. Then it was his turn: 'I moved to the escape hatch and just toppled out. I had my hand on the parachute D-ring but I don't remember those few moments of free-fall. I just felt the tug when the canopy opened and then I was floating down in dead silence.'[17]

Everyone got out except Wynne: 'When I attempted to leave the aircraft, I became entangled in the oxygen lead and, after much difficulty, got free. Having relieved myself of the responsibility of the crew, I felt it was my duty to try at all costs to save my machine.' After some time the fire died down. Wynne trimmed out the aircraft and climbed down into the nose for Heal's maps; it took three trips to find the right ones.[18] Meanwhile, as the fire continued Wynne grew increasingly concerned and he decided to leave the aircraft. This time his parachute became snagged and he had to return to the controls. He made for the emergency airfield at Reims. The fire then went out and the vibration eased. He couldn't raise Reims so he decided to try for England. He made it to Bassingbourn, Cambridgeshire, where he landed safely – a pilot without a crew.[19]

Wynne returned to 214 Squadron in the mistaken belief that his crew had baled out over Allied territory: 'I was sent on leave while I waited for my crew to turn up. I was at my parents' home when I got a telephone call. They had back-plotted the navigator's log and realized that the crew had not jumped into France, as we thought. They were in Germany. It was a real shock. There I was thinking that the buggers were running around somewhere in France … I couldn't believe it.'[19]

Wynne was extremely lucky to get back. At one point he had to stand between the two cockpit seats in order to control the aircraft. When the Fortress finally touched down, the port tyre burst but it ran on for 1,000yd before going down on the rim. During this ground run the No. 2 engine's propeller fell off and cut into the nose.[20] Wynne's solo return was the talk of 214 Squadron's mess.

Less than three weeks after the destruction of Pforzheim, Johnny Wynne's crew had the misfortune to bale out near the ruined city. Flight Lieutenant Pow, the bomb aimer, broke his ankle on landing and was taken to hospital. The navigator, Flying Officer Heal, landed some distance from the others, was apprehended and held in solitary confinement. Initially, Heal was thought to be a member of another crew, probably because most heavy bombers had a crew of seven. Wynne's remaining crew – Hall, Tate, Vinall, Frost, Matthews, Percival and Bradley – landed close together and were taken into custody.[21]

Subsequently, the seven were marched through burnt-out Pforzheim, where they received abuse from survivors. Tom Tate stood on the valley crest and looked down on Pforzheim: 'I had never seen anything like this. I had seen the damage in London,

The perpetrators. Top row, left to right: Kreisleiter Hans Knab, Pforzheim's top Nazi; Bannführer Max Köchlin, 'a real SS man'; and Kreisstabsführer Niklaus of the Volkssturm. Centre row: Sturmbannführer Eugen Weiss escaped justice by committing suicide; Friedrich Hauser was executed for his part in the murders; and Kurt Kroll, who participated in the churchyard shootings. Bottom row: Huchenfeld Bürgermeister Gustav Schmidt could have asked locally billeted troops to intervene; Gerd Biedermann, Vinall's killer; and Wilhelm Maxeiner, who was acquitted of beating Vinall owing to problems of identification. *Photos: via Stephan Paetzold.*

where the docks had been destroyed, and in Sheffield, too, but never a whole city in ruins. The shock was tremendous. Our escort walked us down a hill towards what had been the centre. The main roads had been cleared and there were narrow paths between the rubble on each side. There was no traffic whatsoever, but lots of people were about and when they recognized our blue RAF uniforms they started bombarding us with anything they could lay their hands on. I didn't blame them. The utter devastation was awful to see. Afterwards, I still thought there was a good reason for what Bomber Command had done and Pforzheim was a legitimate target. But there is a difference between talking about targets and seeing the reality of what it was like on the ground. There was complete desolation. This was the awesome power of the Lancaster bomber.'[22]

Their guards protected them as best they could, but they were pelted with stones and rocks. Eventually, they arrived at nearby Huchenfeld and were led into the village school's cellar. It was now the evening of Saturday, 17 March and Kreisleiter Hans Knab – Pforzheim's top Nazi – had plans. He arranged to have the seven airmen murdered by a small group of 16-year-old Hitler Jugend leaders. Those who lacked weapons were armed and the youngsters were told to report in civilian clothes. The SA and Volkssturm were also involved. These killings were to be carried out under the guise of the 'people's fury', directed against 'air gangsters'. Later, during a war crimes trial, this plan was described as a bogus display of public indignation following the Pforzheim bombing, a cover for murder.[23]

During the evening of that Saturday the plan unfolded. An armed group burst into the cellar, pushed aside the two Luftwaffe guards and led the airmen upstairs and into the street. The plan was to shoot all seven in the school cellar, but Huchenfeld's Bürgermeister, Gustav Schmidt, protested. He said that if they had to be shot it should be done in the village cemetery.[23]

That was the limit of Schmidt's protest. He returned to the wedding party he was attending, despite having heard shots on his way back. Subsequently, in court, he struggled to explain why he didn't ask the 500 Wehrmacht troops then stationed in Huchenfeld to intervene. In his statement he said he went to the cemetery the next morning, saw the bodies and rang up the Pforzheim Kreisleitung. He was told: 'Just bury the bodies.' He then added: 'At an earlier meeting of Ortsgruppenleiters I heard Kreisleiter Knab say that enemy airmen were to be buried in mass graves without church ceremony. I arranged for the bodies of the four British airmen to be buried in a common grave in the cemetery, without church ceremony.'[23]

Three of Wynne's crew had escaped in the evening gloom, on the way to the cemetery: Tate, Bradley and Vinall made a break for it in the dark lane leading to the church. Their comrades – Hall, Frost, Matthews and Percival – were shot and their bodies left overnight where they fell, sprawled on the ground. The following morning, a Sunday, the congregation walked past the bodies as they made their way into church for a confirmation service.[24]

Where the prisoners were confined: the seven airmen were held in a cellar room at Huchenfeld School. *Photo: Tony Redding.*

War crime: the view the prisoners had as they were frogmarched to their execution in the churchyard. The street is much changed; in 1945 there were only a few houses. *Photo: Tony Redding.*

Murder scene: a view towards the original north gate of Huchenfeld churchyard (this has since been replaced by a new gate, at a different location). The cross at the far hedge marks the approximate position of the original gate and is where Frost's body lay. His killer is not known. Hall was killed on the lawn, towards the memorial near the centre of the picture. He received a bullet in the back of the head. *Photo: Tony Redding.*

Later, Vinall was taken into custody again. He was held at Dillweissenstein's police post, in the old town hall. Later, he was taken out, beaten severely and shot in the head. Dillweissenstein villagers, including children, participated in the beating. His body was dumped in a nearby quarry. An attempt was then made to murder one of the surviving two of the group of seven, but both Tate and Bradley managed to enter the system as POWs and survived, along with Heal and Pow.[24] In the early post-war years they helped to ensure that justice caught up with the perpetrators, but Johnny Wynne remained unaware of what had happened for nearly fifty years.

All five murdered men were married. Four had been decorated for bravery. Vinall was shot by a 16-year-old boy, Gerd Biedermann. The Hitler Youth leader admitted that he had given Vinall the *coup de grâce*, shooting him in the back of the head. One of Biedermann's family had been a Bürgermeister of Pforzheim. Biedermann knew nothing but the Nazis: he had been five when Hitler came to power. He joined the Jungvolk in 1938, and by 1944 he was a Hitler Youth Jungzugführer.

Pforzheim researcher Stephan Paetzold has put together a detailed picture of how Frost, Matthews, Hall and Percival were murdered at Huchenfeld and how Vinall was killed at Dillweissenstein the next day. Tate narrowly escaped death. Having participated in the murders of five airmen, the Hitler Youth leaders were ordered to go to Eutingen railway station, remove Tate from custody and dispatch him, before returning to Dillweissenstein to report. On arriving at Eutingen, however, they discovered that Tate was securely under guard, awaiting a train to Ludwigsburg. His military escort refused to give him up and the Hitler Youth returned empty handed.[24]

Huchenfeld in 1945 was a 'street village'; virtually all its houses were grouped along what was then Adolf Hitler Strasse. Neighbouring Dillweissenstein – an amalgam of the Dillstein and Weissenstein communities – had been incorporated into Pforzheim in 1913. This village was the local Nazi stronghold. Kreisleiter Knab occupied the most impressive house and he used the building next door to stable his prized Arab stallions (to the private disgust of locals, who had been forced to give up most of their horses to the Wehrmacht). Just a few metres away was the old town hall, then serving as the registry office and police post. The school next door had a temporary building extending behind the town hall. This provided extra classrooms but, at that time, accommodated the Hitler Youth. This single-storey timber building, erected in 1921, was not especially temporary – it stood until 1982. This is where the Hitler Youth underwent paramilitary training, including those bombed out from Pforzheim.[25]

Dillweissensteiners were accustomed to keeping their mouths shut. Yet one local, Fritz Trautz, got fed up and used a community meeting to protest against Nazi behaviour in Dillweissenstein: 'The next evening I had the Gestapo at my house. I was taken to the Kreisleitung, where Knab yelled at me and threatened to have me taken to a concentration camp.'[26]

Dillweissenstein was also home to Knab's *Kreisleiter Stollen*, or tunnel. Sarcastic locals called this the *Heldenkeller* (hero's cellar). In fact, this was not one tunnel but a complex of tunnels, with four separate entrances. Pforzheim's Nazi headquarters had been destroyed in the 23 February raid. One of the tunnels was then occupied by the Kreisleitung; bombed-out refugees were evicted. These tunnels were adjacent to the paper mill, a long-established Nazi centre. During the economic crisis of the early 1930s, any Party member looking for a job could be sure to find work at this mill.[27]

Other local Nazi 'landmarks' included Dillweissenstein's Post Inn (now an Italian restaurant). At the time of the killings, Kreisstabführer Niklaus had his Volkssturm office at the Post Inn. Next door was a large, partially constructed bunker. The village men were required to work on this bunker during the evenings, having finished their day shift at the mill.[27]

The paper mill's canteen was a regular meeting place for SA, Volkssturm and Hitler Jugend. Those who participated in the killings at nearby Huchenfeld first reported to the mill canteen, then set out to commit murder. Next to the mill is the house once occupied by Bannführer Max Köchlin, a former SS officer and another central player, along with Knab and Niklaus, in the five murders.[27]

Rendezvous for murder: Dillweissenstein paper mill. The canteen, where the perpetrators met before proceeding to Huchenfeld, was on the ground floor, right. The mill closed in 2001. *Photo: Tony Redding.*

Köchlin is described by Stephan Paetzold as 'a real SS man'. He served with SS Regiment Nordland and the SS Freiwilligen (volunteer) Division Prinz Eugen. He was released in 1943 to supervise Hitler Youth training in Pforzheim. He ran the Dillweissenstein paramilitary training camp. Köchlin and his wife occupied the second floor of what was then his father-in-law's home, near the mill – Kirsauerstrasse 239. The mill itself still stands but is now closed. Köchlin married Luise Friedrich; her father, Wilhelm, was the mill's yard manager. Still standing, close by, is the large, ramshackle timber building once used by the Hitler Youth for military training. Their shooting range became a car park.[28] Köchlin was in charge of Hitler Youth Unit 172 (Pforzheim).

As the seven airmen were led to their execution in Huchenfeld cemetery, during the evening of Saturday, 17 March, Tate suddenly struggled free of his escort and ran back up a slight hill, past the school where they had been held. He soon found himself in fields. Bradley and Vinall then broke free and went in another direction, a lane at ninety degrees to the road leading to the church. They ran downhill towards a wooded area and separated. There was no escape for Frost, Hall, Percival and Matthews. Stephan Paetzold has interviewed eyewitnesses who confirm that bodies were found that Sunday morning at three locations within the churchyard. One body was at the north gate, the entrance used to bring the prisoners to their place of execution. This was Frost, who is thought to have made a break for it. He was shot in the head. It may be that he made this desperate attempt to escape on hearing the shots that killed others.[28]

Another body, that of Hall, was in the middle of the small cemetery, nearer the church and opposite the north gate. He had been shot in the back of the head. Two more bodies were found behind the church – at the boundary of the cemetery, where it looks down into a valley. Stephan Paetzold: 'These events must have happened very quickly. They arrived with their prisoners in two or three groups. The first two airmen, in all likelihood Percival and Matthews, were led into the churchyard. Two men called Weiss and Hauser (and, possibly, also Biedermann – who later claimed that his weapon jammed four times in the churchyard) took them behind the church and shot them, just as the second and, possibly, third group entered the north gate. Frost made a run for it and was shot; his killer is unknown. Hall was taken just a few more metres across the grass and also killed. The bodies were left where they fell. It may be that the killers wanted to get on with the search for the three who had escaped.'[28]

The murderers went on to claim their fifth victim. Jimmy Vinall was at the police post in Dillweissenstein's old town hall, just a few metres from Kreisleiter Knab's private residence and close to the Hitler Youth paramilitary training accommodation at the bottom of the old town hall's yard. On that Sunday Volkssturm leader Wilhelm Niklaus left his office at the Post Inn and made the short walk to the police post. He later said he wanted to move the prisoner as the police post telephone was out of order. He wanted to use the Post Inn's telephone to call the local airfield and ask the Luftwaffe to pick up the airman.[29] He never explained why he didn't just make the call without removing Vinall from police custody.

Just a few metres from the inn, a small crowd stood outside the entrance to the incomplete bunker. It was alleged that Niklaus told them that he was fetching a 'black' prisoner (Vinall was Maltese) and that they should arm themselves with sticks. Niklaus denied this allegation. Dillweissenstein historian Helmut Schmitt: 'Vinall was led down the road towards the inn with his Hitler Youth escort in a U formation, the prisoner being on the inside of the U's curve. When they reached the crowd outside the bunker, a man struck Vinall a blow to the back of the head with a large piece of wood – probably a timber used for tunnel building.'[29]

Stephan Paetzold has concluded that paper mill labourer Wilhelm Maxeiner struck Vinall.[30] This blow was probably not the first, according to local historian Helmut Schmitt. The prisoner was almost certainly beaten by his Hitler Youth escort during the couple of minutes it took to cover the distance to the bunker entrance, next to the inn. Niklaus was said to have encouraged violence by shouting that Vinall was one of those who had left Pforzheim in ruins. In fact, Wynne's aircraft never carried bombs, as it was deployed in the radio-countermeasures role.

Stephan Paetzold: 'During the main beating, in front of the air-raid shelter, some claim that a number of young children took part.' An eyewitness, Helene Kramer, confirmed that children were present, on the fringes of the small crowd. It seems that Vinall fell twice. When a blow brought him to his knees, he was dragged upright, to make it easier to continue the beating. Vinall then fell again. He was shot in the head by Hitler Youth leader Gerd Biedermann. This bullet caused a large exit wound in the front of the head. Helene Kramer remembers the pool of blood on the ground. Sixteen-year-old Biedermann later said he was ordered to shoot, but Paetzold says that, according to Helene, he took the decision himself.[30]

Stephan Paetzold adds: 'There is some confusion over whether Vinall was shot once or twice in the head. At his trial, Biedermann insisted that he had fired only once. A French pathologist, on examining the body, concluded that Vinall had been

Teenage killer: a drawing of the killing of Jimmy Vinall by 16-year-old Gerd Biedermann, with Niklaus looking on. This drawing was created with the assistance of Helene Kramer, who witnessed the shooting as a 15-year-old. It is also based on sketches produced for the war crimes trial. Helene heard Niklaus say 'Get some sticks' as he walked past the crowd outside the bunker, on his way to pick up Vinall from the police post. There were many more people at the scene when the killing took place. *Graphic: Norbert Scholtyssek (via Stephan Paetzold).*

shot twice – once in the back of the head and again through the cheek.' The first exhumation and examination of Vinall's body was on 7 May 1945. It was carried out by Dr Hommel, a local doctor. Hitler Youth leader Biedermann could have fired once or twice. He could have fired once, with the second wound caused by a ricochet from the cobbled street. In subsequent years it has been claimed that a second shot was fired by a 15-year-old referred to as 'Herbert X', who was said to have lost most of his family in the Pforzheim bombing. This is regarded by some as a convenient fabrication. Both Stephan Paetzold and Helmut Schmitt dismiss Herbert X as 'pure fantasy'. Indeed, Paetzold knows the identity of the family concerned. He has spoken at length to the man said to be Herbert X's brother. The latter has spent years explaining that Herbert X does not exist.[30]

The Hitler Youth leaders ordered to dispose of Jimmy Vinall's battered body used a plasterer's handcart to take him to a nearby quarry at Hinteres Tal, in the Nagold valley, opposite what is now the Sports Association building. They dumped the body in a garden at the edge of the quarry, in a very shallow grave. The corpse was barely covered with earth. The Hitler Youth members returned to Dillweissenstein and received immediate orders to drive to Eutingen, to murder Tate.

Some of Vinall's limbs remained exposed. The locals knew the body was there and the quarry owner and his daughter feared the consequences. They went to Knab to

The graves, as described in correspondence with the widows: the British war crimes investigators found five separate graves in Huchenfeld churchyard, following the initial exhumation by the French. Vinall's body was brought here from Dillweissenstein. Four of the five bodies were buried originally in a common pit, without church ceremony. *Photo: Stephan Paetzold.*

complain, but it did them no good. They ran into Köchlin in Knab's outer office. The quarry owner's daughter told Köchlin that they should get rid of the body, as the Allies would soon arrive. Köchlin told them to shut up. They insisted on seeing Knab, but nothing was done and the airman's partially exposed body remained in the quarry garden. When the French arrived, a local eccentric sought favour by informing the occupation forces. In reward, he was given an attic flat in the house of Dillweissenstein paper mill manager Dietl, which stands on the hill overlooking the site.[30]

Three war crimes trials attempted to give justice to the five murdered airmen and their families. There were twenty-seven accused. The main proceedings, against twenty-two of the accused, were heard at Essen-Steele, in the British Zone, between 14 August and 3 September 1946. Eight accused were from Dillweissenstein. Five served prison terms, two were acquitted and another was declared medically unfit to stand trial. The members of Hitler Youth were sentenced to terms ranging from five to fifteen years, but all were released in the spring of 1949.[31]

The ringleaders – Hans Knab, Max Köchlin and Wilhelm Niklaus – were sentenced to death and hanged at Hamelin prison on 23 January 1947. A fourth man, hardline Nazi Friedrich Hauser, was also executed for his part in the murders, following another trial. Kurt Kroll, suspected of participating in the Huchenfeld shootings, escaped trial as he had advanced TB. Maxeiner was acquitted owing to insufficient evidence. Stephan Paetzold says, however, that eyewitnesses are still alive who confirm that it was Maxeiner who struck Vinall the blow that first forced him to his knees.[32]

At his trial, Knab said he didn't know the airmen were taken to Huchenfeld. He denied knowledge of any 'demonstration' in Huchenfeld. He denied sending the Hitler Youth leaders there. He denied giving orders for the SA to go to Huchenfeld. In short, he denied everything.[33]

Stephan Paetzold found himself deeply moved when he read Max Köchlin's plea for clemency: 'It is a difficult read. He begged for the chance to become a better man. He explained how he had grown up experiencing nothing but National Socialism. He pleaded for the opportunity to form his own, independent views.'[34] It was too late for Köchlin. He kept his appointment with Albert Pierrepoint, the British executioner. As for churchyard killer Sturmbannführer Eugen Weiss, he was beyond reach, having committed suicide.

Stephan Paetzold has spent several years researching the murders of Allied airmen and, in particular, the Huchenfeld and Dillweissenstein killings. He lives in Pforzheim and has close friends in the city and its outlying districts, including the two communities associated with the killing of Johnny Wynne's crew members. Paetzold's researches focus on local people, including the families of those tried for war crimes. He has also reviewed evidence of similar murders: 'The Huchenfeld/Dillweissenstein killings were far from unique. There are other examples in the Pforzheim area. Significantly, some pre-date the February 1945 bombing of Pforzheim. In other words, it did not

'Father forgive': the plaque on the wall of Huchenfeld church, commemorating the five murdered airmen. *Photo: Tony Redding.*

require a catastrophic air raid to prompt unlawful killings of Allied aircrew. Indeed, this seems to have been the policy of many local and regional Nazi officials. The evidence suggests that aircrew murders often followed a pattern. An aircraft goes down. The local Nazi leadership responds. Measures are taken to organize a lynch mob. The Huchenfeld/Dillweissenstein killings, however, may be unique in that there was a carefully planned, cynical attempt to pretend that these murders were the result of public outrage. I have no knowledge of another case of this type.'[34]

Only a week after the Huchenfeld/Dillweissenstein killings, on Thursday, 22 March 1945, five aircrew were captured after baling out during a raid on Dreierwalde airfield at Hopsten, North Rhine-Westphalia. The attack killed around forty civilians and Luftwaffe personnel. The prisoners were marched into a wood and shot in cold blood. A wounded Australian airman, Flying Officer Keith Berick, managed to escape. Almost exactly a year later, in March 1946, a British military court convened at Wuppertal. The man who led the guards that day, Oberfeldwebel Karl Amberger, was hanged on 15 May 1946. Personnel at Dreierwalde were also involved in the killing of eight unknown prisoners, who took part in a follow-up attack on the airfield. Four were taken out in the middle of the night, ostensibly to fill craters on the aerodrome, and were shot and killed by their escort. Immediately afterwards, another three prisoners were taken out and shot. The eighth prisoner was not taken out as he had an injured leg. Later, he was driven out in a motorbike side-car and shot in cold blood.[35]

Justice caught up with other perpetrators. Baden Gauleiter Robert Wagner was arrested by the Americans, tried and executed.[36] Strasbourg Gestapo's Julius Gehrum, responsible for the murders of 108 members of Réseau Alliance at Natzweiler, the 'Black Forest Blood Week' killings of Resistance prisoners (including those held at Pforzheim) and much more besides, was executed on 10 November 1947.[37]

Strasbourg Gestapo head Erich Isselhorst was sentenced to death twice. Isselhorst was an Einsatzgruppe administrator in 1942. He was sentenced to die for the murder of British paratroopers in the Vosges in the autumn of 1944. He was also brought to trial for the Réseau Alliance killings. He was shot in Strasbourg on 23 February 1948.[37]

As for Wynne's murdered crew members, the widows were left to grieve. Problems of identification were resolved with the help of laundry marks and dental records. The victims were taken to their final resting place at Durnbach War Cemetery in 1949. On 20 September 1946, Iris Matthews received an invitation to attend Buckingham Palace on 29 October, to receive her husband's DFC. The Distinguished Flying Cross is awarded for courage while flying on active service against the enemy. She was accompanied by Sidney Matthews' mother, Maud Louise, and her own father, William Baden Farr. Ten days after the invitation, the Air Ministry wrote to Iris, setting out the results of the trial of Knab and his fellow perpetrators.[38]

Notes

1. Neillands, R. (2002), The Bomber War, 368–9.
2. Ibid., 144.
3. Ibid., 368–9.
4. Ibid., 141.
5. The National Archives: WO 309/2158.
6. The National Archives: WO 309/1148, 1945–1948.
7. Milton, G. (2011), Wolfram, 208–11.
8. Interview with Doris Weber and Sigrid Kern (née Weber), November 2013.
9. Newsletter No. 25, 28 October 2002, 550 Squadron and RAF North Killingholme Association.
10. Rolfe, Mel (1998), To Hell and Back, 179–87.
11. Hermann Bogner, interviewed by Roland Watzl – via Stephan Paetzold.
12. Pforzheimer Zeitung, 12 February 2005.
13. The National Archives: WO 309/1889.
14. Middlebrook, M. and Everitt, C. (1990), The Bomber Command War Diaries, 680–1.
15. James, R. (1989), Avenging in the Shadows: 214 (FMS) Squadron, Royal Air Force, 165–6.
16. Sweetman, J. (2004), Bomber Crew, 238–9.
17. Nichol, J. and Rennell, T. (2004), Tail-End Charlies, 337.
18. Sweetman, J. (2004), Bomber Crew, 239.
19. Nichol, J. and Rennell, T. (2004), Tail-End Charlies, 333–7.
20. James, R. (1989), Avenging in the Shadows: 214 (FMS) Squadron, Royal Air Force, 165–6.
21. Ibid., 166–8.
22. Nichol, J. and Rennell, T. (2004), Tail-End Charlies, 340.
23. The National Archives: WO 235/235.
24. Interviews with Stephan Paetzold, 2013.

25. Interviews with Helmut Schmitt, 2013.
26. Interviews with Stephan Paetzold, 2013; Footnote 11: GLA 465a/55/5/27/29 441 5153.
27. Interviews with Helmut Schmitt, 2013.
28. Interviews with Stephan Paetzold, 2013.
29. Interviews with Helmut Schmitt, 2013.
30. Interviews with Stephan Paetzold, 2013.
31. The National Archives: WO 235/235.
32. Interviews with Stephan Paetzold, 2013.
33. The National Archives: WO 235/235.
34. Interviews with Stephan Paetzold, 2013.
35. The National Archives: TS 26/626.
36. Milton, G. (2011), *Wolfram*, 307.
37. Federal Archives, Ludwigsburg, B114 AR-Z 67/67.
38. Various correspondence, including letters to Iris Matthews from the Air Ministry Casualty Branch.

Chapter Sixteen

Occupation

On 8 April 1945, a French armoured unit occupied the area north of the Enz. Territory to the south of the river was defended by German infantry, supported by artillery. The defences around and in Pforzheim were finally overcome on 18 April. The occupying French Colonial troops showed poor discipline; they plundered homes and there were hundreds of rapes.

By 11 April Allied forces had crossed the Enz and were just a few kilometres from Mönsheim, the village where the Katz family now lived. Their home on Pforzheim's Schwarzwaldstrasse was now a burnt-out ruin. Nearby German artillery positions were in action, provoking strafing runs by Allied fighter-bombers. Adolf Katz and stepson Robert helped with the firefighting, while Katz's wife, Ruth, put up with constant nagging from their host, Mrs Bauer. Marianne and Robert moved to a nearby château, under an arrangement with the resident Gaisberg family. On 19 April Ruth helped two shellfire victims, including a 9-year-old boy. Civilians began

Occupation: French Colonial troops enter Pforzheim's ruined centre. *Photo: Stadtarchiv Pforzheim.*

to show animosity towards the weak German units who continued to resist, as they were prolonging the agony.[1]

Katz's diary describes how the people of Mönsheim went out to greet French Colonial troops as they entered the village on Friday, 20 April. The welcome evaporated when night fell. Three 'Africans' broke into the Bauer home but Katz persuaded them to leave. Later, he vented his feelings: 'My first experience is that these Africans are like children but, once they are overwhelmed by their instincts, they are like beasts. The French officers show cold hatred. They tolerate the excesses of their units and point to the atrocities that our soldiers are said to have committed during their retreat in France.'[1]

Katz describes looting and rapes, including a case involving a 70 year old: 'It was worst in the houses along the main road.' His young daughter, Marianne, reacted differently to the French Colonials: 'I saw dark-skinned people for the first time in my life and stared at them.' Katz feared for the older girls, Annina and Erika von Gaisberg. They were warned not to show themselves at the windows.[1]

The dangerous transitional phase was over by 23 April, when the first soldiers moved on. The next day Adolf Katz made a note in his diary: 'Ruth has a lot of work. Women and girls are coming to her who have been raped and are now afraid they might have contracted sexually transmitted diseases or become pregnant. We are completely puzzled to see how easily they take these acts of rape. One woman told Ruth, when asked how she was doing: "I've been raped but, other than that, nothing happened!"'[1]

French Colonial troops were responsible for a wave of sexual attacks against women living in Baden Württemberg's villages. One source, Norman Naimark, refers to the French Moroccan units as 'similarly undisciplined' to Soviet troops and that women in Baden-Württemberg were especially exposed to sexual assault, as in the Eastern Zone.[2] According to another source, Marc Hillel, there were 385 rapes in the Konstanz area, 500 in the Black Forest town of Freudenstadt and 600 in Bruchsal.[3]

Brigitte and Gerhard Brändle have researched acts of violence against women during April 1945 in Pforzheim and the Pforzheim Landkreis (administrative district). This has revealed that there were cases of rape in almost half of the thirty-three communities/areas of Pforzheim studied: Eisingen, Kämpfelbach-Ersingen, Keltern-Ellmendingen, Kieselbronn, Königsbach, Stein, Neuhausen, Neuhausen-Schellbronn, Niefern, Öschelbronn, Pforzheim, Pforzheim-Eutingen, Pforzheim-Hohenwart, Remchingen-Wilferdingen, Straubenhard-Langenalb and Tiefenbronn-Lehningen. In the other seventeen areas there are no documented cases of rape. Further research is pending, extending to a larger area.[4]

The Brändles are aware of one grotesque case, at Pfinzweiler, when the French commandant told the Bürgermeister to provide three women 'volunteers'. If he failed to do so, the troops would be permitted to do what they wanted. Gerhard Brändle: 'There were three volunteers. This is a very small community; everyone knew what happened and the women concerned faced no discrimination.'[5] The risk to women, as the French took over, depended on several factors, especially the character of senior officers. Some incited criminal behaviour by reminding troops of what the SS had done. 'Much depended on whether the French encountered resistance. There were very few rapes in villages flying white flags. In some villages there were no sexual attacks as French POWs and forced labourers, who were treated well in these communities, interceded. There were obvious difficulties, however, when displaying white flags. You could be shot by the Wehrmacht or SS for doing so. You could also be shot for refusing to build barricades. It was hard to know what to do for the best.'[6]

It didn't take much to deter potential rapists – perhaps the women gathered together inside the local church, with the door shut and the pastor outside. 'This was the case in Heimsheim. In Ersingen, Pastor Fertig, who spoke good French, negotiated with the local commander and got an agreement that women sheltering in his church would be guarded by soldiers at the door.'[7] Women in Tiefenbronn were put under military protection.[8] Brändle adds: 'It is very difficult – but not impossible – to gain access to French records of this time. There are also a few first-hand accounts. One example is a letter written by a woman to her friend, telling of a night of rape in Neuhausen.' This describes events when 'several of these beasts came into the cellar again and again and fetched their victims for abuse … Then, after these severe tests, the pastor put us up in his house … we thank the good Lord every day that at least we were spared from the black beasts.'[9]

In some instances, French officers acted to stop the rapes. In the case of the Freudenstadt rapes, eighteen perpetrators were court martialled and shot.[10] In some villages close to Pforzheim, including Würm, French officers ordered women and girls to report to the town hall in the early evening, in order to shield them from the threat of rape.[11] In Hohenwart, rape cases prompted French officers to issue orders on 17 April 1945 for women to gather in the local school for their own protection.[12]

Giles Milton gives an account of those early April days in 1945, when artillery could be heard from the north-west. Local Nazi diehards, including August Issel of Eutingen, still clung to fantasies and claimed the Allies would be thrown back. He instructed all local boys born in 1930, and now fifteen, to assemble. When none of them answered the call to arms, Issel ordered a house-to-house search. 'He managed to gather forty-six young lads but forty of them slipped away before they could be deployed and only six were actually sent to the Front.'[13] Then the Nazi bigwigs themselves disappeared.

On the early morning of 11 April Allied troops arrived in Eutingen but, to the dismay of the locals, they were French Moroccans rather than Americans. Their first action was to search homes for concealed weapons.[13] Raimund Frei's future wife, Hildegard, kept a diary account of the approach of occupation. On Saturday, 31 March 1945, she was on night duty with the DRK (German Red Cross). The night was filled with explosions. The Autobahnbrücke was demolished at 8pm and the Eisenbahnbrücke at 6am the following morning. An entry for Tuesday, 3 April refers to minor fighter-bomber activity, but this intensified the next day, with enemy aircraft active in the area before 8 am. Nevertheless, Hildegard made a trip to nearby Kieselbronn, where anti-tank defences were being dug. The entry adds: 'The French are at Bruchsal.'[14]

Events moved swiftly on Friday 6 April. There was an alarm in Eutingen at around 5.30am. Allied forces were flowing forward. They stood before Göbrichen and tanks reached Kieselbronn that night. Niefern was shelled by tanks and artillery. On the Saturday morning there were signs that the end was close. Hildegard's diary reads: '7am: two white flags on top of the church spire, one each at the station, the sawmill and the town hall. Suddenly, there is gunfire and thirty minutes later the flags are gone. The German soldiers were still there and want to defend our village. Will our home be spared or will it be turned into a pile of rubble during the battle? Agonizing hours of uncertainty.'[14]

By Sunday, 8 April the French had made progress. Hildegard: '11.45pm–00.15am artillery fire on our village. Terrible explosions. How will we get out of here? All of a sudden an explosion very close to our house and the windows are rattling. Nobody could even think about sleeping.'[14]

French infantry began to occupy the high ground on Monday, 9 April. Hildegard noted: 'Hard battles south-west of our village. Now the artillery on the hill right next to us starts firing. It's uncanny to hear the shells whistle over our heads. The thought that they are aimed at German soldiers tortures me to death.' Fighter-bombers attacked the German positions near Eutingen Woods the next day: 'This doesn't bode well. Maybe this is the preparation for the invasion of our village. I am feeling fidgety and afraid of all that is to come. It is today that I am really feeling what it means to be all alone, without my father. About 8pm heavy artillery fire back and forth from hill to hill, with us right in the middle.'[14] Hildegard's father had been killed the day after the 23 February air attack; a cellar ceiling collapsed on him as he attempted to retrieve possessions.

The French troops pushed forward before 6.00am on Wednesday, 11 April: 'Strong resistance in the western part of the village by our few but brave soldiers. Unfortunately, everything was in vain. Between 8.15 and 8.30am our house is being searched by a Frenchman. I wore my DRK dress, which made him treat us with respect. Now fighting flares up in the east but, unfortunately, the resistance of our soldiers was too weak. The first vehicles come dashing through the village. Now, all of a sudden, we're all destitute, without any kind of power. Shouldn't we envy the dead, who don't have to endure this? Yes, we should, because they are spared the humiliation we're experiencing.'[14]

Teenager Sigrid Kern (née Weber) was waiting for the Moroccans to enter Eutingen: 'We girls were taken down into the cellar and stayed there, out of sight. I was in the cellar for several days. I'd heard people talking about "rape", but I didn't know what the word meant. I was afraid the French would torch the cellars with flame-throwers.'[15]

The Webers' garden provided a campsite for eight Moroccans. Sigrid's younger sister, Doris, protected her pet rabbit. It was hidden in a large wooden box in the kitchen: 'One day, one of the Moroccans came in and sat on the box. I thought my rabbit would suffocate. Anyway, it escaped a Moroccan cooking pot. A number of things helped us deal with the soldiers. Firstly, Father could speak French. Secondly, a number of French POWs vouched for us. Father had helped them by giving them cigarettes, potatoes and coal, which was generally forbidden.' As the Moroccans left, several French officers called on them. 'They talked to Father and were invited to stay for dinner. Sigrid, now out of danger, rejoined the family group.'[15]

Ten-year-old Doris had a young girl's outlook: 'I was very excited. The Moroccans were exotic. One was bald, except for a ponytail. I went outside with a red ribbon and put it around his ponytail. They were very friendly and gave me biscuits and chocolates. They brought their stolen chickens to mother, for cooking. She may have been a country girl but she had never got her hands dirty plucking chickens! When they left, I watched out of the window as they drove away. It was a very sudden departure. The soldier with the ponytail looked up and pulled his helmet down, to show that he was still wearing the red ribbon. However, they also caught sight of Sigrid and shouted that they would be back.'[15]

Raimund Frei's future wife, Hildegard, missed her father: 'There are so many things I would like to ask him right now and I could be so much calmer with him around. But that's just the way it is. In your darkest hours you're always on your own. The occupiers – some mulattoes among them – are allowed to freely access houses. The commandant ordered that all wirelesses, binoculars and cameras have to be delivered to the church by 6pm. I wonder whether we will ever see them again. There is a curfew from 7pm.'[16]

Pforzheim had yet to be occupied. Kreisleiter Hans Knab, the city's top Nazi, was still making plans to defend his fiefdom of ruins. Meanwhile, the Moroccans settled into Eutingen. Max Weber had worried about Sigrid, his teenage daughter; he had made her disguise herself as an old woman. After four days the Moroccans had left. The Tunisians then moved in, together with French European officers. Max Weber was shocked when the officers told him about the concentration camps. There was then great confusion. Suddenly, the French left and German soldiers reappeared. They vanished, in turn, when more Moroccans arrived. Then an angry French officer banged on the Webers' front door and told Max that, as civilians had shot at his soldiers, they intended to burn down the town hall. This threat was then extended, to encompass the entire village. Fortunately, some newly liberated French POWs – who had been well treated in Eutingen – persuaded them to burn down just the one building.[17]

In the second week of April, as Allied troops approached Pforzheim itself, Knab continued to make bellicose noises. With the ruins surrounded, the French showed no immediate inclination to storm the city. Instead, artillery spotters circled overhead, directing shellfire. The last few days before occupation saw Gerd Fleig fulfil the dream of many a schoolboy. He was still on the strength of an artillery unit and was called up for duty at the last gasp: 'Our unit was based at Huchenfeld and they used my local knowledge to range onto buildings in Pforzheim already occupied by French troops. The targets included my former high school. As far as I can recall, there were only a few Wehrmacht soldiers in town. Most resistance to the French came from a few snipers.'[18]

Hildegard's diary entry for 12 April records fighting in Niefern village and in the hills towards Öschelbronn. She expressed her fear of having her home commandeered by French troops: 'hopefully we will be spared. The French are taking revenge for what our SS did. Today, I remembered a sentence I heard three months ago and which I couldn't believe back then: "The worst is yet to come." And now the time has come. The Schweizers have ten soldiers in their house. For these "gentlemen" roads don't seem to exist. They climb over garden fences and walk right across the meadows and fields. It is terrible! What is happening to civilization? And you have to agree to just anything or else you are for it. These are supposed to be our liberators!'[19] In fact, Hildegard was mistaken. The Allies had reached an understanding that, during the invasion and occupation of Germany, Allied forces would behave as conquerors rather than liberators. The American troops found it difficult to assume this role. The French, for obvious reasons, found it less challenging.

In Pforzheim, Knab slipped away after a week of shelling, leaving his people in the lurch. Indeed, all senior Party officials made a run for it. As a parting gift, Knab ordered power, gas and water utilities – still under emergency repair after the big attack – to be destroyed in a series of demolitions. Knab wanted to apply Hitler's so-called 'Nero Decree', under which retreating German forces were expected to destroy all surviving infrastructure.[20]

In nearby Stuttgart Max Rodi was ordered to play his part in robbing the German people of the means of survival. His job was to destroy Stuttgart's bread ovens. He refused, left his post and returned to Pforzheim. Meanwhile, the non-commissioned officer charged with carrying out Knab's demolition orders in Pforzheim was persuaded to do otherwise. Nevertheless, the city's remaining bridges were blown, with the exception of the rail bridge (a group of courageous civilians intervened and disabled the charges).[20]

When French Colonial troops finally arrived in the city they opened the occupation with the wholesale theft of chickens and rabbits from back gardens. By 18 April the last German snipers had been killed and Pforzheim was secure. The celebrated French commander General Jean de Lattre de Tassigny made a ceremonial entry through the ruined streets. The news of Hitler's death was broadcast less than a fortnight later, in an announcement that included the last lies.[21]

Hans Ade, then 9 years old, has vivid memories of the final days of National Socialist Pforzheim: 'The city was declared a "fortress" but there were very few soldiers around. Some were dug in along the slope of the Nagold, below our villa. The men had no supplies. Some of us broke into empty homes, grabbed whatever we could find and carried it down to the troops. There was no real fighting. They took off when the French appeared, leaving most of their weapons behind. Later, we went down to their trenches and played with hand grenades. We went fishing with them in the Nagold.

'The only fighting I saw involved French tank spearheads positioned on the cemetery hill. This overlooked the entire valley, including Würm. They could see all roads and bridges and fired at anything that moved. Before the German soldiers left, they warned us boys about moving on the roads. At Kupferhammer, the Kreisleitung set up a command post. This was strafed and bombed by fighter-bombers and one blast shattered our villa's windows. I went to have a look at the bomb craters. In one there was an injured policeman. He bled to death.'[22]

When the hospital was destroyed Hans' sister moved to the tunnel complex at Dillweissenstein. It was damp in the hospital tunnel and she suggested that some wounded be moved to the doctor's villa. This building then flew the Red Cross flag, which kept it safe when the French arrived. 'Our temporary home became a field dressing station. We heard French tanks moving in from Huchenfeld. The first French to arrive were Moroccans and Tunisians; they set up a machine gun on the terrace. We were all in the cellar. My sisters were in Red Cross uniform. The French moved out the German wounded and occupied the building.

'Father had got hold of a cow from a nearby farm. It was slaughtered in the garage of Lameystrasse 61. We shared the meat with neighbours. We were cooking stew for the hospital patients when the French arrived. One of the soldiers went into the large room used by the doctor as an office, took out his brass knuckles and attempted to demolish the desktop. An officer, also a Tunisian, slapped him across the face. Later, a gynaecologist set up a clinic at the villa, to treat rape victims.'[22]

The confusion and uncertainties of early occupation continued to be documented in Hildegard's diary. Friday, 13 April: 'Our house has still been spared. Now we're off to Pforzheim to get coal. On the way we found steel helmets, gasmasks, waist belts and field dressings. The sight of it makes me sick. Poor German Wehrmacht. What have you been fighting for? I carried home six bags of coal and coke. I never thought I would be able to, or have to, haul coal sacks one day. More and more I realize how we are all alone because once you're in misery even the best friends are worthless. However, Mother and I will make it somehow. I am wearing my DRK armband, which is the only thing they still respect. Today, I noticed how they often said 'Croix Rouge' to each other as I passed. Today, I made the decision to always wear my DRK dress because there are more and more cases of young girls and women being raped every day. Complaints at the town hall always result in the same answer: "What the SS did was even worse and now we have to pay for it." Apparently, some [perpetrators] have been executed, though. I am trying to go out on the streets as little as possible.'[23]

The ebb and flow of troops left everyone in limbo. On Saturday, 14 April Hildegard wrote: 'The resistance of our soldiers has hardened … Hopefully, we won't get hit as they are shooting back and forth all the time. At about 3pm two blacks came walking down the road and rang our bell.' Hildegard, her mother and a friend found themselves face to face with the enemy. One immediately greeted her with a handshake. They then went upstairs to the guest room. 'The short one had a terribly avaricious gaze. The tall one then asked me to sit on the bed. This made me feel a little uncomfortable and I refused. Then he said I should not be afraid – he would be a *guter Kamerad* and I would be a *guter Kamerad* as well.' The men knew no German and Hildegard used a dictionary to find out what they wanted. She gave them fruit juice rather than alcohol but the shorter of the two was dissatisfied: 'I will never be able to forget that gaze of his.' Her friend became so afraid she made a run for it. The soldiers moved downstairs, sipping fruit juice, and eventually left: 'The goodbye was so affectionate it gave me hot and cold chills.'[23]

While she was relieved to see the back of them, this was tempered by their promise to return that evening: they wanted to sleep in the house. Meanwhile, the short man went over the road and behaved badly towards a neighbour. Hildegard and her mother went to the town hall to plead for protection. 'After a long discussion they promised to send over a Frenchman to sleep at our house. Hopefully, this black plague will be gone soon or else we will be emotionally dead. On top of that, the captain made fun of me and told me he would send over two Moroccans.' They heard heavy artillery fire during the night. In the morning the door bell rang again: 'And guess who was there: the tall black guy from yesterday. The little guy was in front of our garden. Fortunately, the door closed immediately behind me, so I was able to handle them outside, in the garden.' They drank more juice and left.[23]

The French troops pulled out during the night, leaving Eutingen unoccupied. Suddenly, Hildegard saw German troops outside. Her mother called to a lieutenant, who promised to return with reinforcements. Instead, the French returned. On Tuesday, 17 April the town hall was set on fire, in retaliation for the alleged shooting of a French soldier by civilians the day before. They were warned that any further resistance would result in the reprisal shooting of fifty civilians. Her diary continues: 'There are lots of soldiers in town now, negroes from Senegal among them.' Civilians were ordered to stay indoors. On Wednesday morning they watched the French advance from the windows. They saw Haidach Farm burst into flames and smoke rise from Buckenberg. This time the French were there to stay.[23]

Among those desperate to see the French take over and the last vestiges of Nazi control fall away was 15-year-old forced labourer Roger Riblet-Buchmann. He was among hundreds deported from the Vosges to work in Pforzheim's armaments factories. They had recently moved from the Italian camp to the Russian camp. Then, in April 1945, the Vosges deportees and a large group of Russians were moved to another camp, at Tübingen. They left the Russian camp as French artillery shells began falling on the outskirts of Pforzheim. Roger was not impressed with the daily menu at Tübingen: a brownish 'coffee' – universally known as 'the brew' – served in the mornings and at midday, followed by unpleasant-looking soup in the evening.

'Food became the main problem, but the spring was warm. As the camp was directly on the Neckar, we spent most days on its bank, delousing ourselves, playing cards and dreaming of release.'[24]

As warm, sunny weather persisted, they pursued the daily search for lice and looked nervously at the nearby flak batteries and station – targets too close for comfort. When the station was bombed they took refuge in a sewer tunnel. They were uninjured by a near miss, thanks to this tunnel's steel door: 'Shaken and covered in dust and dirt, we stepped outside, into the open, ignoring the body of a German soldier. We ran like frightened animals along the Neckar towards Lustnau. As panic subsided, we slowly returned to camp.'[24]

Following the bombing, Roger and his friend, René, formed a small group determined to reach the French lines as the spearheads approached Tübingen. They had a stroke of luck. A train stopped at the top of the camp, as the track had been damaged, and the passengers were told to get out and walk. Roger, René and the others blended with the crowd and were soon well beyond the camp and its guards. They entered the village of Oberndorf as a German artillery column passed through. They took cover but were then confronted by a German civilian carrying a rifle. He decided not to challenge them and slipped away. They stayed in Oberndorf, encouraged by French POWs in the vicinity and the friendly villagers. The mayor found them lodgings; it felt like a holiday after Tübingen camp. Shortly afterwards they linked up with French forces occupying Pforzheim and the surrounding area.[24]

The occupation of Pforzheim began badly. On Monday, 16 April the French reached the southern districts. It took them some time to clear as far as the northern area. Former Stadtarchiv director Christian Groh: 'The last-ditch Nazis refused to allow people to hang white sheets from their windows. Knab warned that anyone attempting to surrender would be hanged, but he saved himself when the moment came. The top Nazis took flight, escaping through the Black Forest to Alsace and Switzerland.'[25]

A hospital doctor may have granted Gerd Fleig indefinite leave, but his own side might well have treated him as a deserter during those final, confused days of collapse. Now, as the occupation began, Fleig had other reasons to be careful: 'I put on civilian clothes. Fortunately, I had a very youthful face. I looked too young to have been in the army. I knew what the French might do if they found out I had been in the Waffen SS. I went to see a doctor in Enzberg and asked him to remove my SS tattoo. He helped out lots of people in this way.' Fleig had a bad moment when the French summoned all young men to report. Fortunately, his ability to speak French was appreciated and he was taken on as a translator for a French officer.[26]

In those first days of occupation, however, ruined Pforzheim was enveloped in fear. Young Dieter Essig was without his father, who had stayed in France and was now a prisoner. Essig remembers the initial chaos: 'The Moroccans were the first to arrive. They were barbarians who plundered, pillaged and raped. My mother took my 10-year-old sister and smeared her face with soot. She then covered her head with

'I had a very youthful face': Gerd Fleig arranged to have his SS tattoo removed. *Photo: Gerd Fleig.*

a scarf, to make her look like an old woman. Then the European French soldiers arrived and they were more civilized.'[27]

Klaus Feucht, a 4-year-old survivor of the Pforzheim raid, was taken in by an Eutingen family. He was then reunited with his family and evacuated to a school in Iptingen. 'Later, we roved the countryside on foot until we reached Leinfelden. I remember very clearly the time my mother and I went to get water from the village fountain. A soldier – presumably French – followed us, entered the house, threatened those inside with a pistol and forced people to hand over jewellery.'[28]

With occupation now a reality, civilians were issued with new food ration cards. Hans Gerstung, then a teenager: 'The three families living in our apartment decided to pool their cards and buy for everyone. In April 1945 the Reichmanns left us. They went to stay with the professor's two brothers in the Black Forest. Our empty room was assigned to a French colonel, as my mother spoke French. At first, the French combat troops were Colonials. Only the officers were white. We called all the Colonial soldiers 'Moroccans'. There was much raping and looting at that time. Opposite our apartment, at Hohenzollernstrasse 96, Dr Irma Feldweg set up a surgery at her home for raped women. Dr Feldweg was a gynaecologist at Siloah Hospital, which had been bomb-damaged. Downstairs, at the front door, an armed French soldier stood guard. I never went into this building, but Mother used to talk about things during the evening. On one occasion I remember her saying: "The other day seventeen women came in for treatment." Irma Feldweg-Strasse is named after this doctor, who later became head of gynaecology.'[29]

Hans Gerstung saw no looting but remembers the 'Moroccans' at Weinkellerei Brenk, on Bahnhofstrasse. The Brenk winery's vaulted cellars were soon discovered by the occupiers, who set up a trading post – swapping wine for food and valuables: 'These troops were even worse off for food than we were. I visited the winery with Mother. We took a jug and handed over jewellery for wine.'[29]

Adolf Katz often went into Pforzheim, to check on the bank. His 8 May diary entry makes no specific mention of the unconditional surrender, other than to reflect that worse was to come. From the banker's point of view, Thursday, 10 May was worse. He arrived to find Deutsche Bank's vault blown and many safes robbed. He

Rape clinic: Dr Irma Feldweg set up a surgery for rape victims at what was then her home. *Photo: Tony Redding.*

blamed French officers. His protests to the military authorities brought Katz and his excellent French to their attention. He was appointed a district administrator – a job with an awkward dimension. He was expected to enforce decisions concerning the requisitioning of beds, clothing and livestock.[30]

Meanwhile, his 8-year-old daughter, Marianne, was enjoying her new-found freedom. Fine spring weather developed into the summer of 1945: 'The bombing had stopped and the grown-ups were too busy organizing the fundamentals of life to bother us. They left us to our own devices. The weather was very warm and it was a summer of anarchy for the kids. We had enough to eat as summer is a time of plenty in rural South Germany. Food supplies held up well in those early months of peace, although things changed later.'[30]

Marianne's father discovered the challenging nature of his new position. On 11 June Pforzheim's French commandant ordered him to produce 500 beds, mattresses and blankets for a Russian transit camp in Mannheim. Katz responded by ordering that beds be taken from well-known National Socialists. The next demand, four days later, was for livestock. The French Army required 7,000kg of meat within the week. Meanwhile, theft cases were piling up: they could not be prosecuted as there were no functioning German courts. Cars were a favourite target for crooks. Yet, for all the problems, Katz enjoyed his new responsibilities. He described it as the job he was made for. He had a good working relationship with the French, but also understood that his position was under threat. The Americans were about to take over and Katz didn't speak English.[30]

The significance of Pforzheim's popular name, Goldstadt, was appreciated by the French. Teams from Strasbourg began a methodical search for strongboxes. Hundreds of small jewellery businesses still had their wealth buried in the ruins, and whenever the French found a safe, they blew it open. Hans Gerstung: 'You could hear the detonations downtown. Much later, in 1960, I was a regional sales manager for a company producing electrical contacts. One of my trips was to Strasbourg, to negotiate a deal with a French customer. My company's owner came along and introduced himself to the French boss. The latter suddenly cut across the pleasantries: "I was an officer with the engineers in Pforzheim, blasting open safes and, among others, I blasted yours! Now, you can either be mad at me or you can simply let me make it up to you by sealing this deal." We shook hands and a very personal Franco-German friendship was born.'[31]

The French occupation was a violent, lawless time. Police files – now held in the Stadtarchiv Pforzheim (B1-513) – tell one community's story. On 29 April 1945, police officers at Brötzingen took a statement from Friedrich Staib, proprietor of an inn, zum Anker. He complained about drunken Moroccans and Tunisians abusing women in the pub. That day three Moroccans came in and assaulted the waitress. One pulled a knife in an attempt to intimidate her into giving in. Staib said he would close the pub (popular with the occupiers) unless he received protection. The station also received complaints that day about a Moroccan who had forced a family to take him in and now roamed the area on a horse, stealing poultry and other food.

Drunken Colonial troops were a big problem in Brötzingen and, presumably, throughout Pforzheim and its surrounding villages. Brötzingen police took details of assaults on 7 May by two French soldiers who arrived at a house and demanded jewellery. The wife refused and had her face slapped. She was then struck with a rifle butt. A man attempted to intervene but was slapped and punched. The offenders did the same in neighbouring houses.

Some episodes were more violent and occasionally had tragic consequences. On 17 May police at Wartberg station took a statement from a pensioner residing in the air-raid shelter of the Nordstadtschule. It concerned the murder of caretaker Hermann Enghofer. The evening before, the pensioner had gone upstairs to cook potatoes. Three French soldiers, two white and one black, had come in. As the pensioner went to return to the cellar the black soldier 'grabbed me by the throat and squeezed it, threw me on the bed, took out his genitals and said "bock!".' The victim fought off the assailant several times and rushed to Enghofer to seek help. The caretaker and his son went into the cellar. The black soldier stabbed Hermann Enghofer nine times during the confrontation and the caretaker died of his wounds.

In late April police received a series of complaints about harassment, sexual assaults and rapes by French Colonial troops, including deserters. One such complaint, to Wartberg Police, concerned armed soldiers living at a local pig farm. Two auxiliary policemen on patrol the next day saw one of the deserters. He was armed with a sub-machine gun. A woman gave a statement on 2 May. She told how a French colonial soldier held a rifle to her chest and tried to rape her. She escaped but he went on to rape her cousin. Her husband was taken away by the Moroccans. The next morning she found him with severe head and back injuries. 'At first I took him back to the apartment and tried to warm him. Since his brain was exposed I had to drive him to St Trudpert Hospital. Dr Rueff told me that, unfortunately, there was no hope of saving his life. He died two days later.'

The attacks continued, some involving deserters.. In one case, a girl was repeatedly raped. Later, it was agreed to billet one Moroccan as protection against the others. On 16 April this man was taken by a German reconnaissance patrol but then returned after eight days in captivity. He had sex with the woman billeting him on one occasion, but her statement is ambiguous as to context. This Moroccan and an associate resisted arrest by two French soldiers and a lieutenant on 30 April. There was an exchange of fire and the lieutenant was wounded. A neighbour said that the two Moroccans involved constantly harassed women and one had raped her niece several times. The other raped two more women.

The Stadtarchiv Pforzheim files show that violence continued into June and July. On 7 June Brötzingen Police took a statement from Wilhelm Mayer, a railway inspector living at Auerhahnstrasse 2, concerning the death of his 14-year-old son, shot by a French soldier earlier that day. It seems the incident began when two Russian railway workers arrived with a French soldier and identified Wilhelm Mayer as 'the man'. One Russian punched him in the mouth. He was told to go with the soldier. When he turned to put on his coat a shot was fired, killing the son.

The French were determined to make Pforzheimers confront Nazi crimes. They exhumed the bodies of the murdered French Resistance fighters of Réseau Alliance. Civilians were forced to view the twenty-five bodies (seventeen men and eight women), but Giles Milton says this backfired: 'Although there was widespread revulsion, the reaction of the populace was not "How terrible that this happened", but, "What a disgrace that we're being forced to look at such things". The French mounted these gruesome displays out of concern that people might refuse to believe the enormity of the atrocities carried out in the name of Nazi Germany.'[32]

There was a dangerous moment when the bodies were exhumed. The French rounded up nearly fifty men and took them to the factory yard of Metallwarenfabrik Wolf. Teenager Hans Gerstung's father, Karl, was listed as Hostage 21. 'They were to be executed in retaliation. This factory, in the northern part of town, was just 150m from my home in Philippstrasse. My father was snatched from our house, right before our eyes. My mother, together with a group of other women, pleaded with the French colonel billeted with us. They begged him to do something. The condemned men were released after just one night. I recall the colonel as a very likeable person. He never took his shoes off at night. He went to bed wearing a white bathrobe, with his sub-machine gun underneath the bed. A Moroccan orderly stood by his door.

I remember the Moroccans as very friendly, at least towards me. They always said: "*Salut! Ca va? Tu veux un bonbon?*" [Hello! How are you? Do you want a sweet?].'[33]

Things were particularly dangerous for those living near the crater where the executions took place. Hans Ade: 'The French commandant put up posters, warning that if people did not turn up for the exhumation of the bodies, in order to show shame and sympathy, he would take hostages and have them shot.'[34] Coffins were made, together with the sign: '*Propagande Francaise ou Crime Nazi?*' The first idea was to force the entire population of Pforzheim to file past the bodies.

The Ade family rented a vegetable plot near the bomb crater. Hans and his mother were working in the garden on the day of the exhumation. They went over, joining those already present: 'The French had ordered former Nazis to do the digging. The crater was full of mud. They were told to remove the bodies and clean them, ready for examination. French soldiers with sub-machine guns ringed the crater. We were among the forty or fifty people at the scene, including several doctors. They looked over the bodies, trying to determine the cause of death. They were then put in the coffins and taken away to the main cemetery for more detailed examination. Many more people witnessed the scene at the cemetery.

'I stood just 3m from the crater rim. It was filled to the top with brown mud. I saw bodies removed from the mud. They took off their clothes and washed them. The two doctors, wearing white coats, looked at them before they were placed in the wooden coffins and carried up the road. We stood and watched four or five bodies exhumed. The stench was terrible.' [34]

People in the neighbourhood knew the bodies were there. A friend of the Ades had a habit of collecting firewood along the forest road bordering the crater. He saw an arm sticking out of the mud and told the police. They cordoned off the area and put up a sign: 'No entry – unexploded bombs!' Hans Ade: 'Mother said nothing as we walked away from the crater. There was total silence on the subject; no-one would talk about it. That persisted over the years. It took me from 2006 to 2008 to persuade the city council to put up a memorial to the victims.'[34]

On Sunday, 8 July 1945, Adolf Katz said farewell to Commandant Pelletier. Katz later wrote: 'He is the only one who leaves here with clean hands.' His adjutant, Capitaine Tabellion, was from a different mould: 'He returned 438 watches stolen from our vault.' He wanted to buy them for a friend, a capitaine at Karlsruhe, for 17,000 Reichsmark. The friend had only 11,000 Reichsmark on him, but asked for a receipt for the full amount. Katz was told the outstanding amount would be brought to him that very afternoon. The capitaine from Karlsruhe never showed up.[35]

The Americans took over later that Sunday. They were less concerned than Katz about his lack of English. He was appointed Oberbürgermeister of Pforzheim on 23 July. The family then moved into a relatively undamaged house, at Friedenstrasse 82. Marianne, just turned 9, had wanted to stay at Mönsheim and continue her summer in the countryside. There were, however, certain compensations. The house was large enough to accommodate a family of refugees who had a son her age. She also found a new friend in a girl from Erfurt, living nearby. The children, with their roller skates, sported grazed knees from their many falls on pot-holed Friedenstrasse. They learnt how to charm chocolate and chewing gum out of the Americans. They went prospecting in the rubble. Marianne Pross: 'We dug in the ruins of the jewellery factories. We found treasures – molten jewellery and coloured stones. What we dug up we carried round in little boxes. Our greatest find was half a gold bracelet. We traded these treasures, copying the grown-ups. During that summer people traded jewellery for food from the farmers. Later, however, they refused to take jewellery. People became more flexible. I remember fine linen napkins being used as diapers. They were not very effective as they were not really absorbent.' Robert showed new talents: he built a small radio receiver and listened in to AFN (American Forces Network). Later, he passed this set to Marianne: 'What I heard corrupted my musical tastes for the rest of my life.'[35]

Things were much improved in Pforzheim after the French left. Christian Groh: 'When the American Military Government took over they set up a checkpoint at Birkenfeld village, south-west of Pforzheim, where they relieved the withdrawing French of stolen property. The Americans even made some show of attempting to return the stolen goods. They were highly critical of the French, concluding that they had done nothing to establish order and security in the city and surrounding districts.'[36]

Giles Milton adds: 'Most Pforzheimers were glad to see the back of the French. They had fleeced and exploited the local population with all the enthusiasm of a medieval army, looting and requisitioning food, cameras and electrical equipment.' Convoys of French vehicles were halted by American troops manning the checkpoint and their booty confiscated, including large numbers of farm animals.[37]

The Pforzheimers' reaction to the Americans was positive. Dieter Essig, then a small boy: 'What a contrast! It felt as if someone had opened the gates of paradise. The GIs were very nice. My mother was fearful at the first encounter, but the American reached down, picked me up and gave me my first chewing gum. I didn't know what it was for. The Americans continued to be friendly and some let us ride around in their jeeps. The answer to good relations between occupiers and occupied was simple – chocolate!'[38]

On 7 August 1945, Oberbürgermeister Katz made a speech before the newly convened city council and representatives of the American Military Government: 'With deepest emotion I am opening this first session of the city council. It is the first step on a long road that will – God willing – lead us towards a better future after the long night of National Socialist terror, after the horrors of war and the atrocious destruction of the city. I do not fail to recognize the enormous hardship most of our fellow citizens live in and I know that probably the most terrible winter that we have ever experienced is in store for us. However, we share the belief in reconstruction.'[39]

In the midst of ruin, Katz made the point that Pforzheimers were suddenly rich in human terms: 'Even today we have more freedom than we have had for many years and, step by step, we wish to achieve greater freedom, up to complete self-determination. The heavy moral constraint under which we have lived for the past decade has fallen. The National Socialist propaganda that distorted and falsified everything and poisoned our lives with endless untruthfulness has been disposed of. The shameless corruption of the Party bigwigs has been removed. We are on our way to install a clean administration in which law and justice will prevail, an administration from the people and for the people.

'The rule of a small minority who oppressed the majority with endless brutality challenged the whole world with megalomaniacal arrogance. It led our people into the most terrible catastrophe we have experienced in our long history. It is our job to lead our people out of the depths. Certainly, we all share the blame for this terrible downfall and, thus, we all have to suffer for it. Nobody can take the consequences of the lost war off our shoulders; no organization, no financial trick can undo the destruction of our city, our industry and the exhaustion of all our reserves.'[39]

Later in his speech Katz said: 'Let us ask the question: "What ideals inspire the American people?" Let us see whether we can find similar ideals in our own past. Three ideals present themselves to us:

1. All sovereignty lies with the people, because only free people can bear the full responsibility for all decisions. Here, I'd like to add that German democracy pre-1933 was only a caricature of a democracy, in which not the people but interest groups prevailed. Things got even worse after 1933, when a small minority seized all power and suppressed the majority with brutal terror. The new democracy we want to build has to wear a different face.
2. Every department must always feel responsible for the big picture. They are not an end in itself. They have to act, not from the viewpoint of their own area of responsibility, but as representatives of an entire people, at all times.
3. Nobody is allowed to claim any kind of privilege for himself that is not available to everyone else.'[40]

Katz made some interesting comments on this third point. He said a German interpretation might be: 'No privileges of rank whatsoever are permitted.' He then observed: 'the American version is much deeper. It recognizes that it is impossible to establish a world without injustice and privileges and thus transfers the decision to the conscience of the individual.' He contrasted this with National Socialist opinion, which held that only the Führer decides right and wrong, 'where the individual has to follow orders without ever being allowed to follow conscience. All these cruelties – which we are horrified at – would not have been possible without this doctrine, that orders have to be obeyed at all costs because only the Führer can decide what was good or evil. People stopped being people and became machines.'[40]

Just four months earlier, only a line or two from this speech would have been enough to cost Katz his head.

The surviving British aircrew who played their part in bringing Nazi cruelties to an end now faced sweeping change in their own lives. Bruce Burrows' wireless operator, Ron Germain, had married before joining 550 Squadron. When his aircraft failed to return from the Hanau raid on 18 March his wife was not informed, as his mother was still named as the next of kin: 'The telegram went to Mum, rather than Peggy. On my return I was given six days' leave and went home to Peggy. My mother and my wife's mother lived very near each other and everyone was in the picture by that stage. They were hugely relieved to see me.'[41]

Tour-expired, surplus aircrew at RAF North Killingholme were remustered for other trades. Ron Germain remustered as a radar mechanic, which involved a return to Yatesbury for more training: 'I remember going to bed one night and suddenly being awakened by the station commander, announcing on the Tannoy that the war with Germany was over. There was a deathly silence, then the whole place erupted. I went home and stopped there for two weeks. I got a lift to London in a Baby Austin. There were six of us in it!' Ron Germain left the Air Force in February 1947 with the rank of warrant officer. His papers carried a useful character reference: 'A most conscientious, thoroughly good and hard-working senior NCO.'[41]

Ken Sidwell's Lancaster crew survived their tour. Mid-upper gunner Frank Woodley had found his future: 'I met the girl who was to be my wife during the crew's first visit to Grimsby. We spotted two young ladies in the Rose and Crown. They were soon surrounded. I married Phyllis without permission, which is an offence in the Air Force. I had a tendency to do things on impulse in those days. I had a fortnight's leave and decided to get married. Why not? We had a son. Sadly, Phyllis died in a car accident. I married again, and today I have grandchildren and great-grandchildren.'[42]

With his operational tour over, Frank was posted for Flying Control duties in northern Scotland, spending some time on Orkney and Shetland: 'Back in Aberdeen, the sergeants' mess was in a big hotel. There was a vacancy for a barman and I took the job. I left the Air Force in August 1946 and did all sorts of things. I even took up fishing, joining my wife's brother, who had served in the Air Sea Rescue Service during the war. I did several North Sea trips, then went on the big boats fishing in Norwegian and Icelandic waters. When I'd had enough, I took a job at Scunthorpe steelworks, where I became a foreman.'[42]

Sam Lipfriend's war was over. He went on end of tour leave after his last sortie on 4 April, the attack on Lützkendorf refinery: 'I spent most of my time dancing at the Royal Tottenham. I went most days and enjoyed myself – I was something of a dancer!' With his leave over, Lipfriend joined a flight mechanics' course but, with the end of the war just days away, his brother had other ideas: 'My brother had a kidney removed in September 1940. He had volunteered for the Air Force but wasn't 100 per cent fit and eventually became an RAF tailor. He said he could wangle a posting for me and I joined him at Felixstowe. I learned about tailoring and became a tailor after the war. Later, I started my own business and carried on in this trade until the early 1970s, when I became an estate agent.'[43]

Bomb aimer Bill Thomas, of 153 Squadron, suffered no obvious ill-effects from operational flying, but others had seen the signs of strain: 'After my ground loop incident, I had three weeks' leave. I called in at the county council offices and chatted to the boss. The next time we met I had finished operations. He then told me he was glad the tour was over. He had seen that it was getting to me. I didn't know it, but I had the "twitch". After the war I remained his "blue-eyed boy", as I had been flying in the RAF!'[44]

Squadron losses rarely affected the Potter crew, but Bill vividly remembers the night one of his mates, fellow bomb aimer Bob Marne, went missing: 'Bob and I were great pals and I had every reason to think he was dead. Three weeks later he suddenly appeared in front of me, in the corridor. That frightened the life out of me! He had baled out when his aircraft was hit during a minelaying op. He had injured his shoulder but was soon found by friendly locals, who hid him from the Germans. The Germans then did the usual: they told the community that six of them would be shot unless Bob was produced. He became a prisoner but was soon freed by the Americans. He returned with a prize – an American leather flying jacket. He sent it away for cleaning and was horrified when it came back. It had shrunk and was then several sizes too small.'[44]

Bill Thomas left the Air Force as a flight lieutenant in 1946. 'Civvy Street presented no difficulties, as I had a job to go to. I returned to Cornwall County Council and married Muriel the following year. We had a son and, today, I have a granddaughter, a grandson and four great-grandchildren.'[44]

Raimund Frei remained a prisoner of war in the United States: 'We learned languages, had lessons in all sorts of subjects and kept ourselves busy with handicrafts. We had teachers and professors in all subjects and experts including architects, botanists and so on. The prisoners had the chance to improve their artistic abilities. Plays and concerts were diversions. We began correspondence courses at various universities and colleges. I signed up with Berkeley for a forestry course.

'After the war ended the food ration became smaller and we were advised to volunteer for work. I put my name forward during the summer of 1945. Since I had brushed up on my English I was assigned twenty men. After helping with the beet, potato and onion harvests in Idaho, we were taken to Camp Stoneman at Stockton, near San Francisco, which was a reception centre for troops coming home from the Pacific. At first, we cleaned trains for the Rail Transportation Office. Later, we were employed in one of the mess halls. This lasted until we went home.'[45]

One of Raimund Frei's fellow prisoners was from Pforzheim: 'He sent a pre-printed card home indicating that I was safe. The last mail we had received dated from Christmas 1944. I had no idea what had happened to my home town until early 1946, when the US major in charge took me to the cinema. One feature was

Germany – the final battle. It was a film showing the ruins of Pforzheim, among other things. It also showed the occupation of the city by French troops.' Frei wrote to a friend in Frankfurt. She replied, saying that she had no news from Pforzheim.[45]

In the ruins, meanwhile, Dieter Essig got used to new realities: 'I learned a lot in those days. I got by on minimal clothes and food and developed my scavenging skills. What is left on plates today was the size of my meal at that time! I was a small child during the final war years and the early occupation period. It is easy to be happy when you are young! Despite everything, I had a happy childhood. I always saw the Jungvolk as attractive and I wanted to be part of it. I was too young, of course, but I was given an aluminium dagger for my birthday and I was very proud of that. 20 April was Hitler's birthday and 30 April was my birthday. I asked Mother why everyone hung out the flags for Hitler, but I got no flags and, what's more, I didn't have enough to eat.'[46]

Ellen Eberle, her mother and future stepfather, Karl Weber, were staying at Dobel, in the Black Forest, when the Moroccans arrived. They were ordered out of their rented rooms but were allowed to return after a fortnight. Everything was wrecked. Ellen Eberle: 'They were very deliberate, ruining food, linen and everything else mother had brought from Pforzheim. Yet, the Moroccans were very friendly with children.' Ellen's mother married Karl Weber in October 1945. Ellen went to live with her grandmother at the Pforzheim apartment. On one occasion, when looking out at the ruined city, Ellen remembers her mother saying: 'If the 20 July assassination attempt on Hitler had worked, Pforzheim would still be standing.'[47]

With Karl Weber absent from Pforzheim, French troops stole the contents of his Bayernstrasse apartment. When the Americans took over, he retrieved his piano and stove. Ellen Eberle: 'With the two apartments, our possessions were consolidated and we used the surplus to trade for food in the countryside. It was a strange time. At one point my stepfather received a letter from two families, asking him to adjudicate on who should be using his stove at Bayernstrasse. This came as a shock to him, as he had no idea that anyone was using it!'[47]

In 1945 there was no immediate prospect of children returning to school, at least in a conventional sense. Virtually all schools had been flattened. Hans Gerstung: 'Instead, we were tutored by professors working from their homes. Private lessons began in late 1945, after the Americans arrived. The Military Police rode around in jeeps with the front window folded down. They smoked cigarettes and clutched sub-machine guns. They were headquartered on Sachsenstrasse, in a former watch factory my father had designed. We knew the roads the jeeps used, in the relatively intact northern areas of town. The roads to and in the southern districts were still blocked with rubble. Every now and then, when "*die Amis*" saw us sitting by the side of the road, they flipped their half-smoked cigarettes in our direction. We'd pick them up, take a drag, then put them out and save what was left in metal "cigarette boxes". This paid for our private lessons. At that time, we had to pay a couple of Reichsmark per lesson. One of our professors, a heavy smoker, told us to bring tobacco rather than money. Eventually, tobacco became a quasi-currency.'[48]

The Americans were hailed as providers of all good things, including food parcels from relief organizations. The Katz family received parcels from relatives in New York, although the clothes they sent never seemed to fit young Marianne. What she really needed was a pair of good shoes, to replace her wooden-soled sandals.[49]

Her father had more serious problems. The Americans began the wholesale requisitioning of property. This involved a series of evictions. Adolf Katz had to navigate between rival senior American officers. He was also the target of rumours about his links with National Socialism. He knew it would take time to establish a city administration, yet he seemed to thrive on difficulties. Marianne Pross (née Katz): 'He certainly had plenty to do. Early on, when filling positions of responsibility, the Allies sought people who had not been Party members and were free of involvement in National Socialist crimes. This meant that they had a relatively small pool to choose from and appointments were made almost at random. Many people with little or no experience of public life found themselves in post. The "Old Guard", of course, ducked away and kept a low profile. Within two years, however, they had more confidence and surfaced once more. These people understood how to manipulate the system and play politics. Gradually, the men given their jobs by the Military Government were pushed aside.'[49]

Difficult times approached. In the late autumn of 1945 the nights drew in. Marianne Pross: 'It was getting dark on my way back from school and I had to walk through the ruins. There were crosses marking where the dead remained buried under the rubble. Candles placed by the bereaved flickered in the gloom. This was frightening. It was easy to "see" dead people sitting beside their crosses.'[49]

Hans Gerstung noted positive developments under American rule: 'The supply situation slowly improved. Now there was milk and even meat once in a while. If we needed bread we knocked on the door of American Headquarters and received two or three leftover white loaves.' Work continued to clear the rubble: 'A bomb disposal unit was based near the infantry barracks at Hagenschiess – the wooded area near Buckenberg. This was where they detonated unexploded bombs. Frequently, they didn't bother to defuse them before transporting them up to the detonation area.'[50]

When the Americans succeeded the Moroccans, Sigrid Kern (née Weber) and her father went into the tobacco business. They picked up the GIs' butts and made their own cigarettes from them. Two American soldiers, Robert and Serry, often visited their home. Mrs Weber did their laundry. They paid in soap, butter, petrol and other precious goods. They felt at home with the Webers. Serry, a mixed race American, tried to persuade Sigrid to return with him to America: 'We couldn't communicate. I didn't speak any English, but I managed to find a dictionary. Serry fell in love with me. One day I showed him my box of "medals", for Winter Relief collecting and so on. He took that box home with him as a souvenir. Some girls from Eutingen did become GI brides. One went to live in Honolulu.'[51]

Gerd Fleig may have had his SS tattoo removed, but he was still reluctant to engage with the occupiers. When the Americans arrived he had no choice but to report, in order to obtain food ration cards. At that point he was asked questions about his military service. He decided to answer directly: 'The Americans were using German interpreters to ask the questions and there were no problems.'[52]

Psychologically, Fleig felt torn: 'I was extremely happy that the war was over. On the other hand, Pforzheim was in ruins and I had spent most of my life being told – in the Hitler Youth and, later, in the Waffen SS – that National Socialism was the only way. It took a long time to be convinced otherwise. When the occupation began, I was in a state of mourning over the collapse of National Socialism.

'When first drafted into the Waffen SS I felt no different from the ordinary soldier. Later, however, I discovered that the Waffen SS were political soldiers, with all the associated consequences. One turning point for me was the restoration of political life. For the first time I was exposed to political ideas other than National Socialism. I found myself supporting the FDP, the German Liberal Democratic Party.'[52]

In June 1945 the British moved prisoners to a big camp at Laboe, Schleswig-Holstein. This soon became full and an attempt was made to reduce numbers by asking for volunteers to work as farm labourers. Naval Cadet Werner Baroni: 'My buddy in the camp was Artur Okas. He and I both wanted to work on the land, but he said he knew nothing about farming. I said: "You know the difference between a cow and a bull, don't you? Tell them you are an expert!" He had no home to return to. Everything he knew was in Silesia, now overrun by the Russians.

'That's how we ended up on a two-week rail journey to South Germany. We were still prisoners. When we arrived at Mannheim a woman working for the railway warned us: "Don't go to Heilbronn. If you do, you'll end up in a French coal mine." Artur and I decided to clear off. We left our rail wagon and hid in a small trackside hut. We were there only a couple of hours when a railway worker came in. He shouted with surprise: "My God! Did you escape?" He said he was a First World War veteran and promised to help us. At 3am we boarded a coal train making for Karlsruhe, where we took a passenger service on to Pforzheim. Arriving that Sunday morning, I gazed out at a gutted city.

'I went to Grandmother's apartment and found that only the cellar was intact. Later, I learned that Anna and Lisel were alive and staying with

Fellow prisoner: Artur Okas became Werner Baroni's 'camp buddy'. Artur's home was in Silesia, occupied by the Russians. *Photo: Jürgen and Margit Okas.*

Jehovah's Witnesses in Weissach, near Stuttgart. On that first day back, Artur and I just stood there in the cellar. Then we went outside and sat down in the ruins. A neighbour's daughter appeared. When she saw us sitting there she started to cry. She said: "Where are you living?" I replied: "In the cellar." She said she would ask her widowed mother if I could stay. I told her that if I moved in, it had to be with Artur. She returned and announced: "You are both invited." She gave up her bedroom, but we couldn't sleep on the bed. We were used to the ground in the prison camp, so we ended up sleeping in front of the bed.

'This arrangement didn't last. One day the bell rang and I opened the door. I looked up at the biggest American soldier in the world. I was 6ft 3in but he was at least 7ft. He was a black American and he walked in and made himself at home. He was carrying bags of food. It soon became obvious that he had an arrangement with both mother and daughter. I said to Artur: "Well, we have been guests here but it is time to say thank you and leave." We went to Weissach and tried to find somewhere to stay near Anna and Lisel. We must have looked unattractive, as we were still wearing our old, dirty uniforms. A farmer refused us his house but offered an empty pigsty to sleep in. We stood it for a few nights but eventually had enough. I told Artur I intended to return to Pforzheim. He went to stay with a girlfriend's family; later, he married the girl. I walked back to Pforzheim.'[53]

Werner Baroni stayed with his Aunt Martha, his mother's sister: 'She had a very small apartment. I slept under the kitchen table for several weeks. During the day I helped clear the streets. Everyone was required to join work gangs moving rubble, to allow people and vehicles to get around. After a while I went to the city authorities and explained about having to sleep under a table. I was told about elderly Mrs Gossweiler. She had a cellar with two rooms in the Nordstadt, at Bayernstrasse 34. I moved in and stayed there for several months. I had food stamps as I worked on street clearance. Mrs Gossweiler sometimes shared leftovers with me and a very religious family living in the house occasionally gave me something extra. When working on the rubble I occasionally saw a friend from my Navy days. Now and then he passed me food from his mother.'[53]

Werner had no news of his brother Arno, who had been drafted into a flak unit during the final months of the war. Werner was still wearing his uniform, as the rest of his clothes had been lost. Pforzheim Police had been ordered to arrest anyone still wearing German uniform. 'My local policeman had been a soldier. He told me: "Baroni, you have to get rid of that uniform." I replied: "What do you want me to do? Run around naked? I have nothing else." My Navy friend told me to stop messing around and find civilian clothes. He suggested a trip to Karlsruhe railway station, where there were always lots of US Army trucks. I stole an Army blanket from the back of a truck. My buddy's father was a tailor and he made me a civilian suit. It was the wrong colour – khaki – so it was dyed a nice shade of navy blue. That suit cost me nothing. Turning it navy blue cost twenty Pall Mall.

'One day I bumped into Arno at Karlsruhe station. I spotted him and shouted: "Arno! Where are you going?" He told me what happened to his schoolboy flak unit. He and his classmates manned a 20mm, four-barrelled flak gun. They joined other guns covering a bridge across the Rhine. Then an American plane bombed the bridge and their post. The boys who were unhurt – including Arno – were sent back to Pforzheim. He told me the whole cellar shook during the February attack. Anna and Lisel prayed aloud and everyone else joined in. Phosphorous trickled in through the cellar's small window. They escaped but Lisel was injured by the phosphorous. Anna couldn't crawl through the hole but Arno saved her life. He knocked through into the next cellar and got her out.

'My father was released from hospital in March 1945 and received fresh orders to report to the so-called Alpenfestung in Bavaria (a proposed last stronghold). He told his colonel he needed Arno to accompany him, as he was still walking on crutches. He was given permission and they travelled together to a unit stationed near Lake Constance. They were walking down a village street when a French tank suddenly turned the corner. A lieutenant jumped down and made them prisoner. Father was a fluent French speaker. After a while he and Arno were given release papers and they found work with a local farmer.'[53]

During the early occupation period, Irma Facoltosi, who later married Arno, set out with her mother on an expedition to the village of Bad Liebenzell, where friends George and Anna Heiley had taken refuge after the bombing. Irma: 'We took their sausage dog with us. On the way, a car drew up. Mother could speak French. The officer in the car offered us a lift to Bad Liebenzell, a generous and very human gesture.'[54]

There was sad news concerning other family friends, Franz and Ida Schlong: 'In their struggle to break out of their cellar, Franz was badly injured and blinded. Acid was required for metal refining and containers were damaged by the bombing. Acid splashed his eyes and his hands were also badly burned. He was taken to a Red Cross ambulance train, where a surgeon removed some of his fingers. Franz was very bad and it was a mercy that he died within a few hours. Ida came to live with us at Arlinger. She had suffered smoke inhalation but was otherwise unhurt. Later, she found accommodation in Neuenbürg, 12km away.'[54]

Notes

1. Documents/interview with Marianne Pross, September 2013.
2. Brändle, ref. Naimark, N.M. (1995), *The Russians in Germany: a history of the Soviet Zone of Occupation, 1945–1949*, 106.
3. Brändle, ref. Hillel, M. (1983), *L'Occupation Française en Allemagne, 1945–1949*, S.84, 108–11.
4. Research by Brigitte and Gerhard Brändle.
5. Brändle: Pfinzweiler – source: conversation, 18 November 2013.
6. Interview with Brigitte and Gerhard Brändle, 2013.
7. Brändle, citing Vögele, Rudolf (1997), *Ersingen, unsere Heimet*.

8. Knöbel-Methner, Judith (2005), *900 Jahre Tiefenbronn, Heidelberg, Ubstadt-Weiher*, and Lindner, Hubert (1990), *Das Buch von Tiefenbronn mit seinen Ortsteilen Lehningen, Mühlhausen und Tiefenbronn.*
9. Brändle, citing Boger, Eugen et al. (2001), *Neuhausen einst und jetzt.*
10. Information provided by Brigitte and Gerhard Brändle.
11. Ruff, Herbert (1995), Würm im Zweiten Weltkrieg, in: Ortsnachrichtenblatt Pforzheim-Würm, Ed., Ortsverweltung Pforzheim-Würm No. 38.
12. Amann, Alois (1992), Hohenwarter Heimatbrief, No. 14, Pforzheim-Hohenwart.
13. Milton, G. (2011), *Wolfram*, 266–8.
14. Diary, Hildegard Frei, via Thomas Frei.
15. Interview with Doris Weber and Sigrid Kern, November 2013.
16. Diary, Hildegard Frei, via Thomas Frei.
17. Milton, G. (2011), *Wolfram*, 269–73.
18. Interview with Gerd Fleig, July 2013.
19. Diary, Hildegard Frei, via Thomas Frei.
20. Milton, G. (2011), *Wolfram*, 266–75.
21. Ibid., 276–7
22. Interview with Hans Ade, November 2013.
23. Diary, Hildegard Frei, via Thomas Frei.
24. Riblet-Buchmann, R. (1993), *Unerwartete Begegnung – Als junger 'Fremdarbeiter' in Pforzheim 1944/45.*
25. Interview with Christian Groh, April 2013.
26. Interview with Gerd Fleig, July 2013.
27. Interview with Dieter Essig, April 2013.
28. *Pforzheimer Zeitung*, 23 February 2005.
29. Interview with Hans Gerstung, April 2013.
30. Documents/interview with Marianne Pross, September 2013.
31. Interview with Hans Gerstung, April 2013.
32. Milton, G. (2011), *Wolfram*, 304–5.
33. Interview with Hans Gerstung, April 2013.
34. Interview with Hans Ade, November 2013.
35. Documents/interview with Marianne Pross, September 2013.
36. Interview with Christian Groh, April 2013.
37. Milton, G. (2011), *Wolfram*, 304–5.
38. Interview with Dieter Essig, April 2013.
39. Documents/interview with Marianne Pross, September 2013.
40. Pross, M. (1995), *Die Einschläge kommen näher, Aus den Tagebüchern 1943–45 von Friedrich Adolf Katz, 1945–1947 Oberbürgermeister der Stadt Pforzheim.*
41. Interview with Ron Germain, April 2013.
42. Interview with Frank Woodley, March 2013.
43. Interview with Sam Lipfriend, March 2013.
44. Interview with Bill Thomas, June 2013.
45. Interview with Raimund Frei, July 2013.
46. Interview with Dieter Essig, April 2013.
47. Interview with Ellen Eberle, November 2013.
48. Interview with Hans Gerstung, April 2013.
49. Documents/interview with Marianne Pross, September 2013.
50. Interview with Hans Gerstung, April 2013.
51. Interview with Doris Weber and Sigrid Kern, November 2013.
52. Interview with Gerd Fleig, July 2013.
53. Interviews with Werner Baroni, 2013.
54. Interviews with Irma Baroni, 2013.

Chapter Seventeen

The Phoenix

Pforzheim's ruined inner area remained sealed off long after the occupation began. The area of greatest devastation was out of bounds for several years. The first plans for reconstruction were put forward in 1948. Former Stadtarchiv director Christian Groh: 'The decision to reconstruct Pforzheim as it appears today was taken in 1951. The pre-bombing street plan was followed where sufficient fabric remained on the ground, but some streets disappeared and others were created. The new city arose – built with the car very much in mind. Flats and large apartment blocks dominate. The population of Pforzheim in 1939 was around 70,000. Post-February 1945, the population had fallen to 46,000. The figure today is 122,000, although this is misleading, as it includes outlying communities which came within the city boundaries following administrative reorganization in the 1970s.

'During the early months of American occupation rules against fraternization were relaxed. People with memories of the late 1940s and early 1950s have only good things to say about the Americans. Cultural life in the city made a slow but steady recovery.

Desolation: a view of the Marktplatz and Stadtkirche, *c.*1950. *Photo: Stadtarchiv Pforzheim.*

Transformation: the Marktplatz and Stadtkirche in 1959. *Photo: Stadtarchiv Pforzheim.*

Milestone: Pforzheim's new town hall opened in 1972. *Photo: Tony Redding.*

Pforzheim's theatre reopened in the spring of 1946. It was housed in a school, as the theatre building had been destroyed. Political life began in the late 1940s with the first local elections. Over the years, the reopening of bridges and the reconstruction of major public buildings marked additional progress. The completion of the new town hall in 1972 was a significant milestone.'[1]

The early years were tough and Pforzheim Oberbürgermeister Adolf Katz felt the weight of responsibility. In his 7 August 1945 speech to the first meeting of the city council, he concluded: 'For twelve years the people have been silenced. The city council had lost all significance. Today, it is the place where the population gets a chance to speak about their needs …' He said it was the council's job to inform the people and teach them to participate, accustom them to responsibility 'and prepare them so that they can assume full sovereignty and full responsibility again'.[2]

In these early weeks of American occupation, Katz acknowledged a major obstacle: the 'cleansing of the city administration and industrial companies of Nazi elements' had still to be achieved. 'This will have to take place as soon as possible, because the uncertainty weighing on many has a paralysing effect on the course of the administration.'[2]

Katz knew what he was talking about. He had to live with that uncertainty for several years. He continued as the appointed Oberbürgermeister, ran for election to his own office on 12 July 1946, and won. He continued in post until 1947, when he left – frustrated at a stream of allegations about his supposed Nazi connections. His reasons for leaving public office were complex but the essential fact was that his decision to join Stahlhelm, taken so long ago and which, by default, led to membership of the SA, came back to haunt him. He went as far as to request a public hearing to clear the air. These proceedings closed with Katz classified as an 'exonerated person'.[3]

It was time for former naval cadet Werner Baroni to find work other than shifting rubble: 'In 1946 I applied for a job on a local newspaper. It was at Hohenzollernstrasse 42. I went to see the city editor and he took me on. It wasn't glamorous. I had to get on my bike and deliver newspapers to Pforzheim's outlying villages. I did this for six months, became bored and left. Later, I went to work for the *Süddeutsche Allgemeine*, published by the Military Government, with Pforzheim Oberbürgermeister Dr Brandenburg [Adolf Katz's successor] as co-publisher. I was a greenhorn reporter with a two-year contract. One of my first stories was a court case involving the young son of a jewellery businessman. The boy had been involved in dirty dealings and was sentenced to four years. The father offered me 1,000 Reichsmark to leave his name out of the story. I refused, explaining that perpetrators in all cases involving sentences of over three years had to be named. Later, I was telephoned by the editor-in-chief, who said the boy's father was in his office, making a complaint. I told my boss about the 1,000 Reichsmark and the complainant was asked to leave. I was rewarded: my salary was increased from 50 to 75 Reichsmark a month as I had refused the bribe.'[4]

Wasteland: the scene on Barfuessergasse. *Photo: Stadtarchiv Pforzheim.*

Baroni's job brought him into contact with the Military Government: 'The military governor, Major Lascoe, was an outstanding character. He was from Chicago. I remember him declaring: "We need roofs on the houses in Pforzheim". He and his Military Government colleagues, together with Dr Brandenburg, did a tremendous job sorting things out.'[4]

It took three years to clear the worst of the rubble. It was used to increase the height of a natural hill which became known as Wallberg (a *trümmerberg* – rubble mountain). Much of old Pforzheim was dumped on the Wallberg and across a large area of the Brötzinger Valley set aside for debris. The Wallberg monument to the dead of 23 February 1945 was dedicated in 2005, on the sixtieth anniversary of the raid.

The cleared sites in town were soon occupied by timber shacks, allowing businesses to reopen. By 1948 some of Pforzheim's larger companies were rebuilding their premises. Private individuals began to rebuild their homes with financial assistance under a programme funded by the American Marshall Plan. Gradually, the grip of American occupation eased. In 1949 the Western Allies devolved some powers and Konrad Adenauer became the first Chancellor of the Federal Republic.[5]

Relations between Americans and occupied were not entirely harmonious early on. According to Milton, Pforzheimers were seen to be submerged in apathy. In one call for volunteers to help clear the ruins, only 800 men responded. Conditional access to food cards soon dealt with the labour shortage. Teams worked day after day to recover human remains and reduce the risk of disease. Work continued to improve electricity supply and the gasworks began to function. Telephone lines were laid and schools began to reopen on an improvised basis. The Rodi family's dining room now served as a classroom.[6] The shortage of male rubble workers reflects the fact that most able-bodied men were still in captivity. Women and children, therefore, cleared the rubble and cleaned bricks for re-use. Hans Gerstung was a teenager: 'Usually, the rubble clearers were required to work several times a week. Orders were spread by word of mouth: "Tomorrow it's our turn." No-one could take materials like timber and bricks out of Pforzheim. Everything was needed for reconstruction and building materials were very scarce. Gigantic machines were built to crush rubble and mix it with concrete. This material was used to rebuild the city.'[7]

The Gerstungs attended the first memorial service: 'We had lost Aunt Anna and Uncle Richard and, like all the other survivors, we wanted to attend. I don't remember much about it. Most of the mass graves had been closed, but there were still open graves, for the bodies found during rubble clearance.'[7]

Adolf Katz faced his first big challenge as Oberbürgermeister when the Military Government endorsed a provisional constitution for Pforzheim and agreed to the re-establishment of the city council. Elections were still some time away, so Katz chose councillors from anti-fascist political circles. He named twenty-two men, from factory owners to doctors, lawyers and pensioners. His first proclamation as

City of grief: the scene at the graves on 23 February 1946 – one year after the attack. *Photo: Stadtarchiv Pforzheim.*

A tough job: Oberbürgermeister Adolf Katz gives an interview. *Photo: Stadtarchiv Pforzheim.*

Heading for home: an amputee and his CARE package. *Photo: Stadtarchiv Pforzheim.*

Oberbürgermeister, dated 7 August 1945, reflects the tenor of his speech to the city council's inaugural session. It captures the flavour of the times and carries a blunt heading: 'The reconstruction begins – Cooperate!' It opened: 'Our city has been fearfully affected by the war. The number of deaths was unusually large. Our homes are destroyed. But the rule of National Socialism is now broken. The intellectual and physical suppression of our people has come to an end. In the clearer air that is ours, we will breathe more freely. We stand on ruins, that is true, but we live! Therefore, to work and reconstruct! We can, indeed, attain only a modest life, but a decent and, therefore, happier one.'[8]

Katz addressed three core issues: reconstruction, accommodation and food. He called for 'the cooperation of all the people' to tackle the most urgent work – the clearing of thoroughfares, the reconstruction of bridges and the rebuilding of factories and homes. He called it the 'Start Programme'. Every man, from 15 to 50, was required to devote six weeks to rubble clearance. Katz talked about 'volunteering' but his proclamation left no doubt about the alternative: 'whoever does not help now, and attempts to avoid his natural duty, can have no right to a home, food or employment in our city, neither now nor later'.[8]

As for accommodation, he added: 'The need for homes in our city is steadily increasing. Every day, former soldiers and concentration camp prisoners return, who, naturally, must find somewhere to live in their home town or at least in the surrounding country districts. And, lastly, Pforzheim families who found refuge from the air raids in other parts of our country are being expelled and are coming back.' He added that it would take time to relieve the situation: 'Therefore, the city administration is forced to take emergency measures which will, indeed, be hard in the face of the present state of distress, but will surely find the required understanding.' Here, the proclamation fell short of explaining exactly what 'emergency measures' would involve.[8]

Turning to the vital subject of nutrition, Katz pointed to progress: 'It was possible to improve considerably the insufficient allocations of the last months. In particular, the rations of bread and meat were brought to a more bearable level. The efforts to bring other important foods to a more satisfactory level continues.' The Oberbürgermeister declared: 'Our goal, which is supported by the Military Government, is to raise food supplies in our city to the general norms of the American Zone of Occupation ...'[8]

Katz turned to the acute shortage of basic equipment for living, such as pots and pans, clothing and furniture. He said great efforts were being made to provide the essentials, albeit at a modest level. He even found space in this first proclamation to offer a few words on cultural life. He said this 'can arise but slowly from the ruins'. He continued: 'There is a shortage of books and reading material. We therefore call upon everyone to voluntarily give suitable books and music, which will be assembled at a circulating library.'[8] Presumably, 'suitable books' meant books free of Nazi taint. In reading these words, some Pforzheimers might have cast their minds back to that evening in 1933, when the Hitler Jugend made a pyre of what was then considered unsuitable literature.

In conclusion, Katz identified the clear priority: 'to alleviate the distress of the many who have lost everything'. He called on survivors to help by 'voluntary emergency aid action to supply those possessing little or nothing with the most essential articles of furniture, clothing, shoes, etc. We hope to gain the support of other cities, too. Above all, the citizens of our city must really participate in this action. The results must reflect the depths of the distress.' His parting sentence linked community service with new values. He said participation 'will be a touchstone of your worth ...'.[8]

The essentials of life: a CARE package is handed over to a family. *Photo: Stadtarchiv Pforzheim.*

A sense of the hardships of life in early post-war Pforzheim is conveyed by Raimund Frei's experiences. He and another Afrika Korps veteran were released by the Americans in 1946. They crossed the Atlantic in a Liberty ship, landed at Le Havre and travelled on by train. They continued to Pforzheim as free men: 'I knew by then that my father and sister were dead. The girl in Frankfurt had checked with the local authorities. My family was now in a mass grave. Our house and the shop were gone – just rubble. Only the cellar was intact. I took up residence in the kitchen of my friend's grandmother. I had to go to the town hall to register and get food ration cards. They refused me. I was told I could stay in Pforzheim only if I had a family and a room. I explained that my family and the house were gone. They just told me to find somewhere else to live. I said I had a bed in a friend's kitchen, but that wasn't good enough. All they offered were "travelling cards" for one month, allowing people on the move to draw rations for their journey.

'Someone who knew my parents told me what had happened in our cellar on the night of the bombing. People were trapped in neighbouring cellars and, since our cellar had not collapsed, they knocked through. Unfortunately, all they found were dead bodies. He added that our belongings, which had been stored in the cellar, had been removed to a distribution point at Dillweissenstein, where they were given to locals.

'A boy from the neighbourhood, who had been wounded and was in a military hospital near Pforzheim at the time, looked for his grandmother after the attack. With the help of some soldiers he broke open an air-raid shelter that she and my parents often used. He told me that everyone, more than a hundred people, had died from lack of oxygen.'[9]

Raimund Frei had to find work if he was to stay in Pforzheim. He went to Karlsruhe to report to the Forestry Administration. To his great good fortune, he was told that a forest ranger was needed for Pforzheim. He began work on 1 October 1946. With his new job he had food and other cards, together with the right to continue to live in the city. How did he find the strength to carry on, having lost everything? 'That's a question I have often asked myself. I suppose I carried on by keeping busy. I had to get food. I had to fix up somewhere to live and take care of personal matters. I travelled to Allgäu, to see whether my father had stored any of our belongings with his relatives.'⁹ Raimund's job was demanding, but the unspoilt forest provided a shelter from loneliness: 'The forest became my second home. Since I lived in Brötzingen I rarely went into Pforzheim. There was no reason to. Only the forest was unchanged – the way I remembered it before the war.'⁹

Frei soon discovered that he was not alone. Families who had been close friends of his parents gave him help and support. 'Most of all, I owe special thanks to the family of my wartime comrade for taking me in, despite the already cramped conditions.'⁹

In January 1947 a future began to unfold for the former prisoner of war. Raimund Frei met his future wife, Hildegard, who lived at her parents' house in Eutingen. Following his engagement to Hildegard, Frei moved into the house. He lives there to this day.

On one occasion Max Weber was playing the piano by an open window when an American soldier passing by stopped and rang the bell. He wanted to meet the person responsible for such beautiful music. Doris Weber: 'He was a black guy. I couldn't stop looking at his hair. I asked him if I could touch it. He smiled and said "OK". He then went to the piano and played jazz, stomping his feet to the beat.'¹⁰

Towards the end of the war Max Weber had been told by the Nazis to stop playing the organ in church. He refused and was punished by being sent to work on the fortifications in Alsace. He was accompanied by his friend, Erwin Aichele, a Freemason. Weber's daughter, Sigrid Kern: 'Father could see his friend was suffering. Erwin Aichele became depressed and Father worried that he might become suicidal. It was at this point that Father had an opportunity to return home, but he gave his place to Mr Aichele, who never forgot that. He vouched for my father at his de-Nazification hearing, as did a number of French POWs, family members and friends.'¹⁰

Nevertheless, Max Weber ran into difficulties. Sigrid: 'One day he had to report to the town hall. He never came back. Instead, he was taken to Ludwigsburg. As he was leaving Eutingen he scribbled a message and threw it out of the jeep, towards a couple we knew. That's how we found out he had been taken into custody; his links with the Party were being investigated. He was imprisoned at Ludwigsburg and Ulm for a year. We were allowed to send him packages; he passed the time by carving a set of chess figures.'¹⁰

The Weber family lived hand to mouth. Sigrid Kern: 'My mother was a capable woman. She made enough from sewing, working in the fields and general trading to keep things going. It was very hard to live on food ration cards alone. Only people in work got food coupons and I had lost my job. I took up art lessons with Mr Aichele. He now headed a basement art school – only the cellars of the Kunstgewerbschule were left intact. I discovered a talent for drawing and design and decided to work in that field. I spent a year with Mr Aichele. I wanted to go to the Academy of Art in Munich, but there was no money.' With the war over and the Americans in town, Sigrid began to live as a teenager: 'I loved dance music and took dancing lessons. Things slowly improved. Father had returned with permission to work again as a teacher, albeit on the lowest grade. Nevertheless, he was earning once more.'[10]

Sigrid's sister felt differently. Doris Weber: 'I wasn't having a good time. My school had been destroyed. I now had to go to school in Brötzingen. That meant a 6km walk. Later, tram services were restored. We received lessons in a former elementary school. Life was poor but we were not starving as such – we were fed at school.' Sigrid also started her day with a long, cold walk during the winter. 'In the first year of my apprenticeship I had to walk to town and that meant setting out before breakfast. I often arrived cold, wet and hungry.'[10]

Pforzheim's ruins posed a threat to life. The demolition of gutted buildings, too far gone for repair, progressed slowly. On 19 September 1945, Oberbürgermeister Katz requested explosives for more blasting operations. Naturally, he was aware of the sensitivities – the city ruins were, in effect, a gigantic cemetery. He indented for 1 ton of explosives, together with fuses and ignition cord. The main priority was to remove bridge debris in the river channels before winter. In his covering letter to the Military Government, Katz warned: 'If blasting cannot be done very quickly, there will be a danger of a flood catastrophe and, as a consequence of the many dead bodies buried in the ruins, a danger of contagious illness and epidemic disease. Moreover, it is necessary to level the many houses in danger of collapsing. If this is not done before the beginning of the cold and wet season, they will fall owing to the effects of weather and pose a great danger to passing traffic and pedestrians.'[11]

A couple of weeks later, on 10 October, Katz sent a polite reminder to the Military Government. He renewed his request for explosives and also took the opportunity to repeat his 2 October request for acetylene equipment, to cut up bridge wreckage and clear the river channels.[11] As if to reinforce this call to action, a report from the Pforzheim Police (Sedan District) on 26 October 1945 noted that walls had collapsed during a violent storm and damaged a passing American jeep.

On 2 November 1945, Pforzheim's demolition master Schwarz listed his programme of blasting work for the five days to 10 November. This was sent to the Military Government following approval by the 'Buildings Police'. It included properties in Westliche Karl-Friedrich-Strasse, Calwerstrasse, Lindenstrasse and Wörthstrasse, together with three bridge sites: Würmbrücke, Rossbrücke and Altstädterbrücke. The following round of blasting was in Bleichstrasse, Hohlstrasse, Dillsteinerstrasse, Ebersteinstrasse and Mackensenstrasse. In December, the blasting locations included Leopoldstrasse, the former hospital (Holzgartenstrasse) and Lindenstrasse.[11]

The New Year opened with more demolitions at existing work sites and new clearance locations. Formal procedures were followed: newspaper notices, aimed at the owners of private property, were published in advance. The notices listed the property, the owner (if known) and the assessed extent of the damage. Owners had a right of appeal before blasting. Work proceeded in the absence of contact from the owners or a lack of intent to appeal. The occupants of nearby properties were warned to open their windows during blasting. In the first quarter work began on bombed properties at a number of fresh locations. By 13 March 1946 Oberbürgermeister Katz was asking for yet more explosives. He wanted to speed up the work by establishing a second blasting squad. [11]

Many Pforzheimers had not lost their sense of irony. In January 1946 Katz received a note recording the colourful graffiti daubed on the sides of tipper trucks carting away the rubble. They included: 'KdF' (*Kraft durch Freude* – Strength through Joy: the Nazi State's leisure organization), 'Reserved for Party Members. Where are they?'; 'Gold City Express'; and 'For Göring's state funeral'. [12]

Hans Gerstung never discovered how many of his schoolfriends died that night in February 1945: 'It was two years before I returned to school. By then, many families had moved away. As for my education, the authorities took children born in the years 1931, 1932 and 1933 as one group, performed a rudimentary academic test and merged everyone together into classes. Most kids were complete strangers to me.' [13]

When organized schooling began Hans was taught in a shack in the backyard of the bombed school in Dillweissenstein. Although two years had passed since the raid, part of his route to school still required him to clamber over rubble. 'Later on, the tram took me from Bleichstrasse, in front of the Kollmar & Jourdan building, to the school.' [13]

Dieter Essig started elementary school: 'I was already older than some and jumped straight into the second year.' Over the next ten years Essig progressed to high school and college: 'I wanted to go to university but Father said: "You choose. Either you go to university or your sister gets married. There isn't enough money to do both." That was that. At the same time, it must be said that it was rather uncommon then to go to university. I left college in 1957 and began working for the city. Most of my colleagues were former soldiers; many had been in POW camps. You could tell – there was plenty of yelling and giving of orders. The City Police, in contrast, now had a more relaxed attitude. I gave them a talk on one occasion. Before I could start, they stopped me and said: 'Sit down for a while. Let's have a drink!' Out came the schnapps. Things had changed.' [14]

The winter of 1945/6 was every bit as bad as Adolf Katz had feared. The family at Friedenstrasse got by thanks to food supplied by those of Ruth's patients living in the countryside. In some ways it was more difficult for the family when Katz became Oberbürgermeister. Marianne Pross: 'During that first winter it was impossible to survive on the official food ration. Bombed-out families foraged in the countryside, illegally trading possessions for food. We couldn't join them as father was the Oberbürgermeister. We had to set an example! Ruth solved the problem by asking some of her patients to pay in food. This period really was "the time of women". They took care of everything; they kept things running. The Nazis and the war created a wave of emancipation. Women stepped out of their traditional roles, filling jobs previously done exclusively by men. There was no choice as most men in the 20–50 age bracket were either dead or in prison camps. Only the old men and boys were left. Even today, it is a mystery to me how men managed to regain control.'[15]

The Katz family environment was far from typical, as the Oberbürgermeister received many guests at home. Marianne, now a 10-year-old, listened to their talk about National Socialism and the war years: 'I heard a lot and there were also letters from Ruth's many Jewish friends who had emigrated. As a young girl, in 1947, I even managed to read a very disturbing book about National Socialism [Eugen Kogon, *Der SS Staat*]. Yet most people remained silent on this subject for many years. Their silence reflects a sense of shame. This is why Germans took so long to come to terms with National Socialism. One of Ruth's closest friends, Anni Hermann, was the Jewish partner in a mixed marriage. She had been deported to Theresienstadt in late 1944. She told her story. Gradually, I came to know about the crimes and the deaths.'[15]

Slowly, year by year, the city recovered and its people built new lives. Reconstruction gathered pace in the early 1950s, yet the survivors continued to mourn their dead. Even so, a new spirit of hope was abroad. Hans Gerstung: 'The first small shops opened in 1946, often in the cellars of bombed buildings. The first factories opened in 1948 and currency reform gave a tremendous boost to the recovery. Things really took off in the 1950s – there was more employment and money around. Things finally looked up. The precious metals industry was up and running, as were exports. My father died in July 1948 and that was a real break with the past. It was also a heavy blow to his architectural practice, which had been responsible for some important buildings, including the Sparkasse, a number of factories and Lutheran churches in Bruchsal. Mother married again in the early 1950s, shortly after I graduated from school. My stepfather, a structural engineer, took over my father's firm until his own death, when the business was liquidated.'[16]

Gerd Fleig, his SS tattoo removed during the first weeks of occupation, went on to build a new and valuable life. He graduated in 1949 and began a career as a choirmaster and *répétiteur* at Neues Theater in Karlsruhe-Durlach and, subsequently, the Stadttheater in Pforzheim. In an unlikely twist of fate, he found that theatre rehearsals were held in an enlarged space that included what had once been Room 35 at the Hindenburg Lazarett. This is where he was, reading on his bed, when the bombers came on 23 February 1945.[17]

Gerd Fleig took over the music school from his father. This is now based at Neulingen-Göbrichen, just outside the city. In 1985 Fleig received the Bundesverdienstkreuz from President Richard von Weizsäcker, in recognition of his accomplishments as a freelance conductor of various choirs, with many guest appearances abroad.[17]

Surviving on the streets: barter was the basis of street dealing. This is Leopoldplatz in 1949. *Photo: Stadtarchiv Pforzheim.*

Teenager Bernhard Mauderer, orphaned in the big raid at the age of 13, struggled through the spring and summer of 1945. Having left his aunt and uncle's small farm, he found his new beginning in Freiburg during the late afternoon of 12 August 1945. He was asleep at the station when a man woke him and asked where he wanted to go. Bernhard then discovered the kinder face of humanity. He was taken home and given supper and a bed for the night; the next morning he set off with a packed lunch. After a lift on a truck, Mauderer was walking towards Neuenweg – to catch up with his fellow evacuees, who were now working on farms – when a jeep drove up. Three French soldiers jumped out, knocked him down, pointed a sub-machine gun at him and searched his kitbag. The boy said: 'Shoot me if you want to.' The men were German speakers from Alsace and asked why he had said that. Bernhard told them his story. 'Suddenly, they packed up my belongings, threw the bag into the jeep and told me to jump in.' He got a ride to a village inn and was treated to a meal. The landlady got talking. Her husband was a POW and she asked Bernhard to stay, but he said he had to go on to Neuenweg. 'This experience showed me that people who are enemies still have a heart.'[18]

Mauderer eventually found a home with a farming family. Anna and Theodor Senn became his foster parents. He worked with the animals and in the fields. He discovered that his sister, Rosemarie, was living with Aunt Elsa in Pforzheim. Elsa was his father's sister, and Rosemarie was treated no better than Bernhard had been at his uncle's farm. 'Somehow, my aunt managed to obtain orphan payments for my sister and kept all the money. Rosemarie was 12 years old. She had to clean the house after school, do the washing by hand and anything else that was required.' She finished school in 1947, went to work and had to hand over her earnings. One day she wrote to Bernhard, saying she could no longer stand it. Theodor and Anna said she could live at the farm, and she enjoyed life with them until eventually returning to Pforzheim to work. She married in 1951.[18]

Bernhard Mauderer, then 17, became an apprentice carpenter in 1948. He joined a company in Müllheim, was paid 56 Deutschmark per month and assumed responsibility for any damage to his tools. He and another apprentice lived in a washhouse equipped with a double bed. He had to do two hours' overtime for the use of the washhouse. Later, Mauderer worked in Basle as a foreman carpenter and he married in 1954. He and Magda had a daughter and a son. Life took a new direction in 1956, when he and Magda began running a sports club. Bernhard continued as a carpenter but studied precision engineering and became head of production at a factory. In early 1964 they got talking to a customer at the sports club restaurant, in the company of friends in South Africa who were originally from Brötzingen. Subsequently, the Mauderers decided to emigrate. The family arrived in Cape Town on 12 December 1964. Bernhard found work as a production engineer, started his own firm in 1977 and built his first factory in 1985, offering precision engineering. In 1997 the couple sold up and retired.[18]

Arno Baroni and Irma Facoltosi also enjoyed a new life in South Africa. At the war's end, with central Pforzheim completely destroyed and conventional schooling out of the question, Irma's education took a more practical direction: 'I began to take lessons in dressmaking. I learnt how to make a new dress from old clothes.' Another lesson was the importance of taking whatever work was available: 'I sold material for clothes and worked in a butcher's. I enjoyed the company – people kept each other going.' They didn't go hungry: 'We had our own garden and grew vegetables. In the summer we went into the forest to pick berries. We also traded valuables for food. We went on expeditions. We had to go 20km or more to reach the big farms with surpluses to trade. We bartered jewellery for flour, potatoes and milk. We cycled out to farms and loaded up our baskets. The big joke at that time was a question: Why do farmers need Persian carpets for their pigsties?'[19]

Irma and Arno married on 5 March 1953: 'He made a career working for Philips, the Dutch electronics group. We moved from Pforzheim and lived in several cities, including Düsseldorf and Wesel. Then Philips offered him the opportunity to develop a business in South Africa. My husband and I, together with our 11-year-old daughter, arrived in Durban on 5 January 1966. Later, Arno had the opportunity to pursue his early interest in flying. When he was very young he had built a detailed model of a Grunau Baby glider (then in widespread use for basic flying training). He flew the real thing in the Hitler Jugend. Later, in South Africa, he got his private pilot's licence and flew many different types of aircraft.'[19]

In 1956, Irma's friend, Karl Mössner, married Virginia, who was born in Pennsylvania. Her father had moved to the United States before the war because of his inability to find work in Germany. A convinced Nazi, he returned in 1938, volunteered for the Waffen SS and served as an artillery spotter and, later, as a translator.

Survivors and victims of Nazi persecution put all their energies into building new lives. Karl Schroth had been imprisoned by the National Socialists for refusing to bend to them and was later drafted into a penal battalion. He was captured and ended up in a Saharan labour camp. Schroth learnt of Pforzheim's fate in a strange way. He saw a column of tanks and other vehicles passing by, just outside the POW camp wire. Each tank seemed to carry a familiar name. These were the names of communities close to Pforzheim. He gaped as his eyes took in Kleinsteinbach, Königsbach, Bilfingen, Stein, Ersingen. He tried to attract the attention of passing motorcyclists, but to no avail. Eventually, a young soldier told him that the unit had been stalled for a time in these villages. He then told Schroth, as gently as he could, about Pforzheim: 'Your city' – spreading his arms wide – '*tout cassé, kaputt, total kaputt.*' Schroth returned to Pforzheim in August 1947, served his local community as a councillor for nine years and took an active role in workers' welfare. He was also instrumental in founding the Volksbühne Theatre.[20]

Gerhard Brändle knew Karl Schroth well: 'He was great – really impressive. A tall, strong man, he had an actor's presence. He was the only man in Pforzheim to publish a book about what happened in Pforzheim pre- and post-1933. After the end of the war, left-wing politics – like the SPD's - shifted to the right a little, producing plenty of arguments, but we reached an understanding not to discuss such matters when we were together.'[20]

Politically, Schroth had much in common with Wilhelm Künzler, a communist jailed and tortured by the Nazis. On his release from Ludwigsburg prison, on 10 April 1945, he returned to Pforzheim. The French Military Government appointed him Bürgermeister of Singen, an office he held until 1953. He became an insurance agent and was involved in the work of VVN, an organization representing victims of Nazi oppression.[20]

Max Rödelsheimer, the courageous Jewish owner of a photographers, who sat in his shop window in 1933 in protest at the activities of Nazi street thugs, died in Auschwitz. His partner later claimed compensation for the Aryanization of the business and managed to obtain something. Gerhard Brändle: 'Compensation was available after the war but the process of making a claim was very difficult. There were a few notable successes. In one case, a survivor came back from the USA and succeeded in recovering his business, a well-known store selling general goods.'[20]

Julius Moser, in a '*Mischehe*' (mixed marriage between an Aryan and a Jew), was forced out of business by the Nazis and ended the war in Theresienstadt; he was freed by the Russians. On his return to Pforzheim he founded a jewellery and watchmaking business, served as president of the Chamber of Commerce and Industry and was honoured by both the Federal Republic and the city for his distinguished service. He was made an honorary citizen of Pforzheim.[20]

Adolf Baier, who had fought with the International Brigade in Spain and was imprisoned by the Nazis, returned to Pforzheim. He was closely involved in the development of free trade unions and was the first chairman of the newly formed Metalworkers' Union. In 1952, Adolf Baier moved to East Germany. In 1963 he was imprisoned in the Federal Republic for involvement in the then banned Communist Party. He died in East Berlin in 1982.

Heinz Kappes, the former pastor exiled from Baden for his outspoken behaviour and who eventually went to Palestine, returned to Karlsruhe in 1948. He became a teacher and co-founder of the Society for Christian-Jewish Cooperation. He died in Stuttgart in 1988.[20]

Watchmaker Werner Schultz's family survived. 'One brother became a forced labourer in a Rhineland coal mine. My oldest brother, who, as a *Mischling*, had been refused permission to marry, held a senior position in a Munich watch factory. As for my sisters, one was conscripted as an apprentice at a foundry. She did well, as her boss was anti-Nazi. The other sister was drafted for factory work in Pforzheim. Again, she was lucky. Father knew the factory owner and she was well treated. My mother was left on her own; she helped out father in his workshop until he was deported.'[21]

After the war the family sought compensation for the Aryanization of the business. The Americans had a command post on Hohenzollernstrasse – ironically in a factory building owned by the brother-in-law of the Nazi who had exploited Schultz senior's import permit. 'When Father asked for compensation the Americans stalled him. It became obvious that he wouldn't get anywhere. Meanwhile, the Nazi prospered. During the war he milked the permit to purchase from Switzerland. He stashed the imported components at safe locations. After the currency reform of 1948 he had sufficient reserves to open up a very large factory.

'Father started again. He hired watchmakers who were still working on rubble clearance. This was the "time of silence". No-one talked about the war, or what Pforzheim's factories had made during the war. Even victims were silent – no-one wanted to embarrass their friends. The perpetrators, of course, were very happy with silence. Gradually, former Nazis began to spread their lies, and it was this climate that allowed some politicians to claim that Pforzheim was the most innocent city ever bombed by the Allies.'[21]

At the personal level, the sports club attempted to mend fences with the Schultz family: 'Our friends at the club asked us to rejoin. We said yes, but only on one condition. Everyone had to pretend that we never left. We were not signing any membership application forms! We never talked about what happened as we had no desire to confront our friends with such cruelties.'[21]

Notes

1. Interview with Christian Groh, April 2013.
2. Pross, M. (1995), *Die Einschläge kommen näher, Aus den Tagebüchern 1943–45 von Friedrich Adolf Katz, 1945–1947 Oberbürgermeister der Stadt Pforzheim.*
3. Badische Neueste Nachrichten, 28 August 1946.
4. Interviews with Werner Baroni, 2013.
5. Milton, G. (2011), *Wolfram*, 311–13.
6. Ibid., 306–7.
7. Interview with Hans Gerstung, April 2013.
8. Approved, No. 1. 6 August 1945, Mil. Govt. DET G2 E2, Pforzheim, Ger.
9. Interview with Raimund Frei, July 2013.
10. Interview with Doris Weber and Sigrid Kern, November 2013.
11. Various correspondence, Pforzheim City, to the US Military Government, Stadtarchiv Pforzheim.
12. Stadtarchiv Pforzheim, B1 802.
13. Interview with Hans Gerstung, April 2013.
14. Interview with Dieter Essig, April 2013.
15. Documents/interview with Marianne Pross, September 2013.
16. Interview with Hans Gerstung, April 2013.
17. Interview with Gerd Fleig, July 2013.
18. Mauderer, B., personal memoir.
19. Interviews with Irma Baroni, 2013.
20. Interviews with Gerhard Brändle, 2013.
21. Interview with Werner Schultz, November 2013.

Chapter Eighteen

Bombing Germany – Perspectives

The intention was to finish the European war by Christmas 1944, but Allied hopes were crushed by the failure at Arnhem, Germany's capacity to form a 'hard crust' defence on its western borders and the surprise winter attack that developed into the Battle of the Bulge. These factors contributed to the decision that the strategic bombing of Germany must continue and intensify if war was not to continue into late 1945. Millions of lives were at stake.

How much did strategic bombing contribute to German defeat? One answer is offered by Dudley Saward. The RAF group captain wrote: 'For Germany, the bombing offensive was disastrous, not only because of the devastation to industry, but also because it forced the Germans to divert more and more production to the needs of defence against the bombing, at the expense of the requirements for the Army's offensives on the Eastern Front, in North Africa, in the rest of the Mediterranean theatre of war and, latterly, in North West Europe.'[1] In short, Allied strategic bombing dictated how the Germans spent a significant proportion of their military capital.

Saward interviewed Nazi Armaments Minister Albert Speer, who said that bombing in 1943 resulted in a loss of 10 per cent of German armaments production (estimated at 9 per cent by the US Strategic Bombing Survey) and at least 20 per cent in 1944.[1] Some commentators argue that strategic bombing had relatively little impact on German war production. Here, Richard Overy makes the crucial point: 'The critical question is not so much "What did bombing do to Germany?", but "What could Germany have achieved if there had been no bombing?"'[2] German military power was so strong that only a long war of attrition brought Germany to the point of defeat. Round-the-clock bombing tied down human and military assets which would otherwise have filled out both front lines defending Germany, so prolonging the war.

At the end of the European war, Bomber Command had nearly 2,000 heavy aircraft and the Americans (8th and 15th USAAF) 4,850. In the final months Germany faced a force of over 6,000 four-engined bombers, of which around 70 per cent could be put into the air at any one time. Not surprisingly, 85 per cent of total bomb tonnage dropped on Germany was dropped after 1 January 1944 (72 per cent after 1 July 1944). In the final twelve months the Allies had the aircraft, navigational/bombing systems and air supremacy over Germany to do what they wanted, rather than what the German defences would allow them to do.[3]

Bomber Command's onslaught in the October 1944–April 1945 period reached an intensity which would have been regarded as pure fantasy in 1940. There were

17,562 sorties in October and 61,204 tons of bombs were dropped, with 15,008 in November (53,022 tons) and 15,333 in December (49,040 tons), despite the adverse weather. From 1 January to 30 April 1945, Bomber Command flew 54,742 sorties and dropped 181,403 tons of bombs on oil, communications and other targets.[4] This is the equivalent explosive capacity of around nine Hiroshima atomic weapons, although, of course, a significant proportion of these conventional bomb loads consisted of incendiaries, rather than high explosive bombs.

The total for the four months to 30 April included 2,647 tons on Dresden, 4,087 tons on Chemnitz (two raids) and 1,058 tons on Leipzig, bringing the total for the three major eastern city/communication targets to 7,793 tons. When the 1,825 tons is included for the western target of Pforzheim, the total of 9,617 tons still represents just 5 per cent of total tonnage dropped in the final four months. In January Bomber Command dropped 34,381 tons, followed by 45,889 tons in February, a staggering 67,637 tons in March and 33,496 tons in April. Most of this tonnage was dropped in support of the advancing armies on the Western Front.[4]

By the war's end, seventy major German cities had suffered area attack and 45 per cent of the target areas in these towns had been destroyed. Twenty-three of the cities were more than 60 per cent destroyed. It had taken just over 10 tons of bombs to destroy each acre of city. According to the British Bombing Survey Unit, around a million people became air-raid casualties, half occurring in the final year of the war. About 50 per cent of these casualties belonged to the German labour force.[5] A civilian death toll of over 600,000 has long been generally accepted, although some recent studies arrive at significantly lower figures. In any event, hundreds of thousands of civilians died.[6] Civilian air-raid deaths in Britain totalled around 60,400. In the Moonlight Sonata raid on Coventry on 14 November 1940, the German attack killed some 568 people (an exact figure was never arrived at).

The British report refers to the much larger American bombing assessment effort and adds: 'According to the enquiries of the United States Strategic Bombing Survey, some 3,600,000 dwelling units in the major German towns (about 20 per cent of all dwelling units in Germany) were destroyed or heavily damaged and some seven and a half million people rendered homeless.'[7]

The report continues: 'A variety of factors were responsible for the resumption of area attacks (following the battles in Normandy) and a large number of German towns were attacked in the period September 16 (1944) to the conclusion of the war. The tonnage expended in these attacks amounted to some 52 per cent of the overall total dropped by the Command in the seven months concerned. Some of these attacks were carried out in support of Army operations, when small towns in the immediate rear of the enemy front lines were obliterated. The question of the continued destruction of German towns was discussed at a political level at the end of March 1945, when the view was expressed that the further destruction of German cities would very likely soon prove a far greater inconvenience to the Allies than it would be to the Germans.'[7] Area bombing ceased in the first week of April.

For Churchill, strategic bombing shifted from a military imperative to a political embarrassment. Churchill had been a strong advocate of Operation Thunderclap but now, suddenly, he stepped back. On 28 March the prime minister attempted to distance himself from the bombing campaign. In a memorandum to the Chiefs of Staff, he declared: 'It seems to me that the moment has come when the question of bombing cities simply for the sake of increasing terror, though under other pretexts, should be reviewed. Otherwise we shall come into possession of an utterly ruined land ... The destruction of Dresden remains a serious query against the conduct of Allied bombing. I am of the opinion that military objectives must henceforward be more strictly studied in our own interests rather than that of the enemy.'[8]

This volte-face caused great offence. Had it been widely known, the comment about 'other pretexts' would have gone hard with young Allied infantrymen struggling to stay alive in the final weeks of the war and grateful for any help they could get from the bombers. Only a few weeks before, Churchill the war leader was calling for attacks on the eastern cities. Now Churchill the politician sought to transfer his responsibilities to Harris and Bomber Command.[8]

Portal, Chief of the Air Staff, refused to accept Churchill's note. His angry protest made the point that the Allied purpose had always been to destroy transportation and industrial facilities in German cities, rather than to terrorize civilians. He demanded the memorandum's withdrawal. Churchill responded with a new text: 'It seems to me that the moment has come when the question of the so-called area bombing of German cities should be reviewed from the point of view of our own interests. If we come into control of an entirely ruined land there will be a great shortage of accommodation for ourselves and our allies ... we must see to it that our attacks do not do more harm to ourselves in the long run than they do to the enemy's immediate war effort.'[8]

In the desperate days of July 1940, with the invasion of Britain and total defeat a real prospect, Churchill had the vision to recognize that Nazi Germany could be brought down by 'an absolutely devastating, exterminating attack by very heavy bombers on the Nazi homeland'. The fact that German defeat was not realized by bombing alone relates solely to a lack of means. It was certainly achieved a few months later, in the skies over Japan.[8] As for area bombing, for most of the war Bomber Command had to operate at night and it lacked the technologies required for precision bombing. The choice was between making the entire city the target – area bombing – or surrendering Britain's only means of offensive warfare. As John Terraine put it, in the context of total war this 'meant no choice at all'.[9] In any event, with Bomber Command's war virtually over, Portal told the Chiefs of Staff on 4 April 1945: 'it is recognized that, at this advanced stage of the war, no great or immediate additional advantage can be expected from the attack on the remaining industrial centres of Germany, because it is improbable that the full effects of further area attacks upon the enemy's war industries will have time to mature before hostilities cease'.[10]

In essence, Churchill did not rule out further area attacks, if required to assist the Allied advance into Germany, but was saying that area bombing purely for destroying or disorganizing industrial areas should be discontinued.

Given the scale of destruction visited upon German cities, it is difficult to see how anyone can seriously suggest that area bombing had only modest effects on German industry. As Neillands points out: 'Even if the production of tanks, guns and aircraft proceeded unabated, what heights that production would have reached *without* the bombing of Germany can only be wondered at.'[11]

Neillands has some interesting observations about bombing and morality. Later in 1945 the atomic bombing forced a Japanese surrender: 'The belief that strategic bombing could end wars without a land campaign, therefore, has some basis in fact and, it could be argued, a moral dimension. If bombing could bring the war to an end without a land campaign and a great expenditure in lives, then the attempt to bomb Germany into surrender had a certain moral validity. Finally, there was a war on. Moral arguments which overlook, dismiss or devalue that point are fundamentally flawed.'[11]

A land campaign was required to defeat Germany, but there is no sound basis for claiming that strategic bombing did not shorten the war. It must be remembered that many thousands of people were dying every day and continued to do so until the very end of the war (and for some time thereafter). No moral argument should lose sight of this fact and the overriding imperative: ending the war as quickly as possible. This objective also served the interests of the German people, as the country continued its descent into chaos.

The definition of 'war crimes' applied at Nuremberg included 'wanton destruction of cities, towns or villages, or devastation not justified by military necessity'. Here, Neillands has a clear view on Dresden: 'The order to attack Dresden was not illegal. There were cogent reasons for bombing Dresden and, though hindsight indicates that it probably was an unnecessary operation, that was not the opinion at the time.'[12] No-one knew when Germany would surrender. The Nazi propaganda machine was active to the last and there was always the possibility that, even at five minutes to twelve, Hitler had an ace to play. Would he be tempted, in desperation, to use radiological weapons or nerve gas? Furthermore, German resistance was still potent in the final months. During the January–April 1945 period, for example, Bomber Command lost 590 aircraft - representing around one-third of its maximum operating strength.[13]

It seems to the author that a viable military case can be made for the late attacks on the eastern cities, *given the perspectives and priorities of that time*. Much the same can be said of the attack on Pforzheim, on the military grounds that the city was in the path of the advancing armies, was a communications target and had a considerable concentration of war materiel in its marshalling yards. There may be a parallel to Dresden, in that the destruction of Pforzheim may have made only a modest contribution to the swift occupation of Germany, but this view benefits from hindsight, rather than perceptions at the time. The Pforzheim attack was one of many designed to bring the war to an end as quickly as possible. Indeed, it would appear that Pforzheim's significance as a major producer of precision components for ordnance, especially fuses, would have justified a heavy air attack in 1944 – certainly following the resumption of the city attacks in September. The city's war production had less significance by late February 1945, as this could have little impact in the final weeks of fighting. According to Adolf Katz's diary, recent production could not be moved from the marshalling yards: it was stuck there owing to constant fighter-bomber attacks on the local rail network. This stalled rail traffic, of course, made Pforzheim an even more inviting target.

The Second World War was a total war. Harris was one of many senior Allied commanders charged with achieving victory. It is pointless to criticize him for pursuing this aim with all means at his disposal. According to Neillands: 'The harshest criticism that can be seriously maintained is that Harris could have done more to attack oil targets from September 1944. Not to do so was a mistake, but Harris is not accused of making mistakes. He is accused of being a monster, even in some circles a war criminal, but there is no basis for the charge. While he was not without faults, Harris was a fine and resolute commander, the right man in the right place to fight and win his corner of the war.'[14]

Equally, there is the view that, given two world wars and the bestial nature of Nazi rule, Allied political and military leaders felt that, 'this time', the German people needed a very harsh lesson on the price of war. Some might even argue that this, in itself, was a legitimate war aim. Certainly, no effort was made to disguise such views at the time. For example, the United States Strategic Bombing Survey report reflected that the bombing of Germany had 'brought home to the German people the full impact of modern war, with all its horror and suffering. Its imprint on the German nation will be lasting.' Few would dispute that this has been the case over the past seventy years. Neillands concludes: 'The bomber offensive of 1939–45 finally brought war home to Germany ... If the price of European peace and a final freedom from chronic German militarism was the physical destruction of Germany, many may argue that the price was well worth paying.'[15]

The bombing 'whirlwind' was delivered in the final four months. Harris believed the European war could be ended by conventional bombing, followed by unopposed occupation. Albert Speer had worried that this might come about and warned Hitler. Commenting on the destruction of Hamburg in 1943, the former Reichsminister told Dudley Saward decades later: 'attacks like that on six such towns and we would have been finished'.[16] At that time, Harris was not in a position to turn that threat into reality. He lacked the means to produce another six Hamburgs. Bomber Command's *Review of Operations* stated: 'This was at a time when the striking power and effectiveness of Bomber Command was still progressing and was far from attaining maturity. Had the striking power, aids and weapons of 1945 been available then, the effectiveness of the force would undoubtedly have ended the German war as abruptly as the Japanese war was ended by concentrated and overwhelming bombing, without need of contested invasion by armed forces.'[17] Had its mature power been available in mid-1943, Bomber Command might now be recognized as the key instrument in a swift end to the European war, with many millions of lives saved.

As it was, Bomber Command's war became one of attrition. More than the cities, the oil campaign was of central importance in the final months. Bomber Command's end of war report comments: 'the combined bomber offensive against oil targets resulted in practically the whole industry being immobilised by the beginning of April'.[17] A total of forty-two German synthetic oil plants and refineries were attacked. Bomber Command and the Eighth USAAF dropped a total of 109,291 tons of bombs on these targets, which were of critical importance to the German Air Force and the Wehrmacht's armoured units.

A review of the distribution of Bomber Command's effort in the January–May 1945 period is instructive. Oil targets received 26.2 per cent (47,510 tons) but cities received 36.6 per cent (66,482 tons). Oil targets received 9,028 tons in January, 14,109 tons in February, 18,936 tons in March and 5,432 tons in April, when the oil campaign ended. As for the cities, they received 11,931 tons in January, but this doubled to 21,888 tons in February and continued to rise, to a total of 30,278 tons in March, before falling back to just 2,322 tons in April, when city bombing virtually ceased.[17]

There was a rather different pattern to attacks on troops and defences. Not surprisingly, the bomb tonnage increased through to the end of April: 2,072 tons in January, 3,756 tons in February, 8,042 tons in March and 12,056 tons in April. Troops and defences received 26,081 tons, or 14.4 per cent of all tonnage dropped in the January-May period. Transportation targets received a little more (28,102 tons; 15.4 per cent).[17]

Bomber Command's *Review of Operations* commented: 'By the end of 1944, 45 of the 57 German towns with a pre-war population of 100,000 or more had been either virtually destroyed or heavily damaged by Bomber Command attacks. During the last few months of the war, in 1945, new targets were attacked and old ones further disintegrated. The Ruhr and Rhineland cities were finally wrecked …'[17]

In an echo of the situation in the summer of 1940, when Luftwaffe bombers occupied French airfields just across the Channel from England, hostile air power was now Germany's unwelcome near-neighbour. The bombers may have stayed in England but their radar and navigational systems moved forward, together with the escort fighters.[17]

The *Review* added: 'The bombing of industrial towns augmented the critically serious effects of the attack on specific railway and communication targets. They intensified the confusion of transportation and disrupted the remaining cohesion of the German war effort. At the same time, they had a most serious effect on the German will to continue the war. It was with the object of impressing the enemy with the futility of continued resistance and to demonstrate the virtually unchallenged and overwhelming air superiority possessed by the Allies that the decision was made to devastate the densely populated Ruhr. The remaining undamaged areas in this great concentration of enemy and military resources were, therefore, subjected to very heavy attacks in the closing months of 1944 and these were renewed during the period under review (January–May, 1945).

'The climax came on the days of 11th and 12th March. Between 14.55 hours on 11th March and 17.07 hours on 12th March, a period of 26 hours and 12 minutes, a total of 9,513 tons of bombs was dropped on Essen and Dortmund. As a consequence, both towns suffered damage that finally destroyed them beyond hope of recovery. As the overall weight of the attacks increased, so, too, did the accuracy and concentration. Densities of over 200 tons per square mile were achieved.' In a remark pertinent to the destruction of Pforzheim, it added: 'The effect of heavy attacks, such as the Command was able to deliver in the early months of 1945, was all the more effective and demoralising when it fell upon towns that had hitherto been spared from bombing.' Here, then, is another reason (among many others) for the Pforzheim raid: the city was attacked because it was still intact. Dresden was the largest of the intact cities: 'Apart from its industrial significance, Dresden had become of great importance as a communications centre and control point in the defence of Germany's Eastern Front. The effect, not only on the local population but on the whole nation, is known to have been very great.'[17] Speer himself said the impact was comparable to that of the Hamburg attack of 1943.

Finally, in early 1945, Bomber Command had the power to produce six Hamburgs in quick succession, but by this time all the main cities, with the exception of Dresden, were already in ruins. This destruction had been a largely incremental process, beyond those targets such as Dresden and Pforzheim, which were subjected to a single, catastrophic onslaught. The opportunity to produce a strategic bombing shock so severe as to trigger total collapse and thus bring about an early end to the European war (as Speer had feared in 1943) had long past. The war continued for another two years and ground Germany's cities to rubble. Those towns more than 60 per cent destroyed included Pforzheim. Eighty-three per cent of its built-up area was destroyed – a figure exceeded only by Würzburg (89 per cent) and Wuppertal/ Elberfeld (94 per cent). According to the Bomber Command *Review*, 304 acres of Pforzheim were destroyed. The surveys also found that 83 per cent of Bochum and Remscheid was destroyed. Pforzheim is small compared with Hamburg, where 6,200 acres were destroyed, representing 75 per cent of the built-up area. The figure for Dresden was 1,681 acres (59 per cent).[17]

In October 1944 Roosevelt approved plans for an American evaluation of the strategic bombing of Germany. The president of Prudential Insurance Company headed the US Strategic Bombing Survey. He received the rank of general and was given immense resources, including access to specialists across all key industries. The size of the effort matched the extent of the brief: to study the effects of bombing on oil targets, railways, canals, bridges, viaducts, aircraft and aero-engine plants, U-boat and other naval construction yards, tank manufacturing facilities, V-weapons targets, munitions factories, dams, chemical works, ball-bearing manufacture, airfields, underground plants and, of course, the cities. The US Strategic Bombing Survey employed over 1,000 people and its field elements began moving into Germany in March 1945, as the Allies crossed the Rhine. It produced 208 reports on the European bombing war.[18]

The British effort was on a far more modest scale. Proposals for a substantial survey were rejected by Churchill, almost certainly with political considerations in mind. The first proposals called for an eighteen-month study involving military experts and specialists from the Ministry of Economic Warfare and other bodies. The plan was scaled back to a study by a small team of twenty to thirty, but even this became stalled in committee. The Royal Air Force finally got on with it, funding the work from its own resources. The British Bombing Survey Unit, chaired by Air Commodore Pelly, began work in late May 1945.[18] The unit concluded that disruption of transportation was the biggest single contributor to the collapse of Nazi Germany, with the area campaign and attacks on oil targets making lesser contributions. On the role of the bombers in achieving final victory, the report concluded: 'three major factors were associated in Germany's defeat. The first and most obvious was the overrunning of her territory by the armies of the Allies. The second was the breakdown of her war industry, which was mainly a consequence of the bombing of her communications systems. The third was the drying-up of her resources of liquid fuel and the disruption of the chemical industry, which resulted from the bombing of synthetic oil plants and refineries.'[19]

The single most important commentator on strategic bombing results was Albert Speer, Hitler's armaments minister: 'The real importance of the air war consisted of the fact that it opened a Second Front long before the invasion of Europe. That front was in the skies over Germany. The fleets of bombers might appear at any time over any large German city or important factory. This front was gigantic. Every square metre of our territory became a front line. Defence against air attacks required the production of thousands of anti-aircraft guns, the stockpiling of tremendous quantities of ammunition all over the country and the holding in readiness of hundreds of thousands of soldiers, who had to stay in position by their guns, totally inactive, often for months at a time.'[20]

The Germans were forced to deploy many thousands of 88mm guns – the war's most effective anti-tank weapon – in the anti-aircraft role, together with just over a million military personnel. Here, the British Bombing Survey Unit commented: 'United States observers calculate that the strength of the artillery provided for the German armies might have been almost doubled if it had not been thought necessary to produce anti-aircraft guns for the defence of the home front against air attack'.[21] In the crucial year of 1944, defending Germany against heavy bombers required 30 per cent of all artillery produced, 20 per cent of heavy shells, 33 per cent of the optical industry's production of sights and 50 per cent of Germany's entire electro-technical output.[22] Around 2.3 million men were engaged in building shelters, clearing debris, repairing houses and factories and restoring services. Had these assets been available for deployment elsewhere, the progress of the war may have been changed – and not necessarily in Germany's favour. In the absence of the bombers, the D-Day landings and subsequent breakout may have been paralysed or even defeated by 88mm gun screens and more men on the ground in the front line. Had D-Day failed, a second attempt would have been unlikely before 1946. Yet the Allies had a 'Germany First' policy and atomic weapons became available in the late summer of 1945. Without a large-scale conventional bombing campaign, it is entirely possible that the first use of atomic weapons might have been against German cities, rather than Hiroshima and Nagasaki.

Around 5 million Germans were evacuated from the cities. It must be said that the German civilian population withstood Bomber Command's whirlwind with great courage and resolution. As Neillands observed: 'Certainly, the bombing depressed the civilian population and worried their menfolk at the front, but there is little evidence that it ever seriously damaged the German will to fight on. The Germans defended their cities under Allied air attack in much the same way that the British had done during the Blitz in 1940–41, and with equal courage and tenacity. The British Government's long-held belief that the Germans would be less resolute and that their morale would crumble under continual air attack proved quite unfounded.'[23] This is freely acknowledged in the reports of the British Bombing Survey Unit.

German war factories were dispersed and kept producing, but two important points are often overlooked. Firstly, as Richards and others emphasize, the central issue is to compare what the Germans *actually* produced against what they *planned* to produce. Secondly, the lion's share of increased German armaments production had to be devoted to air defence, primarily fighters and flak guns.[24]

The primary benefit of the bombing offensive was the opening of a Second Front in the air, which went on to assist and support the Second Front on the ground. This was the key to Allied targeting policy. After the support period for Normandy and the campaign against V-weapon sites, the bombers returned to the cities, but generally only when other, priority, targets were not being raided. In the period March 1943–March 1944, around 85 per cent of the bombing effort was directed against cities, but this fell to 30 per cent for the rest of the war.[25]

Bomber Command cut back frontline German armaments deployment, denying guns and men which would have made the Wehrmacht even harder to defeat. The bombers supported the Allies' great land offensives in West and East. Strategic bombing was a cost-effective way for Britain to wage war on such a powerful continental enemy. The fundamental British aim was to build and deploy a huge fleet of heavy bombers. This was achieved at an initial cost of around 7 per cent of Britain's total war effort.[26] This increased, in the final thirty months of the war, to around 12 per cent. This was a cost-effective Second Front in the air. The core investment was the Lancaster bomber. A total of 107 Lancasters were available for operations in January 1942, rising to 627 in January 1944 and 1,096 in January 1945. By 8 May 1945, there were 1,320 Lancasters with the squadrons.[27] Bomber Command would have grown even larger but for the fact that substantial resources were required to build up British land forces, to the point where they were capable of large-scale operations on the Continent from mid-1944 onwards. This cost around eight times more – in terms of manpower – than Bomber Command. Even so, the total manpower cost of British strategic bombing is estimated at 3 million man-years.[28]

Bomber Command flew 387,416 sorties and lost 8,953 aircraft (2.3 per cent). Around 125,000 aircrew served with Bomber Command (some 93,000 were British and most of the rest were Canadians, Australians and New Zealanders); 47,130 were killed on operations. A further 8,305 aircrew died in non-operational circumstances. A total of 10,838 British bomber aircrew became POWs, of whom 138 died in captivity. There are minor variations in statistics, from source to source. Neillands estimated the loss rate at 51 per cent: 'This was the highest casualty rate of any of the British Empire armed forces in the Second World War.'[29] The figures for Germany's U-boat arm (also active for the entire war period) offer a comparison. A total of 40,900 men served in U-boats and 25,870 were killed.[30]

Bomber Command's aircraft loss rate averaged 5 per cent during some periods of the war. The chance of a man completing a first tour (typically thirty operations) was as low as one in five during Bomber Command's 'black periods', when the pendulum of the long war with the German defences swung in the enemy's favour. This meant that perhaps twenty of every hundred aircrew starting a first tour of thirty ops would finish. At the end of the second tour of twenty operations, just seven or eight might remain alive. Arthur Harris himself put the odds of surviving a first tour as 'scarcely one in three'. Many crews were lost before reaching ten operations and only optimists hoped to reach fifteen.[31]

Casualty rates, as a percentage of total sorties flown, declined as the war progressed, but losses remained serious. Over one-third of all Bomber Command casualties occurred in 1944. By way of example, thirty-five Lancaster crews joined 582 (PFF) Squadron in April 1944. By the end of August, fifteen crews had been lost and ninety-two airmen had died.[32]

Bomber Command's volunteers were, for the most part, in their very early twenties. In a study of 1,590 aircrew buried in the war cemeteries of Rheinberg and Durnbach, the average age of the pilots was found to be 24.3 years. One per cent were in the 18–19 age range, 7 per cent were 20, 10 per cent were 21 and 27 per cent were 22-24.[33] The casualty rate was appalling but there were always more volunteers than places. Many young men who stepped forward were sent home on 'deferred service' until required.[34] In the final six months of the bombing war, Bomber Command's loss rate fell to just over 1 per cent, but 649 bombers failed to return. Around 15,000 young men died in the Lancasters – around a quarter of Bomber Command's war dead.[35] At the squadron level, 220 complete crews, totalling 1,540 men, flew on operations with 550 Squadron at North Killingholme. One in four did not survive.[36]

The Lancasters dropped 608,612 tons of bombs on primary targets. This amounts to around two-thirds of the total weight dropped by Bomber Command in the March 1942–May 1945 period. The Lancasters dropped 51.5 million incendiaries.[37] Bomber Command, of course, represents only part of the strategic bombing effort. The Eighth USAAF lost 26,000 men (a 12.4 per cent loss rate). Another 18,000 were wounded and 20,000 became POWs.[38]

Lancaster rear gunner Warrant Officer Sidney Knott, DFC, survived two tours, totalling sixty-four operations. He has this to say about the price of victory: 'In my own mind I am quite sure that their sacrifice shortened the war. At the individual level, however, every young man lost was some mother's son. They died for us, our children and grandchildren. I was very lucky to survive, to enjoy over sixty years of tomorrows – a future denied to so many of my friends.'[39]

The German Air Force fought to the last. In the final phase of the bombing campaign, from mid-October 1944 to early April 1945, 550 Squadron lost nineteen Lancasters. Seven of the pilots were Canadians. These Lancasters were crewed by 134 men and there were just thirty-one survivors. Eight complete crews of seven were lost. This data was compiled by a former 550 Squadron pilot, Wing Commander Jack Harris, OBE, DFC (in later years Secretary of the 550 Squadron and RAF North Killingholme Association). He comments: 'The contrast between the large number of aircrew killed and the small number surviving as POWs is very sobering.'[40]

The price of victory: Warrant Officer Sidney Knott, DFC, at the Runnymede Memorial to the missing. *Photo: Sidney Knott.*

In his analysis of the loss of fifty-six Lancasters from 550 Squadron, Jack Harris notes that, not surprisingly, a high proportion involved inexperienced crews (nineteen losses; up to five operations). There were nine losses involving crews in the six to ten ops category, eleven in the eleven to fifteen ops group, eight in the sixteen to twenty category, six in the twenty-one to twenty-five ops group and three in the twenty-six to thirty ops group. Harris puts forward two reasons for the high losses among new crews. The first was the obvious factor – they were inexperienced. The second reason is related to 'safety in numbers' within the bomber stream: 'New crews were positioned to bomb in the last wave of the main force. At the end of the bomber stream and last to bomb, they were most vulnerable to night fighter attack near and over the target.'[40]

The most experienced crews were also vulnerable, but for the opposite reason: 'Crews on second tours or approaching the end of their first tours were selected to bomb in the first wave. At the head of the bomber stream the "Window" cover they received was at its thinnest. The Window that helped to mask your presence from German radar had to be dropped by bombers ahead of and higher than you. There were not too many ahead of them, only a small Pathfinder force and their supporters. So, aircraft at the front of the bomber stream could be picked up as individual targets by radar-controlled searchlights, flak and night fighters.

'Experience was clearly a factor affecting survival prospects, but it was by no means the only factor. In my view, the skill and ability of the navigator, in keeping the bomber in the middle of the bomber stream, was extremely important. This had two big advantages. It maximized the cover the bomber would get from Window and reduced the chance of being picked up as an individual aircraft by the radars that controlled searchlights, flak and night fighters. Secondly, night fighters assembled at beacons on either side of the bomber stream and were fed in as the stream went by. Night fighters tended to pick off bombers on the outer flanks of the stream. There was no way a night fighter wanted to enter the middle of the stream, for the bomber gunners let fly at any twin-engined or single-engined aircraft.'[40]

Air gunners who opened fire were required to file a combat report on their return. The gunners of 550 Squadron opened fire on seventy-nine occasions. Their targets were: twenty-three Ju88s, eleven Me109s, nine Me110s, eight Fw190s, five Me410s and one Me262 jet, together with twenty-two unidentified aircraft (some of which may have been jets). There was also one 'friendly fire' incident involving another Lancaster.[41]

The squadron's gunners were credited with five night fighters destroyed. Lancaster captain Jack Harris: 'It is interesting that the greatest number of combats in a month, eleven, occurred in March 1945. This is explained by several factors: a "last ditch" defence by the night fighters, who put everything into the air; the Germans' ability to predict likely targets with greater certainty, as Allied armies were already in Germany; and the fact that Bomber Command was putting a huge number of bombers into German airspace.'[41] The five kills are believed to have been three Ju88s and two single-engined fighters. To be classed as destroyed, the enemy aircraft had to be seen to blow up, crash into the ground or be confirmed as a kill by other bombers.[42]

One question – why Pforzheim? – echoes down the years. For those who still seek answers, perhaps to understand why their parents or grandparents lost their lives, all the cogent arguments in the world cannot set aside the understandable conviction that the raid was unnecessary at that late stage of the war. In February 1945, however, the planners lacked the benefit of hindsight. They had no way of knowing the war would be over in early May. Certainty of a fast-approaching end came only with the Rhine crossing and the Russian crossing of the Oder. In February 1945, on both Eastern and Western Fronts, the aim was no longer to smash German industry and break morale but, rather, to clear the way for advancing ground forces and get it over with as quickly as possible.

Here, Richards comments: 'In most, though not all, of the area attacks of this period there were two aiming points – the local railway yards and the town centre. Between mid-February and the end of March Bomber Command made at least 20 area attacks. A few ranged far afield, but, in accordance with the current directive, most were concentrated on the Rhineland-Ruhr zones facing the armies of the Western Allies. In the second half of February, after the raids on Dresden and Chemnitz, the towns which Bomber Command hit most heavily were Dortmund, Duisburg, Essen, Worms and Mainz. Most destructive of all these raids during the latter half of February, and the last predominantly area attack to be delivered by night, was that on distant Pforzheim, in South Germany.'[43]

Richards reviewed the strong moral objections to the bombing of German cities and then considered counter-arguments: 'Among them are that 'Germany began it first', with Warsaw and Rotterdam; that the British intention was not to kill civilians but to destroy their homes and drive them from the centres of industry; that civilians are so important for war production that they are a legitimate objective …' There was the overriding need to gain victory over a ruthless enemy, responsible for the deaths of millions of innocent men, women and children merely on grounds of their race or religion. There is also the 'practical argument' that, for a long period, area bombing at night was the RAF's only way of damaging Germany. Richards dismisses the view that the Americans held the moral high ground as they bombed 'precision targets'. He points out that their results, very often, were no different from area bombing at night. He also points to the fire bombings that razed Tokyo and other Japanese cities and, of course, the atomic bombing of Hiroshima and Nagasaki, using the ultimate area bombing weapon.[44]

Addressing fundamentals, Francis Mason made a key point: 'the tragedy of the Allied bombing was that it was never possible at 20,000 ft, on a dark night, to distinguish the guilty from the innocent'.[45]

Area bombing was the product of *what was possible*, in the technological sense, in the first half of the 1940s, rather than any moral failings among politicians and senior military commanders. The Western Allies lacked any other means of bringing the war home to Germany until the final year of conflict. The strategic bomber of the time had inherent limitations. These dictated the need for the area attack method, in the face of strong German defences, target-finding difficulties and often adverse weather. What can be said with certainty is that the absence of a strategic bombing campaign would have meant millions of additional deaths and a longer period of enslavement for millions of others. It is all too easy, today, to forget what was at stake – for both the British and German peoples. A victorious Hitler would have condemned hundreds of millions of people (including the Germans) to live out their lives in a perpetual nightmare. The Western Allies decided not to enter Germany as liberators, but many Germans must have regarded the British and Americans as such and many more must have rapidly reached that view, following the initial shock of defeat and occupation.

Neillands reflects: 'One can admire the courage and tenacity of the German fighter pilots, flak gunners, soldiers and private citizens in defending their homeland against terrible attacks, but that should not be allowed to obscure the fact that Nazi Germany was a vile and murderous tyranny, attempting to impose its will on the civilised world. In rooting out that tyranny, a great many harsh actions were necessary and can therefore be excused. The Dresden raid and Auschwitz are not the same thing.'[46]

As for the British, so close to total defeat and subjugation in 1940, nothing less than national existence was at stake. Here, Bomber Command veteran Sidney Knott, DFC, offers a view: 'This was a just war, in so much as any war may be described as "just". Hitler's Germany revelled in an orgy of industrialized mass killing and the victims were, for the most part, the weak and defenceless. Beyond genocide, the ruthless exploitation and degradation of Europe's conquered peoples continued unabated, in many instances until the very last day of the war. We had an unspoken appreciation of the fundamentals. This, perhaps, is the real key to the resilience of morale on the squadrons. We were not philosophers and the key issues were black and white for most. The appalling character of Nazi Germany gave the whole filthy business a stark clarity.'[47]

Sidney Knott adds: 'It is important to understand that we were within a hair's breadth of losing the war in May 1940. Our leaders were poor and our military capability virtually non-existent. Britain was about to tumble into the abyss and only the English Channel and Fighter Command kept us free. Rather than discuss the immorality of bombing (within a free society bought with the lives of too many of my contemporaries), I would rather talk about the moral duty – clear to us at the time – to crush Nazi Germany.'[48]

A comment from British politician Michael Howard says it all: 'The defeat of Nazi Germany gave humanity a future. Almost everything we value about our life today – freedom, democracy, prosperity, let alone an existence without the constant fear of the firing squad, the death camp and the torture chamber – exists only because Hitler was crushed.'[49]

Notes

1. Saward, D. (1985), *Victory Denied*, 360.
2. Overy, R. (1997), *Bomber Command 1939–45*, 199.
3. Document prepared by Wing Commander Jack Harris, OBE, DFC.
4. Saward, D. (1985), *Victory Denied*, 347; 353.
5. The strategic air war against Germany: The official report of the British Bombing Survey Unit (1998).
6. Neillands, R. (2002), *The Bomber War*, 379.
7. The strategic air war against Germany: The official report of the British Bombing Survey Unit (1998).
8. Neillands, R. (2002), *The Bomber War*, 372–3.
9. Terraine, J. (1988), *The Right of the Line*, 502–3.
10. Saward, D. (1985), *Victory Denied*, 357.
11. Neillands, R. (2002), *The Bomber War*, 382–3.
12. Ibid., 392–3.
13. Ibid., 396.
14. Ibid., 399.
15. Ibid., 400.
16. Saward, D. (1985), *Victory Denied*, 313.
17. The National Archives, AIR 14/3454: Bomber Command Review for 1945: Part 1: War Operations, 1st January to 8th May, 1945.
18. Newsletter 33, 24 October 2005, 550 Squadron and RAF North Killingholme Association.
19. The strategic air war against Germany: The official report of the British Bombing Survey Unit (1998), 161.
20. Neillands, R. (2002), The Bomber War, 384–5.
21. The strategic air war against Germany: The official report of the British Bombing Survey Unit (1998), 98.
22. Neillands, R. (2002), *The Bomber War*, 385.
23. Ibid., 141.
24. Richards, D. (1994), *The Hardest Victory*, 300–2.
25. The National Archives, AIR 20/3181: 1946-7, Report on the effects of strategic air attacks on German towns.
26. Overy, R. (1997), *Bomber Command 1939–45*, 202.
27. The National Archives, AIR 20/3181: 1946-7, Report on the effects of strategic air attacks on German towns.
28. The strategic air war against Germany: The official report of the British Bombing Survey Unit (1998), 34, 37.
29. Neillands, R. (2002), *The Bomber War*, 379.
30. Document prepared by Wing Commander Jack Harris, OBE, DFC.
31. Redding, T. (2008), *Flying for Freedom*, 116.
32. Ibid., 209.
33. Hampton, J. (1993), *Selected for Aircrew*, 141.
34. Redding, T. (2008), *Flying for Freedom*, 223.
35. Ibid., 258.
36. Newsletter 25, 28 October 2002, 550 Squadron and RAF North Killingholme Association.
37. Holmes, H. (2001), *Avro Lancaster, The Definitive Record*, 165.
38. Neillands, R. (2002), *The Bomber War*, 379.
39. Redding, T. (2008), *Flying for Freedom*, 258.
40. Newsletter 39, 25 January 2008, 550 Squadron and RAF North Killingholme Association.
41. Newsletter 35, 2 November 2006, 550 Squadron and RAF North Killingholme Association.

42. Newsletter 48, 19 March 2011, 550 Squadron and RAF North Killingholme Association.
43. Richards, D. (1994), The Hardest Victory, 276–7.
44. Ibid., 300–2.
45. Mason, F. (1989), *The Avro Lancaster*, 7.
46. Neillands, R. (2002), *The Bomber War*, 388.
47. Redding, T. (2008), *Flying for Freedom*, 118.
48. Ibid., 258.
49. Neillands, R. (2002), *The Bomber War, 388,* quoting the Rt Hon. Michael Howard, QC, MP.

Chapter Nineteen

Reconciliation and Remembrance

Bomber Command's war became a popular target for the revisionists, among them authors, TV producers and media commentators. They argued that the Allies lost the moral high ground by engaging in the area bombing of German cities. Most of the critics were born after the war. They grew up (as did this author) in a comfortable, affluent society offering unfettered freedom of speech. This freedom was bought with the lives of, inter alia, over 50,000 Bomber Command aircrew. Naturally, the criticism had an impact on some veterans. In recent years, however, the wheel has turned. A more balanced understanding of the bombing of Germany has taken root.

One of the more notorious examples of simplistic, partisan treatment was the 1992 Canadian television (CBC-TV) production 'Death by Moonlight' (one of three programmes in the series *The Valour and the Horror*). This programme caused deep offence among the thousands of Canadian veterans who flew with Bomber Command. The programme suggested that Bomber Command hid the truth about aircrew survival rates and concealed the deliberate targeting of civilians. The CBC ombudsman found that many of the programme's assertions were not supported by the evidence. Some claims were untrue and information differing from the producers' views was ignored. This heated row became the subject of a Canadian senate inquiry and feelings ran so high that the veterans took the programme-makers to court. The senate inquiry concluded that 'the criticisms levelled at *The Valour and the Horror* are for the most part legitimate. Simply put, although the film-makers have a right to their point of view, they have failed to present that point of view with any degree of accuracy or fairness.'

In this area, James Hampton made the important point: 'During the war, the aims and execution of the strategic bombing offensive against Germany had seemed clear and uncomplicated. They had enjoyed the fullest support and approval of almost every member of the population, from the Prime Minister downwards. However, in the post-war years, with the country safely delivered from the prospect of defeat and the imposition of an unspeakable tyranny, Bomber Command became the subject of much controversy.'[1]

Some aircrew veterans felt ostracized. There was no campaign medal. There was no memorial. These wrongs were addressed only when they were in their late eighties – with the award of the Bomber Command Clasp and the dedication of a fine memorial in London. This depicts a bomber crew safely back on the ground, having just emerged from their aircraft.

Years of negative comment had led some former aircrew to question their wartime role. There were feelings of guilt. The long-running controversies over Dresden dogged many a brave man as he entered old age. Equally, many former aircrew – in all probability the majority – have been sustained by their understanding of what was at stake and the true nature of the enemy. They have lived their lives in the belief that what was done was regrettable but right, in the context of a total war not of their making. When they came home, most – Sidney Knott, DFC, included – did their best to forget the war. They kept tight lipped and got on with building a new life.

Sir Arthur Harris' *Despatch on War Operations* was published in 1995. It has an interesting section, 'Harris – a German view', by the author and historian Horst Boog. He wrote: 'In talking to former airmen of RAF Bomber Command I have never felt that they were proud of the destruction they had wrought on German cities and civilians. On the contrary, some even regretted what, in those days, had been their duty.' Boog added: 'The impact of Bomber Command's area offensive and the remembrance of ruins and burnt civilians, as much as the burden of the Holocaust and the launching of a ruinous war or, in other words, the experience of their own sufferings and the feelings of guilt for having made others suffer, have developed in the German people a high sensitivity to any kind of war and inhumanity, and a feeling that such events should never be allowed to occur again. This certainly is a positive result …'[2]

Those who experienced the bombing and lived with its consequences do not consider matters of grand strategy but, rather, what happened in their own town, street, apartment block and shelter. How is the destruction of Pforzheim perceived by today's Pforzheimers? Christian Groh, former director of Stadtarchiv Pforzheim: 'The first commemoration of the raid was in October 1945, only six months after the attack. The annual memorial service – on 23 February – continues to this day. Thousands attended the service in the 1950s. Numbers declined in the 1960s but there was a strong recovery in the 1980s. People here were not afraid to show their grief. Of course, the Allies have been our friends for many decades and it is hard to criticize. Perhaps the public attitude today is best summed up in simple terms: war is a bad thing and *we know*, as we suffered so much. Sorrow at our own losses, however, needs to be managed. It should not be used to paper over difficult issues associated with the Nazis. It is too easy to think that dues have been paid and the account settled. In many German cities it took a long time – certainly well into the 1960s – for the Holocaust and other Nazi crimes to be recognized. This became a political football.'[3]

Hans Gerstung was a teenager at the time of the attack: 'This year [2013] was the sixty-eighth memorial service. I have attended every one. My life is always arranged to make time for the memorial service. Today, I make every effort to explain to my son and grandchildren that life always goes on. Things are never easy, but you have to go on, take care to stay decent and never give up hope.'[4]

A city mourns: Pforzheimers continue to gather at the Hauptfriedhof every year, on the anniversary of the raid. This was taken at the 1975 service of remembrance. *Photo: Stadtarchiv Pforzheim.*

The passage of time: 23 February 2014, the sixty-ninth service of commemoration. *Photo: Tony Redding.*

Remembering: an elderly mourner stands in front of temporary grave-markers. *Photo: Stadtarchiv Pforzheim.*

Yet Gerstung still puzzles over why Pforzheim was bombed: 'I have to accept what the historians say. Some say Bomber Harris had old cities destroyed because he wanted to demoralize the German population. Others say that Pforzheim supplied the armament factories. Both may be true. What I refuse to accept is the argument that the people of Pforzheim got what they deserved as they were making weapons. That argument is macabre. After all, the Allies were waiting just across the Rhine at the time and it was only a couple of months to the end of the war.'[4]

Raimund Frei, who loved old Pforzheim and returned to the ruined city after his time as a POW in the United States, has strong views on the bombing: 'I could understand it if there had been anything of military significance in Pforzheim. In my view, this was a genocidal attack. Bombing such a target was just murder. Certainly, we Germans did the same – look at Coventry and Guernica. The problem, of course, is that two wrongs don't make a right. Yet Harris' plan – which was supported and demanded by Churchill – to bring a second "Sodom and Gomorrah" to the Germans was nothing less than genocide. Let me cite the 65,000 [*sic*] dead of Dresden and the 18,000 dead of Pforzheim.

'If the Nuremberg War Crimes Tribunal had not been initiated by the *Siegermächte* [the victorious powers], then I am sure that these murders, also, would have been avenged. You should not forget the USA, because all of this matched US Secretary of the Treasury Morgenthau's concept. He wanted Germany turned into an agrarian state by destroying its industry. You could read in the US newspapers that he thought there were 24 million Germans too many. After all, we were only rats, Huns, bastards and God knows what else. But, thank God, there were also many individuals and organizations, like CARE, among our enemies who thought differently and helped devastated Germany with food and clothes.'[5]

There was an alternative point of view in Britain, a country victorious but on the verge of bankruptcy in 1945. Former Bomber Command rear gunner Sidney Knott, DFC: 'Churchill gave a speech after the war, saying that, with hostilities over, we must help to rebuild Germany. This did not go down well with me and many, many others, given all the problems at home. Those coming back to Civvy Street were changed men. Our country was struggling to cope. It must have taken two years for all the troops to be demobbed. Churchill did not consider our problems. The country was in a weak position, with rationing, bombed buildings, nowhere to live and the tremendous national debt. It was fifteen years before things started to get better.'

Adolf Katz never harboured doubts over why Pforzheim was destroyed. His daughter, Marianne Pross: 'He stuck to "moral guilt" as the reason and never looked for any military justification. He saw it as a purely moral issue and, consequently, could not regard the bombing as a crime.' These thoughts have an important personal context – Adolf Katz had a sense of what he called 'heavy collective guilt'. Remarkably, he used the phrase 'collective guilt' in a diary entry for 1 March 1945, just one week after the attack and years before this term formed the very heart of countless debates in post-war Germany.[6]

Supplementing the low basic ration: an elderly lady clutches her CARE package. *Photo: Stadtarchiv Pforzheim.*

Many British veterans remember by visiting crash sites and the cemeteries where their young crewmates are buried. Vic Cassapi was the flight engineer in the crew of 550 Squadron's Flying Officer A.W. Lohrey, RNZAF. He made annual pilgrimages to a village near Nancy, to pay his respects to the men who died when their aircraft was involved in a collision with another Lancaster. They were returning from Ludwigshafen on the night of 1/2 February 1945, when they were struck from underneath by an aircraft from 170 Squadron (believed to be corkscrewing at the time, to shake off a night fighter). Both starboard propellers were damaged and these engines were feathered. The port engines then lost power and Lohrey gave the order to jump. Five got out, but wireless operator Sergeant Tinsley and mid-upper gunner Sergeant James died. Their bodies were never found. The 170 Squadron Lancaster made it back to Hemswell, but the rear gunner was badly injured and later died. Tinsley and James were 20 years old. In 1997, a roadbuilding team at Fleville found the remains of RA502, Lohrey's Lancaster. Subsequently, a memorial was erected; it is now tended by local people.[7]

Westerbeek is a small village 15 miles south of Nijmegen. On the night of 3/4 February 1945, 550 Squadron Lancaster PD221 ('R'), captained by Flying Officer R.G. Nye, crashed at Westerbeek on the return from Bottrop. All seven crew were killed. The wreckage was widely scattered, suggesting that it blew up in mid-air. The tail unit came down half a mile from the main fuselage.[8]

Nye and his crew are buried in Westerbeek churchyard. The plot is carefully tended by villagers. A special ceremony was held in 2005, to mark the passage of sixty years. The gathering at Westerbeek included the daughter of the navigator, Sergeant Jack Holding, the sister of wireless operator Warrant Officer W.J. Howson and the nephew of rear gunner Sergeant L.C. Taerum, who was killed at the age of 18.[8]

The memorial to Pforzheim's dead, on the Wallberg, reads: 'Total war – provoked by Nazi Germany – was also directed at our city.' A memorial plaque on the wall of Huchenfeld church, dedicated in 1992, includes the phrase: 'Father forgive'. It names the five airmen from Johnny Wynne's crew murdered on 17/18 March 1945. The last line of the inscription reads: 'Let the living be warned.'

In Britain, BBC Radio 4 broadcast a programme on 19 December 2002, telling the story of Wynne's crew. The prime mover for the Huchenfeld memorial had been Curt-Jürgen Heinemann-Grüder, who moved to Huchenfeld in the 1980s. A retired pastor, he got to hear about the killings and took the view that the crime should be acknowledged. There was strong local opposition. It was seen as 'raking over the coals', but Heinemann-Grüder had the backing of Horst Zorn, then village pastor, and eventually got his way.

Tom Tate narrowly escaped execution at Huchenfeld and, later, at Eutingen. Having given evidence at the main war crimes trial, he swore never to return to Germany, but that was not to be. Marjorie Frost-Taylor, Flying Officer Harold Frost's widow, visited Huchenfeld; she attended the dedication of the memorial in 1992. In church were several men involved in the events of that night in March 1945. She offered forgiveness. In November 1992, as a mark of reconciliation, the Community of the Cross of Nails at Coventry gave a Cross of Nails to Huchenfeld Church. Another was presented to Pforzheim on 23 February 2005, the sixtieth anniversary of the raid. Johnny Wynne, the pilot who returned without his crew, became a hill farmer in North Wales. He got to hear of the 'reconciliation village' in 1992 and was horrified to discover that his five comrades had been murdered. When the anger subsided and following contact with Marjorie Frost-Taylor, Wynne and his wife took part in the reconciliation process. The former pilot presented a rocking horse to Huchenfeld's village nursery. The rocking horse is called 'Hope' and it carries the inscription: 'To the children of Huchenfeld from the mothers of 214 Royal Air Force Squadron.' Tate also became aware of what was happening. He spoke to Johnny Wynne for the first time since the order to bale out was given. Wynne asked him to come along on his next visit to Huchenfeld; it proved to be the first of many such trips by Tate. Wynne went on to establish a school exchange between his village, Llanbedr, and Huchenfeld. The two communities have since cooperated in supporting a small hospital in Tanzania.

When Tate was a prisoner he was minus his flying boots. Subsequently, Emilie Bohnenberger, recently widowed, gave Tate her dead husband's boots when she saw he was barefoot. They met again when Tate visited Huchenfeld. Only a fortnight before the murders, Emilie Bohnenberger had prevented another killing. At around noon on 1 March 1945, a captured British airman was escorted along Huchenfeld's main street, towards the town hall. Several people rushed up and began to beat him. Emilie was in the street. She intervened, seized one of the attackers and began shouting: 'Stop beating him! Behave like a human being!' Emilie was threatened but, somehow, the moment passed and the airman's wounds were tended. He left Huchenfeld by car shortly afterwards.[9]

The Nazis' victims and resisters within Pforzheim and in surrounding communities are also remembered. Gerhard Brändle became a teacher in 1974: 'In my history lessons, I wanted to deal with the years of National Socialism in the context of Pforzheim, but found only a few paragraphs on the important subject of resistance. There was also very little on Pogromnacht ['Kristallnacht'] and the deportation of Pforzheim's Jews. I wrote the first paper on this subject in 1978. This led me to research what happened at Gurs camp. In 1980, in association with the City's Cultural Department, I published a list of deportees to Gurs. This formed part of the first exhibition on Gurs camp. I continued to research the fate of these victims, in France and elsewhere. By 1985 I had a database of 830 victims – the persecuted and resisters. To my mind, we must confront our National Socialist past by a "clearing" process; this means working through the stories of individuals. These stories need names and, whenever possible, faces.'[10]

There are good reasons why Brändle's 2013 publication on the 'euthanasia' killings at Grafeneck Castle is titled *Names instead of Numbers*. He says: 'People need to realize that these things happened to PEOPLE. I often think about my own family's past. My mother's family were Waldensian Huguenots with a strong Protestant spirit. They were persecuted for their background of conscientious objection, opposition to war and the struggle for basic rights. This is not a religious spirit but, rather, an emphasis on the "protest" in "Protestant". We protest, whenever protesting is necessary and imperative.'[10]

These issues have a particular resonance in the German context: 'Germany has had a profound impact on the world and vice versa. The struggle goes on. There are German right-wing politicians who welcomed Pinochet's coup in 1973. They haven't changed – they failed to see the cruelties of that regime. Walter Rauff, the inventor of mobile gas chambers in 1941, lived in Chile in 1973 and is thought to have worked for Pinochet and his Secret Service.'[10]

There are many views on the meaning of resistance but no formal definition. In Germany, the term *Zivilcourage* (a citizen with moral courage – the courage of his or her convictions) is used to embrace all forms of behaviour which may be described as resistance (*widerständiges Verhalten*). Gerhard Brändle: 'The debate on German resistance to the Nazis passed through several phases. Immediately after the war there was total silence on the subject – there was no resistance. Gradually, however, concentration camp survivors, people held in prisons and prisoners of war returned. Then the discussions began. At first, the focus was on Stauffenberg and resistance within the Wehrmacht. Then the focus switched to resistance within the Church. Later commentators found it convenient to ignore the evidence of the prison lists and the fact that 80–90 per cent of all resisters in cities such as Pforzheim and Karlsruhe, going back as early as 1933, were of left-wing persuasion. In the Cold War era, the major contribution of communists and small political groups to the left of the SPD went unacknowledged.

'I have a wide definition of resistance. Whatever form it takes, resistance must be active rather than passive. The resister's actions must be intended to have consequences extending beyond that individual's immediate circle. To give a clear example, listening to the BBC – *Rundfunkverbrechen* – was an act which could result in serious punishment. It was dangerous but it was *not* an act of resistance. If, however, a person listened to the BBC, wrote down the news and passed it to others, that was resistance under my definition. In contrast, even those who circulate literature critical of the regime within their own immediate circle, perhaps a religious group, are not engaged in active resistance. In essence, they are "preaching to the converted".'[10]

Those resisters from the Pforzheim area taken into custody included: forty members of the KPD, KJVD, Rote Hilfe and Rotfrontkämpferbund; twenty union members; twenty SAP members; fifteen Jehovah's Witnesses; ten SPD members; ten Adventists; six Jews; six Protestant clergymen; five 'religious socialists' (Protestants); four former members of the International Brigade and four Catholics (three clergymen and one layman). Resisters murdered or classed as 'deceased in custody' included six KPD members, three Jews, two *SAP* members, two Jehovah's Witnesses, one Adventist and one Catholic layman.[10]

As for *Zivilcourage*, in 1995 Gerhard Brändle supervised the exhibition 'Mut zum Widerstand [Courage to Resist], Pforzheim 1933–45'. He has written papers on National Socialism and resistance and has spoken on this subject in Pforzheim. He believes in associating remembrance with geographic location: streets, places where people used to live and locations where they were arrested, so as to underline meaning and consequence. This exhibition, linked to the fiftieth anniversary of the raid, provided a public opportunity to pay tribute to all who fought Nazi oppression, from all religions and cultural backgrounds. The exhibition sought to relate events in the Nazi era to the eventual destruction of the city.'[10]

Gerhard and Brigitte Brändle are a team. Their current work includes studies relating to the rapes that occurred during the early days of occupation in April 1945. They continue to research what happened to those who survived Nazi persecution by escaping abroad, together with the fate of French resistance prisoners in Germany. They also have a research project concerned with members of the International Brigades who came from Pforzheim and elsewhere in Baden.[10]

As a former pastor and church representative, Hans Ade – who witnessed the exhumation of French resisters from a bomb crater – pressed for a memorial to the murdered members of Réseau Alliance. He worked together with Gerhard Brändle and members of various parties of the city council. Hans made contact with Mireille Hincker, who lives in Strasbourg and is the head of Souvenir Francais. She wrote to Pforzheim's lady Oberbürgermeister at that time, saying that, if necessary, she would raise the money from relatives of the victims. Subsequently, Pforzheim City financed the memorial, via a sponsor. The memorial was opened on 25 January 2008, in the presence of the victims' families.[11]

Dr Alan Russell, OBE, is founder and president of The Dresden Trust. He continues to play a central role in the work of the Trust and in the wider movement for reconciliation and closer understanding between Britain and Germany. He believes reconciliation must be founded on a mutual understanding of history and culture. Alan Russell points out that city bombing in Europe began with German aircraft over Guernica. As a boy, he witnessed the London Blitz: 'My grandfather's business was bombed out three times. Aerial retaliation was inevitable, not least because Britain had no other means of prosecuting the war. I regard the development of the bombing campaign in that strategic light. The cost of the campaign, in the lives of Bomber Command's crews, was appalling and we should never forget the courage and sacrifice of these young men. At the same time, it is my view that the bombing campaign got out of hand towards the end of the war. By that time we had won air superiority over Germany. We had a new capacity for precision bombing. For these reasons alone the bombing campaign could – and should – have been modified to concentrate less on city centres and more on specific military targets.'[12]

Dr Russell underlines the importance of recognizing the realities of war: 'War is the use of violence to achieve political ends. It is true that the main concern was to end the war as quickly as possible. It is also true that, by early 1945, many Germans regarded the advancing Western Allies as liberators rather than conquerors. Unfortunately, not enough Germans felt that way. The issues, of course, are never clear cut. Take the example of Victor Gregg, the British Army prisoner condemned to death and in custody in Dresden on the night of the raid. He experienced the firestorm and wrote graphically about its power and the terrible toll of human life. I also think of the words of Simon Barrington-Ward, a former Bishop of Coventry. He described the war as a storm so fierce that all sides lost touch with their principles. Today, as memories dim, it is important to take steps to remind people of what war really means.'[12]

Alan Russell spent some months in Germany as a National Serviceman. He became friends with a young German who wanted to improve his English: 'We are still in touch sixty years later. Naturally, we talked about the war in those early days. I asked him why people had indulged in the horrible persecution of the Jews. He asked me why Dresden was destroyed. I became interested in the subject and read many books about the raid. Decades later, while working for the European Commission, I had lots of friends from the various member states, including Germany. At that time – in the early 1990s – some underlying sensitivities in Anglo-German relations were exposed. During the Queen's visit to Dresden, in 1992, the royal car did not stop at the ruins of the Frauenkirche. This was, in fact, at the request of the city's Chief of Police, who feared a revenge attack, but it was widely misinterpreted. Then, in the same year, the Queen Mother unveiled a statue of Arthur Harris outside the RAF Church of St Clement Danes, in The Strand, erected in honour of Bomber Command's crews. On that occasion, I stood across the street holding a placard, reminding people of the dreadful effect that the bombing of Dresden had had on civilians.

'A couple of years earlier a small group of dedicated Dresdeners, who had long campaigned for the rebuilding of the Frauenkirche, issued a call for international help. I founded The Dresden Trust in 1993, in direct response to this call. The Trust is now part of a wider effort to build relationships founded on reconciliation. Today, these relationships include links with Pforzheim.'[12]

Dr Russell, as might be expected, has clear views on the destruction of Dresden: 'The bombing of Dresden was an incomprehensible act of war. It did us no great credit. The Trust is always careful not to criticize Bomber Command aircrew and has never accepted the charge that Harris was a "war criminal". He was a strong leader, when a strong leader was needed. When the Bomber Command Memorial was opened by the Queen on 28 June 2012, some claimed this was a memorial to those responsible for the destruction of Dresden. This is not true. It commemorates over 50,000 airmen who lost their lives. On that day I found myself in Dresden, holding a candle for those brave young bomber crews, so that our German friends would understand the true meaning of the memorial.'[12] Today, St Clement Danes and Lincoln Cathedral hold the Rolls of Honour, listing men of Bomber Command who lost their lives in the cause of freedom.

The Dresden Trust's initial aims were to promote the rebuilding of the Frauenkirche, as a memorial to all who died as a result of bombing. These aims broadened in 2001 and now include cultural relations in the wider sense. 'Perhaps our most important achievement, over the past twenty years, is a general rapprochement. Rightly or wrongly, the Dresden raid destroyed one of Europe's most beautiful cities. We have since shown the German people that we are capable of regretting some of the things we did in a war which was certainly not of our making. One tangible sign of rapprochement was the making and gifting of the orb and cross for the Frauenkirche. This is a replica of the original by Johann Georg Schimdt. The services of Grant Macdonald, head of the London firm of that name, were retained and with them the skills of the late Alan Smith, head of the team that undertook the work. Interestingly, Smith was the son of a bomber pilot who took part in the 1945 Dresden raid. In February 2000, the fifty-fifth anniversary of the attack, the orb and cross was handed over in Dresden by the Trust's patron, HRH the Duke of Kent. It was raised into position on the rebuilt Frauenkirche in 2004. The new church was consecrated the following year.[12]

Dr Russell is forthright about the bombing of Pforzheim. 'This city was no Schweinfurt, which was an industrial target of strategic significance and, therefore, had to be bombed. In contrast, Pforzheim was a collection of small artisan industries. This city was obliterated when it was obvious to all that the war was coming to an end. For this reason, its destruction is open to criticism. Three years ago people in

Reconciliation: Dr Alan Russell, of The Dresden Trust, speaks at the service of remembrance on 23 February 2010. Standing with Dr Russell is Oberbürgermeister Gert Hager. *Photo: Stadtarchiv Pforzheim.*

Reconciliation: 'Father forgive'. *Photo: Tony Redding.*

Pforzheim made approaches to The Dresden Trust and, as a result, I have visited the city and, at the annual commemoration of the raid of 23 February 1945, I have expressed the regret of the British people about the large-scale loss of life.'[12]

Over the years, Alan Russell's concept of reconciliation has not changed. It does, however, lay more stress on the vital importance of forgiveness and of mutual understanding: 'Reconciliation is the willingness to shake hands and make peace with former enemies, to forgive the wrongs they have done but, at the same time, to understand the forces that drove them to commit them, to recognize one's own faults and wrongs without necessarily admitting moral equivalence, and to take all possible moral and practical steps to ensure that past wrongs, misunderstandings and suffering are never repeated.'[12]

Notes

1. Hampton, J. (1993), *Selected for Aircrew*, 7.
2. Boog, H., 'Harris – a German view', in Harris, Sir Arthur T. (1995), *Despatch on War Operations*.
3. Interview with Christian Groh, April 2013.
4. Interview with Hans Gerstung, April 2013.
5. Interview with Raimund Frei, July 2013.
6. Documents/interview with Marianne Pross, September 2013.
7. Newsletter 30, 23 June 2004, 550 Squadron and RAF North Killingholme Association.
8. Newsletter 32, 23 May 2005, 550 Squadron and RAF North Killingholme Association.
9. Beck-Ehninger, R., *The Plaque*, 57–8.
10. Interviews and documents/information provided by Gerhard Brändle, 2013.
11. Interview with Hans Ade, November 2013.
12. Interview with Dr. Alan Russell, August 2013.

Chapter Twenty

Aftermath

Buried in the ground, beneath Pforzheim's buildings, pavements and open spaces, is the legacy of the Lancaster raid – missing Pforzheimers and unexploded bombs. In November 2002, during the construction of a new shopping centre, a digger bucket struck a 500lb bomb. People were evacuated as a bomb disposal team dealt with another unwelcome reminder of the night of 23 February 1945. Around 500 police, firefighters and other emergency services secured the area around Bohnenberger Schlössle.[1]

Gerd Fleig's attitude towards the bombing of Pforzheim changed over the years. Even at the time, his views were out of step with most: 'Back then I felt it was an act of revenge, but not completely unjustified. It took years for the facts to emerge. Pforzheim's factories were engaged in war production and, to my mind, this makes the raid more understandable.' Today, he avoids discussing politics with young people: 'I have had my share of political indoctrination. When it comes to politics, it is better for young people to find out for themselves.'[2]

In 1946 prisoner of war Raimund Frei returned to the wasteland of Pforzheim: 'There were some good things about the National Socialists. They got rid of a lot of misery, which weighed heavily on our people because of the peace treaty after the First World War. But, unfortunately, these good things were negated by a lot of the actions of the Party leadership, carried out in the name of the people. This includes the murder of the Jews, here and in the occupied territories, the extermination of so-called *unlebenswertes Leben* [a reference to euthanasia] and racist arrogance.'[3]

In 1948 Raimund Frei met and married Hildegard. They lived in Eutingen. Their son, Thomas, was born in 1949. They also had a daughter. Thomas Frei: 'The war was a closed book in our family. We knew the bare essentials about Father's service in Eastern Europe and North Africa and the fact that he had been a prisoner in America, but that was about all.'[4]

During the 1950s the children went to school in Pforzheim. 'This was a difficult time financially. The five of us – parents, two kids and grandmother – lived on Father's small salary.' Fortunately, they had extra income from renting out the ground floor of the house, which had been built in the 1930s by Hildegard's father. 'Immediately after the war up to thirty people were crammed into our house. They were bombed out and billeted on us. Subsequently, the ground floor was home to just the one family. Later, they had a new house built, moved out and were succeeded by a young couple. The husband was a travelling salesman in office supplies and toiletries: he dished out free samples on Fridays!'[4]

Thomas Frei had two godfathers. One was in the jewellery business and quite wealthy: 'He was a good source of sweets, chocolate and pocket money. This was much appreciated. My paternal grandfather died in the raid. My maternal grandfather survived but died shortly afterwards; he was rummaging for things in the cellar when it collapsed on him. He had taken good care of his family and must have been a wonderful person.'[4]

The Frei household had strict rules against wasting food: 'We ate simply but well. Grandmother was a good cook and there was always food on the table. As for Pforzheim, kids of my generation never saw the city intact. We only knew Pforzheim as a city in ruins. The rebuilding was slow but, gradually, new buildings went up in the late 1950s and early 1960s. The street shacks and other temporary buildings disappeared.'[4]

The school curriculum of the early 1960s avoided Hitler and the war. Thomas Frei: 'In grammar school we were taught history that, apparently, ended with the Treaty of Versailles and the Weimar Republic. This is why, even today, many people know surprisingly little about life in the 1930s and how we arrived at the catastrophe of the Second World War.'[4]

During the early 1970s he made friends in Poland: 'These contacts led me to take an interest in the past. A deep conflict had developed between the generations. Nothing was said about the time of the Nazis, at home or at school. The questioning began in the late 1960s, at the time of the student rebellions. My father's generation stood accused. I was deeply shocked in 1973, during my first visit to Poland. I went to Auschwitz. You can't imagine the impact … the mountains of hair and teeth, the gas chambers. It was overwhelming, indescribable.'[4]

Thomas Frei became a journalist. He spent ten years with a Ludwigsburg newspaper, then returned to his home town. He has been an editor with *Pforzheimer Zeitung* for many years: 'I came back to Pforzheim in 1985 and my position with the newspaper required me to understand what happened on 23 February 1945. I now appreciate that many people who lived through those times want to tell their stories. Every year, on the anniversary of the attack, we cover the events of long ago and the service of remembrance. Every year something new emerges – a letter or a diary from that time – offering fresh insights.' Thomas Frei published a book (*Pforzheim – On its Way to a New City*), which covers the period from its destruction in February 1945 to the currency reform of 1948.[4]

What of Pforzheim today? Thomas Frei: 'Well, many people dislike the modern town. They resent the way it was rebuilt, with factories in the central area and cheap residential blocks. At the same time, it is only fair to say that Pforzheim also has some very beautiful little parks and its three rivers, lying in a basin surrounded by forests. As for the Pforzheimers, many people made a lot of money from the jewellery business in the 1950s, 1960s and 1970s. They made their money in Pforzheim but

On the streets: anti-Nazi marchers gather on 23 February 2014. *Photo: Tony Redding.*

tend to spend it elsewhere. Now their children enjoy a very comfortable lifestyle. They know how to spend but are careful not to display their wealth.

'Modern Pforzheim, of course, is much more than this community. Perhaps 40 per cent of the population of around 120,000 have an immigrant background. They include some 10,000 people from Eastern Europe, another 20,000 from Italy, Turkey and Spain and, more recently, around 2,000 from Iraq. Many ethnic Germans from the former Soviet countries also found a home in Pforzheim. Today, this city has the highest unemployment rate in Baden. The inability of many immigrants to speak German creates a huge social problem; kids learn quickly but are held back as they live in homes where German is never spoken.

'Today, efforts are made to tackle the worst excesses of 1960s construction. Apartment blocks are spruced up and modernized. Architects are clever at making buildings look new and more interesting. Whenever new development takes place, plans are reviewed by an independent panel of architects who seek to promote good design. As building proceeds, of course, there are occasional reminders of the past. A bomb disposal expert is required on site whenever foundations are excavated. Very occasionally, a neighbourhood is evacuated as an unexploded bomb is dealt with. On one occasion I couldn't get into my office until lunchtime, while a bomb was defused.'[4]

Art student Gisela Bär became a sculptor, with her own studio in Pforzheim. She came to terms with that catastrophic night in February 1945, but also wrote about vivid flashbacks to childhood dreams of thousands of bodies and the *Jabos* (fighter-bombers) overhead.[5]

Dieter Essig, a young boy at the time of the raid, now partners Hans Gerstung, a teenager in February 1945, in giving talks to schools in Pforzheim and the surrounding area: 'The history teachers organize the talks. The pupils learn about the Second World War and, of course, the bombing of Pforzheim. They are asked to write down their questions and then get the chance to put them, face to face.' During these talks, Essig hammers home the point that today's freedoms should not be taken for granted: 'We talk to different age groups. I know I can't reach everyone, but one in ten is enough for me. Kids in elementary school tend to be more interested. They ask the best questions. Older pupils and young teachers are less interested.'[6]

Dr Christian Groh, the former director of Stadtarchiv Pforzheim, adds: 'Young people get their history lessons and are told about the bombing. Yet many people who now live in Pforzheim are not from this town, or even from Germany. How can they connect with the Second World War, the bombing and the importance of commemoration when, for many of them, it just isn't important? Arguing for acceptance of this reality is always controversial. The 9 November ceremonies marking Pogromnacht are already regarded by many as a "forced" commemoration. Perhaps the best way forward is to drain some emotion from commemoration. This would help those with no direct emotional tie to the events being remembered. Today, many people in our communities have had direct and painful experience of more recent conflicts – in Iraq and Yugoslavia, for example. Perhaps they should play a role in explaining war, in ways which do not focus entirely on loss.'[7]

There is a dualism in Hans Gerstung's feelings about the time of National Socialism: 'Firstly, knowing what we know now about the Nazis and their concentration camps, it would have been terrible for the entire world had National Socialism triumphed. The regime mistreated its own population and was responsible for the suffering and misery of the Germans. Yet, at the personal level, I remember my years in school and as a Pimpf with the Jungvolk as a time of great camaraderie. We were brought up with the same ideals, did sports together, went on camping trips and had flags, drums and uniforms. This was wrapped up in a package with nothing negative about it, except that we had to be very tidy and keep our uniforms clean.

'What we now know, of course, is the importance of being free. We have the right to vote. We live in a free world and we are doing fine. Most of us have jobs. Life is balanced and we do not live under a dictatorship. We can only understand what dictatorship really means by looking back. Then you can clearly see the terrible things. Dictatorships, however, always perish, as you can't go on abusing people forever. These are lessons which must be taught to our young people and exemplified through our own lives.'[8]

Wolfram Aichele was still a prisoner in Oklahoma in September 1945. In May he had read about the Pforzheim raid in a German-American newspaper. During October he received news that his parents had survived. Meanwhile, he was shocked to the core by a film of the British takeover of Belsen. The prisoners filed out of the camp cinema in silence; no-one could bring themselves to speak.[9]

Peter Rodi came close to starving to death in a French prison camp. He was lucky to be picked for a job in the kitchen; his hunger oedema disappeared within a month. He then worked on the land and his body began a slow recovery.[9] Rodi escaped from the French camp in June 1946 and eventually reached the American Zone and ruined Pforzheim. In that month, Wolfram Aichele discovered that he was to be returned to Europe. On arrival at Le Havre he was free to travel on to Germany.[10]

Some young people decided to make a new life abroad. Former naval cadet Werner Baroni took to journalism and enjoyed his life as a newspaperman. 'I covered all subjects. I met my wife, Edith, when covering an important boxing match. There was a party going to the fight but Edith didn't have a ticket. I went as a news photographer and gave Edith my press pass. We married in July 1949 and our first child arrived in 1952. We lived in Pforzheim until emigrating to the USA in 1957. The twins arrived two years later. Today, there are four grandchildren; two have graduated and two are still at university.

'Back in the 1950s I knew I had to go abroad to get ahead. I went to New York and aimed high. I had an interview at the *New York Times*. They told me to come back when my English had improved. At that point my wife and child were still in Pforzheim and I needed money to bring them over. For a time I found work with a jewellery manufacturer. The owner had a workforce of 400 Germans and he had known my grandfather in Pforzheim. I also freelanced for newspapers and DPA, the German Press Agency. I got an assignment in South America from a German magazine. When I returned I became editor-in-chief of a daily, the *Staatszeitung*.' Later, Werner Baroni moved to Chicago, to become editor-in-chief of the Chicago daily *Abendpost*. 'I spent ten years there but eventually fell out with the publisher. I launched my own newspaper and sold it in 1994 after twenty-five years.'[11]

Reflecting on wartime Germany and those harsh first years of peace, Werner Baroni recalled Anna's words: 'When in the first prison camp I decided she was right. I made a terrible mistake when I volunteered to serve criminals. Hitler and his gang were just that – criminals.' Anna died in 1948, before Pforzheim's recovery really began, but Lisel saw the transformation before she died in 1993. Werner's brother, Arno, built a new life in South Africa with Irma. Werner Baroni now lives in Florida.[11]

In 2012, a walker in the forest near Krefeld found a section of Lancaster fuselage. The 12in by 18in panel carried the number 319. This once formed part of the aircraft of Flying Officer H. Dodds. His 550 Squadron Lancaster was PD319 ('BQ-G'). Dodds and his six crew lost their lives when this aircraft failed to return from the 14 October 1944 attack on Duisburg. It had been Dodds' eleventh operation.[12]

The seven men killed in action included two members of another Lancaster captain's crew. The navigator, Flying Officer D.J.K. White, and the bomb aimer, Flying Officer H. Black, usually flew with Warrant Officer R.A. Tapsell. This pilot was unlucky. Earlier in the month he lost both gunners, Sergeants J.P. Shendon and J. McVey, who were killed in an accident while flying with yet another Lancaster captain, Flying Officer Hayter, on 4 October 1944. Tapsell had lost four of his crew in less than a fortnight. He re-crewed and finished his tour. The panel found in the forest was later presented to the 550 Squadron Museum by the son of Flying Officer Black.[12]

Mid-upper gunner Frank Woodley and the rest of Warrant Officer Ken Sidwell's crew had a lucky escape in a 550 Squadron Lancaster when it aquaplaned on landing at North Killingholme in the early hours of 20 October 1944. They were returning from Stuttgart. The Lancaster ended up in a field but, fortunately, with only superficial damage, as 'B' was the celebrated 'Phantom of the Ruhr', a veteran of over 100 operations. This aircraft's striking nose art, depicting the phantom, was recreated for the Battle of Britain Memorial Flight's Lancaster in April 2007.[13] Sidwell and crew had several close shaves. They were hit by flak (on one occasion losing an engine), struck by a cloud of incendiaries tumbling down from above, and experienced engine fires. Nevertheless, they survived the tour.

When the European war finished, 550 Squadron took part in a series of special operations. These activities began in April 1945, just before the German surrender. An understanding was reached with the Germans, permitting low-flying heavy bombers to drop food to the starving Dutch. Operation Manna had its origins in the previous autumn's Market Garden, the failed attempt to seize a series of bridges and then penetrate Germany's western defences. When Market Garden began, the Dutch Government in exile, in London, issued a call for a national rail strike. The attack stalled and the Germans took harsh retaliatory action against the Dutch people. They banned the movement of food from the farmlands of the eastern Netherlands to the densely populated west, including the big cities – Amsterdam, Rotterdam and The Hague. The result was the 'Hunger Winter', or 'Tulip Winter', so called because the Dutch were reduced to eating tulip bulbs.

Operation Manna involved Lancasters from 1, 3 and 8 Groups. They dropped food in the south of the country. USAAF Fortresses dropped emergency supplies in the north. The Lancasters of 550 Squadron began to contribute to Operation Manna on 26 April, when they experimented with the free drop of food sacks at low speed, from around 500ft. After a weather delay, food-dropping sorties to the Dutch began on 29 April. The squadron had flown 189 Manna sorties by 8 May 1945.[14]

A few days later Bomber Command aircraft began repatriating British prisoners of war. The 550 Squadron Lancasters flew to Brussels, to pick up recently released POWs and return them to Westcott and other reception airfields. This was Operation Exodus. The squadron flew forty-eight Exodus missions on 10–11 May 1945. Everywhere, people were going home. On 24 May 1945, all RCAF and RAAF aircrews were withdrawn from 550 Squadron, in readiness for their repatriation to Canada and Australia.[14]

The 'Cook's Tours' began on 1 June 1945. Ground crew and other non-flying personnel with 550 and other Bomber Command squadrons were taken on low-level flights around the Ruhr, to view the bomb-damaged cities. Later in June Operation Post-Mortem began. Bomber Command aircraft, including 550's Lancasters, flew exercises to test the effectiveness of the Mandrel screen, Window and other jamming systems. The German short and long-range radars were now manned by British personnel. The 550 Lancasters flew sixty-eight sorties to Flensburg, contributing to this post-hostilities evaluation.[14]

In July 1945 the heavy bombers were employed to dump surplus ordnance in the North Sea. The Lancasters of 550 Squadron participated and, in late July, went on to join Operation Dodge. This involved flights to Italy, to repatriate British Army personnel due for leave or release. These flights continued through to the October/November period. There were two accidents involving 550 Squadron aircraft. Pilot Officer Matthews took off from Bari on 29 September 1945, and went missing, with the loss of six aircrew and twenty passengers. On 7 October Warrant Officer Graham crashed shortly after take-off from Pomigliano/Naples. Two passengers were killed.[14]

Jack Marshall, the bomb aimer with Flight Lieutenant W.R.B. Parker's crew, recalled an Operation Dodge flight returning Army personnel to Italy after UK leave. They took off on 16 October 1945, for Pomigliano, with nearly twenty passengers on board. The Lancaster lost an engine passing through the 'Toulouse Gap' – the passengers had no oxygen so the Lancaster kept below 8,000ft. When there was bad weather over central France the Toulouse route was preferred, as conditions tended to be better: it took aircraft through the valley between the Pyrenees and the Massif Centrale.[15]

As they neared Marseilles a second engine failed and the prop was feathered. As Parker's aircraft reached the Mediterranean a third engine failed and he turned for an emergency landing at an airfield occupied by the Americans, who were astounded at the sight of a four-engined heavy bomber landing safely on one engine. They flew on the next day, following work on the engines. They had to wait seventeen days at Pomigliano for an engine change and bad weather to clear. They left Italy on 5 November and were routed over Austria, Germany and Belgium, owing to bad weather in the Mediterranean area. More hostile weather over eastern England forced them to divert to St Mawgan in Cornwall. They finally reached North Killingholme on 6 November, only to find that 550 Squadron had disbanded seven days before and that their base was on 'care and maintenance'.[15] Until mid-August and the Japanese surrender, 550 Squadron had trained for Tiger Force, the British contribution to the planned attack and occupation of the Japanese homeland. The intention was to base up to thirty-six Lancaster squadrons at five airfields on Okinawa, with raids on Japan commencing in September 1945. Following the atomic bomb attacks and the Japanese surrender, the squadron disbanded at the end of October.[16]

Don Robson completed his second tour of operations in November 1944. He had completed twenty-six trips as a Fortress waist gunner with 214 RCM Squadron at Oulton. He should have stopped at twenty rather than twenty-six. In any event, Bomber Command's brief and distasteful sleight of hand counted some sorties as only half an operation, so reducing his second tour to an official nineteen and a half operations. Putting aside such dubious mathematical engineering, Robson finished combat flying with fifty-five trips in his logbook. He took it all in his stride. Ever the pragmatist, he turned down the offer of a commission. He refused it on financial grounds: 'I was better off as a senior NCO rather than a junior officer.'[17]

Johnny Wynne's Fortress III was scrapped on 11 March 1947. Robson had heard stories of aircrew murdered after baling out. He left 214 Squadron three months before five of Wynne's crew were murdered: 'I suppose I was always aware of this possibility but I never gave it a second thought. Later, after the war, I read a newspaper article about the murder of some of Wynne's crew. I was shocked and surprised. I don't remember them. They must have started their tour just as I finished. Looking back, I find it hard to blame the Germans in any way. If you get the hell knocked out of you, you are going to retaliate in some way.'[18]

Many aircrew reached out to old comrades as they neared retirement. The son of Fortress pilot George Wright made sure his dad celebrated his sixtieth birthday in style. He managed to trace all nine members of his Fortress crew, including Don Robson: 'His son took him out for the day to the RAF Museum at Hendon. He returned home to a surprise birthday party. George turned to me and said: "Where the bloody hell did they find you, Robbie?"'[18]

Robson wasn't hard to track down. After the war he returned to the village bakery in Kent and continued working there until he reached seventy. On his role in the bombing campaign, over two tours, Don Robson had no qualms: 'As far as I was concerned, the Germans got what they asked for. At the same time, I can't say I harbour any bad feelings against the Germans. Many years after the war I found myself in conversation with a German fighter pilot. He wasn't really interested in me. He was too busy chatting up my wife!'[18] Sadly, Don Robson died in April 2014, while reading the draft of this book.

On 17 December 1945, 100 (Bomber Support) Group was disbanded. Earlier in the year, on 27 July, 214 Squadron was disbanded. As for 214 Squadron's base at Oulton, the tower was demolished in December 1999. Only a few scattered huts now survive. The squadron colours are laid up in Ely Cathedral and Oulton is farmed once more.

July 1945 was not the end of 214's story. On the very day of disbandment, 614 Squadron, based in Italy, was renumbered 214 Squadron, with a bombing role in the Middle East region. In addition, victory in Europe did not bring Flight Lieutenant Johnny Wynne's RAF career to an end. He stayed in as an operational pilot. During 1946, 214 Squadron was re-formed and equipped with the Lancaster's successor, the Avro Lincoln. It was disbanded in late 1954 but re-formed again in early 1956 to

Standing by the guns: the late Don Robson at the rear turret of a Lancaster (this example is fitted with the twin 0.5 guns of the 'Rose Turret'). *Photo: Don Robson.*

fly the Vickers Valiant, the first of the four-jet nuclear bombers of Britain's V-Force. The squadron was based at RAF Marham, Norfolk, and one of its pilots was Johnny Wynne, DFC, who, eleven years earlier, had struggled back alone to England in his battered Fortress. Wynne, now a squadron leader, became a flight commander and saw action once again during the Suez Crisis. His Valiant attacked Abu Sueir, which, ironically, had been a 214 Squadron base in 1919. The Valiant attempted to crater the runways, but missed when the bomb release malfunctioned.[19] Subsequently, in 1962, 214 became a tanker (in-flight refuelling) squadron. It disbanded in 1965, when the Valiant force was grounded, but re-formed the following year with Handley Page Victor tankers. The unit was disbanded in 1977.[20]

Former 550 Squadron air gunner Frank Woodley found steady work at Scunthorpe steelworks: 'Subsequently, I moved around and finished up as a manager before being made redundant when four steelworks went. Mrs Thatcher closed us down. By then I was fifty-eight. We moved south as my wife wanted to be near my stepdaughter. I kept busy doing small jobs locally until I took my pension. Just by chance, I was talking to a neighbour who had flown in Blenheims. He was going to Shoreham Airport for an exclusive get-together, reserved for wireless operators and gunners. I went along with my wife and we became members. There were fifty of us at one point, including four members of the Guinea Pig Club.' The Guinea Pig Club was for aircrew who had suffered burns and had undergone pioneering reconstructive surgery by the renowned Sir Archibald McIndoe.[21]

Jack Harris, OBE, DFC, a Lancaster captain with 550 Squadron, survived thirty-seven operations. The night raids included three trips to Cologne and two each to Essen and the Merseberg oil plant. The Harris crew also attacked Saarbrücken, Stuttgart, Düsseldorf, Dortmund, Karlsruhe, Ludwigshafen, Nuremberg, Dresden and Duisburg. It took five and a half months to complete the tour: 'There were several reasons for this. Crews on bomber squadrons were allowed one week's leave every six weeks. Secondly, weather at base or over the target, especially during the winter months, was a big problem. We were briefed many times for operations that were cancelled shortly before take-off. Thirdly, I was a deputy flight commander and there were restrictions on too many senior officers of the squadron flying on ops at the same time.'[22]

Harris received his DFC in May 1945. It recognized the completion of a solid tour, free of early returns, and a collection of excellent bombing photos over primary targets. During this long operational tour Harris adopted a phlegmatic attitude: 'You couldn't go on ops unless you thought you were coming back. There was a lot of manufactured banter in the briefing room and on the crew bus. There were comments like: "If you don't come back, can I have your camera?" On the other hand, reality often intruded. I was not overly affected by losses, unless I knew them well. One crew had two officers billeted in our hut. When they failed to return, the empty room was a harsh reminder of what could happen. It was even worse for all-NCO crews. When an aircraft was lost, half the hut would empty.'[22]

Some crews went in for good luck charms and rituals. Jack Harris: 'I wasn't superstitious as such, but I wore one particular pair of long pants on every raid. They went unwashed for over five months. All crews on ops drew survival kits before flying. I had something extra. The left breast pocket of my battledress held an old tobacco tin containing a razor, shaving soap and a cut-down toothbrush, together with sweets, chocolate and a small mirror. My personal survival kit sat over my heart, providing a last line of defence.'[22]

Harris was 'rested', returning to Sandtoft Heavy Conversion Unit as a flying instructor. This HCU had re-equipped with Lancasters. Harris became deputy flight commander of D Flight. The flight commander was a 'movie star'. He had been the second pilot of a Wellington – sitting next to the renowned bomber pilot Charles Pickard – in the hit film *Target for Tonight*. Pickard was killed leading the Amiens prison Mosquito raid, to free Resistance fighters facing execution.[22]

Harris was posted to a junior commanders' course at the RAF College, Cranwell, but took the controls of a Lancaster again on 17 July 1945, flying to Germany. This was a 'Cook's Tour' of the Reich's ruined cities: 'I took eight ground personnel on a five-hour grand tour of Arnhem, Wesel, Emmerich, Essen, Duisburg, Düsseldorf, Cologne and Aachen.'[22] Subsequently, Harris received a permanent commission and joined the Air Ministry's Directorate of Personnel Services. In the spring of

1948 he took a flying refresher at RAF Finningley, where one of the instructors was Bill Bedford, who went on to test-fly the Harrier jump-jet prototypes. Harris flew transport aircraft in the Far East until he was selected for the RAF Staff College. He converted to Meteor jet fighters and Canberra jet bombers. In late 1955 he became officer commanding 542 Canberra Squadron. His later postings included a period as wing commander, operations, at RAF Wildenrath, Germany.[22]

Harris retired from the RAF in 1967 and took on the running of the British Healthcare Export Council, a position he held for sixteen years. His first wife died in 1981 and he married Bobbie three years later. Sadly, Bobbie passed away in 2013. Harris has a large family: two daughters, three stepchildren and two step-great-granddaughters. In 2013 he applied for his Bomber Command Clasp. The reply commented: 'Please be aware that due to the high volume of applications which we have received, it may be a while before your application is assessed.' One is left with the impression that Jack Harris would have sorted this out very quickly had he still been resident at the Air Ministry.[22]

Some brave survivors did not live long enough to enjoy decades of peace. Heinz-Wolfgang Schnaufer, the German night fighter ace, died in a prosaic manner after a flying career filled with drama and danger. His Bf110 night fighter was put on display in Hyde Park, London, after the war. One of its tail fins, decorated with 121 victories, can still be seen at London's Imperial War Museum. Schnaufer died in a road accident in France in 1950, killed by a French truck with faulty brakes.[23]

Dresden became a symbol for the horrors of total war. Ron James served with 214 RCM Squadron. He has this to say: 'The name conjures up visions of the massacre of a defenceless civilian population and a condemnation of our war leaders. Whatever the facts of the matter, I can only relate my feelings at that time, and those of some of my compatriots. The Germans, who started the war, had for five years been bombing open cities all over Europe, without thought of civilian casualties, and waging all-out warfare against several neutral countries besides the lands of their enemies. In 1945 our forces were winning on all fronts and could see an end to the fighting before the year's end. Our main task was to get the war over as quickly as possible. We were not heartless, but could not have carried out this work if we had allowed our minds to dwell upon the consequences of our bombing. If we killed civilians, so be it. It was as well we fought an impersonal war, from miles up in the sky, for if we had seen our victims at close hand, ours would have been a harder case to bear.

'On every raid carried out, we were always apprised of our target, its military importance and the reason for bombing it. Dresden did not differ in this respect. I am still asked if I feel any remorse over bombing this town and the answer is "No". To our knowledge, we were attacking a vital military target. If we had been told that this was an undefended town full of refugees and of no military importance, I can well imagine a mutiny starting up between us and the powers that be. My own guess is that no-one knew the real situation in Dresden and that this was one of the terrible mistakes made in the war.

'At the briefing, we were told the bombing attack was against an important rail junction which was supplying the German Army with reinforcements for holding back the Russians, who were then only 50 miles away, and that this attack was to help our Allies. The intelligence officer did mention that Dresden's factories also produced porcelain and chocolate. This black humour was not unknown at briefings and was always good for a nervous laugh but, like the rest of us, the officer concerned was convinced that the target markers would fall over the railway station.'[24]

British public opinion at that time was firmly in favour of the bombing, to give the Germans 'a taste of their own medicine'. Equally, it is important to acknowledge the men of conscience who, against the tide of opinion, expressed opposition and took a highly unpopular stance. Perhaps the most prominent critics were Labour MPs Richard Stokes and Alfred Salter, together with George Bell, Bishop of Chichester. Bell failed to gain the support of the Archbishop of Canterbury. The Bishop of York firmly opposed him.

In the House of Commons, Home Secretary Herbert Morrison was asked, in October 1943, whether he was prepared to intern the 'pro-German' Bombing Restriction Committee. Morrison evaded this mild challenge with ease: 'I am aware of the existence of this committee and I have seen specimens of the leaflets issued by them. The scope of their propaganda is very limited and its influence on public opinion is negligible. I have no evidence that their sympathies are pro-German, nor do I have any reason to question the sincerity of their motives, which they conceive to be purely humanitarian. I should not feel justified, as things are, in using emergency powers to prevent them from giving expression to their misguided views.'

The past caught up with some perpetrators. Hans Knab was hanged for his instigation of the murder of five of Johnny Wynne's crew. After the war, the Knab family left their large house in Dillweissenstein. As a high-ranking Nazi, Knab's assets were seized and that included the house. Later, this building was occupied by city employees. Just eleven years after the aircrew murders, Helmut Schmitt, now a Dillweissenstein local historian, found himself at a school desk in the very room the Hitler Youth killers had occupied during the final weeks of the war.[25]

18 March 2009 was a fine spring day. Exactly sixty-four years had passed since James Vinall was beaten and shot in Dillweissenstein. A small crowd of around forty people had gathered by the old town hall, where Vinall was held. A memorial to Jimmy Vinall was dedicated by the group. They stood only metres from the site of the old school building, once the base of the Hitler Youth perpetrators and, later, Helmut Schmitt's classroom. Sadly, on this occasion, only a few of those attending were from Dillweissenstein. Helmut Schmitt: 'Everyone in this village knows about Vinall's murder but no-one talks about it.'[25]

On 7 June 2013, various events were held to celebrate the hundredth anniversary of Dillweissenstein, the incorporation of the communities of Dillstein and Weissenstein into Pforzheim. Helmut Schmitt made a speech and talked about the National Socialist years. He included a description of Vinall's killing: 'I could see from the faces of my audience that they were moved.'[25]

With the war in Europe over, Vera Atkins made determined efforts to trace the fate of the twelve women of the Special Operations Executive who had parachuted into France and remained unaccounted for. Atkins had helped prepare them for their missions. Her investigations led to the concentration camps of Natzweiler, Dachau and Ravensbrück. Among the victims was 'Madeleine', Noor Inayat Khan, who had been held in Pforzheim.[26]

In 1946 Vera Atkins was nearing the end of her work as a war crimes investigator. Then she read a letter from Yolande Lagrave, the sole survivor of the Réseau Alliance group executed on the outskirts of Pforzheim during 'Black Forest Blood Week'. Lagrave wrote: 'At Pforzheim, where I was imprisoned in a cell, I was able to correspond with an English parachutist who was also locked up there. She was very unhappy. Her hands and feet were chained and she was never allowed out. I heard the blows she received from prison guards.'[26]

Noor Inayat Khan described herself as 'Nora Baker'. Atkins knew this was her missing agent's alias. She had thought she had been killed at Natzweiler in July 1944, but Lagrave said she was still alive, at Pforzheim, that September. The investigation into Madeleine's fate reopened.[26] Gradually, her story came together. There had been two escape attempts in Paris. She had arrived at Pforzheim prison in November 1943 and was shackled on security grounds. War crimes lawyer Alexander Nicholson visited Pforzheim and interviewed the former prison governor, who said the British agent had been kept in solitary confinement, in chains and on the lowest of rations. Subsequently, she died in Dachau, at the hands of a sadist.[27]

The killings of aircrew at Huchenfeld and Dillweissenstein in March 1945 were cold-blooded, premeditated murders, warped into a crude propaganda trick by the false claim that they were the product of a spontaneous outburst of civilian anger. Yet there can be no doubt that some aircrew murders were genuine expressions of fury after heavy bombing and large-scale loss of life. Sidney Knott, DFC, a veteran of sixty-four bomber sorties: 'There were many reports (some subsequently confirmed) of shot-down British aircrew being attacked and even lynched by civilians in heavily bombed German towns. I can understand the power of such bitter emotion. I felt it myself – perhaps to a lesser degree – early in the war, when I sat on the cliff top with my father and watched over 100 German bombers fly along the Thames to London. I felt elation when one was hit and went down. I always thought it would be very bad news to bale out over Berlin or a Ruhr city.'[28]

In a contribution to *Narratives of Trauma*, Dr Christian Groh, the former director of Stadtarchiv Pforzheim, considered aspects of remembrance: 'In a city like Pforzheim, in which 17,000 people died after one bombing raid, it was hard to address the role of Germans as perpetrators. As a consequence, well into the 1970s, the city's public memory concentrated on its suffering, not on the complicated entanglements of competing roles as perpetrators, sufferers and beneficiaries.'[29]

The annual ceremony and service at Pforzheim's main cemetery, on 23 February, includes a speech from the Oberbürgermeister. Christian Groh: 'During the 1950s and 1960s, their speeches focused on reconstruction and reflected a kind of pride in the progress made.'[30]

Unfortunately, German neo-Nazi groups attempt to hijack ceremonies in cities such as Dresden and Pforzheim. The anniversaries in Pforzheim are typical. They usually feature a largely left-wing demonstration and march, protesting against the presence of neo-Nazis. This led to a serious confrontation in 2013, resulting in violence and many arrests. Some blamed heavy-handed, provocative police tactics. These were moderated in 2014, and 23 February passed peacefully enough.

Doris Weber graduated in 1955 and began working for an import-export company: 'Money was tight. I remember using my salary to buy two summer dresses and being told off by mother for wasting money. I had to remind her that I had worked for it!' Doris' new life was to centre on an international career: 'I applied for a job in London and went to work in Foyles bookshop. I had to learn to stand on my own two feet and I enjoyed it. My ambition was to live and work in Paris. I joined the Foreign Service, spent time in Bonn and eventually got my wish. I moved to Paris and began working for what became the OECD. I spent ten years in Paris and became personal assistant to the ambassador. In all, I was fortunate enough to spend twenty-eight years abroad, working in Bonn, Paris, Pretoria/Cape Town, Belgrade, Washington DC and Luxembourg, before returning to Bonn.'[31]

Sigrid Kern finished her apprenticeship, worked in a boutique, married and had three children. She remembers the shadows that war cast over her young life: 'You couldn't ask questions and Mother wouldn't say anything about National Socialism. Father carried a heavy burden. He had a stomach ulcer during the Second World War and his First World War experiences still haunted him, as did the loss of his brothers. He had also lost his parents in the big attack. As a former Party member, he found it difficult to find work. Then there was Hannelore, our eldest sister. She suffered from a serious condition that affected her physical development. Our parents feared she would die young, but she confounded the doctors, living on into her eighties. My father loved to spend time with his grandchildren. The highlight of his later life, perhaps, was a visit to the French town where he had been held prisoner in the First World War. He was invited back by the mayor. On the day of that visit he became reconciled with his past. It was the most important milestone in his life.'[31]

Ellen Eberle started school at the age of eight, in 1946. 'My mother taught me to read and write at home. I attended the Nordstadtschule. I developed a habit of visiting the local library. It was run by the Americans but staffed by Germans, and there were some German language books. I was fascinated by English and American lifestyles. I liked English authors, especially Charles Dickens. At home, however, it was thought inappropriate for a girl from a family like mine to have direct contact with Americans. My stepfather was very conservative. I wouldn't say he was anti-American, as such, but he did resent them. He would let me speak French during meals, but not English. He hated jazz, calling it "negro music". Some years later, when I was 21, I went to a jazz club in Pforzheim. When I came out, he was standing outside, yelling at me.'[32]

The family often talked about National Socialism, the war years and Nazi atrocities. 'I knew about the Holocaust when I went to school. My stepfather told me about it. He had seen trains full of deportees on their way to Gurs camp. I remember 9 November 1950, and the moment the teacher asked the class what had happened on that date in 1938. That's when I first learnt about Pogromnacht, which happened the year I was born. I went home and asked Mother point-blank: 'Where was Father on 9 November 1938?' She was taken aback by my hostile attitude. Ever since, I have made a point of reminding people of what happened on Pogromnacht.'[32]

Ellen had touched a raw nerve. She was told later that her father had been ordered to take part in the Pogromnacht action in Ludwigsburg. 'Mother said he didn't come home that night. When he got back early the next morning he told her that terrible things had happened, adding: "It won't be all right with Hitler in power."'[32]

Ellen Eberle was a teenager in a ruined city. 'There was rubble everywhere. Money was tight and there were no funds for school fees, but my grades were so good I didn't have to pay. My stepfather was very strict. I couldn't go out. I wanted to go to college but we couldn't afford it. When I turned 15 I started to work in the afternoons and during the holidays – packing for a mail order company. I was also involved with the church, helping with services and running summer camps. The summer camps were important. Most of my classmates had lost their fathers in the war and there were lots of single mums around. I looked for a commercially sponsored university place but had no luck. Eventually, I got a job with a jewellery merchant who took me on because I could speak English. The work was well paid but I decided to join Pforzheim police in 1961. I had married – probably just to get away from my stepfather – but that was a mistake. My husband had a problem with me working. I had joined the police as a secretary. I had a ninety-minute lunch break and had to go home to cook his lunch. I used to be a good housewife. Anyway, people at work encouraged me to join the criminal police. I was still a secretary but I managed to go out on investigations and gradually learnt the job. I needed a background in social work to become a criminal policewoman. It was decided that my church work and a reference from the pastor would cover this. I joined the police as a female officer. There were two others. One was a former Nazi who had escorted prisoners to Ravensbrück. The second was

harmless enough. Eventually, I became the first criminal policewoman in Baden to have the same duties as male colleagues.'[32]

Ellen became widely recognized as an experienced crime scene investigator. Later in her career she became deputy head of the Police Juvenile Delinquency Unit. She remarried in 1968 and started a family the following year.[32]

Dave Davidson's wireless operator, Howell Evans, became a specialist in airborne radars and went on to fly with RAF Transport Command. His pilot, George Blackler, flew the Avro York, a transport version of the Lancaster. Evans left the Air Force in March 1947, having married the previous September. He and Pat went to live at Hendy village. Sadly, Pat died in 2006. Today, Howell has four grandchildren and three great-grandchildren. As the years slipped by, he decided to look for

Remembering: Ellen Eberle (top left) with her mother and daughter. *Photo: Ellen Eberle.*

Brothers in arms: Davidson and comrades. Left to right: Fred Decker, Dave Davidson, Howell Evans and Dicky Lloyd. *Photo: Jo Cowen (née Davidson).*

his crew: 'Comradeship has been very important to me. I am a founder member of the 100 Squadron and 550 Squadron associations. I had trouble tracing the crew, but bomb aimer Dicky Lloyd found me. Dick had married his girl from Pontypool and, after twenty years in London, had returned to Wales. He knew my father had kept the post office at Hendy. His rugby club visited ours. Dick spotted one of our members with an RAF tie and asked about me. He was then taken to my house. When we met, it was as if we had never been apart.'[33]

Howell Evans suffered no long-term effects from flying, other than the hearing loss so common among aircrew in later life. His son escorted him to London for the Bomber Command Memorial opening ceremony. He also received the Bomber Command Clasp. Howell and Dicky Lloyd have visited the Battle of Britain Memorial Flight on several occasions: 'When we climbed inside the Lancaster there wasn't a dry eye in the house – nostalgic memories of a magnificent aeroplane.'[33]

Howell Evans adds: 'I felt terrible about dropping the bombs. I know they killed innocent people – including women and children – and I never got over that. I never had the "that's what they deserve" feeling. At the same time, I witnessed the bombing at home – the "Swansea Blitz". I saw what happened to Swansea; they absolutely flattened it. My final view is that I don't think we would have won the war without Bomber Command. I am very proud to have served.'[33]

Evans' pilot, Dave Davidson, toyed with the idea of staying in the Air Force after the war but came out. Later he became a manager for Atlantic Tubes. William 'Dave' Davidson has a daughter, Jo, two grandchildren and two great-grandchildren.[34]

Ron Germain, Flight Lieutenant 'Buzz' Burrows' wireless operator on 550 Squadron, retired in 1983 after spending many years with the engineering department of the Post Office (later BT). He has a son, two daughters and two grandchildren. Comradeship is also important to him: 'I joined the Aircrew Association and became treasurer of the Plymouth branch. I made many friends through the Association. As for the bombing, we have often been told how important it was to victory and it was important. Yet I keep thinking about the women and kids on the ground. It must have been appalling. Dresden was less than three months before the end of the war. I think Dresden was probably an attack too far. I remember North Killingholme's briefing officer telling us: "Tonight you are going to smash up Dresden's china." It didn't mean a thing to us then.'[35]

Sam Lipfriend, Flying Officer 'Eddie' Edlund's flight engineer on 550 Squadron, left the Air Force: 'I turned my back on the war. I wanted to get on with life. I didn't attend a reunion until 1991. Today, looking back, I think the bombing campaign was particularly effective when supporting our armies on the ground. They fought their way through as we bombed Germany all the way back to Berlin.' Recognition for Bomber Command's veterans was a long time coming. Sam Lipfriend again: 'I was never bothered about that but I must say that the London memorial, including its position, is absolutely marvellous. It's a fantastic memorial – the best in London.'[36]

Reunion: 550 Squadron veterans in front of the Battle of Britain Memorial Flight's 'City of Lincoln'. *Photo: Phil Rigby.*

In March 2013 Sam Lipfriend attended 10 Downing Street to receive his Bomber Command Clasp from Prime Minister David Cameron. Sam died later in the year, leaving Pam, their two sons and six grandchildren. In 1995 he had been fortunate enough to fly in *City of Lincoln*, the Battle of Britain Memorial Flight Lancaster. He recalled: 'That day I flew in a Lancaster rear turret for the first time. I came out with even greater respect for rear gunners. It took me thirteen attempts to get in it!'[36]

Bill Thomas, Flying Officer Bruce Potter's bomb aimer on 153 Squadron, also closed his mind to the RAF when peace came: 'I concentrated on family, work and studying for more qualifications. Later in life, however, I decided to trace the crew. I put a letter in various journals. At that time, I also saw a letter seeking members for the 153 Squadron Association. Eventually I found Jack Boyle, the navigator. We corresponded but he died within the year. I also found Harry Hambrook, the rear gunner. We have both been inside the Memorial Flight Lancaster and *Just Jane* at East Kirkby. Harry never had any trouble getting into the rear turret when he was younger, but he had more difficulty now.'[37]

Bill Thomas has no reservations about the bombing of Germany: 'I have no particular view, other than the belief that they deserved it. I bombed Dresden and,

Historical record: the late Bob Stone, who assembled a vivid pictorial record of 550 Squadron at North Killingholme. *Photo: Bob Stone's family, via Phil Rigby.*

frankly, I don't care, as bombing Germany made an important contribution to victory. The Battle of Britain pilots saved Britain in 1940. Our job was to take the war back to Germany and we did much to destroy their war effort.'[37]

Many years after the war Bill Thomas had a strange encounter with a former target: 'A friend and his wife often joined us for holidays. One year we drove down to Austria. We had planned to stay the night in Stuttgart but my friend suggested a stopover at a small town nearby – a place called Pforzheim. We went into the town centre during the early afternoon. Everyone was polite and spoke good English. Pforzheim was modern and we took a stroll by the river. I kept turning the name over in my mind as we returned to the boarding house. Suddenly, I realized and whispered to my mate: "I bombed this bloody place!" He replied: "Shut up. Our host has got a very large knife in her hand!"'[37]

What he saw of the final events of the war, together with what he learned later, shook Hans Ade free of the 'hero cult': 'In the autumn of 1945 I got involved in the Jungschar, the church youth organization. One Jugendleiter, a bit older than me, had been with the Flak. He opened my eyes to the truth – there is nothing heroic about war. I realized that war should not be glorified. The real turning point for me was watching a film about Auschwitz. When I saw what my own people had done, I changed my mind.'[38]

His eldest sister underwent no such transformation: 'She didn't reflect on those days. She was just happy that life could begin again. She went dancing and had boyfriends. If she did think about such things, she certainly didn't talk to me about it.'[38]

Hans Ade became a glazier and carpenter. He was to have taken over the shop owned by his boss, who wanted to step back yet continue working, but the shop was destroyed in the raid. Hans, at 17, then heard a sermon that took him on a very different path: 'The theme was the need for more pastors. I couldn't get it out of my head and told Father I wanted to study theology. He and the boss didn't appreciate the idea, so I had to fund my studies myself. Yet Father did pay for a nice suit; I didn't have to attend class in leather pants! Eventually, I became a parish and youth pastor.'[38]

Today, Hans Ade sees the bombing of Pforzheim as a boomerang: 'We started the area bombing, in Holland and in England. We had sown the wind and we had to reap

Not forgotten: Gerhard Brändle at the memorial for two deportees to Gurs Camp. *Photo: Tony Redding.*

the whirlwind – to face the consequences.' Later in life, Hans Ade taught religious studies at the school where Gerhard Brändle taught. They have cooperated on several projects concerning the victims of National Socialism, such as documenting the fate of the elderly, handicapped and sick people murdered under the Nazis' 'euthanasia' programme and also recognizing men and women of the French Resistance murdered by the Nazis in Pforzheim.[38]

Oberbürgermeister Adolf Katz eventually fell victim to the 'Old Guard'. His daughter, Marianne Pross: 'There were many factors behind his resignation in 1947. Rebuilt political parties now wanted their people back in the driving seat. My father had no political ties and, consequently, no power base. He had no background in politics and administration. All his life he had worked as a bank manager, yet his world was one of books, with a special interest in philosophy and the philosophy of religion.' The old hands found it easy to engineer a 'no confidence vote' and he was soon out of office.[39]

Adolf Katz's difficulties were rooted, to some extent, in his own personality. He disliked compromise. He preferred to make decisions and implement them in what was seen by many as an authoritarian style. His opponents also found his incorruptibility disturbing. Those who knew him could expect no special treatment. He served as Oberbürgermeister until June 1947. When it was over, he felt great relief at being a private citizen once again. Marianne Pross: 'He had been appointed to a job he didn't seek, but he had fully recognized its importance at the time. Now he returned to a familiar world. He began work at a bank in Karlsruhe.'[39]

Adolf Katz died in 1956 after a long illness. In his final years he became a student of Eastern religion. Marianne Pross dropped out of university in Munich and took up a career in periodical journalism. Her husband, Harry Pross, was a leading journalist in post-war Germany and, later, a distinguished professor of journalism at Freie Universität Berlin. A former student of her husband, Dr Alfred Hübner – who later became cultural spokesperson for Pforzheim city – urged her to publish parts of her father's diary.[39]

The role of foreign workers during the Nazi years received little attention in political circles during the first thirty-five years of the Federal Republic. Things changed in the 1980s, with the appearance of academic papers and other published work relating to the use of forced labour. Some accounts looked at the record of specific major companies during the war years, prompting much media discussion of the case for financial compensation for foreign workers.[40]

Human nature being what it is, there came a time when some former forced labourers *wanted* to return. In September 1964 the Vosges villages of La Bresse, Ventron and Cornimont made an approach and, in association with the 'Peace Initiative' and the German Federation of Trade Unions, a group of over 100 people visited Pforzheim, where they had worked on war production in 1944 and 1945.[41] In May 1987 a larger group of former forced labourers visited the city. Other groups followed, in August 1988 and in May 1989.[42]

On 31 May 1950, Mrs Olive Swales opened the South African Air Force Memorial in Pretoria. Her son, the recipient of Bomber Command's last Victoria Cross of the war, is buried a long way from home, at Leopoldsburg War Cemetery, Limburg, Belgium. Pforzheim was Swales' forty-third operation with 582 Pathfinder Squadron.[43] Warrant Officer Sidney Knott, DFC, completed a second tour with 582 Squadron. He suggests that Swales' posting to the Pathfinders, despite his lack of operational experience (which was almost unheard of), might have been a 'political appointment' contributing to South African representation.[44]

Swales had to learn his trade. His fourth operation, to Kiel on 23/4 July 1944, ended badly. On the return he was short of fuel and had to divert to an airstrip at Handley Page's Radlett factory, in Hertfordshire. The approach was misjudged and they crash-landed. Swales and his flight engineer were injured and the Lancaster (JB417) was a write-off. Yet Swales put this behind him and made remarkable progress, eventually achieving master bomber status.[45]

Swales' commentary over Pforzheim was remembered by another 582 airman, gunner Flight Sergeant John Smith, DFM: 'The master bomber always broadcast in plain language, so we could hear Ted's aircraft being attacked and him calling for his deputy to take over. Then we could hear that the attack was over as he called the deputy and resumed control of the commentary. We knew he had been in trouble, though, and when we all got back a large group of us hung around, waiting for his return. After a little while we decided he wasn't coming back and were surprised when most of his crew did.'[46]

Group Captain Stafford Coulson, DSO, DFC, was the commanding officer of 582 Squadron and he wrote the recommendation for Ted Swales' Victoria Cross: 'Ted was such a jolly nice chap and had a fine crew, very well trained. He wasn't what you would call a squadron "character" – he wasn't that type – and apart from his uniform he didn't really stick out. But he was just very good at what he did and really stuck to the task. The recommendation was accepted just like that.'[47] Swales is not forgotten. His school, Durban High, has a Swales House. One of Durban's roads became Edwin Swales VC Drive.

Notes

1. *Pforzheimer Zeitung*, 25 November 2002.
2. Interview with Gerd Fleig, July 2013.
3. Interview with Raimund Frei, July 2013.
4. Interview with Thomas Frei, September 2013.
5. Schmalacker-Wyrich, Esther (Ed.), (1980), 'Pforzheim 23. Februar 1945, der Untergang einer Stadt', in: *Bildern und Augenzeugenberichten* (third edition).
6. Interview with Dieter Essig, April 2013.
7. Interview with Christian Groh, April 2013.
8. Interview with Hans Gerstung, April 2013.
9. Milton, G. (2011), *Wolfram*, 278–80.
10. Ibid., 288–301.
11. Interviews with Werner Baroni, 2013.
12. Newsletter 53, 15 October 2012, 550 Squadron and RAF North Killingholme Association.
13. Newsletter 35, 2 November 2006, 550 Squadron and RAF North Killingholme Association.
14. Newsletter 32, 23 May 2005, 550 Squadron and RAF North Killingholme Association.
15. Newsletter 33, 24 October 2005, 550 Squadron and RAF North Killingholme Association.
16. Newsletter 32, 23 May 2005, 550 Squadron and RAF North Killingholme Association.
17. Redding, T. (2008), *Flying for Freedom*, 163.
18. Interview with Don Robson, March 2013.
19. James, R. (1989), *Avenging in the Shadows: 214 Squadron, Royal Air Force*, 183–7.
20. Halley, J.J. (1980), *The Squadrons of the Royal Air Force*, 217.
21. Interview with Frank Woodley, March 2013.
22. Interviews with Jack Harris, 2013.
23. Redding, T. (2008), *Flying for Freedom*, 79.
24. James, R. (1989), *Avenging in the Shadows: 214 Squadron, Royal Air Force*, 163–4.
25. Interviews with Helmut Schmitt and Stephan Paetzold, 2013.
26. Helm, S. (2005), *A Life in Secrets*, 302–4.
27. Ibid., 318–24.
28. Redding, T. (2008), *Flying for Freedom*, 256–8.
29. Groh, Dr. Christian (2011), 'Expressions of memory in Pforzheim', in *Narratives of Trauma: German Monitor No. 73*, 75–87.
30. Interview with Christian Groh, April 2013.

31. Interview with Doris Weber and Sigrid Kern, November 2013.
32. Interview with Ellen Eberle, November 2013.
33. Interview with Howell Evans, June 2013.
34. Interview with Dave Davidson, April 2013.
35. Interview with Ron Germain, April 2013.
36. Interview with Sam Lipfriend, March 2013.
37. Interview with Bill Thomas, June 2013.
38. Interview with Hans Ade, November 2013.
39. Documents/interview with Marianne Pross, September 2013.
40. Becht, Hans-Peter (1993), 'Der Arbeitseinsatz von Kriegsgefangenen und ausländischen Zivilarbeiten, in Pforzheim 1940–1945 – Ein Rekonstruktionsversuch', in: Riblet-Buchmann, R. (1993), *Unerwartete Begegnung – Als junger 'Fremdarbeiter' in Pforzheim 1944/45*, 65–103.
41. *Pforzheimer Zeitung*, 10, 11 and 14 September 1964.
42. *Pforzheimer Zeitung*, 7 to 11 May 1987, and 24 August 1988; also *Pforzheimer Kurier* of 27, 28 and 29 May 1989.
43. Redding, T. (2008), *Flying for Freedom*, 219–20.
44. Interview with Sidney Knott, March 2013.
45. Feast, S. (2008), *Master Bombers*, 172.
46. Ibid., 130.
47. Ibid., 196.

Final Words From Germany

'As the years passed, I took an interest in Jewish life. I used to spend time with Jewish friends in Karlsruhe. I have also been to Israel and Palestine. A friend in the Jewish community once said to me: "After what the Germans did to the Jews, they must pay, generation after generation." That can't be right. Those who were small children at the time committed no crime.'

Dieter Essig

'My daughter grew up with the answers to important questions about the past. She is a musician and a teacher. I have shared the lessons of the war years, including the importance of realizing that political involvement is the only way to stop repression and persecution. Looking back, I now see that the bombing of Pforzheim was the answer to Goebbels' famous question: "Do you want total war?" It was also a response to National Socialist crimes. My mother and grandmother were not bitter at the end – they were just grateful to be alive.'

Ellen Eberle

'Many people here still see Bomber Harris as a war criminal. This is wrong. In the war some 50 million people died – or an average of around 20,000 lives lost per day. During the final phase the actual figure was probably in the region of 40,000 deaths every day. Every twenty-four hours, another 40,000 lives! Harris acted correctly, to bring the war to an end as soon as possible. He was no war criminal. He did the right thing. The longer the war went on, the more would have been murdered in the gas chambers.'

Werner Schultz

'People today grow up in a society at peace. There is no *fliegeralarm*. When their grandparents open up they are astounded. Our reality is so far away from the good life they enjoy today. At the same time, people of my age often don't want to share their experiences, but when we do talk we must talk honestly and truthfully.'

Irma Baroni

Bibliography

Bowman, M.W., *100 Group (Bomber Support)* (Pen and Sword Aviation, 2006)

Bowman, M.W. and Cushing, T., *Confounding the Reich* (Patrick Stephens, 1996)

Feast, S., *Master Bombers* (Grub Street, 2008)

Hampton, J., *Selected for Aircrew* (Air Research Publications, 1993)

Holmes, H., *Avro Lancaster, The Definitive Record* (1997; Airlife, 2001)

Longmate, N., *The Bombers* (1983; Arrow Books, 1988)

Middlebrook, M. and Everitt, C., *The Bomber Command War Diaries* (1985; Penguin, 1990)

Milton, G., *Wolfram* (Sceptre, 2011)

Neillands, R., *The Bomber War* (2001; John Murray edition, 2002)

Nichol, J. and Rennell, T., *Tail-end Charlies* (2004; Viking/Penguin, 2004)

Overy, R., *Bomber Command 1939–45* (HarperCollins, 1997)

Probert, H., *Bomber Harris* (Greenhill, 2001)

Redding, T., *Flying for Freedom* (2005; Mulberry TRS, 2008)

Richards, D., *The Hardest Victory* (Hodder and Stoughton, 1994)

Saward, D., *Victory Denied* (Buchan and Enright, 1985)

Schmalacker-Wyrich, E. (ed.), 'Pforzheim 23. Februar 1945, der Untergang einer Stadt', in: *Bildern und Augenzeugenberichten* (third edition, 1980, Verlagsanstalt J. Esslinger, 1963)

Sweetman, J. *Bomber Crew* (Little, Brown, 2004)

Terraine, J., *The Right of the Line* (1985; Sceptre, 1988)

Glossary

ABC: Airborne Cigar – a system for disrupting German fighter controller voice transmissions.

AI: Airborne Interception radar.

Airspeed Oxford: twin-engined training aircraft.

Artificial horizon: an instrument allowing the pilot to control the orientation of the aircraft relative to the horizon.

ASI: airspeed indicator.

Astrodome: perspex observation bubble set in a bomber's upper fuselage, behind the cockpit.

ATC: Air Training Corps, for training 'air-minded' youth.

Atlantic Wall: German coastal defences, from Norway to the Spanish border but concentrated on the French coastline.

Backers-up: aircraft briefed to assist in maintaining target marking.

Battle Order: list of crews required for a raid.

BDM: Bund Deutscher Mädel: 'League of German Maidens' – the girls' branch of the Hitler Youth.

Beaufighter: twin-engined aircraft, employed as a night fighter.

Benzedrine: an amphetamine.

Bf110: twin-engined aircraft, employed as a night fighter.

'Big Three': Roosevelt, Churchill and Stalin, the leaders of the principal Allied Nations.

Blackout: extinguishing/hiding artificial light, to help protect cities from air attack.

Blind-bombing: systems/tactics for accurate bombing of an obscured target.

Blockbuster: or *'Cookie'*, a 4,000lb high-capacity blast bomb.

Blockleiter: 'Block Leader', or Blockwart (block warden) – a minor Nazi official responsible for supervision of a neighbourhood.

Bomber stream: the main body of aircraft flying to and from a target.

CARE: an organization founded in 1945 to deliver CARE packages to the hungry survivors of war in Europe. Twenty-two American agencies established CARE; $10 bought a package, with delivery guaranteed within four months.

Carpet: airborne device to jam German Würzburg ground radar.

Christbäume: 'Christmas trees' – flares dropped to mark a target at night.

Corkscrew: evasive action – a diving turn, followed by a climbing turn in the opposite direction.

Corona: the use of German-speaking RAF personnel to broadcast false orders to enemy night fighters.

Crewing up: the informal RAF system allowing aircrew to join others to form bomber crews.

Deflection: shooting ahead of a moving target.

DFC: Distinguished Flying Cross.

DFM: Distinguished Flying Medal.

Dicey: dangerous, risky.

Dina: development of Mandrel airborne jammer.

Dispersal: a system for distributing, over a wide area, aircraft, buildings and other facilities, to reduce losses in the event of air attack.

DSO: Distinguished Service Order.

Einsatzkommando: 'Task Force' shooting Jewish populations, communists and 'partisans'.

Elsan: chemical toilet.

ETA: estimated time of arrival.

Feathering: propeller blades turned edge on, to reduce drag and prevent windmilling.

FIDO: 'Fog, Intensive Dispersal of' – use of petrol fires along a runway, to burn off fog and allow an aircraft to land.

Finders: aircraft locating the target.

Fishpond: radar device warning of an approaching fighter.

Flak: anti-aircraft fire/guns.

Flarepath: runway illuminated for use at night or in bad weather.

Flensburg: device allowing German night fighters to home onto Monica tail-warners.

Flight: a squadron sub-unit (typically of six or eight aircraft in a heavy bomber squadron).

Fortress: B.17 – American four-engined heavy bomber, from Boeing.

Freya: German ground radar system.

Fw190: German single-seat fighter (radial engine).

Gardening: an operational sortie involving the dropping of mines.

Gauleiter: regional Nazi leader – the head of a Gau.

GEE: navigational aid utilizing signals from ground transmissions (pulse-phasing position fixer).

Gestapo: Geheime Staatspolizei – the Nazi Secret Police.

GH: blind-bombing system.

Gremlins: mischievous sprites said to interfere with RAF aircraft and, in particular, their engines.

Ground Grocer: ground-based transmitters for jamming German night fighter radars.

Ground loop: rapid rotation of an aircraft when one wingtip touches the ground.

H₂S: navigation and target identification radar system (pulse reflector).

Halifax: four-engined heavy bomber, from Handley Page.

Hang-up: a bomb that has failed to drop.

HCU: Heavy Conversion Unit.

Heimatflak: anti-aircraft defences manned by civilians, including factory workers and schoolchildren.

Hitler Jugend: Hitler Youth.

Illuminators: flare-droppers, providing illumination over the target.

Intruder: heavily armed aircraft on an offensive patrol in enemy airspace.

Jostle: airborne jammer to disrupt German VHF communications.

Jungvolk: junior branch of the Hitler Youth.

Ju88: twin-engined fast bomber with variants developed for night fighting.

KPD: Kommunistische Partei Deutschlands – the German Communist Party.

Lancaster: four-engined heavy bomber, from Avro.

Lebensborn: a programme devised to increase the Germanic/Nordic population of Germany.

Liberator: B.24 – four-engined American heavy bomber.

Lichtenstein: German night fighter radar.

Lincoln: Avro's successor to the Lancaster.

LMF: 'Lack of Moral Fibre' – refusal to fly.

Luftschutz: Luftschutzwarndienst – a civilian-manned air raid warning service.

Lysander: high-wing monoplane used for landing agents in France.

Main force: a large group of bombers attacking a target.

Mandrel: system for jamming German radar stations.

Master Bomber: operationally experienced pilot using VHF to broadcast instructions to control the progress and accuracy of a raid.

Maximum effort: an order for mobilization of the maximum number of aircraft to attack a given target or targets.

Me109: single-seat day fighter.

Me163: rocket-powered point defence fighter capable of very high speeds.

Me262: twin-engined German jet fighter.

Me410: twin-engined heavy fighter.

Monica: a tail-warning radar, to warn (by audible bleeps) of fighter attack.

Mosquito: fast, twin-engined multi-role aircraft.

Musical Parramatta: Oboe blind-marking.

Mustang: highly successful single-engined air superiority/escort fighter.

Newhaven: visual ground marking of a target.

Nissen hut: a building of semicircular section, constructed from corrugated steel sheet.

NSDAP: Nazi Party.

OBE: Order of the British Empire.

Oberbürgermeister: Lord Mayor.

Oboe: blind-bombing system.

OECD: Organisation for Economic Co-operation and Development.

Op: operation – an operational flight.

Operational tour: a series of combat missions, typically 30 for a first tour and 20 for a second.

Orderly Room: a room used for general administrative work.

OTU: Operational Training Unit.

Overshoot: to fly too far down the runway before touching down.

Panzerfaust: German hand-held, one-shot anti-tank weapon – shoulder fired.

Parramatta: blind ground marking by H_2S.

Percival Proctor: single-engined training aircraft.

Perimeter track: concrete/tarmac tracks allowing aircraft to taxi from the runway to other locations on the airfield.

PFF: Pathfinder Force.

Piperack: Dina/Mandrel-type jammer used to counter FuG 220 AI radar.

POW: prisoner of war.

Prang: to bomb a target or have an accident or crash in an aircraft.

Primary Markers: responsible for initial marking of the target.
Pundit Beacon: high-powered coloured lights flashing Morse, to aid navigation.
RAAF: Royal Australian Air Force.
Radio-countermeasures: RCM – systems to jam or otherwise confuse enemy communications and radars.
RCAF: Royal Canadian Air Force.
Reserved occupation: an occupation excluding the individual from military service.
RNZAF: Royal New Zealand Air Force.
R/T: radio-telephone/telephony.
Run-in: final approach to the target.
SA: the Sturmabteilung – 'Stormtroopers', or 'Brownshirts' – a Nazi paramilitary organization.
SBC: Small Bomb Container.
Schräge Musik: twin 20mm cannons, fuselage-mounted to fire upwards, just forward of the vertical.
Scrub/scrubbed: cancelling of operation, owing to adverse weather or other reasons.
Second Dicky: Second pilot.
Serrate: device homing onto German Lichtenstein night fighter radar.
Siegfried Line: the German defence line opposite the French Maginot Line.
Skipper: Captain of the aircraft; pilot.
Sky markers: parachute-equipped flares for marking obscured targets.
Small Bomb Container: SBC – container for incendiary bombs.
SN2: a variant of Lichtenstein German airborne interception radar.
SOE: Special Operations Executive – created to organize sabotage and subversion in Occupied Europe, in cooperation with Resistance groups.
'Spare bod': airman no longer part of a permanent crew and available to cover for others unavailable to fly.
Special operator: crew member responsible for operating radio-countermeasures.
Spoof: hoax; attempt to deceive.
Stand-down: release from operations, typically owing to bad weather.
Steiner Movement: a philosophy developed by Rudolf Steiner to investigate the spiritual world with scientific precision.
Stooge: fly around aimlessly.
Sufi Movement: Islamic mysticism.
Target Indicators: TIs – pyrotechnic flares used to mark targets.
Tiger Moth: biplane, primary trainer.
Time over Target: TOT – time allocated to arrive over and bomb the target.
Tinsel: airborne system broadcasting engine noise on German night fighter frequencies.
Toc H: originally a rest house for troops in the First World War – Talbot House, or TH (Toc H in signallers' parlance). Toc H developed into a major network of hostels and, later, became responsible for many community support projects.
Tracer: incendiary ammunition that can be observed in flight.
U/S: unserviceable.
V1: Flying Bomb.
VC: Victoria Cross – Britain's highest award for bravery.

Versailles Treaty: treaty between the combatant powers at the end of the First World War.

Volkssturm: German militia, consisting of the elderly, Hitler Youth, invalids and men previously considered unfit for military service.

WAAF: Women's Auxiliary Air Force.

Wanganui: radar-assisted blind-marking of an obscured target using parachute-equipped pyrotechnics – 'sky markers'.

Watch Office: Flying Control (control tower).

Wehrmacht: German Army.

Weimar: the German federal republic established in 1919.

Wellington: twin-engined bomber.

Westwall: the Siegfried Line, on Germany's western border.

Whitley: twin-engined heavy bomber.

Wilde Sau: 'Wild Boar' – night fighting tactics employing single-seat day fighters using illumination over the target to find the bombers.

Window: aluminium strips dropped to swamp enemy radars.

Winter Relief: Winterhilfswerk, an annual campaign to provide food, clothing, coal and other essentials.

Würzburg: radar used to control searchlights, flak and fighters.

W/T: Wireless telegraphy.

Yalta: the conference between Roosevelt, Stalin and Churchill to discuss post-war European reorganization.

Zahme Sau: 'Tame Boar' – an air defence strategy based on the infiltration of night fighters into the bomber stream, allowing them to accompany the main force.

Index of Names